# Praise for *Smart (Enough) Systems*

"Automated decision systems are probably already being used in your industry, and they will undoubtedly grow in importance. If your business needs to make quick, accurate decisions on an industrialized scale, you need to read this book."

*Thomas H. Davenport, President's Distinguished Professor of Information Technology and Management, Babson College, author of* Competing on Analytics

"James Taylor and Neil Raden are on to something important in this book—the tremendous value of improving the large number of routine decisions that are made in organizations every day. While experienced business intelligence professionals may recognize the individual pieces, the authors do a wonderful job of integrating the component parts and providing frameworks, concepts, technology discussions, examples, and implementation guidelines to help companies make the potential a reality."

*Dr. Hugh J. Watson, C. Herman and Mary Virginia Terry Chair of Business Administration, University of Georgia*

"This is a very important book. It lays out the agenda for business technology in the new century—nothing less than how to reorganize every aspect of how a company treats its customers. The book is very comprehensive in its coverage of the concepts, the underlying technologies, and implementation techniques. If you read one book on Enterprise Decision Management this year, this is the one."

*David Raab, President, ClientXClient*

"Throughout business, every day, critical decisions are made by people—people who may have just the right information and understanding to make good decisions, but just as likely do not. Many of these decisions could be made correctly and consistently if the rules that govern them were understood and the information needed to shape them was readily available. Despite three decades of progressively more comprehensive business automation and the accumulation of a rich "digital history" of business, too few organizations really understand and apply critical business rules. In *Smart (Enough) Systems*, James Taylor and Neil Raden lay out a well-reasoned path to attacking this situation and improving business operations through the understanding and consistent application of business rules using readily available technologies. The book is an important contribution to business productivity because it covers the opportunity from both the business executive's and technologist's perspective—essential; if the two sides are to come together in an understanding of what can be done and what's needed to do it. This should be on every operational executive's and every CIO's list of essential reading."

*John Parkinson, Chairman and Managing Director, ParkWood Advisors, LLC. Former CTO Capgemini North American Region*

"An important book that finally, for the first time, addresses the topic of enterprise decision making not by relying on IT "geekspeak" but by taking a holistic view of why business people require EDM, why past approaches have failed, and why the changing landscape such as ESOA will make EDM even more critical for the changing business landscape. The authors have an excellent, deep grasp of most concepts, and they presented it in a readable, comprehensive, logical way."

*Roman Bukary, Vice President SAP Labs, LLC*

"Enterprise Decision Management (EDM) is a key facet of high-value operational business intelligence. James Taylor and Neil Raden do an excellent job explaining EDM and helping the readers work those concepts and technologies into future BI development to the benefit of their organizations."

*Alan Simon, author of 27 books, including* Data Warehousing for Dummies *and* BI for Dummies

"James Taylor and Neil Raden provide a clear, concise, and well-written book offering both the breadth and depth to make sense of an exciting yet difficult subject. Not only does *Smart (Enough) Systems* cover all aspects of decision automation, from the technologies and approaches needed to their impact on existing and future technology architectures; it is a very easy, interesting read. A must-have reference for business and technology people alike.

Well-organized and comprehensive, this book provides pragmatic guidance on how to use proven, existing technology to make systems smarter. It makes a compelling case that in order to survive and indeed thrive, all organizations need to focus on controlling and then optimizing their operational decisions. I would strongly recommend this book to both business and technical managers who want to make their information systems smart enough for the 21st century."

*Christine H. Pratt, Research Director for Consumer Banking & Credit, Financial Insights*

"This is the first book I have read that brings together the technologies and techniques needed to make systems smart enough for a modern business. James Taylor and Neil Raden have provided a concise and accessible book that both business and technical managers can use to make their business processes smarter. *Smart (Enough) Systems* is very well organized and thorough, covering all the technologies and techniques needed for decision automation.

It shows how to use proven technology to make business processes smarter. It clearly makes the case that organizations need to optimize their operational decisions. It is a must-have reference for process professionals throughout your organization."

*Jim Sinur, Chief Strategy Officer, Global 360, Inc.*

"James Taylor and Neil Raden have produced a substantive work that explores what will soon be recognized as the next arena for competitive advantage in our fast-paced global economy. Their central thesis is that organizations must treat decisions as an enterprise asset and take action to increase their "decision yield." The combined effect of improving the hundreds of routine operating decisions that an organization makes day in and day out is analogous to the effect of compound interest, where the value of an initial amount of capital begins to increase exponentially over time.

Companies presently focus their attention and energy on the big strategic decisions and overlook the enormous opportunities to be found in consistently improving the accuracy and responsiveness of the many seemingly routine decisions they make. The book is organized into chapters that introduce the core concepts and then explore these concepts in greater and greater detail. The authors present their case in a scholarly and articulate manner."

*Michael Hugos, Principal, Center for Systems Innovation,*
*author of* Building the Real-Time Enterprise: An Executive Briefing

"*Smart (Enough) Systems* blazes a new trail in the crucial territory of finding the business value in information systems. With a well-tuned blend of technology and business, this book is a great read for anyone trying to discover the potential of decision management in the enterprise.

The book contains dozens of helpful case studies that illuminate the potential for real dollar return on investment from decision management solutions. The authors do a superb job of identifying the opportunities for improving business rules through the application of decision management to the enterprise.

The authors have a remarkable level of depth and insight about how enterprises can benefit from decision management, as well as a thorough appreciation for how to get the task done in practical terms—including situations where the best option is to go slowly."

*Hugh Taylor, CISM, UC Berkeley School of Information, author of* The Joy of Sox

"A thorough examination of the business value and technologies enabling decision management, positioned as the next major wave of business process automation. The book is filled with examples that should help the reader learn from the experiences of other organizations in deploying decision management technologies. Traditional business intelligence addresses the delivery of information, but not the selection of the optimal decision in the face of uncertainty. Taylor and Raden provide a comprehensive survey of the business and technology dimensions of establishing a policy hub for decisions across the enterprise."

*Henry Morris, Group VP/GM for Integration, Development, and Application Strategies, IDC*

"While growing up, the big rhetorical question I often heard asked was, "If we can send people all the way to the Moon and back, why can't we.... ? (Fill in the blank with a frustration—predict tomorrow's weather, design a car that runs on something besides oil, make a good omelet...). The same kind of question might be asked of today's businesses: With all the vast amounts of information technology and data that are abundant in today's corporations, why can't companies still comprehend what their customers want, what their employees know, and what future directions they should take?

In *Smart (Enough) Systems*, James Taylor and Neil Raden—who have been leading the charge for more engaging business intelligence for a number of years now—attempt to finally answer this question, by looking at the current state of technology and how it is employed, or underemployed, within today's organizations.

In fact, James and Neil point out that most organizations already have the technology in place from which they can make better decisions. It's not technology that's holding things back, it's the way that decision making is managed and measured—which, in many cases, is no management or measurement at all.

This book is a must-read for any manager or professional who seeks to understand how human-machine interaction can be better leveraged to make sense of all that data now flowing through organizations—and make smarter decisions. And, ultimately, the lesson learned is the same with any other major technology change that has swept today's organizations: it's not technology that means the difference between failure and success—it's adroit and informed management that makes the difference."

*Joe McKendrick, Industry analyst and contributing editor, ZDNet,*
*Database Trends & Applications magazine, ebizQ*

"Enterprise decision management (EDM) is a leading-edge concept that brings together business intelligence, business rules, and business modeling: three areas that have heretofore been progressing along separate paths. By bringing them together, businesses could realize substantial gains through more effective and understandable enterprise decision making, and apply automation where possible to overcome the cost and complexity challenges that are plaguing most BI efforts. Neil Raden and James Taylor have written a book that is unique in its ability to explain EDM in depth, shows how it represents an advance over earlier concepts, and describes why businesses will attain new competitive advantages by adopting EDM. I recommend this book highly.

With so many distinct applications but interrelated decision processes at work in most large organizations, it's time that business and IT leaders look more comprehensively at what it takes for employees and partners to make good, informed decisions to accomplish a business goal or serve a customer. Since most BI and DW systems were set up for a different sort of information gathering and strategic analysis of historical data, organizations need to look at fresh approaches that may be more relevant to solving their problems. This book describes well the problems with current BI and DW approaches and why EDM deserves careful consideration—especially as organizations look at service-oriented architecture and greater implementation of process management.

While the authors show the shortcomings of current BI and DW implementations, they do not recommend "boiling the ocean" and changing to something completely different. Rather, the authors describe how EDM can take the current investments and apply them to address business challenges and seize new opportunities. Leading-edge companies want to sharpen and deepen how they use information for decisions that must be made with blinding speed, including loan processing, financial trading, and fraud detection. To do this, they need to push forward, not get mired in massive redevelopment or reengineering of BI and DW systems. The authors are sensitive to this constraint and present EDM as an additive approach.

The writing is clear, perceptive, and enjoyable to read. This is not an academic or theoretical treatise; it is rooted in experience with real-world information and rules systems, including current frustrations with implementing them. The in-depth discussion of what EDM is and how it fits with other relevant rules, BI, and information management initiatives is highly valuable, even if the reader ultimately decides that EDM is not exactly what their organization needs or can implement at this time. Readers gain a better understanding of what's ahead for businesses trying to become 'intelligent' businesses."

*David Stodder, VP & Research Director, Ventana Research,*
*and founding chief editor of* Intelligent Enterprise

"The book is more than a primer and handbook—it is an instruction manual that can be used collaboratively by both sides of the organization. The business-oriented sections of the book justify and explain the need for the technical requirements, which ought to make for constructive leadership and better decisions that are understood throughout the process by all parties.

An ambitious dive into a complicated topic, *Smart (Enough) Systems* delivers a big menu of valuable opportunities balanced by the pragmatism of the authors' experience. I could immediately relate the advice in this book to the experiences of the corporations I talk to on a daily basis."

*Jim Ericson, Editorial Director, DM Review, BI Review Magazines*

"A must-read for anyone who is serious about improving the art and practice of organizational decision-making."

*Mark Clare, Vice President, Parkview Health. Adjunct Faculty, Northwestern University*

"This book is an excellent introduction to Enterprise Decision Management. It is sufficiently detailed to help choose which decisions are ripe for automation and to develop the rule sets for them. It explains how EDM fits in the organization and how to interface with existing IT systems. Most sections have brief real-world examples that help with understanding.

I now feel that I have sufficient knowledge to determine what decisions can benefit from automation, the ROI on the effort, and what problems to expect along the way. I may or may not be able to build an EDM system, but I am knowledgeable enough to spec one, I know what questions to ask, and I can manage its development. Further, it has given me a broader view of the field of decision management."

*Dr. David G. Ullman, author of* Making Robust Decisions

"Very thought provoking! After spending 10 years in the business rules space, *Smart (Enough) Systems* takes EDM to a new level for me. This book is a blueprint to creating systems that are in tune with the customer and their needs. Real-time decisions that are consistent, accurate, and specific to the situation would give any company embracing this thought process the competitive edge! The book is well balanced, written with the novice to expert in mind. Well Done!

**Buy the book!** But only buy it if you are serious about reading it. Don't leave it on the shelf with all those other business rules books you bought and never read.

**Read the book!** *Smart (Enough) Systems* will help create an EDM culture in your organization. It will change the way business rules technologists think about their work.

**Embrace the concepts!** It is time to make the jump, from systems that are designed and driven by the developers, both business and IT, and create EDM that truly meets the customers needs throughout their entire experience with your organization. Your competitors won't know what hit them."

*Michael Koscielny, CPCU CIC, Assistant Vice President, American Modern Insurance Group*

"*Smart (Enough) Systems* delivers razor-sharp insight into the power of people and technology to deliver organization impact and competitive advantage. Taylor and Raden do a masterful job providing depth and color around industry and technology trends, illuminating some hard truths about organizational change, and exposing the delta between business strategy and operational reality. They deliver a call to arms and provide a power playbook on how to execute. *Smart (Enough) Systems* is a must-read for anyone focused on unlocking the power of information to drive competitive advantage."

*Patrick Morrissey, SVP Marketing, Savvion*

"A masterful presentation of an important new idea, Enterprise Decision Management (EDM). Like BPM, EDM is destined to provide a focal point where business minds and IT engineers can find common and very fertile ground to plan for success.

As the authors say, the business rule approach has evolved and proven itself convincingly over the last decade. With Enterprise Decision Management (EDM), business rules finally have a compelling architectural voice and clear business motivation. EDM essentially turns the world inside out. The book shows in highly pragmatic fashion that seemingly the most mundane thing in operational business—everyday operational decisions—are actually key to success in today's vastly altered business and computing landscape.

If you are doing BPM, SOA, CDI, MDM, compliance, data quality, business rules—or simply seeking a more informed way to conduct scalable, intelligent business in the 21st century—don't miss this book!

This book explains why your business should be decision-centric, rather than system-centric or even exclusively process-centric. EDM brings intelligence to your business processes and IT architecture in a pragmatic, proven fashion. It makes them smart. There's simply no alternative if you want your processes to be agile, adaptive, and comprehensively compliant.

This book shows you how to prosper in the face of massive data overload and pervasive inconsistency in the application of basic operational knowledge. More importantly, it shows you how to manage rapid-fire change, not just so you can survive it, but to turn it into a structural competitive advantage."

*Ronald G. Ross, Co-Founder, Business Rule Solutions, LLC,*
*and Executive Editor,* Business Rules Journal

"Even though Business Rules has been around as a discipline and a methodology for many years, it is a field that is poorly understood by management. Because Business Rules is dominated by technologists and a confusing mix of data modeling and artificial intelligence, managers and executives struggle with the benefits and necessity. *Smart (Enough) Systems* overcomes the jargon and hype of business rules by reframing the challenge as the strategic necessity to control decisions.

Business agility cannot be achieved without enterprise decision management. Without a clear vision, the journey to effective decision management can be long, complicated, and expensive. *Smart (Enough) Systems* presents a well written guide to this topic. Many parts of the book detail useful activities that companies can start today. *Smart (Enough) Systems* should be on every thoughtful manager's bookshelf. The information James and Neil present is an absolute must-read for every executive or manager working with business strategy and tactics."

*Tom Debevoise, author of* Business Process Management with a Business Rules Approach

"Taylor and Raden's central manifesto highlights that it's critical to embody more intelligence in today's business decision-making and have consistent, automated decisioning built into business processes in order to remain agile and competitive in today's fast-moving market. They take you through the core concepts of enterprise decision management (EDM), dive into the underlying technologies, and then address how to integrate EDM into your business processes to create your own Smart (Enough) Systems.

By focusing on operational decisions that contribute to corporate strategy, *Smart (Enough) Systems* provides the ability not only to create agile business processes, but to have these processes be self-learning based on historical results. Instead of simply capturing operational process statistics in a data warehouse for later analysis, *Smart (Enough) Systems* uses that knowledge to inform the business rules and allow them to adapt their guidance of the decision-making process. By extracting the decisions from legacy applications, static enterprise applications and manual procedures, and managing them within a shared enterprise decision management system, operational decisions can be applied consistently—and modified easily for processes in flight—across the enterprise.

As a business process management specialist, I see this book as a great resource for exploring how EDM can simplify and improve business processes."

*Sandy Kemsley, BPM analyst and architect. Kemsley Design Ltd, www.column2.com*

"The data warehouse and business intelligence industry has been struggling for two decades to figure out how to deliver compelling business value. What we see is a return to our roots of figuring out how to help organizations leverage data and analytics to make better decisions. James and Neil outline what companies need to do to realize the value from many years of investment in data and technology infrastructure by introducing the concepts that support a true decision platform."

*Bill Schmarzo, Vice President, Advertiser Analytics Yahoo Inc. Formerly Vice President,*
*Analytic Applications Business Objects*

"This is a good survey book of the subject of smart systems and many related fields. If you want to understand what they are and why you should care (and you should), read this book."

*Charlie Lewis, Air Products and Chemicals, Global IT Chief Architect and Innovation Champion,*
*Instructor Pennsylvania State University*

"This book provides an excellent introduction to the key issues addressed by the technology, the related core concepts, and it also provides guidance for its implementation, including readiness assessments for your business units and technology departments."

*David Luce Information Technology Architect*

"Rules-based technology deserves to play a greater role in modern computing. And James Taylor is one of its most persuasive advocates."

*Curt Monash, Ph.D., President, Monash Information Services*

# Smart (Enough) Systems

## How to Deliver Competitive Advantage by Automating the Decisions Hidden in Your Business

**James Taylor** *with* **Neil Raden**

PRENTICE
HALL

Upper Saddle River, NJ • Boston • Indianapolis • San Francisco
New York • Toronto • Montreal • London • Munich • Paris • Madrid
Cape Town • Sydney • Tokyo • Singapore • Mexico City

Many of the designations used by manufacturers and sellers to distinguish their products are claimed as trademarks. Where those designations appear in this book, and the publisher was aware of a trademark claim, the designations have been printed with initial capital letters or in all capitals.

The authors and publisher have taken care in the preparation of this book, but make no expressed or implied warranty of any kind and assume no responsibility for errors or omissions. No liability is assumed for incidental or consequential damages in connection with or arising out of the use of the information or programs contained herein.

The publisher offers excellent discounts on this book when ordered in quantity for bulk purchases or special sales, which may include electronic versions and/or custom covers and content particular to your business, training goals, marketing focus, and branding interests. For more information, please contact:

> U.S. Corporate and Government Sales
> (800) 382-3419
> corpsales@pearsontechgroup.com

For sales outside the United States please contact:

> International Sales
> international@pearsoned.com

**This Book Is Safari Enabled**

The Safari® Enabled icon on the cover of your favorite technology book means the book is available through Safari Bookshelf. When you buy this book, you get free access to the online edition for 45 days.

Safari Bookshelf is an electronic reference library that lets you easily search thousands of technical books, find code samples, download chapters, and access technical information whenever and wherever you need it.

To gain 45-day Safari Enabled access to this book:

- Go to http://www.prenhallprofessional.com/safarienabled
- Complete the brief registration form
- Enter the coupon code 6NFV-KLLG-NNB9-PRGB-FSK5

If you have difficulty registering on Safari Bookshelf or accessing the online edition, please e-mail customer-service@safaribooksonline.com.

Visit us on the Web: www.prenhallprofessional.com

*Library of Congress Cataloging-in-Publication Data:*

Taylor, James, 1965-
  Smart (enough) systems : how to deliver competitive advantage by automating hidden decisions / James Taylor with Neil Raden.
    p. cm.
  ISBN 0-13-234796-2 (pbk. : alk. paper)  1.  Decision support systems.  2.  Decision making.  I. Raden, Neil. II. Title.
  T58.62.T39 2007

  658.4'03—dc22

                                 2007013166

ISBN-13: 978-0-13-234796-9
ISBN-10: 0-13-234796-2
Text printed in the United States on recycled paper at R.R. Donnelley in Crawfordsville, Indiana.
First printing June 2007

**Editor-in-Chief**
Mark Taub

**Acquisitions Editor**
Bernard Goodwin

**Development Editor**
Deadline Driven
Publishing

**Managing Editor**
Gina Kanouse

**Senior Project Editor**
Lori Lyons

**Copy Editor**
Lisa Lord

**Indexer**
Erika Millen

**Proofreader**
Gayle Johnson

**Technical Reviewers**
Mark Smith
Katherine Knowles
David Stodder

**Publishing Coordinator**
Michelle Housley

**Cover Designer**
Alan Clements

**Composition**
Gloria Schurick

**Graphics**
Hucks Graphics

*To my boys, Theo and Dylan*
*—James*

*To my parents, Joe Raden and Lillian Sonnenfeld Raden*
*—Neil*

# Contents

CHAPTER 4 **Core Concepts** 125

CHAPTER 5 **Data and Analytics** 147

## CHAPTER 10   EDM and the IT Department   317

## CHAPTER 11   Closing Thoughts   367

# Foreword

What single characteristic distinguishes humans from other known life forms? Some say it is our serious lack of instincts. Lacking instincts, we exhibit a shortage of behaviors that are universal among us. And yet, from this characteristic emerges our intelligence, creativity, character, and perhaps wisdom.

In place of instincts, however, we rely on other guidance systems to direct and monitor our behavior, including the mental abilities to absorb complex information, apply reasoning, comprehend abstract ideas, and learn from experience.

And yet, a human's innate intelligence cannot be changed. Sadly, each of us is destined to remain at the intelligence level from which we begin. However, unlike human intelligence, organizational intelligence can be altered, alluding to the idea that we can improve it.

Therefore, it was alarming when David Taylor proposed in 1996 that, as an organization grows larger, it becomes less intelligent. In fact, Taylor's Law of Corporate IQ was computed as Corporate IQ = 100 divided by $n$, where 100 is the average individual IQ and $n$ is the number of employees in the corporation. This deterioration of organizational intelligence does not bode well for large or growing organizations, let alone for the rapid globalization of business partnerships today.

Yet Taylor offered hope by noting exceptions. One is that a small team of humans, in fact, can outthink its brightest member. Another is that, although a single person can't design a highly engineered product, an entire corporation can. So what is at play in teams? It seems that organizational or group learning is at play. A corporation can become smarter by learning, and learning is the opposite of instinct. Instinct is hard-wired, resistant to change, but learning is soft-wired, amenable to change and to rapid change.

So in 1996, the smart organization was one that learned. Therefore, learning organizations delivered accessibility to quality information, defined processes, partnerships, and proper organizational placement of decision power. And now, James and Neil focus on a new immediate future, where the smart organization is one that's high-performance in execution, customer centered, data driven, real time, loosely coupled, focused on learning, and agile. The last two, focused on learning and agile, imply rapid learning coupled with corresponding dynamic improvements in decision making.

For this new immediate future, James and Neil have produced a book that goes beyond information sharing and organizational decision power. Raising the bar for the decision process is the introduction of enterprise decision management (EDM) as a new formalization for the company of the immediate future.

EDM is not about narrow learning, but about learning from experience in a broad and deep manner and learning quickly. With this in mind, the book focuses on selecting appropriate decisions for EDM, managing the business rules behind those decisions, and instituting model-driven, analytical feedback loops based on past decision performance. James and Neil drive home the value of EDM when they state, "Making information more readily available can be important but making better decisions based on it is what pays the bills."

Equally important, EDM is emerging as a critical necessity in a world where business processes are globally outsourced, regulatory compliance is critical, and systems development occurs offshore. EDM can be the unifying discipline behind all these situations, as James and Neil outline how EDM will affect all of us:

- "BPO vendors can deliver innovation and optimize processes only if they make the key decision points in their processes available so that customers can control them."

- "Business rules are ideally suited to showing that a decision has been made in a compliant way."

- "Outsourcing development and maintenance of nondifferentiating code can be cost effective, but outsourcing code representing your IP is a big risk. The code that business rules replace is core IP."

- "The most important change to your software development lifecycle is the separation of rules and requirements."

- "Business rules and their interrelationships can be visualized and managed more easily than code, so more of the application can be managed more visually."

This book makes you stop and think. It starts a new conversation between business leaders and IT specialists. The conversation begins with the core of the business by bringing important business decisions back into the boardroom with a new purpose. It continues by delivering them in innovative configurable technology.

After all, if humans were rich in instincts, we would run all businesses in a predictable, universal, and admittedly boring fashion. Fortunately, instead, we possess other talents that lead to organizational intelligence and distinction. Your enterprise's decision management is the backbone of its future. Delivered as configurable business rules, your EDM framework reveals a whole enterprise that's smarter than its parts.

Use this book as your guide to your company of the future. It's time to abandon outdated hard-wired instincts that no longer lead to organizational survival and success. It's time to deliver important decisions as agile soft-wired services for the enterprise.

—*Barbara von Halle*

# Preface

This book is about how organizations can deliver systems smart enough to cope with the modern world. Doing so requires a focus on decision making and on automating and managing those decisions. Most organizations struggle with dumb systems and think that they face a difficult choice—between esoteric "artificial intelligence" straight from the lab and mindless systems where all the intelligence comes down to "peopleware." In most systems today, people do all the intellectual heavy-lifting, and computers are used only to store and move information. Flipping that around is completely feasible: Have people do what they do best, and let computers do the hard work. Organizations can apply proven technology in a new way to get the systems they need.

If you're interested in how to make your organization function more effectively by improving the behavior of your information systems, this book is for you. You might be a manager, wondering what's possible with your systems, or an IT professional looking for a framework for thinking about these aspects of information systems. Perhaps you know something about data mining, predictive analytics, optimization, or business rules and are looking for better ways to apply these concepts. You might be in an organization that has never attempted this kind of work or one struggling with getting these technologies out of pilot projects into the mainstream.

We have tried to move gradually from a nontechnical to a moderately technical point of view. The initial chapters are designed for any business reader; the later chapters are aimed at readers who are more technical. None of the chapters requires a detailed understanding of or experience with the technologies described. Plenty of books describe the component technologies; this book is about how, and why, they fit together. The real case studies scattered through the book and, in the more technical sections, the real architecture diagrams are meant to be illustrative rather than comprehensive. Similarly, several sections of the book discuss SmartEnough Logistics, an imaginary company that illustrates some key points in the book.

A companion Web site is available at www.smartenoughsystems.com. This companion site is designed to be a useful ongoing resource to support the book and those using the concepts described in it. The site has an enterprise decision management wiki that supports errata, links, additional materials, and more for the subjects covered in the book. The wiki is open to anyone who registers to participate. News and updates are available through the site's blog, and additional information is available to help you learn more about the subjects covered—everything from webinars and podcasts to training and books.

# Acknowledgments

It would not have been possible to develop the ideas behind this book, or produce the book itself, without considerable and ongoing support from Fair Isaac as well as current and former employees. Fair Isaac gave me an opportunity to meet very smart people, to work with them on developing new concepts, reworking old ones, and developing a breakthrough framework for viewing the world of information systems: enterprise decision management, or EDM.

Many people have helped in different ways, but I want to acknowledge a number explicitly. Ken Molay and Jeff Kilbreth who, among other things, were there when we came up with a new name and who worked with me on some of the first EDM materials. Michael Chiappetta, John Nash, Todd Davis, Brian Kane, and others in Fair Isaac management supported the adoption of enterprise decision management within Fair Isaac and made improvements too numerous to mention. Frank Rohde developed the original decision yield concept and Ian Turvill extended the concept and applied it to many industries. Larry Rosenberger and the fantastic analytic R&D folks at Fair Isaac explained their magic to me in words of one syllable, and Dave Shellenberger gave me some great insight on where enterprise decision management might go next. Mark Eastwood and other members of the Fair Isaac Professional Services staff validated and improved the practical parts of the book, and Joe LaLuzerne contributed based on his work on the Fair Isaac methodology. Andy Flint and Mac Belniak of Fair Isaac helped enormously on analytics and related technology, and Tom Traughber, Chaitan Sharma, Lisa Buonpane, Eric Wells, and Sally Taylor-Schoff helped me with the adaptive control chapter. Stuart Crawford gave the whole book a thorough review, which greatly improved it, and Scott Olsen and Dave Ross were of enormous help with case studies and examples of architectures. Carlos Serrano-Morales, Carole-Ann Matignon, Tom Travis, Paul Vincent, Don Griest, and many others educated me on the power of business rules. Mark Layden supported the book through thick and thin and made sure I had the time and focus needed to complete it. Other current and former Fair Isaac staff who provided material assistance in everything from graphics to concepts to writing include Darcy Sullivan, Marc Friedland, Dennis Gaines, Beth Carr, Sunny Frantz, Brenda Lewis, Jamie Nelson, Cath Davis, Sean Logan, Jeff Zabin, Lori Sherer, Renee Jackson, Laks Srinivasan, Larry Feinstein, Wendell Larson, Lamont Boyd, Senthil Kumar, Chisoo Lyons, and Dan Rich.

Outside Fair Isaac, I would like to acknowledge the boost that the idea of enterprise decision management got from the work Curt Hall did in the 2005 Cutter Group report as well as the editors who accepted articles about EDM, including Mary Jo Nott, Dan Power, Jim Erickson, and David Stodder. Elizabeth Book and the folks at ebizQ deserve my thanks for their support of my blog and various articles over the years. Mark Peterson and Bill Cox at Experience Communication and the whole Fleishman Hillard public relations team

(Alan, Jamie, Nina, Rory, and Michael) did sterling work over the years promoting the concepts, and the team at Hodgson Meyers created some nifty graphics concepts for us.

The people we worked with at Prentice Hall have been great throughout: Bernard Goodwin backed the proposal long before the book was written, and Michelle Housley, Gina Kanouse, and Lori Lyons offered their ongoing technical support and editing. Lisa Lord was a wonderful copy editor, managing to correct our English line by line while still keeping the whole manuscript in her head.

I want to thank Barb von Halle particularly for her encouragement, her thoughtful reviews, her foreword, and her ongoing assistance. Without her, we might never have got off the ground.

Last, I want to thank my family. My parents Jill and Mike who always knew I would write a book one day. Meri, Theo, and Dylan for putting up with a very distracted author for the past few months. Meri said, "If I had known the book would become part of the family, I would have given it a name." Even though we didn't name it, the book would not have been born without you all. Thank you, I love you all.

—*James Taylor*

The first person I want to thank is James Taylor for inviting me to be a part of this project. He always accepted my comments graciously and never complained when I couldn't keep up with his prodigious pace. Working with smart, confident people is always preferable to the alternative.

I also want to acknowledge people who encouraged me to write and supported me as I learned the ropes: Bob Evans and Julie Anderson at InformationWeek; Maurice Frank, Dave Stodder, and Doug Henschen at DBMS, Database Programming and Design, and Intelligent Enterprise; Jim Ericson and Mary Jo Nott at BIReview and DM Review; and Katherine Glassey, who suggested that Ramon Barquin and Herb Edelstein invite me to speak at the first Data Warehousing Institute conference in 1995, which was the start of this whole other career of writing and speaking.

I am privileged to have so many brilliant friends in the industry, too, whose counsel, company, and encouragement I appreciate more than they know (in completely random order): Mark Smith, Roman Bukary, Nigel Pendse, Jill Dyche, Evan Levy, Cindi Howson, Wayne Eckerson, Larry Barbetta, Bill Schmarzo, Kim Stanick, Michael Peterson, Dave Menninger, Dave Raab, Tina Jones, Bob Kwartin, Troy Pearsall, Kim Dossey, Jim Sterne, Clive Harrison, Doug Laney, Seth Grimes, Roger Walters, Doug Neal, Aaron Zornes, Dave McComb, Kevin Pledge, Steve Galvan, Eric Rogge, Dan Bulos, Vickie Farrell, and, no longer in the industry but more than ever an appreciated friend and confidante, Doug Hackney. A special thanks to my good friend and volunteer copy editor, Linda Ashton Borling.

Special thanks go to Dr. Ed Sakurai, who inspired me to stretch and revealed the beauty of mathematics to me so many years ago.

My wife, Susie (T.S. Wiley), has gifted me with the best years of her life (so far) and five fantastic kids, Mara, Aja, Jake, Max, and Zoe, and now three grandchildren, Harvey, Liam, and Aengus, and the best son-in-law on the planet, Ian McGuinness. They are all the centers of my universe.

*—Neil Raden*

Despite all the help we received, any errors the book still contains are ours alone, and the opinions and views expressed in this book are ours alone, not those of Fair Isaac Corporation, Hired Brains, or any other entity.

# About the Authors

**James Taylor** is a vice president at Fair Isaac Corporation, where he has been developing the themes of enterprise decision management for the past several years. He has seen many systems that are smarter than most and the value they bring to companies as well as the technologies and approaches that make them possible. James has experience in all aspects of software development, including designing, developing, researching and marketing application development technology and platforms. James writes many articles and frequently presents at trade shows and conferences. He writes a popular blog at www.edmblog.com and has contributed chapters to *The Business Rules Revolution* (Happy About, 2006) and *Business Intelligence Implementation: Issues and Perspectives (ICFAI University Press, 2006).*

**Neil Raden** is the president and founder of Hired Brains (www.hiredbrains.com), a firm offering research and analysis services to technology providers as well as consulting and implementation services in business intelligence/analytics, information integration, and semantic technology throughout North America and Europe. Neil began his career as a casualty actuary with AIG in New York before moving into software engineering, consulting, and industry analysis, with experience in the application of information technology to business processes from fields as diverse as health care, nuclear waste management, and cosmetics marketing. The recurrent theme in his work is the transformative effect of rationally devised information systems for people. He is a popular speaker, his articles appear in industry magazines, and he is the author of dozens of sponsored white papers for vendors and other organizations.

# Introduction

**A**lthough many of the techniques and technologies described in this book are in active use, typically they have been used only in certain kinds of systems. As a result, these technologies have been perceived as solutions only for narrow problems—credit card fraud and loan originations, for example. Meanwhile, ongoing change in the business world has resulted in a broad need for smart enough systems. However, mainstream development technologies and approaches lack critical capabilities, and proven technologies are overlooked. This book is about smart enough systems—why you need them and how to use these technologies to develop them. Why smart enough? In the past, the term "smart systems" has been associated with Artificial Intelligence. The insertion of the modifier "enough" is meant to draw a distinction between Artificial Intelligence and those systems that are capable of automating many decisions without reliance on the esoteric practices of Artificial Intelligence.

The book is divided into two unequal "halves." The first "half," directed at both business and technical readers, explains the need for smart enough systems and describes the core concepts behind them. The second half, aimed at more technical readers, describes in more detail the techniques and technologies required and explains how to implement smart enough systems.

We begin with a manifesto—a statement of our beliefs about smart enough systems. Read first, it might seem like a series of assertions. By the time you have finished the book, however, it will seem more like a statement of obvious truisms.

The following list summarizes this book's chapters to give you an overview of what's covered:

- **Chapter 1, "The Need for Smart Enough Systems,"** shows how current business megatrends are increasing the importance of operational decisions and forcing organizations to treat operational decision making as a corporate asset. This chapter examines the pressures and difficulties of decision making in the future and the

1

particular challenges of decision making when your systems embody your business more than ever before. This chapter also introduces a theoretical company, SmartEnough Logistics, to illustrate concepts discussed in the book.

- **Chapter 2, "Enterprise Decision Management,"** introduces a way to build smart enough systems. It explains the enterprise decision management approach to automating decisions and making them into a corporate asset. It also describes the characteristics of operational decision making problems and finding the hidden decisions in your business. This chapter also discusses how this approach generates a return on investment and presents 11 case studies to show how real organizations have used this approach.

- **Chapter 3, "Why Aren't My Systems Smart Enough Already?"** gives you some historical perspective on the development of information technology (IT) and discusses the challenges and opportunities in managing data, building programs, and analyzing businesses.

- **Chapter 4, "Core Concepts,"** is a transitional chapter that explains the basics of the enterprise decision management approach: data and analytics, business rules, and adaptive control. Although this chapter is more technical, it should still be accessible to most readers. Five more case studies are presented.

- **Chapters 5, "Data and Analytics," 6, "Business Rules," and 7, "Adaptive Control,"** describe these areas in more detail and begin the more technical content of the book. Each chapter contains an architectural overview, definitions of some core concepts, an outline of the critical pieces of technology, and a basic process for using the technologies. You can read the process first and refer back to the concepts and technology or read the basics first and then see how they fit together. Another 11 case studies are presented in these three chapters.

- **Chapter 8, "Readiness Assessment,"** outlines how to consider your readiness for building smart enough systems in terms of business/IT collaboration, data, analytic understanding, organizational change, and management focus.

- **Chapter 9, "Getting There from Here,"** lays out the steps for developing true enterprise decision management competency in four phases: piecemeal adoption, localized decision management, expansion, and steady state enterprise decision management. Another nine case studies are included. The chapter wraps up with a discussion of how SmartEnough Logistics adopted the approach and some thoughts for future developments in enterprise decision management.

- **Chapter 10, "EDM and the IT Department,"** brings enterprise decision management back to IT and ties its impact to your existing IT architecture. It shows how enterprise decision management complements your existing and future architecture, how it solves a number of issues, and how it enables you to deliver on some critical promises. This chapter includes an overview of how enterprise decision management changes your software development life cycle.

- **Chapter 11, "Closing Thoughts,"** wraps up the concepts and technologies discussed in the book.

- **An appendix, "Decision Yield as a Way to Measure ROI,"** is provided to explain a method for assessing return on investment. Few public examples of its use are available, however; so at the moment, it's more of a good idea than a proven technique.

The case studies used throughout the book are real companies that use enterprise decision management. A couple of case studies are amalgams of several similar companies, and all are anonymous to preserve their privacy. In most cases, these are Fair Isaac customers.

This introduction would not be complete without a note about Fair Isaac. The concept of enterprise decision management (EDM) was first developed at Fair Isaac. The technology and applications Fair Isaac's customers use are based on analytics, business rules, and adaptive control. This book—indeed, the whole approach—derives from Fair Isaac's experience in developing these systems and its customers' experience in using them. The phrase "enterprise decision management" was first used to give a handy label to something Fair Isaac, and others, had been doing for some time. It is not now, nor was it ever, a product or set of products. It's an approach proved by hundreds of organizations, Fair Isaac customers and others, over many years. One of the authors, James Taylor, works for Fair Isaac, where he has gotten most of his experience with this kind of system. Product names have been deliberately avoided because it's the approach—the mind-set—that matters. The central issue is not product-specific; it's about taking charge of the operational decisions that run your business and turning them from a liability into an asset, as expressed in this quote:

> "Enterprise decision management (EDM) is emerging as an important discipline, due to an increasing need to automate high-volume decisions across the enterprise and to impart precision, consistency, and agility in the decision-making process."[1]

Our goal in this book is to show you why enterprise decision management is important, how to adopt it, and how to succeed with it.

---

[1] Curt Hall, "Enterprise Decision Management," *Cutter Consortium Business Intelligence,* Vol. 5, No. 6, 2005.

# The Smart Enough Systems Manifesto

The business world has never been more complex or changing more rapidly than it is today. Organizations trying to survive and thrive must act smarter, yet their information systems are not smart enough. They fail to make the right decisions or fail to make any decisions at all, exposing the organization to risks and causing it to miss opportunities. This dilemma leads to the manifesto—a cry for systems that are smart enough for today's business world and the even more complex one coming tomorrow.

## Operational Decisions Are Important

Organizations[1] are perceived through the lens of the decisions they make.

- Some decisions are major (which countries to do business in), and some are minor (what to offer as a cross-sell to a customer on the phone).

- Organizations make far more decisions than they think because they mistake a collection of minor decisions for a single, more major decision.

- An organization interacts with an associate[2] (customer, supplier, distribution agent) and makes a decision about that interaction every time it sends a letter or an e-mail, makes a phone call, serves a Web page, prices a product, and so on.

- These operational decisions are made in huge volumes by all but the smallest organizations, whenever and wherever those organizations operate.

---

[1] Many organizations are being forced to change by changes in the business world, so this manifesto considers both for-profit and not-for-profit organizations.

[2] Companies have employees, suppliers, partners, and customers. Government agencies might have employees, citizens, and regulated companies. All are considered associates of the organization.

**Lots of small decisions add up.**

- Small improvements in the way minor decisions are made have a major effect over the course of many decisions.
- Organizations are much better at recognizing major decisions than minor ones.
- Organizations often spend a lot of time and effort making sure they make major decisions correctly.
- Nevertheless, the cumulative effect of many minor decisions can mean the difference between success and failure.
- Organizations are often unwilling to invest in improving a set of minor decisions, at least in part because they don't recognize the value of those decisions.

**All decisions an organization makes should be managed as though they are deliberate.**

- The recipient of an organization's action regards the action as the result of a deliberate decision the organization has made.
- Regardless of whether recipients like or dislike a decision, they assume it was deliberate.
- Most organizations don't act as though this is the case, allowing decisions to be made at random by aging information systems or poorly trained and informed staff.
- Loyalty to, and a good opinion of, an organization, as well as the quality of experience when interacting with an organization, are affected by these decisions.

## Operational Decisions Can and Should Be Automated

**High-volume, operational decisions can and should be automated.**

- High-volume operational decisions can be identified and automated successfully.
- Automated decisions can be
  - Precise, because they include expert judgment and learn from past successes and failures
  - Consistent across channels, geographies, time, and associates
  - Agile, in that they can be changed to react to new ideas and new opportunities
  - Carried out quickly to speed processes and allow organizations to operate at the pace their associates demand

- Made for the minimum cost required to make good decisions
- None of this automation requires science-fiction technology. You can do this, and you work with organizations that do it already.

**Traditional technology approaches won't succeed in automating decisions.**

- Current business intelligence is focused on delivering reports and hindsight to knowledge workers, not on making better decisions at the point of contact.
- Existing "legacy" systems with hard-coded decisions are too hard to modify quickly in a rapidly changing world.
- Business users can't control or even understand the decisions embedded in systems built with standard programming tools and approaches.
- Enterprise applications don't focus coherently on decisions and don't allow the decisions they do automate to be managed effectively.
- Business process management systems, event-driven architectures, and service orientation aren't sufficient to properly automate decisions, because they lack a coherent focus on those decisions.

**The overall effectiveness of automated decisions must be measured, tracked, and improved over time.**

- No organization is static, no market is static, no customer base is static, and no competitor is static.
- In a rapidly changing world, no decision remains optimal indefinitely, no matter how much has been invested in making it.
- Only measurement, constant improvement, and ongoing revision of decisions in the face of changing conditions can be relied on to ensure effective operations in the future.

## Taking Control of Operational Decisions Is Increasingly a Source of Competitive Advantage

- As the world becomes flatter—that is, more global—the connections between organizations, their suppliers, and partners must become more automated. Therefore, organizations that can automate good decisions will have an advantage.

- As the era of mass-market products makes way for massive Internet-enabled choice, organizations must manage their business at a more finely grained level, giving an advantage to those who can focus on micro decisions.

- As baby boomers retire, organizations that can capture their expertise will have an edge over those that can't. More of the day-to-day work will have to be automated, along with the decisions that need to be made.

- As business processes and supply chains become more electronic, using Internet technologies and electronic data-capture systems such as radio frequency identification (RFID), organizations that can decide faster can move faster.

- As social networks become more important, and consumers are better informed and have more power to influence an organization's success or failure, organizations must be able to react more quickly and effectively to the information about them on these networks.

- Consumers, employees, and partners increasingly want to do more for themselves—to self-serve—meaning that an organization wanting to deliver excellent service must make decisions when its associates want to, not when the organization wants to.

- The pace of change keeps increasing. Therefore, successful organizations will be those more adept at changing their behavior quickly, so the way they make decisions can't be static.

- As organizations become more electronically connected, data volumes continue to grow. Organizations that find ways to turn that data into useful insights and improve their decisions will outperform those that don't.

- As an always-on, interconnected world becomes a reality, organizations must operate so that decisions are made and appropriate actions are taken around the clock.

- As competition becomes fiercer and profit margins smaller, successful organizations will squeeze value from their transactions by managing risk and opportunity more effectively and at a more granular level.

- As government regulations and social-justice issues grow more complex and more important, so organizations must demonstrate compliance in all their decisions.

# CHAPTER ONE

# The Need for Smart Enough Systems

The world is changing fast, and well-documented business and economic changes, such as the growth of outsourcing and Internet retailing, are increasingly affecting the way organizations must operate. Some organizations will see these trends as creating opportunity and adapt to take advantage of them. Others will try to deal with these trends with a minimum of change but will still have to face competitors that are using these trends to their advantage. Given the importance of information systems to most organizations, all organizations need systems smart enough to handle their operations effectively in this new environment.

## The Importance of Operational Decisions

**Smart enough systems** deliver effective automation of the decisions that drive organizations' day-to-day operations. Although organizations have automated standard processes with enterprise software, these operational decisions haven't been the focus of investment. They are overwhelmingly made manually or automated poorly, which is a mistake. Embedding business processes in systems to streamline operations but not managing and improving these decisions leaves half the opportunities for improvement untouched. The means and the resources are now available to close that gap.

For more than a decade, organizations have strived to make their operations more efficient by rationalizing business processes, eliminating the handoffs between people that added latency and cost, driving down the cost of support with software standardization and data center consolidation, and outsourcing. None of these efforts, even the most successful ones, provided much more than a short-term competitive advantage, because they attacked the problem from the denominator—revenue per employee, sales per store—always focused on taking out cost but not emphasizing the numerator: benefits. Unfortunately, this approach is what's known as a "Red Queen" exercise, a reference to the Red Queen observing to Alice in Wonderland, "In this place, it takes all the running you can do, to keep in the same place."

## Operational Decisions Matter

In 2004, an Opinion Research Corporation[1] survey of executives found a clear opportunity to automate and improve decisions. Operational decisions were high-impact, but only a fraction had been automated, and maintenance cost and time to market were real problems. Specifically, the findings included the following:

- More than 90 percent felt that front-line operational decisions affected profitability.

- About half had not yet automated about 25 percent of these decisions, and nearly 80 percent still lacked automation for more than half of them.

- Making the right decisions with a high degree of accuracy and precision was very important to more than 90 percent of respondents. More than 60 percent also rated consistency of decision making and effective management as important.

- 85 percent expressed difficulty in changing decision-making criteria in their systems, with more than 50 percent saying it took months to get business changes implemented in production.

- 60 percent felt that automated decisions were carried out inconsistently or they were forced to deal with redundant logic in multiple systems to prevent this problem.

- 70 percent of chief information officers/chief technology officers (CIOs/CTOs) didn't believe they were getting the most value they could from their data. The most common reason was that their inability to blend business rules with data prevented them from maximizing the value of their data.

In a survey by Teradata[2] in 2004, 75 percent of the senior executives of top U.S. companies said that the number of daily decisions has increased over the past year, and more than 50 percent said that decisions are more complex this year than last year. The overwhelming majority of respondents, more than 70 percent, said that poor decision making is a serious problem for business. The top casualties of poor decision making are profits, company reputation, long-term growth, employee morale, productivity, and revenue.

For many organizations, the only way information technology has been applied to decisions is in the form of business intelligence or **decision support**—analyzing of data to help someone make a decision. Decision support as a discipline has always been aimed at the small segment of the population that uses data to make important decisions in organizations: managers and knowledge workers. It hasn't been effective at more fine-tuned, operational decision making that's just as crucial to the organization's well-being, if not more so. In addition, current enterprise data architectures are cleanly divided between operational systems and those that support the analytical and reporting processes behind decision support. This division leads to excessive duplication of data, latency in its accessibility, and usually a high degree of mismatch between analytical and operational data. Coupled with the rapidly increasing volumes of data being generated and the increasing rate of disparity as data arrives from external sources, the situation needs a better solution.

What's needed is a blueprint for orienting data, systems, and people to manage operational decisions more effectively and a way to automate decisions when appropriate and streamline those that still require some level of human intervention. Smart enough systems are computer applications that have enough intelligence to make these kinds of decisions without intervention. These systems offer a true strategic advantage. To understand why, you need to consider what "strategic" advantages involve, as discussed in the next section.

### Strategy Drives Decision Making

> *"The essence of strategy is choosing to perform activities differently than rivals do."*
> *—Dr. Michael Porter, Bishop William Lawrence University Professor at Harvard Business School*

Dr. Porter's quote is more relevant today than ever. With fewer geographic barriers and always-on connectivity, your organization must *behave* differently to stand out from the crowd. You might choose to perform activities that your competitors don't perform, not perform activities your competitors do, or (most likely) perform the same activities but perform them differently.

---

[1] Opinion Research Corporation. "IT Professionals and Decision Automation." A sample of 200 IT professionals at companies over $100 million in revenue, including 40 CIOs/CTOs. Companies included retail banking, credit card, mortgage, property and casualty, health, life insurance, telecom, retail, and healthcare providers. Survey was conducted July 1–29, 2004.

[2] Teradata 2004–2005 Report on Enterprise Decision-Making, fielded by BuzzBack online market research between July 23 and August 3, 2004, querying 202 executives, with follow-up conducted September 3–9, 2004.

Critical to behaving differently is an ability to *decide* differently. Deciding when to omit or add an activity and when and how to change the way you perform an activity are essential. A strategic advantage must make an impact on strategy, which means it must change your decisions.

The decisions you must change could be occasional strategic decisions, such as whether to acquire a certain company or enter a new market. Or they could be more tactical and operational, focused on how you treat a customer the next time he calls your call center or how you price a product on your Web site. All these decisions must be driven by your strategy if you are to deliver effectively on that strategy. Although your organization probably focuses on getting major strategic decisions correct, you might struggle to keep your operational activities—the way front-line members of staff and applications behave—synchronized with your strategic plans. For example:

- You might want to treat all gold customers a certain way, but you have a self-service application that doesn't differentiate between customers.

- You might want to get more aggressive about retaining customers who are likely to leave, but your call center representatives have too many campaigns to remember, so they treat everyone the same.

- You might want to offer dynamic pricing to suppliers, but the software that drives your Web site does not use the pricing algorithms sales representatives use.

Unless your operational activities reflect your strategy accurately, your organization can't succeed. You can't even be said to be implementing your strategy.

### Strategy Is Not Static

The problem of ensuring that your operational activities match your strategy is exacerbated by the need for **business agility.** Business agility is critical to survival in a rapidly changing world, so your strategy can't be static. You must constantly refine and update it to keep up with competitors, market shifts, and consumer preferences.

Most executives say their companies are facing a more competitive environment than they were five years ago; in fact, 85 percent say "more" or "much more."[3] Organizations that want to compete effectively must change continuously and base those changes on feedback about what is and isn't working. Those unwilling or unable to do so must recognize that they will soon be competing with organizations that have changed, if they aren't doing so already. No organization can remain immune; all will have to change somehow.

---

[3] McKinsey Global. "An Executive Take on the Top Business Trends." Survey conducted 2006.

Not only must your strategy change more rapidly, but you also have more information about why and how it must change than ever before. The growth in business intelligence and performance management systems[4] means you have more insight into how well (or poorly) you are doing. To respond effectively to this new understanding, however, delivering new processes, skills, and expertise rapidly to front-line workers and information systems is essential.

For instance, if your analysis of last week's sales shows that a competitor is eating into your sales, and you decide a new pricing model is required, many factors influence how quickly you can respond. Your cultural willingness to change, for example, or your escalation and sign-off processes determine how quickly you go from recognizing a problem to *intending* to respond to it. The key issue, however, is likely to be how quickly you can move from that *intent* to a change in the operational behavior that implements your new strategy. After all, if your operations haven't changed, no customer or other associate is likely to notice—they won't detect the change in your pricing or how it affects them.

However, changing your operations means changing the way your operational information systems behave. Your information systems characterize your operations in such a fundamental way that you can no longer separate them from your business—your systems *are* your business. The time it takes to change your operational systems determines how fast you can modify your operations and is the ultimate determinant of your business agility.

Agility also contributes to **strategic alignment**—how well your strategies are reflected in your business operations. Without agility, your organization can't consistently carry out a new strategy without an extended period of change. Indeed, you risk never achieving strategic alignment if changes to the strategy occur faster than the organization can respond.

Often this alignment, or lack of it, can be seen in the organization's operational or front-line activities. Indeed, divergent agendas and miscommunication between those working on an organization's strategy and those carrying it out operationally are chronic problems. These disconnects can hinder executive leadership's access to information about what's really going on and their ability to effect change in organizational behavior when they see the need. A recent study[5] included the following statement:

> *"Most devastating, 95 percent of employees in most organizations do not understand their [organization's] strategy."*

---

[4] Business intelligence systems is used here to refer to reporting and analysis tools for managers and knowledge workers, while performance management systems are those driving more real-time monitoring tools such as dashboards.

[5] Q&A with Robert Kaplan, "The Office of Strategy Management," Working Knowledge for Business Leaders, Harvard Business School. March 27, 2006.

Many things contribute to these disconnects between strategy and operations. Among them are a lack of agility (the strategy has changed too often for the employees to keep track), execution problems (the decisions made by front-line employees aren't affected by the strategy), and secrecy (the strategy is confidential, proprietary, and a competitive advantage, so fear that it will "get out" prevents its dissemination). You must solve these problems to ensure that your strategy is carried out continuously and effectively, top to bottom, by both people and information systems.

Therefore, a dynamic, agile strategy means being able to decide to act differently and then being able to apply that decision to the way your operations work. However, to change the way your operations work, you have to change the way you make operational decisions.

## Operational Decisions Matter

*"Most discussions of decision making assume that only senior executives make decisions or that only senior executives' decisions matter. This is a dangerous mistake."[6]*
*—Peter Drucker*

When most organizations think about the decisions that matter, they think about the decisions executives or boards make: the major strategic decisions that can make or break an organization. However, Peter Drucker noted that the decisions front-line workers make matter. They interact directly with your customers, partners, suppliers, and other associates but are often among the lowest-paid staff you have. They probably also have the highest turnover and are among the most likely to work for a third party or on a contract basis, yet they make crucial decisions about how your organization treats associates every day.

However, at least you actually have someone interacting with your customers or other associates when front-line workers are making decisions. Sometimes no one is involved when your computer systems interact directly with your associates. The options your interactive voice response (IVR) system lists, the way your Web site promotes products, the letter your campaign management system decides to send, the price your online booking system calculates for a customer—these operational decisions also influence your associates.

Although the influence of each operational decision is small, their cumulative effect can be huge. As shown in Figure 1.1, the value of individual strategic decisions is much higher than that of individual operational decisions. However, the cumulative value

---

[6] Peter Drucker, "What Makes an Effective Executive," Harvard Business Review, Vol. 82, No. 6, June 2004.

shows a more balanced picture. The large volumes involved in operational decisions mean that their cumulative impact can meet or exceed that of strategic decisions.

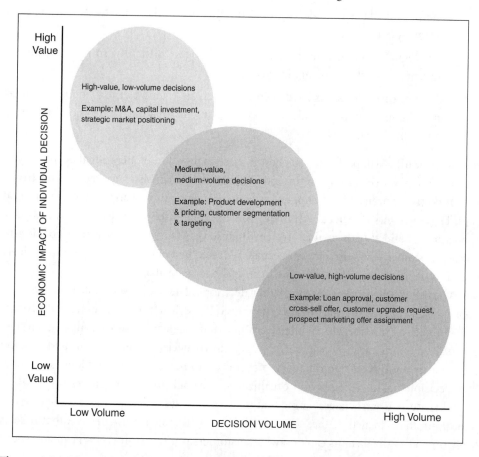

**Figure 1.1   The value and volume of different kinds of decisions**

Although a single big strategic decision has a high value, it's likely to be made with planning and analysis, thoughtfully and by the best minds in your organization. In contrast, operational decisions often aren't made so deliberately. This lack of focus is the result of several factors:

- Each decision has a low individual value; it doesn't seem that important to get the cross-sell offer for this customer just right, for example.

- The sheer volume of decisions involved is high—hundreds, thousands, and even millions for larger organizations.

- The number of workers who handle operational decisions makes managing these decisions seem impossible.
- The time available to make most operational decisions is short, not lending itself to time spent in analysis.
- The "right" way to make these decisions changes constantly, so investing in the current approach can seem ill advised.
- Many of these decisions have been effectively delegated to the IT department by embedding them in the code of an existing system, making the decision logic hard to find or change.

Your organization will perform at its best if these high-volume operational decisions can be made at a lower cost, in real time, and with maximum consistency. The systems front-line workers use aren't smart enough to make decisions, however—certainly not good ones. These workers also need technology to help them discover, assess, and address new opportunities and threats as they present themselves. The first person in a position to notice a customer who's unhappy or seems interested in a new product or service is likely to be a front-line worker, not someone in an office looking at a report.

What front-line workers need is better decisions. They need to be able to make decisions in high volume and narrow time windows. If they can't make or execute decisions, they can't deliver good service or effective support. If the decisions are wrong or even suboptimal, your organization will suffer. Operational decisions are critical, and making them poorly undermines productivity, prevents customer-centricity, and lowers revenue. Poor decision making reduces your organization's overall ability to be successful.

Likewise, your associates assume that the way your systems treat them is the way you want them to be treated. If the Web site, ATM, or IVR system is ineffective, that reflects badly on you. If the systems can't do what customers want, customers will call and speak to representatives, creating wait times that delay other customers.

The operational decisions at the front-line of your organization are, cumulatively, essential to your ability to run your organization the way you intend. Unless these decisions, too, are driven by your strategy and carried out with maximum effectiveness and efficiency, your organization won't perform at its best. Making good operational decisions, however, is getting harder.

### Operational Decisions Are Under Pressure

Napoleon Bonaparte said, "Nothing is more difficult, and therefore more precious, than to be able to decide." Making the right operational decision is only getting harder as pressures on the decisions you must make grow:

- Decisions that once might have taken days now have to be made at the speed of the transaction, such as while your customer is completing an online purchase.

- Business objectives used to be simpler and set at the local level. Now those objectives are often set at the corporate level and involve trade-offs between risk, resource constraints, opportunity costs, and other factors.

- You're being forced to comply with more new regulations, stricter and more complex rules, shorter deadlines, and more serious consequences for noncompliance.

- You need to change your strategy—such as how to manage customers to retain them in the face of competition—more frequently and more rapidly to deal with competitive forces, environmental changes, and changes in your customer base.

- Decisions once owned by a single group might now be shared by multiple departments and have to be coordinated across channels and regions.

- Some decisions that were handled with manual review processes now occur in volumes or time frames that make manual processes impractical.

- The value of a decision could once be measured in terms of the cost and time needed to make it; now other objectives are also used to measure value.

Implementing your strategy means making decisions that support it every day and at all levels. It means making these decisions quickly and keeping them aligned with a strategy that adapts and changes. It means turning operational decision making into an asset, not a liability.

## Operational Decision Making as a Corporate Asset

If operational decisions must be made well for your organization to deliver on its strategy, they can't be made randomly. They have to be made systematically. You have to turn operational decision making into a corporate asset you can measure, control, and improve. After all, when associates interact with you, they consider every decision you make to be a "corporate" one—that is, a deliberate one.

Every day you must make decisions faster and across more channels and product lines, which makes it harder to ensure that the decisions your organization makes are the best ones *and* the ones you intended to make. What makes an operational decision the right one?

### Characteristics of Operational Decisions

To be effective, an operational decision must be precise, agile, consistent, fast, and cost-effective:

- **Precise**—Good operational decisions use data quickly and effectively to take the right action, behaving like a knowledgeable employee with the right reports and analyses. They use this data to derive insight into the future, not just awareness of the past, and use this insight to act more appropriately. They use information about customers to target them through microsegmentation and extreme personalization. They use behavioral predictions for each transaction or customer to ensure that risk and return are balanced properly, and they use the information a customer (or supplier or partner) has provided (explicitly or implicitly) to improve the customer experience.

- **Agile**—Operational decisions can be changed rapidly to reflect new opportunities, new organizations, and new threats; otherwise, they rapidly decline in value. No modern business system can stay static for long. The competitive, economic, and regulatory environment simply doesn't allow it. When organizations automate their processes and transactions, they often find that the time to respond to change is affected largely by how quickly they can change their information systems. To minimize lost opportunity costs and maximize overall business agility, operational decisions must be easy to change quickly and effectively. The agility of these decisions—both the speed of identifying opportunities to improve and the readiness with which they can be changed—ensures that they remain aligned with an organization's strategy, even as that strategy changes and evolves.

- **Consistent**—Your operational decisions must be consistent across the increasing range of channels you operate through—the Web, mobile devices, interactive voice response systems, and kiosks, for example—and across time and geography. They allow you to act differently when you choose to—to offer a lower price online to encourage the use of a lower-cost channel, for example—but ensure that you don't do so accidentally. These systems support third parties and agents who act on your behalf and the people who work for you directly. They enforce your organization's laws, policies, and social preferences wherever it does business and make sure you avoid fines and legal issues. They deliver a consistently excellent experience for your associates.

- **Fast**—You need to take the best action that time allows. The saying on the Internet is that your competition is three clicks away. Your associates are learning to be impatient and have short attention spans. Meanwhile, your supply and demand chains are becoming more real-time, and the systems that manage them must respond quickly as well as smartly. With fewer employees handling more customers, partners, and suppliers, you must eliminate the wait time for these associates. You must decide, and act, quickly.

- **Cost-effective**—Above all, operational decisions must be cost-effective. Despite the massive efficiency gains and cost reductions of recent years, reducing costs continues to be essential. Good operational decisions help eliminate wasteful activities and costly reports. They reduce fraud and prevent fines. They help your people be more productive and spend their time where it really matters. They make sure you do as many things right the first time as possible and avoid expensive "do-overs." They reduce the friction that slows processes and increases costs.

Operational decisions are what make your business strategy real and ensure that your organization runs effectively, right down to the front-lines interacting with your associates. To ensure that operational decisions are effective, you need to manage operational decision making. The change in mind-set required is akin to the changing view of data over the past few years. Data is no longer just something needed to run systems; it has become visible to many and is managed as a resource for the whole organization—a corporate asset. Managing operational decision making as a corporate asset means treating it as strategic, managing it explicitly, making it visible and reusable across the organization, and improving it constantly.

## Characteristics of Corporate Assets

A focus on operational decision making means treating decisions as corporate assets, which means ensuring that these assets have the following characteristics:

- **Strategic**—A corporate asset is strategic. Planning exercises consider how it can be used and applied to reduce costs, increase revenue, and expand the business. Ensuring that decision making is strategic means considering the process of making low-level operational decisions critical to the business and worthy of executive and management focus.

- **Managed**—Corporate assets must be managed, maintained, and kept in good working order. They must be reviewed and improved dynamically and continuously. Decision making is similar to equipment that needs constant maintenance, replacement of small parts, and upgrading. Because decisions must change and adapt, they must be managed.

- **Visible**—A corporate asset must be available and visible to management if it's to be used correctly. It must be understood as a competitive weapon and subject to reporting and analysis. Making decision making visible means managing decision-making assets as you would other aspects of the organization's infrastructure, storing information about decisions in technology designed for that purpose, and making the use of this technology and supporting techniques standard across your organization.

- **Reusable**—Assets aren't casually duplicated or left idle but are reused and leveraged as much as possible. Decision making must be reusable across manual and automated processes and systems, internally and externally.

- **Improving**—Decision making must improve constantly; in other words, you must close the learning-improvement loop. Closed-loop decision making, as shown in Figure 1.2, enables you to capture results from production systems and put what you learn from them into a useful form rapidly. It means updating decisions based on your results or outcomes. Decision automation requires supporting all these steps.

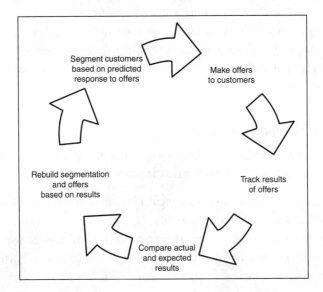

**Figure 1.2    An example of closed-loop decision making for marketing**

Systems that can treat operational decisions as a corporate asset, deliver the best operational decisions, and ensure that those operational decisions reflect your business strategy are what we call Smart (Enough) Systems.

## Introducing Smart Enough Systems

What kind of systems would deliver this vision of operational decisions? The term "smart enough systems" is used in this book to describe them. A smart enough system is not some kind of artificial intelligence device like HAL 9000 (from *2001: A Space Odyssey*). Equally, a smart enough system can't be developed the same way you build traditional "dumb" information systems.

Building smart enough systems means taking a new approach to bringing automation to operational decisions. Instead of hard-coding decision rules into systems, it means using separate tools to build, manage, and carry out decisions in concert with other operating processes. It means developing new services that can deliver operational decisions that perform well enough to be used in real-time front-line systems and processes. It means developing services that are agile enough to keep up with a changing world and, indeed, learn from it. It means services that make customer-centered (associate-centered) decisions and services that can support an extended enterprise.

### Characteristics of Smart Enough Systems

Smart enough systems have some key characteristics. In particular, they are operational and capable of real-time performance. They are agile, capable of learning, and customer- (associate) centered as well as compliant and supportive of an increasingly extended enterprise.

#### *Operational*

The increasingly distributed and always-on nature of organizations puts a premium on **high-performance execution,** which means operating quickly, flawlessly, legally, and profitably at every level. It's about more than how your employees perform; it's about how your *systems* perform.

For organizations to exhibit high-performance execution in day-to-day operations, their top performers' expert judgment must be made available everywhere. This means making sure the systems everyone uses embody that expertise—not in an expert system, ask-if-you-get-stuck way, but with systems that are embedded in the operational processes necessary to the business. This expertise, however, must be balanced by analytic insight developed by a careful analysis of the organization and its operational history. As Malcolm Gladwell said:

> *"Truly successful decision making relies on a balance between deliberate and instinctive thinking."* [7]
> *—Malcolm Gladwell*

---

[7] Malcolm Gladwell, *Blink: The Power of Thinking Without Thinking.* Little, Brown and Company. January 2005.

Not only must the organization's expertise be balanced with an effort to run the organization "by the numbers," but the interaction skills of those who serve as the point of contact with associates also must be considered. For the moment, no system can replace human interaction. Ensuring that these interactions make use of decisions informed with an analysis of past success and experts' judgment can ensure that customers get the best possible experience and organizations can get the best possible results. Smart enough systems make organizational knowledge "explicit, executable, actionable, and adaptable."[8]

### Capable of Real-Time Performance

Smart enough systems must operate in a no-wait, multichannel world where customers and other associates expect responses, actions, and decisions immediately. Suppliers expect immediate updates on the demand chain, and retailers and distributors expect to know about problems in the supply chain instantly. Real-time connections between organizations are also essential, because organizations must become more loosely coupled. They must deliver their products and services by coordinating and orchestrating many distinct organizations, both internal and external.

In the past it was sufficient to coordinate operations within an enterprise, but today successful organizations must be able to operate with both known and unknown entities without delays. Systems can't wait for someone to wake up before acting, and people want to be told what has been done to make their life easier, not asked for decisions. Smart enough systems must make decisions fast enough to be used in operational, real-time systems.

### Agile

An agile organization can effectively change the way it operates when it needs to, but only if it has a good understanding of how it's operating and why it operates that way. Smart enough systems support this agility by making how they operate explicit, easy to understand, and easy to modify. Agility is a measurement of the total time and cost in getting from having the data that means you *should* change your business to actually making the change.

---

[8] Peter Fingar, *The Real-Time Enterprise*, Meghan Kiffer Pr. October 2004.

---

### Agile Compliance

In the heavily regulated environment in which many organizations must operate, agility can't come at the expense of compliance. Every time an organization shifts its strategy and changes its operations, it needs to be sure that the new approach is compliant and can be demonstrated to be so. Compliance, then, can act as a drag on an agile organization by preventing it from making changes as quickly as needed unless the approach it uses to achieve agility allows it to remain compliant—which can be called "agile compliance."[9]

---

Gartner Group Inc. defines agility as "the ability of an organization to sense environmental change and to respond efficiently and effectively to that change."[10] Gartner uses an agility cycle,[11] shown in Figure 1.3, to show how agility is achieved and to indicate that it's ongoing. The basic steps are sensing a threat or opportunity, strategizing about options, deciding on the most appropriate action, and then communicating it before acting. This cycle must be continuous, because each change must be monitored for subsequent changes.

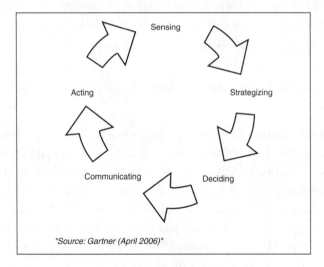

"Source: Gartner (April 2006)"

**Figure 1.3    The agility cycle**

---

[9] A phrase first used by Hugh Taylor in his book *The Joy of SOX*, Wiley, April, 2006.
[10] Daryl C. Plummer, and David W. McCoy. "Achieving Agility: Defining Agility in an IT Context." Gartner Group, Inc. 4/20/2006.
[11] Ibid.

**Human Latency** *People will always be a bottleneck when it comes to change. Gartner defines "human latency" as something that reduces agility, for instance. Some technology approaches make it harder to be agile, and some make it easier. Some help you persuade people to change; others help you make the changes after they have been agreed on. Organizations in the future will have to improve their agility organizationally and in terms of the technology they use and how they use it.*

### Capable of Learning

Smart enough systems need to "learn" as new data is collected. Organizations collect an enormous quantity of data, and the volume of data is increasing steadily. Generally, organizations don't have systems that are smart enough to take advantage of this data. For instance, a PricewaterhouseCoopers Barometer survey[12] in late 2006 gave an accurate summary of how organizations think their data should give them a real competitive edge and why it currently doesn't:

- 71 percent of senior executives describe the data in their company's information systems as potentially very valuable.

- 68 percent of these executives expect this data will become even more valuable as a source of competitive advantage during the next 12 to 18 months.

- 84 percent cited their inability to mine and interpret data as the highest-ranked obstacle to achieving value.

- 75 percent said that an ability to mine and interpret data was key to getting value from data.

You have to do more than collect, organize, and report on your data. You, and your systems, have to learn from it, mine it for insights, and interpret what it means for the future. Doing so is a key to taking advantage of one of your last remaining areas of competitive advantage—knowledge of your associates—and is a way to improve performance by insisting on realism. If your business decisions are based on what your data tells you, you're more likely to get realism than if you rely on hunches and how you have always done something. Even Malcolm Gladwell, in his paean to instinctive reactions, noted that informed snap judgments outperform uninformed ones.

---

[12] Results from interviews with 107 top executives of large, U.S.-based multinational businesses, for PricewaterhouseCoopers' Management Barometer.

### Competing on Analytics

In their book,[13] Davenport and Harris describe competing on analytics as "the extensive use of data, statistical and quantitative analysis, explanatory and predictive models, and fact-based management to drive decisions and actions." They define an analytical competitor as an organization that uses analytics extensively and systematically to out-think and outperform its competition. They see a growing cadre of companies competing this way and identify a number of trends as a result:

- More automated decisions

- More real-time decisions

- Increased use of alerts

- More prediction and less reporting

- More mining of text

Companies wanting to compete with analytics will require far more than a few "PhDs with personality" using data-mining tools on existing enterprise data. They will need a systematic framework for using analytics to make their systems smarter.

You must also realize that a generation of workers, the baby boomers, is retiring. The new generation of workers is more technology-literate but is unlikely to take the kind of jobs their parents and grandparents took. Even if they did, they lack the depth of experience on which organizations have been relying. Those retiring baby boomers know all the tricks, exceptions, and workarounds that make your manual decisions work. Without them, you need some other way to get this knowledge to your workers, and these workers will look to information systems for that knowledge.

---

[13] Tom Davenport and Jeanne Harris. *Competing on Analytics*. Harvard Business School Press, 2007.

## Customer- (Associate) Centered

*"Customers can access more information about more vendors, negotiate more effectively with still more vendors, and switch from one vendor to another whenever they find greater value."*[14]

Much money and energy have been spent using technology to improve customer relationships, ***yet much of it has been used as a technological alternative to talking with customers, not to empower customers.***

Many organizations fail to respond to customers in a consistent, focused, targeted way and have customer processes that are costly in terms of customer satisfaction, operating costs, and profits. As the world moves faster and gets more complex in terms of regulations and competition, this situation will get worse. Customers expect quicker decisions and are no longer willing to wait for them. With all the information about competitors and quick Web-based access to them, they can find an alternative easily.

With the many channels now available, the potential for annoying or ignoring customers unintentionally is rising. Competitors are constantly forcing reactions, because customers might find another supplier who offers them something more compelling. These customers want to self-serve, to actively manage their relationship with their suppliers, and the organization of the future must make it possible for them to do so. As interactive web applications get better, many people will prefer "self-service" over "customer service."

The information an organization has about its associates is widely regarded as one of the few advantages an "incumbent" has. The current frenzy for customer data integration (CDI) is clear evidence that more attention is being paid to managing the resource of customer data. However, it doesn't matter how well managed and integrated this information is unless it contains customer preferences, and unless their preferences and your insights are used to tailor interactions with them.

---

[14] John Hagel and John Seely-Brown, *The Only Sustainable Edge*. Harvard Business School Press. May 2005.

The information you have about associates is a critical advantage only if you can learn from it. This learning can't be static, either; you can't discover an interesting piece of information about your associates and then stop. This insight must make it into your systems. Smart enough systems focus on better decisions for how to treat associates.

### Support for an Extended Enterprise

The growth of outsourcing and smartsourcing[15] is leading to more loosely coupled organizations or groups of organizations. As Hagel and Seely-Brown said, "Loose coupling represents a more modular approach to process management."[16] **Loose coupling** means creating independent activities with clear owners and interfaces and performance guidelines. These activities can then be assembled and disassembled more easily to meet changing needs. This kind of business structure parallels the more flexible approach to information systems represented by a service-oriented architecture (SOA). This approach implies trusting relationships.

Organizations adopting this approach need systems smart enough to work in this environment and smart enough to allow associates to change how decisions are made in the processes that span organizations—that is, processes that require multiple organizations to deliver. Business processes, which once belonged to a single organization, are now composed of agile mini-processes that must be configured dynamically across organizational boundaries. This is impossible without the handshake of industry standards, directory services, and orchestration—and, once again, loose coupling in a service-oriented architecture. The systems supporting these processes must also be smart enough to generate the kind of audit trails and decision outcome logs that build trust between companies and between companies and their regulators.

---

[15] Thomas M. Koulopoulos. *Smartsourcing: Driving Innovation and Growth Through Outsourcing.* Platinum Press, Inc. April 2006.

[16] John Hagel and John Seely-Brown. *The Only Sustainable Edge.* Harvard Business School Press. May 2005.

## Web 2.0

There was a time when trendy expressions were durable. "Groovy" lasted about five years before it was no longer "cool" to say it. In business, "impact" as a verb stuck around for a decade or more. During the Web Bubble, "disintermediation" was cool for a year or so before, as with other trendy words, using it indicated you were a little behind the curve. The problem is that technology moves so fast now that these terms fall out of favor long before they have a chance to prove themselves. This trend is already happening with "Web 2.0."

Web 2.0 has real merit and staying power, however. It might no longer be avant-garde because of overuse and overexposure, and by favoring it we may find ourselves a bit derriere. But the term is an intermediate point between the original "World Wide Web," a collection of pages and a protocol for using them, and "Web 3.0," the truly semantic Web, where the entire collection can be mined for meaning. Web 2.0 offers some fascinating features and capabilities that enable people, organizations, governments, and even machines to interact based on some simple principles:

- **The Web as a platform**—The Web itself becomes the place where computing happens, which is part of the growing interconnectedness or "flattening" of the world. Services on the Internet can be assembled and disassembled at will.

- **Collective intelligence and wisdom of crowds**—Some evidence exists that the collective behavior of large numbers of people is a better predictor than expert judgment.

- **Using data, not just collecting it**—Data is gathered from both internal and external sources with the intent to use it to act differently.

- **The end of release cycles**—Continuous, unnoticed software change without conflicting and overlapping release cycles replaces point releases and disruptive, crippling maintenance efforts that drain IT budgets.

- **Designs for "mashing" and "hacking" applications**—These application designs provide a rich user experience in the corporate IT environment by "mashing" multiple applications together or by "hacking" an application to alter its behavior. This is all made possible by adherence to standards precipitated by the dynamic nature of the Web.

Operational decisions being reflected in services, the use of predictive analytics to apply the implications of group behavior to transactions, the focus on getting insight from data rather than just collecting data, and the ability to refine decisions continually without affecting other systems are characteristics of smart enough systems and Web 2.0.

## Service-Oriented Architecture

Service-oriented architecture (SOA) is one of those phrases that gets thrown around in everything from technical standards to business books. Thomas Erl makes four key points in his books: [17]

- SOA can establish an abstraction of business logic and technology that allows a looser coupling between an organization's processes and its technology.

- SOA is an evolution of past approaches, preserving successful characteristics of traditional architectures and adding distinct new principles that foster service orientation.

- SOA is ideally standardized throughout an enterprise, but achieving this requires a planned transition and still-evolving technology.

- SOA is a technology architecture that supports and promotes service-oriented principles throughout an enterprise.

What SOA does, at a fundamental level, is allow the development of individual pieces of business functionality in a way that lets them be combined and modified effectively and without tightly coupling them to each other.

Organizations must also handle more jobs that aren't located in one building or even one country but are outsourced or "homesourced" by using the Internet and related technologies to connect workers. The systems these workers use must be smart enough to let them do their jobs effectively and to act on behalf of the organization yet ensure compliance with company policy and more.

---

[17] Thomas Erl. *Service-Oriented Architecture (SOA): Concepts, Technology, and Design.* Prentice-Hall, 2005.

Thomas Friedman says, "There are currently about 245,000 people in India answering phones from all over the world or dialing out to solicit people for credit cards or cell phone bargains or overdue bills."[18] He describes a series of trends and technologies that have, in his words, "flattened" the world by making it more interconnected. He explains how this flattening fits with globalization and how companies are reinventing themselves in the face of these changes and describes some of the problems, risks, and effects on political and public policy.

For example, deciding where to locate work is becoming more complex. More options, with advantages and disadvantages, are available, thanks to the overall increase in interconnectedness. Friedman explains that work will go where it can be done most effectively.

Another concept emphasized in the book is that of global, dynamic supply chains that "[coordinate] disruption-prone supply with hard-to-predict demand." For most of history, location has been critical for businesses of all kinds: where to open a store, where to put a factory, where to find customers. Improvements in connectivity and network bandwidth, however, mean that location is no longer a factor. Now the trend is work taking place where it can be done best and for the lowest cost. In addition, organizations find customers as well as suppliers and staff all over the world. They can reach out to new markets, take advantage of new opportunities, and collaborate with new partners worldwide. The parallel growth in information content of products and the overall shift from products to services in the world economy have forced organizations to consider their "digital supply chain." You can no longer consider just how and when physical goods are moved through your supply chain; you must also manage the knowledge and information that flow through it.

This ability to build a more distributed, electronically connected organization has consequences, however. In particular, how do you control it? When you outsource work to India or homesource it to Peoria, how do you make sure the work is done the way you want it done, following your policies? You need to be able to ensure that people working all over the world for you and your partners or suppliers treat your customers, your products, and your employees the way you want them to. You must equip them to act as though you were sitting in the next cubicle, even though they are geographically dispersed and perhaps brought together only temporarily to meet a business need.

Will you rely on just policy manuals and training? Will you assume that the people making decisions on your behalf can interpret data correctly from their reports and apply your business strategy to what the data tells them? With homesourced booking agents, for

---

[18] Thomas Friedman. *The World Is Flat: A Brief History of the Twenty-first Century*. Farrar, Straus and Giroux. April 2006.

example, you want to make sure they offer your best travelers upgrades when they can and know how to prioritize customers who need rerouting. Those 245,000 phone operators in India need an automated system for approving credit and recommending what kind of collections strategy will work. They need smart enough systems.

### Demonstrably Compliant

Each new scandal seems to result in a new piece of regulation. Government and nonprofit organizations struggle under their own burden of reporting and compliance, and the penalties for noncompliance grow for organizations and individuals. For these reasons, governance and compliance are popular topics on the conference circuit.

Not only do organizations face more restrictions, but also many restrictions now demand *demonstrating* compliance. Organizations must be able to *show* that they are compliant with regulations. No one has to sue them or demand the information; they must report it annually, quarterly, or more often. In this environment, allowing front-line workers to make critical decisions is risky. They are less likely to be well trained, more likely to have high turnover, and most likely to be employed by third parties in the form of outsourcing. They don't necessarily make the best decisions. More important, showing that they made legal, appropriate, compliant decisions isn't easy. If more of your decisions are embedded in your information systems, however, you risk pushing the enforcement of these rules onto programmers who don't understand them, not onto businesspeople who do.

Additionally, more organizations must contend with multiple layers of regulation. They are obliged to follow local and national regulations, as they always have, and doing business on the Internet or using outsourcers around the world increasingly involves new sets of national regulations. Many international organizations, from the European Union to the World Trade Organization, also have rules that must be followed. Even knowing which set of local, national, and international rules must be applied to a specific transaction becomes a problem, let alone actually enforcing and demonstrating compliance with those rules.

Formal regulations are not the only rules an organization might need to follow. Socially conscious consumers, activist shareholders, and nongovernmental organizations also play a role. An organization might need to enforce rules to show that it's "green" or to defuse an unpopular perception of it. These "rules" must be enforced just like regulations, but they will be truly valuable only if made public. Those who care about these rules want to know exactly what the organization is planning to enforce. They want accountability—knowing what you did with their money, goods, and so forth. Managed transparency becomes important for most, if not all, organizations. Demonstrated compliance with publicly auditable rules creates new demands on systems and people.

Regulations are also becoming more sophisticated. No longer are they simply a set of rules to be enforced; some are starting to embody best practices and statistical measures. Two examples are Basel II,[19] with its enforcement of best practices in risk management, and court rulings forbidding personnel actions that might reasonably result in discrimination against a class of employee, even when no actions specifically do so. Being compliant won't get any easier.

The push toward compliance has a cost, however. As Taylor[20] notes, "The biggest problem with SOX . . . and [other regulations] is that it assumes a relatively static mode of business operations, and today, to be static is to be dead."

Organizations must deliver agile compliance; they must maintain business agility despite the burden of increased compliance. The increase in regulation tends to slow the rate of change in organizations by making it more expensive to make changes, but it can't stop change. Some organizations will find a way to evolve and be agile despite the regulations they operate under, and their competitors will need to do likewise. Achieving agility despite regulatory burdens requires smart enough systems.

### Current Approaches Fail

*"We have established that you cannot code your way into the future."[21]*

Different approaches to technology and systems development have failed to deliver smart enough systems so far, but why?

*"The problem is that computers and the software that runs on them . . . are notoriously difficult to change with any speed or accuracy."[22]*

First, decision logic (policy rules, formulas, thresholds, regulatory mandates, and other elements used to make decisions) traditionally has been hard-coded into operational systems. As a result, development is time-consuming and costly. Developers have to translate business requirements ("If this condition is encountered, respond in this manner") into abstract representations in programming. This is a laborious process full of possibilities

---

[19] New regulations from the Basel Committee on Banking Supervision (BCBS) in Basel, Switzerland, aimed to produce uniformity in the way banks and banking regulators approach risk management across national borders.

[20] Hugh Taylor. *The Joy of SOX: Why Sarbanes-Oxley and Services Oriented Architecture May Be the Best Thing That Ever Happened to You.* Wiley, 2006.

[21] Unknown Gartner Analyst, 2006

[22] Hugh Taylor. *The Joy of SOX: Why Sarbanes-Oxley and Services Oriented Architecture May Be the Best Thing That Ever Happened to You.* Wiley, 2006.

for error through misinterpretation. Developers have to try to anticipate all possible requirements and conditions because any changes after deployment could affect other parts of the program and require unraveling a good part of their work. Businesspeople requesting a change usually have to wait weeks or even months for the change to be coded and deployed, and because the hard-coded decision logic is buried in a system, it must be written (and rewritten) for each new platform or channel.

In addition, decision logic is difficult to understand. Because it's lodged in application programming code, business managers often have difficulty saying exactly how decisions are made. Different programmers might have coded layer after layer of policies and other types of rules in various ways. Some companies have tens of thousands of rules coded into their systems, including many that are irrelevant because they're based on market conditions and business requirements that no longer exist. Also, as organizations have moved from proprietary programs and applications to packaged applications from independent software vendors, the range of available decision rules and criteria has shrunk to those that could be "configured" with software system tools and workbenches.

Second, good decision making requires insight, especially into the probability of specific outcomes. Retail banking and other credit-extending companies have used this type of analysis extensively in automated decision systems. These "predictive analytics" are equally valuable—and still largely unused—for decision making in other industries. Business managers who want to bring predictive models into their decision processes might be daunted by the complexity of the data and analysis, however. Additionally, there's the impact of analytics deployments on IT resources. Predictive analytics, like decision logic, must be programmed into application code.

Third, although many companies can capture data from front-line systems and have invested heavily in data warehouses to store it, too much time might go by before they draw insights from the data. Most companies, in fact, often operate on stale data, partly because of what must be done to turn the data into a form useful for gaining insight.

Massive investment in business intelligence (BI) and data warehouse technology has undoubtedly helped management understand the impact of their decisions and detect trends in their business. What this technology hasn't done is improve the way employees and information systems that interact with customers make operational, front-line decisions. The purpose of using BI is to put it in the hands of people who can use analytic and business operations skills to understand what it's telling them. No matter how much visualization or smarts are embedded in these tools, they remain focused on knowledge workers who aren't the people making most of the decisions involved in day-to-day operations. These decisions are made by customer service representatives, counter staff, drivers, Web sites, or telephone support staff.

## The Data Tipping Point

More and more data is now available to organizations about their operations, their customer interactions, and their Web sites. With the arrival of radio frequency identification (RFID) chips on every palette, case or box of products, and eventually on every individual product, organizations will have more data about their supply chain than ever before. With mobile devices that are always on and fitted with global positioning system (GPS) chips, every vehicle and employee will be a source of a continuous stream of data. Customers, too, as their mobile phones interact with organizations' systems, will deliver constantly updated information about their whereabouts and activities. Growing sensor networks and the integration of massive external consumer databases with enterprise and government databases will only add to this increase in information. We will, if we haven't already, reach the tipping point where the volume of data overwhelms current data reporting and analysis systems.

Two other factors complicate an organization's ability to take advantage of this embarrassment of riches. First, most tools, techniques, and methods for managing data are largely for transactional, relational data. Much of the new information that's available isn't. It might be unstructured text, as in e-mail or blogs, or structured but not semantically understandable. Social network software accounts for some of the most popular Web sites and can be a gold mine of information, if it can be extracted and understood. Second, all these types of data require technology such as voice recognition, image recognition, and text analysis to turn previously unusable data into information. Bigger volumes of unfiltered data, however, won't be valuable to organizations unless the data can be turned into useful insight.

Fourth, much money has been spent on customer relationship management (CRM) and other enterprise application technology. Too few CRM implementations have successfully created a unified view of customers, identified their preferences, rewarded them for providing information, and then marketed to them and interacted with them the way they want. Many companies fail to respond to customers in a consistent, focused, targeted way, despite massive investments in CRM. Too many call centers and other groups of front-line workers have been neglected. These agents don't have what they need to help customers solve their problems, too much cross-selling and up-selling are done without sensitivity to customers, and the feedback loop to improve interactions is broken. The move to outsource call centers has only exacerbated this problem.

Current practices in coding, data analysis, data capture, and data management and the priorities represented by enterprise applications have resulted in systems that just aren't smart enough anymore. Chapter 3, "Why Aren't My Systems Smart Enough Already?" gives more details on this problem. But if the current approaches to information systems don't work, what can provide smart enough systems?

---

### Modern IT Architecture Is Helping

The recent growth of standards-based service-oriented architecture and related approaches and technology, such as business process management and event-driven architecture, is moderating the negative impact of many of these trends. The approach in this book is complementary to these changes in how IT tackles problems. How this approach interacts with and complements a modern IT architecture is explained in Chapter 10, "EDM and the IT Department."

---

### Decision Management Is Required

Fundamentally, a smart enough system must automate the operational decisions that drive your business. If you identify and automate operational decisions, you can separate them from the rest of your applications so that they can be managed and reused.

*Managing decisions* isolates the logic behind the decisions, separating it from business processes and the mechanical operations of your applications. Treating decision logic as a manageable enterprise resource means you can reuse it across applications in different operational environments and treat your decisions as a corporate asset.

*Managing decisions* means applying analytics to make decisions more precise. Using analytics in this way makes it possible to ensure that your decisions are informed by the data you're capturing. Indeed, with experience, you can apply more advanced analytics, take market and economic uncertainties into account, and arrive at optimal decisions.

*Managing decisions* makes it easier for you to improve decisions over time. You can focus efforts on improving decisions and be certain that improvements will be spread throughout your organization. This focus means your return on investment (ROI) is higher, because any improvements in decisions improve results in *all* applications that use them, essentially multiplying the value of your investment by the number of applications used.

*Managing decisions* has a cultural component. By recognizing and separating out operational decisions, you can focus your business thinking and investment on these decisions more easily. You can apply your strategic vision and management approaches to achieve optimal decisions.

So what might an organization that used smart enough systems to run its business look like? How would an organization that managed its decisions act,?

## Introducing SmartEnough Logistics

SmartEnough Logistics is a glimpse into the immediate future. SmartEnough is a company that ships packages around the world for its business clients and applies smart enough systems to maximize returns and minimize costs.

Customers interact with drivers collecting packages, who can price, up-sell, and cross-sell effectively, thanks to their handheld devices. These devices can record customer preferences and needs, predict whether the service being purchased is more or less than required, match this prediction against the customer's contract and established preferences, recommend cross-sell and up-sell opportunities, and get the price right, given the relevant contracts.

Packages are tracked using RFID and trucks with GPS, so the tracking system knows where each package is (in which truck and at what location). The dispatch system also uses this information to make adjustments. For example, it predicts that a driver's truck won't have the capacity for the second-to-last scheduled pickup because of the volume of orders at that location, so it changes the truck's route dynamically and transmits this information to the anticipated driver, who's used to this kind of just-in-time changes to routes. The historical data from the GPS allows the dispatch system to predict which trucks can make the pickup (by predicting the additional time needed) and select a different truck by balancing this data with each truck's open capacity.

As another example of making just-in-time changes, while a truck is in transit, a customer realizes that one of her packages was shipped with too low a priority. She logs on to the company's Web site to change the shipping priority. The site uses the same decision engine as the driver's handheld device, so it gives her exactly the same information about likely delivery dates, times, and pricing as the driver did, reassuring her that everyone involved knows what they're doing. The customer requests expedited delivery online, and the system responds immediately with available upgrades based on the rules and analytics built into the scheduling system. New pricing is displayed, and the customer accepts; because her relationship with the shipper is established, she doesn't need a credit check or additional credit card.

When the truck arrives at the cross dock, the unloading crew takes each package off the truck. The RFID tags trigger an automated sorting belt that routes them to the correct loading areas for different delivery schedules and destinations. This system routes the changed package differently at this point, given its new information. The manager of the loading area notices this change because he received an automated alert from his activity-monitoring system when a label configuration unusual for the load being assembled was scanned. When he checks, the system can tell him exactly why the routing has been changed.

While the plane carrying the package is in flight, the customer calls the call center from her cell phone on the drive home, worried about her package. The customer service representative (CSR) sees the shipping information, the rerouting and the reason for it, and he has access to the same system for predicting delivery time. This delivery time, of course, now reflects the impact of the rerouting. Despite reassurances from the CSR, the customer is still concerned the package won't arrive on time. The CSR asks the system for other options on the package, and it shows that no additional rush options are available (given the package's current routing). The CSR also sees that an extra notification offer is available for free; this offer is based on the package and its delivery location, and the pricing is based on the customer's status as "concerned" (entered by the CSR) and "long established" (from the system). The customer accepts the offer and goes home to bed.

This package must also go through customs at its delivery location. SmartEnough has another system that applies current rules for the destination (a combination of rules established by the locality and rules from the federal government about exporting the items in the package) and generates the correct customs paperwork. This system ensures that the package won't be held up in customs. Some rules were added just today when new export rules were announced unexpectedly. Fortunately, SmartEnough's system could be updated directly by the legal department as soon as they understood the new rules' implications.

During the flight, bad weather closes an airport on the route, forcing a diversion. This information enters SmartEnough's system directly from the airport's system. Automated routines run in response to see what rerouting options exist for packages on the flight (package by package) and determine that some won't make their scheduled delivery, no matter what. The system immediately notifies these customers of the delay and gives new delivery times. It also makes retention-oriented "we're sorry" offers based on calculated retention risks for those customers and the kind of service they ordered. Packages that can be rerouted are.

Two options are available for the concerned customer's package. The first means it might arrive on time but has the risk of a lengthy delay. The second means it won't be on time but guarantees that it will be only a little late. Given the kind of service ordered, customer preferences, and the package's transit history, the system chooses the first option and informs the customer. At this point, there's time for the customer to change the option if she notices the notification in time (it's now night), but the system has made the best decision it can for now.

When a package is delivered in a foreign country, a third-party delivery company is used. Because SmartEnough makes all its systems available to its extended enterprise, the delivery company's driver has access to the same information and same decisions as the driver of a SmartEnough truck. When the package is delivered—on time, as it happens— the third-party delivery staff are notified that acknowledgment of receipt is important for this package, so they double-check with the hotel staff at the delivery location. The system prompts for a name and phone number from the person signing for the package and transmits this information to the customer.

# CHAPTER TWO

# Enterprise Decision Management

Today's business trends are driving organizations to build systems smart enough to cope with the demands of a more complex world. As a result, organizations must automate and improve far more of the decisions underpinning day-to-day business operations. They must treat these decisions as a corporate asset in the same way they treat their data as one—perhaps even more so. These decisions are too numerous and cumulatively too important to be handled in an ad hoc manner. Decisions (or at least the definition of a good decision) change rapidly and influence your organization's behavior. A new systematic approach called enterprise decision management is needed.

## Introducing Enterprise Decision Management

**Enterprise decision management** (EDM) is a systematic approach to automating and improving operational business decisions. It aims to increase the precision, consistency, and agility of these decisions and reduce the time to decide and the cost of the decision.

To make your systems smart enough, your core problem is knowing what's the right decision to make and how to make it when required. These decisions must be precise (accurate and informed by past experience and actual data), consistent (across staff and channels), and yet agile (easy to change when necessary). Making your systems smart enough shifts the focus away from manual and hidden decisions and toward decisions embedded in systems, as shown in Figure 2.1. Before adopting enterprise decision management and using it to deliver smart enough systems, most operational decisions are made by people, with only a few embedded decisions. Many operational decisions aren't made at all but remain hidden. After adopting enterprise decision management, the balance shifts, with more operational decisions identified and embedded in systems, many manual decisions automated, and the opportunity for people to make new decisions of more value to the business because they are freed from operational decision making.

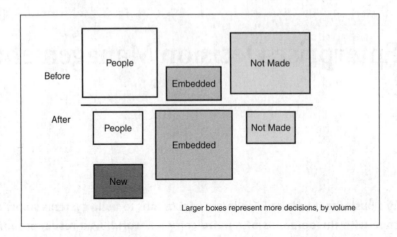

**Figure 2.1    The change in operational decision making when enterprise decision management is adopted**

### The EDM Process

Enterprise decision management involves a straightforward approach, at least in principle. Later chapters cover the technology and key concepts and outline an approach for adopting it. The basic process is as follows:

1. **Remove decisions from applications**—Decisions can't be managed effectively, or even automated effectively, while they're embedded in other applications. You must remove decision making from your applications.

2. **Analyze decisions' potential for improvement**—Realistically, not all decisions lend themselves to the same degree of automation and management. In the later section "The ROI for Enterprise Decision Management," benefits and return on investment (ROI) are discussed. Decisions offering the highest potential return should be addressed first.

3. **Automate key operational decisions**—The key operational decisions, separated into what are called "decision services," can then be automated. Typically, this process involves a set of business rules developed from knowledgeable staff, regulations, policies, and perhaps legacy code.

4. **Apply predictive and decision analytics**—Applying analytics brings insight derived from historical data to bear on your decisions. This step might take place in parallel with the previous one or come later, as a way to enhance decision making.

5. **Give business users control**—At some point in the process, you will hand over control of all or some of the decision logic to business users in your organization. This change of focus is essential for ensuring maximum agility and collaboration.

6. **Keep it simple as "intelligence" increases**—The more complex decision making becomes, the more important it is that the business can control the logic without too much of the complexity showing.

7. **Focus on production performance requirements**—The decision process is running in production, so you must focus on performance and reliability the way you would for any operational system.

8. **Manage change and evolve**—No decision is ever perfectly automated, or at least not for long. You must develop a mind-set of constant testing and refining the way you make these decisions.

## The EDM Definition

You can consider the three parts of the phrase "enterprise decision management" separately to understand the concept better:

- **Enterprise**—You should treat decisions as an enterprise asset. You should make even the most high-volume, operational decisions as though they are *enterprise* decisions. Your customers and other associates behave as though this approach is the case. When you decide to contact them or treat them in a certain way, they assume that decision was deliberate on your part. In fact, most organizations not using enterprise decision management make many decisions incidentally, without thought, or implicitly.

  "Enterprise" is also the "E" word, possibly the most overused term in the software development world. Every product and every approach seem to be "enterprise" class. Despite this, the term is part of the phrase because enterprise decision management is most effective when you can cross information "silos" and use *all* your information to inform decisions and share common decisions throughout your application portfolio. Most organizations operate in silos, with different parts of the organization "owning" different data and making decisions separately. Enterprise decision management involves focusing on decision making as an enterprise asset, not as a departmental one or an individual one. Customers expect the decisions an organization makes to be deliberate, not accidental. The "E" in enterprise decision management is about making sure this approach is followed.

**Note**  *In general, you'll be most successful if you can make use of a common decision-making infrastructure across silos and systems, but enterprise decision management doesn't have to touch every part of your organization.*

*You can apply EDM techniques to a single decision within a single silo and get a great deal of value. If you can apply EDM across multiple silos there is a multiplying effect that will likely be a large part of the value and benefit you get from EDM in the long term. So think "enterprise" even if you start with a single project.*

- **Decision**—A **decision** is a determination arrived at after consideration, a solution that ends uncertainty or dispute about something. It's the act of selecting a course of action. Therefore, decisions

  - Select from alternatives, typically to find the one most profitable or appropriate for the organization and/or associate.

  - Consider various facts or pieces of information about the situation and participants.

  - Result in an action being taken, not just knowledge being added to what's known.

  Organizations make decisions at every level, from strategic decisions the CEO makes to operational decisions customer service representatives (CSRs) or store workers make. Other decisions must be completely automated (for instance, in customer self-service applications), or the people making decisions need a system that helps them do so (such as a call center application supporting call center CSRs). Typically, enterprise decision management focuses on operational decisions. As an approach, it's intensely decision centered rather than process or system centered.

- **Management**—It's called enterprise decision *management,* not enterprise decision automation or enterprise decision improvement, for a reason. Management is about conducting or supervising something and the judicious use of a means to accomplish an end. Management in an EDM context means treating decision making as a business issue and a business asset, focusing on accomplishing an end (taking an action) and on supervision to ensure that improvement and optimization of decisions are ongoing and proactive. You can't just automate decisions and hope for the best; you must manage them over time.

## Large European Bank: Risk Management and Compliance

### Old Way

The bank had different processes for consumers, small business, and mortgage lending, as well as different processes for different countries. The system often generated inconsistent ratings for customers through each channel; for example, the Web site, call center, and branch might assign different risk levels to the same customer, resulting in different pricing. Similarly, customers might get varying risk assessments for different loan types, even if the collateral and amount were the same, because of inconsistent risk calculations for products. Because the risk calculation was run only at application time, some loans were identified as high-risk (forcing a large loss reserve to be held) when they had, in fact, become lower-risk over time.

### EDM Way

A single decision service for credit-rating decisions uses business rules and predictive analytics to ensure consistent customer ratings independent of the system handling sales. This decision service calculates a complete risk profile for a customer across lines of business. The service also performs an expected loss computation and uses all available and relevant data. To prevent any sudden change in creditworthiness, business rules gradually prioritize account activity information and deprioritize generic applicant data over time. In addition, the service allows collateral to support multiple loans, and collateral assignment is handled to minimize expected loss.

As shown in Figure 2.2, the decision service has an impact in all aspects of the credit life cycle, from credit decisions to marketing and back to credit decisions. The automated computation of default probability and expected loss leads to an objective and standardized credit decision. Instead of a yes/no decision, the credit risk drives flexible pricing. Regular monitoring of risk levels generates early warning signals at both the single loan level and portfolio level. Expected loss and default probability are important factors for building loan loss reserves. Workout

*continues*

*Continued*

actions can depend on customer ratings, and marketing can concentrate on customers with sufficient creditworthiness. The new system ensures that the bank gets the best possible rating under the new Basel II banking accord.

**Note:** Basel II is a worldwide banking accord with the stated goal of improving global financial stability by adjusting loan reserves to match risk. The final version, published in June 2004, has an all-encompassing impact on credit and risk management practices.

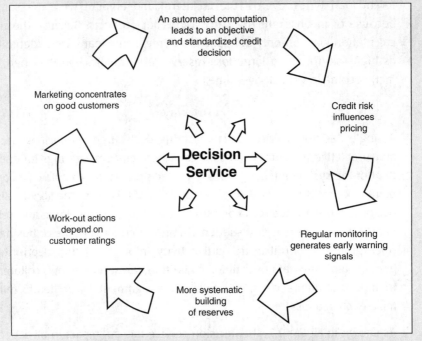

**Figure 2.2**     **A central decision service affects all stages of the credit life cycle**

### Benefits

- Substantial reduction in delinquency rates for new and existing loans
- Reduced internal costs
- Improved response time
- Regulatory compliance

The following list explains some critical phrases in the formal definition of enterprise decision management you saw at the beginning of the chapter:

Enterprise decision management is a systematic approach to automating and improving operational business decisions. It aims to increase the precision, consistency, and agility of these decisions and reduce the time to decide and the cost of the decision.

- **Systematic approach**—Enterprise decision management is a planned, methodical approach to automating decisions. It's not about automating decisions as a side effect of another activity, such as automating a process or implementing an enterprise application, but a deliberate focus on decisions. As Bill Fair, one of Fair Isaac's founders, once said, the key is to "grab the decision by the throat and not let go." You must treat decisions, in other words, as separate entities addressed distinctly.

- **Automating and improving**—It's not enough to automate a decision; you must also improve it continuously. Like automating bad processes, simply automating bad decisions results in little gain in anything except speed. You should identify how you want to make a decision and then automate that improvement. Improving a decision means not only working on every aspect of it to see where you can improve it, but also establishing processes and mechanisms for monitoring and constantly improving that decision over time. This kind of ongoing improvement often offers the most value in enterprise decision management.

- **Operational business decisions**—Operational business decisions are those made in large volume every day. They are clearly different from low-volume strategic decisions, such as where to open a new store or when to drop an unprofitable product line, that are rarely the same twice and simply don't happen that often. Clearly, strategic decisions are important, but you aren't likely to automate them or try to make them in "real time."

**Note** *Some strategic decisions could be improved if the operational decisions derived from them are simulated and the results used to inform strategic decisions. This method would count as using an EDM approach, albeit to consider a strategic decision's operational impact.*

These workaday operational decisions are typically, although not always, part of interactions with associates. These decisions have the highest volume and most time pressure of any in your business. They are often hidden—not specified explicitly, not managed, and not recognized as important. You can probably think of many examples, including approve/decline, benefits eligibility, the next best offer to make a customer, authorization of a sale, fraud detection in a claim, issuance of a permit, and account application processing. Typically, you must make these decisions in real time or near-real time. Indeed, you might find that these decisions *must* be automated to achieve the requisite throughput and timeliness.

There's a gray area between strategic and operational decisions. Decisions falling in this area are called "tactical" decisions. They determine how you manage processes and customers, such as decisions about which segments of a customer base should receive which offer. You might support these decisions with EDM systems, but you're unlikely to automate them completely.

Operational decisions require the shortest decision latency, which is the time it takes to receive an alert, review the analysis, decide what action is required (if any) based on knowledge of the business, and take action.

- **Precision, consistency, agility, speed, and cost**—Enterprise decision management has a wide-ranging set of effects that can be categorized as a combination of these five aspects of decision yield (explained in more detail in "Introducing Decision Yield" later in this chapter):

  - Precision—how targeted a decision is
  - Consistency—across channels, geographies, and so on
  - Agility—time and cost to change
  - Speed—how fast a decision is made
  - Cost—how the decision affects cost

### Key Features

Organizations have tried many different approaches to improve the way they make decisions. Some are described in Chapter 3, "Why Aren't My Systems Smart Enough Already?" Without trying to compare enterprise decision management to each approach in any detail, a few key features of the EDM approach are distinct:

- By focusing on decisions as distinct opportunities for improvement, enterprise decision management delivers solutions that are independent from applications and databases so that you can update decisions in one central location and use them in other systems, making those systems smart enough to run the business.

- By focusing on the power of having business users manage part of the decision directly rather than through a traditional IT process, enterprise decision management builds flexibility into decision processes and improves business agility.

- By using executable, predictive, and decision analytics to derive insight from data, an EDM approach means injecting intelligence into the transaction-processing stream for real-time decisions, not just after-the-fact analysis.

- With its focus on adaptive control and constant improvement, enterprise decision management requires a closed-loop capability for managing and improving decisions over time, which is made possible by the explicit focus on decisions and the use of technology and design approaches that support this focus.

These features are described in more detail in subsequent chapters.

---

### Real-Time Decisions, Not Real-Time Modeling

One of the most common problems in adopting EDM is the misuse of the phrase "real time." Many organizations believe that embedding decision services into real-time systems, such as Web sites or call center applications, means real-time optimization or real-time analytics.

In fact, real-time analytics or real-time optimization are rarely required for real-time decisions. Typically, offline analysis of data and construction of models, offline implementation of optimization models, and simulation of transactions are sufficient and more effective. Real-time calculation of complex algorithms for predictive analytics or use of solvers for optimization is high cost and high risk. These algorithms use a lot of processing power and access a lot of data. Without some expert supervision, these tools can fail to converge on a solution quickly or even produce contradictory data.

These drawbacks make IT departments reluctant to use these techniques in operational systems, and rightly so. Generally, using them offline to develop rules or equations that can perform efficiently at runtime is much preferred.

## Characteristics of Decision-Making Problems

Realistically, not every decision lends itself to automation and management. As noted previously, in most organizations, there's a spectrum from **strategic decisions** (where to build the next distribution center, which new product will make the most profit) to **operational decisions** (cross-sell offers, eligibility). The right approach to supporting these decisions varies, too, from a focus on decision support for knowledge workers to a focus on decision automation, as shown in Figure 2.3. Operational decisions are ideal for automation. **Tactical decisions,** those falling in the gray area between strategic and operational decisions, might also be good automation candidates but usually for partial automation—a guided script, for example—rather than complete automation.

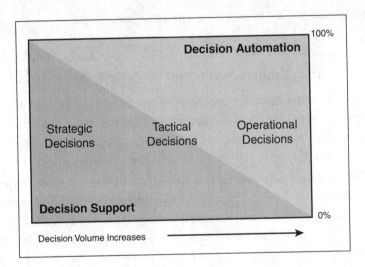

**Figure 2.3    The relative value of decision support and decision automation for different types of decisions**

Strategic decisions might show results only over long time frames, suitable for reporting with standard business intelligence capabilities. Performance management, meanwhile, is particularly good at tracking the effectiveness of tactical and operational decisions. Operational and tactical decisions reward performance management because the time frames, and your time to respond, are much shorter, justifying the near-real-time supervision of results that's more typical of performance management.

## Not Just Business Intelligence

Better decision making from data you have collected, more targeting of customers, and integrated data for decision making sound a lot like business intelligence. Indeed, some organizations have had success with using business intelligence to improve operational decisions.

Many organizations, however, have found a gap between gaining insights from business intelligence and taking action to exploit that insight in operational decisions. This gap, shown in Figure 2.4, arises because although BI gives you insight into business performance, it's largely insight for knowledge workers and decision makers. For instance, business intelligence might show you that customer retention rates are dropping. Although this data is informative for management, it's less helpful in influencing the behavior of CSRs. Only by manually coding a change to CSR systems has a typical organization been able to make use of this insight.

It's easy to use reporting and related analysis tools for a view in the rearview mirror—to show you what has happened in the past. In contrast, EDM is about using technology to understand the view ahead through the windshield. Which way is the road bending? How fast can I safely take that corner? What road rules apply right now?

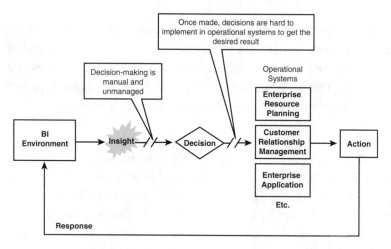

**Figure 2.4    An insight-to-action gap caused by manual decision making and updating operational systems**

The next section expands on what operational decisions are and explains why and how so many of these decisions are hidden. You go on to learn some techniques for finding operational decisions and see how applying enterprise decision management can deliver smart enough systems. Finally, you see when to use and not use enterprise decision management.

## Operational Decisions

*"A robust decision is the best possible choice, one found by eliminating all the uncertainty possible within available resources, and then choosing with known and acceptable levels of satisfaction and risk."*[2]

Given that the EDM approach focuses on problems with operational decisions, considering some characteristics of these decisions can help you identify them more easily. If you look at your operations, the decisions made in those operations—operational decisions—are likely to have some or all of the following characteristics and be suitable for enterprise decision management:

- **Volume**—Perhaps the most common characteristic of operational decision problems is that the number of decisions of a particular type you must make is high—so high you must automate it or high enough that many front-line workers must make it on your behalf. Volume alone can cause problems or exacerbate another decision problem, such as compliance or risk assessment.

  **What Is a Decision?**   *When considering decisions, differentiating between types of decisions and the actual decisions is worthwhile. A type of decision might be "underwrite insurance policy" or "make cross-sell offer." An actual operational decision would be something like "underwrite James's insurance policy" or "make Neil a cross-sell offer." In this context, decisions have volume, not the types of decisions.*

- **Latency**—Many managers now have more timely information about their business. If you can use this information to see trouble coming but can't change how you make decisions in time, you might have an operational decision problem. The latency between knowing something must change and being able to change it probably comes from having systems or people processes that are hard to change quickly. This is often caused by the way operational decisions are handled.

---

[2] David Ullman, *Making Robust Decisions*, Trafford Publishing, 2006.

- **Variability**—Try imagining nightmare scenarios and thinking about what approach you might take. Think about the systems and people interacting with associates. Decisions those systems and people affect that must change to reflect your new approach could well be operational decisions that, although not a problem now, would cause problems if the business climate changed suddenly.

- **Compliance**—Ensuring that decisions are made consistently by using the same set of guidelines and policies and being able to prove to regulators that the correct rules are in place and used for a given decision can be difficult, especially if the decision must be made in any sort of volume. Demonstrating compliance in every operational decision can be particularly time-consuming if the decision isn't automated correctly.

- **Straight-through processing**—"Straight-through processing" or "once and done" processing involves performing every step in a transaction or process without human intervention. A manual review that drags down response time in a process might be hiding a problem-prone operational decision. If you have a mostly automated process that hangs up on manual reviews, you might have a good candidate for an operational decision.

- **Managing risk**—A prime reason for having a person involved in a process is to manage risk, which is often all about making decisions that manage trade-offs or risks and rewards. A risk-centered decision that must be made quickly or in volume might be a good candidate for an operational decision.

- **Unattended**—With some transactions, there's no choice but to automate a decision. Without automation, there's no way to inject expertise or learn what works better and improve the decision; for example, there's no person who can make a decision in transactions on your Web site or at your ATM. These kinds of decisions are often good candidates for operational decisions.

- **Self-service**—Complex decisions are more common in self-service. No longer is it enough for a self-service portal to deliver a document or ask someone to call an 800 number when things get complex. Now you need to automate this decision so that customers can self-serve, even when the decisions involved are complex.

- **Personalized**—Any time you want to personalize interactions with associates, you're making a decision. For most organizations, these operational decisions can create problems because of the need to balance timeliness with personalization.

Many decisions in your organization will have more than one of these characteristics. You might want to personalize a high-volume self-service interaction while taking fraud risk into account, for instance. One characteristic can be enough to consider using an operational decision, but combinations of factors obviously make a decision more problem-prone and likely to need a new approach to solve effectively.

### Hidden Decisions

One of the biggest challenges is finding the right decisions to automate and improve. Although most organizations can identify some operational, high-volume decisions that have the characteristics just listed, most make far more operational decisions than they think they do. These decisions are called an organization's **hidden decisions.** They are often well suited to automation, and finding them is a key step toward smart enough systems. Hidden decisions can be categorized as described in the following sections.

#### Micro Decisions

Probably the most common category is **micro decisions.** They are considered hidden because organizations recognize them as decisions but don't realize how many they actually make. For instance, if you decide to send a marketing letter to a subset of your customers, you might think you have made a couple of decisions—what to put in the letter and who receives it—and so you have. In addition, you have made a decision for each customer to receive or not receive the letter. Therefore, if you have 10,000 customers, you just made 10,000 micro decisions. If your Web site has 1,000 visitors each day, and you have decided to display a promotion, you have made 1,000 micro decisions to display that promotion to each visitor. When you add a new option to your interactive voice response (IVR) system, you have decided that everyone who hears that menu must have that option. When you decide on a product's price, you have decided to offer that product at that price to each potential customer who asks. You could consider the price separately for each customer, offering each a different price based on the value of the product to them and the long-term potential value of that customer to you. You should make micro decisions explicitly and thoughtfully, even if you decide to make them the same way for many associates.

Another way to spot micro decisions is to review your strategic decisions. If you have clearly articulated all the operational consequences in the strategic decision's description, you have probably described a number of operational or micro decisions that need to be managed. If you haven't described operational consequences carefully, you probably have hidden decisions. For instance, a strategic decision to improve customer retention needs a plan for making sure every interaction with customers that might influence their decision to stay or go has been reconsidered in that light. Trying to think through all the ways you hope the organization will change in response to a strategic initiative can reveal many hidden micro decisions that support the strategic decision.

#### Manual Decisions

**Manual decisions** are those hidden under manual processes. In other words, you might not think about decisions front-line workers make every day. Perhaps when your CSRs talk to customers about renewals, they are making an instinctive decision about retention risk before deciding what offer to make. Your delivery drivers might be making a decision about whether to accept a package for a certain delivery date based on their experience. Your store clerks might have to decide whether a customer can return an item without a receipt, or your salespeople have to estimate a prospect's price sensitivity.

You might want to recognize these decisions and leave them to your staff to make. Then again, you might not, or at least you want to think about how you could help them make better decisions that are more aligned with your corporate strategy, more visible to management, and perhaps more sophisticated and data-driven.

### Default Decisions

The third kind of hidden decision is what might be called a **default decision.** The policy controlling the decision was set a long time ago and never updated to reflect changing circumstances. Perhaps you established a return policy when all stores were independent, and you haven't changed it to reflect the more integrated approach used now that all stores are connected and supported by the same Internet infrastructure. Perhaps when your customer profile was quite different, you set up a policy for which claims are paid immediately and which ones are reviewed. Perhaps determinations of elite customer status or preferred supplier status are based on out-of-date views of these relationships.

These kinds of decisions often need to be revisited when technology and associates' expectations have changed. Default decisions can be out of date *and* be made at too high a level—they could be hiding micro decisions, too.

### Long-term Decisions

Many decisions are made with only a short-term or narrow focus. For instance, when you decide to offer a customer a new credit product, you might be focused only on how likely the customer is to accept the offer and use the product. Your decision is driven only by the need to get the customer to use the new credit you're offering. If you consider a longer time frame, however, that decision might be based on the likelihood that a product is a gateway product that allows you to follow up with additional offers or the possibility that customers might not be able to pay their bills and will end up in collections. This longer-term decision often hides under a short-term one, especially because company objectives and employee performance might be measured only in the short term.

**Long-term decisions** aren't automatically better than short-term ones, but recognizing long-term decisions is important, and comparing costs and benefits of both short- and long-term decisions is often helpful.

## Life Insurance Company: Death Benefits

### Old Way

Handling insurance claims for death benefits is a delicate situation, not only because of regulations about who can be told what, depending on the location of the person who died and the person getting the benefits. There's also a need for sensitivity and care in the choice of words; after all, people being told they are eligible for benefits might not know of the death.

The company struggled with making sure the many regulations bound in printed manuals were being followed and had to invest considerable time in training staff to handle a wide range of possible circumstances. Despite the training, calls often took too long and failed to capture the information needed to continue the process. The company also found it hard to capture what had been learned about doing the process well.

### EDM Way

To manage calls, a decision service applies business rules to information about the policy and scheduled call information. The rules control the entire death claims process, including call scripting, data acquisition, and data validation. The decision service applies the right subset of rules automatically, based on information about the person being called, the policyholder, and more. As policies or regulations change, the company incorporates them quickly by updating the decision service's business rules. Staff training focuses on empathy and interaction skills, not mechanics of the regulations. As a result, calls focus quickly, but not disrespectfully, on the information needed to continue the process.

### Benefits

- Reduced call time and operating expenses
- Improved customer and employee satisfaction with the process
- Reduced training time and cost

### Override Decisions

**Override decisions** are hidden in a different way. When you look at the results of decisions made by using overrides, you don't get a true picture, because generally the logic isn't recorded. For example, your policy says turn down applicants age 18 or under. However, your staff sometimes approve applicants of that age who have wealthy parents. You might think this young customer base is a good segment to target, but you're looking at a truncated sample, and you don't know the "rules" used to approve them. Similarly, when you draw conclusions about your customer base without considering that these customers have already passed a screening, your customer base isn't representative because it's composed of people who passed approval criteria or people who were already interested in your company's products. Clearly, manual decision making carries a risk that these override decisions will be hidden.

### Missing Decisions

**Missing decisions** are those you don't think you can make. For this reason, you do the same thing every time. For instance, you have a one-size-fits-all approach to pricing because you don't think your associates would accept variable pricing. Perhaps you think your Web site and IVR system have to be the same for all users, or you include the same information in everyone's monthly statement. Failing to consider these decisions means that your associates do not get the personalized, focused service they deserve and that you do not get as many opportunities to influence them as you could.

### No Decisions

One of the classic ways to hide a decision is to forget that not deciding is, in its own way, a decision. By not making a compelling or competitive offer or not doing so fast enough, you are, in effect, deciding to lose a customer or prospect. If your CSRs don't make a cross-sell offer, you're deciding not to do so. If you don't respond to information you learn about your customers, such as changes in their monthly deposit or payment patterns, you're deciding to do nothing. This category of decisions can be hard to spot and clearly overlaps somewhat with Missing Decisions. Although both are missed opportunities, making no decision implies an awareness of the possibility of making a decision and a failure to do so.

### Conflicting Decisions

Although not really a hidden decision, considering **conflicting decisions** can often be worthwhile. If different parts of your organization treat associates in different ways, they are making conflicting decisions. Identifying, formalizing, and describing these differences can help you see what the real underlying decision is. Like the consideration of long-term decisions, a conflicting approach to a decision could be worse or better, but failing to consider and resolve the conflict "hides" the decision.

### Outside Decisions

**Outside decisions** are those made outside your organization. For instance, a customer decides to choose a certain channel for interacting with you, such as your Web site. If you could have influenced that decision, you might have made a different choice for that customer. Perhaps a competitor makes an offer to your customers. By accepting this offer, your customers cease to be a target for one of your products. In other words, other people, not you, are making the decision. Finding these kinds of decisions can help you determine whether you could do anything to influence them, and if so, what you could do.

These categories of hidden decisions often overlap and complement each other, but considering each category can help you find the hidden decisions in your business. Finding hidden operational decisions and clearly identifying those that aren't hidden becomes easier with practice. Some steps you can take to find them are explained in the following section.

### Finding Hidden Decisions

Finding suitable hidden decisions that have the characteristics of a decision that repays automation and improvement is an important step toward smart enough systems. Many suitable decisions will occur to you simply because you're looking for them, in much the same way you notice a particular model of car after you own one. Using techniques such as brainstorming and facilitated sessions can be effective, too.

The most suitable decisions are typically those an organization uses to manage its interactions with associates, although not exclusively. Here are some straightforward ways to find good candidates for hidden operational decisions:

- Analyze the reports you generate, and find out what prompts *action* from those who read them. From this information, you might be able to identify rules for taking the action and have the system use the data to take action for them—automate the decision that's made when the report is reviewed.

- Read the procedures or your users' cheat sheets. If they work around something in the system or are forced to override the system, you might be able to figure out which rules in the system are wrong. If changing these rules isn't easy, you might be able to externalize them so that you can manage and change them more easily.

- Processes that involve lots of manual review—by your auditors, for example—and are hard to monitor might be worth automating. Other potential candidates include areas where showing compliance with regulations is a problem.

- Supervisors in your call center can give you information on what decisions get referred to them. If some involve no new data collection or are otherwise mechanical, perhaps they can be automated to allow front-line workers to act on behalf of customers without having to refer them to a supervisor. Any supervisor's decisions might be good candidates for automation.

- Get the list of actions your CSRs or their supervisors can take on behalf of associates. Some can be achieved through the IVR system or Web site, but there might be other actions that could or should be. Often Web sites and IVR systems only collect or report information and leave decision making to people.

- Analyze users' requests to see what feature they want so that they can self-serve. Underlying many of these requests are decisions made manually that prevent self-service.

- Change logs might show you that pieces of the system are always being changed. The business or decision logic in your legacy applications is often the cause of these high-maintenance components. You can measure how much time and effort these changes take and assess whether IT is behind schedule in making them. You could externalize this part of the application and make it possible for the business to change the rules itself to improve this part of the application as and when needed.

- Check whether your business users get all the data they need the first time they interact with an associate. If they have to go back and ask for more, or if they can specify what data they want and why and when they want it, you might be able to derive the rules that would let you collect the data they need (but no other data) the first time.

- Analyze the data you have, and consider data mining or predictive analytic techniques. Establish what you could *predict* based on your data. If this information would be useful in running the business, see whether you could improve a decision being made by using your data in this way.

- Find out what your business users want to know. You might be able to find a way to derive this information from the data you have. You might also be able to find out what they would do if they had this information, and see whether you can automate the *action,* too.

Like most skills, finding hidden operational decisions gets easier with practice. It's important to find the operational decisions you're going to focus on before you use an EDM approach to improve them. To understand this point more clearly, consider a utility company as an example:

- A core function of this utility company is to deliver energy to customers, so it must measure and bill for this energy in a predictable way. Applying enterprise decision management to this decision—the amount to bill—is probably not worth the effort, because it's a mechanical calculation.

- If the utility company offers credit terms to customers, using enterprise decision management in the credit department for decisions on who should be offered credit, how much, and at what rate is a suitable choice.

- Even if credit isn't offered, the utility company needs to decide how to treat customers who are behind on their bills—which ones should have extra time, which ones should be called, and which ones should be referred to an outside collections agency. This business decision also would be suitable for enterprise decision management.

- If the company adopts "smart meters" that allow different pricing for electricity at different times of the day, its pricing decisions and customer segmentation decisions (for billing plans, for example) are good candidates for applying enterprise decision management. Pricing will go from simple and mechanical (with the old meters) to dynamic and complex. Working out pricing that incents off-peak usage profitably is hard and results in much more complicated pricing decisions.

- The utility company's maintenance and repair operation is a constant trade-off of staff, contractors, overtime, and priorities and would contain other candidates for automating decisions.

Other kinds of organizations have other suitable decisions. Marketing and promotion decisions in almost any organization are good candidates, because often many choices and options have to be considered before the right offer is made. Product configuration and pricing decisions are also good candidates, especially when the product or pricing model becomes complex. Routing and shipping decisions in an automated supply chain or logistics environment often involve complex sets of rules and regulations and a lot of relevant information. Picking targets for audits, benefits eligibility, tax processing, and regulatory enforcement are examples of government decisions. Most organizations have many suitable decisions buried in their operations, whether or not they are aware of them.

Enterprise Decision Management and Smart Enough Systems

Enterprise decision management means taking control of operational decisions and automating them. Table 2.1 shows how this approach can be used to achieve all the characteristics of smart enough systems discussed in Chapter 1, "The Need for Smart Enough Systems." Unless your organization's operational decisions are automated intelligently and thoughtfully, you will struggle to make your systems smart enough to meet current and future demands on them. Enterprise decision management gives you the approach you want to deliver the systems you need.

**Table 2.1    Enterprise Decision Management Delivers Smart Enough Systems**

| Characteristic of a Smart Enough System | Value of Enterprise Decision Management |
| --- | --- |
| Agile | An agile organization must be able to change its policies and procedures rapidly and make sure those changes are enforced effectively across the extended organization. These policies and regulations drive decisions, particularly operational decisions. Changing operational decisions can be the hardest part of being agile. |
| | Enterprise decision management ensures that all systems have a single source for the rules and regulations that affect operational decisions, enabling them to be changed easily and quickly to achieve agility. |
| High-performance execution | By combining expert judgment, insight from data, and regulations in automated decisions, enterprise decision management helps ensure that a distributed organization has optimal performance at the operational level. Ensuring top performance in high-volume, transactional systems requires that automated systems and front-line workers make the best possible decisions, and enterprise decision management delivers those decisions effectively and efficiently. Front-line workers can be high performing only if they are supported by excellent systems, which requires enterprise decision management. |

*continues*

**Table 2.1    Continued**

| Characteristic of a Smart Enough System | Value of Enterprise Decision Management |
|---|---|
| Customer-centered | Although enterprise decision management doesn't guarantee a customer-centered approach, it's hard for most organizations to be customer-centered without it. Unless customer treatment decisions are managed and optimized, customers can't truly be at the center of an organization's behavior. |
| | Using enterprise decision management for customer treatment decisions ensures consistency of treatment across channels, delivers on the promise of microsegmentation and personalization, and enables self-service. |
| Capable of learning | A learning organization needs a framework for finding out what works, analyzing those lessons, and putting them into practice. When learning is about operational decisions, it means a software infrastructure for automating and improving decisions. It means easy access to the rules for a decision so that they can be modified and improved by business users as they learn. It means using analytic insight to allow new data to influence new decision-making approaches. |
| | Although other kinds of organizational learning are important, a modern organization *is* its systems in a very real way, making learning *systems* crucial. |
| Capable of real-time performance | A real-time organization needs to be able to make accurate, appropriate, timely decisions 24x7. It can't afford to wait for people to come into the office to make operational decisions; it needs to use enterprise decision management to deliver those decisions where and when they're needed. |
| Loosely coupled | When an organization becomes more loosely coupled, it gains efficiency from using different organizations, structures, or approaches in different parts of its business. However, these loosely coupled business components must still act legally, ethically, and appropriately. |
| | Enterprise decision management helps ensure that all loosely coupled components make consistent, effective decisions through access to a single source of decision making |

| Characteristic of a Smart Enough System | Value of Enterprise Decision Management |
|---|---|
| Compliant | An organization with an EDM backbone has one place to go for decisions, and those decisions are automated in a way that makes demonstrating compliance easy. |

Enterprise decision management, although an effective approach, isn't suitable for every type of decision. Taking the characteristics discussed previously and other aspects of decision making, you could summarize the appropriateness of enterprise decision management as good, moderate, or poor, as shown in Table 2.2.

**Table 2.2    Appropriateness of Enterprise Decision Management for Types of Decisions**

| Fit | Types of Decisions |
|---|---|
| Good | High-volume operational, repetitious and consistent across channels, analytical—driven "by the numbers," qualification or eligibility, classification or segmentation, low rates of exception handling, pattern recognition, or rapidly changing |
| Moderate | Circumstantial, certainty analysis, compassionate, or varied across channels |
| Poor | Purely algorithmic, highly iterative or recursive, one-off or ad hoc, collaborative, trust-based, or fuzzy or imprecise |

## The ROI for Enterprise Decision Management

The following definitions give you a brief primer on calculating ROI and total cost of ownership (TCO):

- **Return on investment**—The ROI for an information system is the ratio of value gained compared to the total cost of ownership. ROI is usually given as a percentage rather than a value and is stated for a period or as an annual rate. The value gained must be assessed in terms of the present value of the benefits gained during the period. ROI is often calculated for a three-year period.

- **Total cost of ownership**—TCO assesses the direct and indirect costs of an information system. It should reflect purchase costs and all use and maintenance costs over a defined period. Costs might include training, support, personnel, downtime or other outage costs, delays, building space and electricity, development costs, and more. TCO gives you a true sense of a system's cost over a specified period.

## Risks and Issues

Adopting enterprise decision management has risks and issues. For some decisions, the approach can be complex, requiring sophisticated analytics and technology. Although these techniques and technologies aren't new, they might well be new to an organization, and the processes and training that people in the organization need could be immature. Developing expertise in analytics, business rules management, and adaptive control takes time.

It's also true that organizations can overreact and apply enterprise decision management too quickly or without sensitivity in addressing cultural and labor issues. Enterprise decision management can result in a reduction in staff and often changes job descriptions, expectations, or definitions of success for workers. Underestimating these consequences can cause serious problems, especially in organizations that already have difficulties in these areas. In addition, a lack of focus on ROI can lead to unnecessary costs, and a focus on manually intensive or collaborative processes can result in unnecessary failures. Picking the right decisions is important, and applying enterprise decision management without enough thought about which decisions it's applied to can be a recipe for expensive and difficult implementations.

When applying enterprise decision management to customer decisions with the goal of improving customer interactions, you must also be aware that automating decisions can be another way to put a barrier between you and your customers. Too much customer relationship management (CRM) technology has been used this way in the past. Although enterprise decision management offers the potential to personalize interactions with your customers and make them more valuable, it could also be used to further reduce the human contact your customers get, and they might not appreciate that result. Be sure you're adding value for your customers, not just saving money.

Chapter 9 explains an approach for adopting enterprise decision management in easy-to-manage stages that demonstrate a clear ROI. Enterprise decision management is a good idea, but that doesn't mean it has no risks.

Given these definitions, an EDM approach can show a positive ROI by reducing costs in acquiring, building, operating, or maintaining your information systems and by increasing the value you get from the systems.

Enterprise decision management can help you make better use of existing investments in technology and offers new opportunities for you to use the data you have about associates more effectively across more systems. If "Information is data that changes you,"[3] enterprise decision management helps turn more of your data into information.

To realize benefits, you need a clear vision for any kind of EDM project before you embark on it. To decide whether enterprise decision management is going to offer the kind of returns that make it attractive, you need to consider whether your organization is the right kind to benefit, who will benefit, and how to put a value on the benefits.

Any organization making many dynamic, high-impact operational decisions can benefit from enterprise decision management. In general, however, the more decision focused organizations are, the more they benefit from enterprise decision management. If the key to their core transactions' profitability or effectiveness is a business decision, they are likely to benefit a great deal.

In general, organizations adopting an EDM approach see layers of benefits, as shown in Figure 2.5. At the lowest level are operational cost reductions. For instance, processing a loan application is less expensive when you automate the origination decision; the same number of employees can underwrite more auto policies, and fewer decisions are referred to supervisors or other experts. IT costs can also be lowered, because fewer programmers are needed to maintain and modify a system or add new product lines, customers, or countries. In regulated industries, costs of fines can be reduced or eliminated, because automated decisions ensure compliance with regulations.

An EDM approach can often result in revenue growth, too. Increased precision in decision making can result in more value from *every* interaction with associates. You can also improve associate relationships and retention through more targeted offers, faster responses to service requests, and more consistent treatment. This improvement also tends to result in revenue growth. You can minimize losses by using analytics to make more accurate and consistent risk assessments and do a better job of fraud detection. Revenue growth also comes from enabling front-line workers and systems to make business decisions. Enterprise decision management often enables once-and-done or straight-through processing transactions, and customers often agree to prices, deals, and offers during their first interaction instead of shopping around (which they might have done if you had said you would get back to them with a price).

---

[3] David McComb, *Semantics in Business Systems: The Savvy Managers Guide*, Morgan Kauffman, 2003.

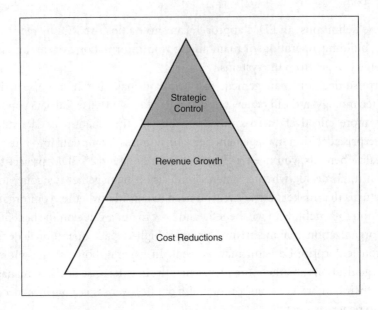

**Figure 2.5    Three layers of benefit from enterprise decision management**

The final layer of benefit, one that's hard to measure but often the most important, is strategic control. Enterprise decision management allows your operations to change to reflect new business strategies quickly and effectively. You can gain a competitive advantage by being more nimble than your competition; you can get new strategic initiatives, products, campaigns, and pricing to market faster and with better precision and consistency. You control how your organization and all its systems make a decision, enabling you to change your business approach quickly to take advantage of even the most narrow window of opportunity and minimizing the opportunity a competitor gets by doing something first.

This combination of strategic control, revenue growth, and cost reduction allows profitable growth. Not only can your organization grow, but it can also decouple its expense growth from its revenue growth. It can add business, respond to opportunities, manage threats more cost-effectively, and use the resources it saves from day-to-day operations to invest and grow. Each layer—cost reduction, revenue growth, and strategic control—can contribute value to your ROI calculation in several different ways, as explained in the following sections.

## Cost Reductions

Information systems that aren't smart enough to cope with current demands waste an inordinate amount of money for organizations of all types. This waste can come in a variety of forms, including costs for buying unnecessary data, wasteful activities, lost opportunities, fraud, and fines. Which costs matter most to you or for a particular decision vary. Applied correctly, enterprise decision management has the potential to eliminate or reduce many costs.

### Time Not Spent

The first element of cost reduction is perhaps the most obvious: time. The amount of staff time required to process transactions in which decisions are automated is reduced dramatically. Many processes have already been automated and streamlined repeatedly but still leave core decisions to be made manually. Typically, leaving some manual decisions means having items queued on work lists; before the process or transaction can continue, there's a wait for staff to access the list and process the item. Many of these decisions can be "rubber stamped" quickly by someone, but even this process consumes a lot of time if the transaction volume gets high enough. Automating these decisions can eliminate extra staffing costs from most transactions. This cost can be significant, especially for decisions made by professionals, such as pricing or authorization decisions.

Few decisions are amenable to 100 percent automation, so there will always be some referrals for manual decisions. An EDM approach can deliver high percentages of automation, however. Auto insurance renewals, for example, have been automated at rates of 95 or even 99 percent. Even when the remaining manual decisions represent a disproportionate percentage of the workload because of their complexity, organizations still save a lot of time. One group of advertising managers, for instance, freed 30 percent of their time when they used enterprise decision management to automate all but the most complex pricing decisions.

**Improved Referrals**   *The process of automating these decisions could even improve referrals. The system can give you insight as to why the decision is being referred, often more than was previously available. For instance, if a pricing engine refers a price decision for an ad insertion because the customer wants a combination of layout and colors for which no rules exist, the advertising manager who gets the referral can be told immediately what the issue is. Understanding the reasons for a referral makes it easier to process an exception.*

## Who Benefits from Enterprise Decision Management?

Enterprise decision management offers benefits to a wide range of people in an organization:

- First, business owners—those who have responsibility for profit and loss or accountability to the outside world—can improve the precision and consistency of customer decisions and take more control of decisions that drive their business. With increased control, they can respond faster and more appropriately to changes in the environment.

- CIOs and IT directors can reduce their backlog by focusing more of their resources on new development, thanks to reduced maintenance costs for existing systems. They can also create systems that are more agile and consistent across multiple existing platforms.

- Those managing analytic modeling or data-mining groups or trying to maximize the value of business intelligence and data warehouse systems can make a bigger impact on decisions by deploying analytic insight to operational systems more quickly and learning at a faster pace through continual feedback loops. They focus on high-volume operational decisions also results in a new range of opportunities for applying analytics, so it increases the return on an organization's information.

You can also eliminate time from a process by removing the need for a "do-over." Typically, a process with manual decision making has a delay from data capture to processing. Data can be captured from a Web form or a call center employee and then queued for decision making by someone else. When the more skilled employee reviews the data to make a decision, the data might be incomplete, so the employee needs additional questions answered. A typical process, shown in Figure 2.6, can lead to constant back-and-forth interaction as the more skilled employee requests more data, which is then gathered, which turns out not to be enough, and so on. In extreme cases, such as commercial underwriting, this process can result in as many as seven attempts to make a decision, with the first six failing because of lack of data. All this rework costs time and money, to say nothing of the negative impact on customer service.

**Telecommunications Network: Network Configuration**

### Old Way

When a customer ordered new service from the company, the order had to be captured and then passed on for fulfillment. An engineer installed and configured the devices needed for the service, and this process was expensive in terms of time and resources as well as slower than customers wanted. In addition, the infrastructure was inflexible and limited in the services it could offer.

### EDM Way

A decision service processes customer orders and configuration requests to determine the correct device configuration, based on the customer's requirements. Configuration of the organization's network devices is done remotely. Business rules ensure that only valid orders are placed and then configure the necessary devices automatically. Engineers maintain the rules to make sure they're correct, and new rules can be added rapidly when new equipment is added or new services are defined. Engineers are free to focus on network maintenance, repair, and troubleshooting.

### Benefits

- Configuration time is reduced from days to minutes
- Delivers a more flexible, faster, and more responsive network
- Frees expensive resources for higher-value activities

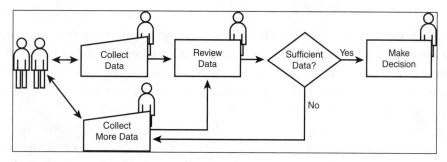

**Figure 2.6    Manual decision-making processes can involve many "do-overs"**

Automating a decision, in contrast, pushes it to the point of contact and allows the people collecting data to make sure they have captured all the data required to decide. The front-line system or worker collects data, and then the decision service tries to make a decision while the initial "conversation" is still open. If it succeeds in making a decision, including one to refer the decision to an expert, the conversation can close. If the decision service can't make a decision, it can identify why and prompt the system or person to collect additional data. The service can repeat this process, shown in Figure 2.7, until a decision can be made. The decision service can then make the decision in many cases, and the customer gets the answer without waiting any longer.

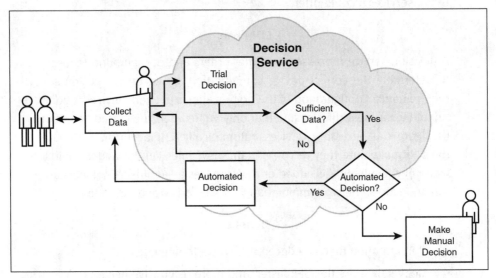

**Figure 2.7    Automated decision making increases the odds that the first conversation results in a decision**

### Activities Eliminated

Some transactions have costly activities, such as property inspections, that are optional. These activities aren't required for every transaction, because they might not make a difference in the actions taken. For instance, if an application for house insurance states that a house is falling down and needs to be completely rebuilt, an inspection isn't likely to change the insurance rate. All it would do is confirm the information on the application. Alternatively, if the application hinges on the truth of a positive comment about the property, an inspection is probably essential. In more complex situations, it may not be immediately obvious whether the inspection is called for. For instance, an unusual combination of property features may meet some legal requirement for an inspection.

In systems using manual decision making, these inspection activities commonly start in parallel to reduce the transaction's total time. This method can result in unnecessary costs when you pay for inspections or other activities that turn out to have no impact on the decision made. Automate the decision, however, and it's easy to order the inspection only if it makes a difference to the decision. The system tries to make a decision without the inspection and then orders one if it can't decide between options.

If more sophisticated decision making is involved, it might even be possible to order inspections only when the difference they might make exceeds the inspection cost. In other words, if the inspection is going to make little or no difference to the price—and, therefore, to your profit on the transaction—perhaps you can't justify its cost and shouldn't perform it.

> **Not Just Saving Money**  *You can extend this approach to nonmonetary costs. For example, if you have an overused system with tightly controlled and rationed access, accessing that system only if you must can reduce operational costs dramatically. If a system is working remotely from a data source, perhaps wireless network traffic can be reduced by not requesting information from that data source unless it makes a difference. This practice can also improve performance if slower parts of the decision are invoked only when they must be.*

### Data Not Purchased

A similar savings can be had with external reports and data, such as government record searches or address validation services. Ordering reports from external services costs money—typically a certain price per transaction. In auto underwriting, for example, more than one motor vehicle report is commonly ordered for the same policy application, because different people in the process order and reorder the report at various steps in the process. In fact, one company with a typical manual decision-making process found that it ordered 1.1 reports per policy. After automating the decision, reports were ordered only when the decision reached the point where a report would make a difference. This practice reduced the use of reports to 70 percent of transactions, eliminating an average of one report for every 2.5 policies underwritten. Again, the system tries to make decisions without additional costly information and requests information only when required.

## Personal Lines Insurer: Underwriting System

### Old Way

A cumbersome, paper-based underwriting processing system resulted in slow and inconsistent decisions. The processing logic was coded in COBOL and hard to change. This logic triggered more referrals to underwriters and therefore used up many hours of underwriter time. If a single application triggered multiple referral conditions, multiple referral reports were generated, causing delays and increased expense. External reports, such as motor vehicle reports, were always ordered, often more than once per application, because the manual process made it hard to keep track of reports ordered or their value to a decision.

### EDM Way

A centralized decision service combined business rules with risk models implemented by predictive analytics. Business rules ensure that external data is brought into the decision-making process only when it makes a difference. This method speeds approvals, increases straight-through processing, and reduces costs. The decision service is used across multiple systems to ensure consistency and is offered to partners so that agents can write policies while a prospect is waiting, avoiding the need for them to return later. Quote counts and new business have increased because agents can write policies immediately.

The risk models are objective, which improves risk management and regulatory compliance, and changes to business rules can be made without IT involvement, resulting in improved agility and business control. This quantitative measure of risk serves as an objective standard for evaluating future performance and makes it possible to track results by agent, geographic region, or other criteria.

> **Benefits**
>
> - In the first year, the decision service contributed to an eight-point reduction in its combined ratio—a standard measure of insurance profitability.
>
> - Resources are applied more effectively, because the decision service has eliminated manual review of clearly unacceptable and clearly acceptable risks.
>
> - Underwriters focus more on book management and agent performance.
>
> - People in the underwriting department manage the rules and don't compete for IT resources.
>
> - Risk management is more effective and pricing is more accurate, because the number of pricing tiers increased four to eight times.

### Fines Not Paid, Errors Not Made

In regulated industries, avoiding fines and penalties by using only manual decision making is becoming more difficult. When a network of agents or third parties is involved, avoiding fines and penalties can be even more complicated. Often the company pays fines even if the misbehavior came from its independent agents. Large sums can be saved by automating regulatory compliance rules to make sure no noncompliant transactions go on the books and by focusing enforcement and audit resources on the highest risk transactions, where there's potential for litigation or fines. For instance, life insurance often has regulations on sources of funds to prevent unscrupulous agents from encouraging customers to "churn" from one product to another. However, often the insurer must pay the fine. Knowing that transactions are compliant can eliminate or dramatically reduce hard costs, such as these fines, as well as soft costs, such as litigation. Indeed, you can become more sophisticated as to which claims you decide to pay, for instance, by considering the potential cost of litigation part of deciding how to treat a transaction.

**Eliminating Bias** *Eliminating bias in decisions through automation has a long history. Replacing human judgment, which is subject to conscious and unconscious bias and hard to police, with a verifiable, mathematically sound approach can reduce bias. This practice can eliminate fines and long-term litigation risk and improve an organization's image.*

*Some people dislike credit scores because they're impersonal, but these scores aren't based on skin color, religion, or any other trait once held against credit applicants. As an early Fair Isaac advertisement for credit scores said, "Good credit doesn't wear a suit and tie."*

Cost reduction can also come from eliminating costly errors. One of the attractions of automation is that the decision logic applies to every transaction. In contrast, manual decision-making processes are often applied to only a subset of transactions. For instance, few insurers using manual underwriting decisions review more than 10 to 20 percent of renewals to see whether they should be cancelled or changed. The remainder are renewed automatically without review. An automated underwriting process, in contrast, can process 100 percent of renewals effectively and efficiently and flag those most worth revisiting and repricing.

Some manual decisions are made in high-stress environments, such as health care, and an automated decision can be used as a "backstop" to catch errors. Eliminating obvious medical errors, such as the wrong dose of a drug for a patient's weight, can reduce medical costs (by getting the treatment right the first time) and potential downstream costs, such as legal bills. Of course, these automated decisions have a clear benefit for patients, although it might be hard for a provider to put a monetary value on this benefit!

### Fraud Avoided

Eliminating or drastically reducing fraud is a classic use of enterprise decision management. For instance, a key issue in claims is identifying fraudulent claims quickly but not annoying honest claimants with unnecessary delays and problems. A company must not pay too soon and have to recoup losses later, nor must it delay legitimate payments. This situation is ideal for rules and analytics to work hand in hand. Predictive models can be developed that estimate the likelihood of fraud initially and can be refined as additional data about the claim is collected. Combined with rules to manage acceptable levels of risk for automatic payment or referral to special investigators, these models allow efficient process automation. In the gray area, rules can be used to give advice to adjusters and capture additional data to explain actions taken. When volumes are particularly high, as after a hurricane, the company could soften the rules to refer fewer claims and/or use the models to prioritize the most suspicious claims for investigation.

**Note**   *An EDM approach introduced in the credit card business, for instance, reduced the overall rate of credit card fraud from 18 basis points (1/100th of a percentage point) in 1992 to just 5 in 2004.*

### Life Insurance: Regulatory Compliance

#### Old Way

Independent agents placed many orders for life insurance products each day. These orders had to comply with state and federal rules for customer suitability, in that certain kinds of customers couldn't be sold certain kinds of products. They also had to be for genuinely new products, because agents couldn't boost their commissions by replacing preexisting products. Finally, the funds for the product ordered could not be borrowed against another product. Manual processes meant that only a small percentage were reviewed, and many noncompliant orders were missed. Even though the agents were the ones not following the law, the company was paying fines.

#### EDM Way

A batch-oriented decision service processes all transactions before they run through the system that records them and places orders. This decision service evaluates and validates new business against customer information by applying business rules representing suitability rules, replacement policy regulations, and restrictions on source of funds. In each case, federal, state, and company rules apply, and all three types of rules are managed by businesspeople who understand them. Therefore, the correct set of rules is applied to each transaction, based on data in the transaction.

#### Benefits

- Business rules are created and updated quickly and easily by business people who understand applicable regulations.
- Insurance regulations are followed consistently throughout the enterprise.
- Fraudulent or illegal transactions are detected automatically.
- Fines and legal costs have been reduced.

> ## Taking Enterprise Decision Management for Granted
>
> In many processes, such as credit card fraud detection or direct-to-consumer marketing, the volume of transactions makes automation essential, and as a consumer you probably take it for granted. If these decisions aren't made well, waste will occur. Expensive marketing materials designed to attract new customers might be sent to existing customers, offers might be made to people unlikely to accept them, and fraud will go undetected. In addition, these decisions often must be made in a narrow time frame, which essentially forces automation; customers expect credit card approvals while they wait, for example. Automating decisions allows most transactions to be processed quickly and accurately. These kinds of systems already use an EDM approach.

### Opportunity Costs Reduced

Opportunity costs, lost revenue, or costs incurred by failing to respond to a change in the market can be a big problem. Taking advantage of an opportunity before a competitor does or while it's still relevant can be complicated if your organization must change how it makes pricing or product-offering decisions. Responding to a competitive threat quickly, so as not to lose revenue and customers, can also mean rebalancing risk management decisions or repricing products. In both cases, an EDM approach can reduce the opportunity cost by allowing organizations to change their systems, or at least the decisions in them, more quickly. For instance, in trade credit insurance, an entire industry's creditworthiness can change rapidly. The Enron scandal affected all energy companies' trade credit for a while, so when Enron crashed, any company offering trade credit insurance to energy companies had extra risk exposure for as long as it took to change its system. One insurance company used an EDM approach to reduce the time to make this change from two weeks to just eight hours, which improved response time and helped avoid potentially bad deals.

## Large Health Insurance Plan: Claims Fraud

### Old Way

Six million claims a year were processed by using a simple rules-based, largely manual method. When fraud was detected, typically it was after payments had already been made, and it was too late to recover the funds. The pace of claims was increasing, which meant more staff were needed. In addition, some fraud was hard to uncover manually, because the small volume of claims per provider made it hard for staff to spot patterns.

### EDM Way

Predictive analytic models—in this case, neural nets designed to spot new and emerging patterns—are integrated with business rules in a fraud detection decision service. The neural net "learns" new fraud patterns as they occur. Combined with dynamic profiling, it identifies a claim as fraudulent much earlier in the process. The decision service flags suspicious claims so that they can be investigated manually, which allows automatic payment of remaining claims without intervention. This method improves straight-through processing rates and meets regulatory requirements for prompt payment. Investigations of fraudulent claims are more effective, because the decision service clearly states reasons for the referral, allowing staff to focus immediately on suspicious elements. The service also detects errors in billing, because it detects any kind of aberrant behavior, from fraud to billing errors to clinical errors.

### Benefits

- Case-targeting effectiveness has increased twelvefold—even higher in high-value cases.
- Fraudulent claims are identified that the manual process wouldn't have caught, according to the staff involved.

## The Growth of Choice

*"The era of one-size-fits-all is ending, and in its place is something new, a market of multitudes."*[4]

The phrase "the long tail" comes from a classic Pareto distribution or power curve that has a head consisting of "hits" and a long tail consisting of "niche" products. Figure 2.8 shows this curve. The area under the curve in the two sections represents the value of traditional "hit" products in relation to the "long tail" of less popular ones. In his book, Anderson begins with three observations:

1. The "tail" of available variety is far longer than we realize.

2. This tail is now within reach economically, thanks to the Internet.

3. All the niches aggregated make for a significant market.

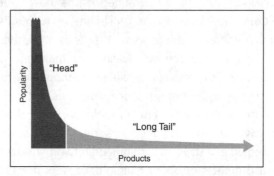

**Figure 2.8    A Pareto distribution showing the relative value of hits (the "head") and niches (the "long tail")**

Anderson presents a case that although the twentieth century was about hits, the twenty-first will be about niches. He illustrates this case with what he calls "the 98 percent rule": 98 percent of online products will be sold often enough to be noticeable. For instance, 95 percent of Netflix's movies are rented in a quarter, 98 percent of Amazon.com's books sell at least once a quarter, and so on. If an online business has 20, 30, or 40 times as many products as an offline retailer, the products available only online amount to 20 to 40 percent of sales. Anderson also states:

---

[4] Chris Anderson, *The Long Tail: Why the Future of Business Is Selling Less of More*. Hyperion, 2006.

*"In an era without the constraints of physical shelf space and other bottlenecks of distribution, narrowly targeted goods and services can be as economically attractive as mainstream fare."*

More niche products are available, and the cost of reaching buyers for them is falling fast. This trend creates an opportunity in the so-called long tail of many industries. However, consumers can and will buy from these niches only if they have ways to quickly find the niches they value. With the explosion of channels and the impatience of Internet-savvy consumers, providing automated tools to help customers find what they want will become more critical. Making cross-sell and up-sell decisions that show customers new niches they find attractive and moving customers from buying in only one niche to buying in several will be required for growth in your customer base.

Organizations also need to segment and resegment their customers as they learn more about them. Those doing business in the long tail must adopt microsegmentation or "markets of 1" to succeed. Complex segmentation requires automation and automated monitoring of the effectiveness of segmentation. Raymond Williams, a Marxist sociologist, said:

*"There are no masses; there are only ways of seeing people as masses."*[5]

Marketing these niches effectively also requires engaging with customers in a new way, such as allowing them to specify some of their own rules, predicting their behavior based on the behavior of others, and learning from what they do and what they say. Anderson quotes Frog Design (a consulting firm): "Information gathering is no longer the issue—making smart decisions based on the information is now the trick." You must use the past behavior of *all* customers to infer the likely future behavior of your *next* customer.

In this environment, choice is king, but choice is hard because there's a lot of "noise" in the system—so many products from which to choose. One person's noise is another person's signal, however. If your products and services lend themselves to mass customization and niche targeting, you had better be good at turning lots of data into useful, predictive insight that lets you connect customers with products they want.

---

[5] Raymond Williams, *Culture and Society 1780–1950*. Columbia University Press, 1983.

Similarly, failing to take advantage of market opportunities can lead to lost revenue, especially if a competitor can respond more quickly. An electronics distributor, for instance, found that changing its rebate management system took too long—so long that its customers couldn't take full advantage of manufacturers' rebates. Changes could take six weeks, during which time the distributor seemed more expensive than its competitors because it wasn't passing along manufacturers' rebates. This delay resulted in lost revenue. Taking an EDM approach to automating rebate calculations more flexibly meant the distributor could change its programs immediately to reflect changes from manufacturers. This practice increased revenue and improved billing accuracy.

## Revenue Growth

When your systems aren't smart enough to cope with current demands, they waste your money and decrease your revenue. You're throwing away revenue if you target customers poorly, respond too slowly, and fail to deliver a compelling, cross-channel customer experience. Enterprise decision management can help increase your revenue by addressing these weaknesses.

### Better Targeting, More Sales

There's much discussion these days of microsegmentation or "markets of 1." Many organizations find themselves dealing with "the long tail" (see the following sidebar "The Growth of Choice") of finely differentiated, small customer segments. You need ways to identify which customer or prospect must be in which micro segment, and you need to target your marketing and customer service to those segments precisely.

You want customer interactions to be based on who they are, how valuable they are to you, what you know about them, and so on. Improved targeting can result in higher rates of cross-sell and up-sell offer acceptance. For example, one company used an EDM approach to target existing customers who purchased only from a single product category in an effort to get them to purchase products from additional product categories. This precise targeting involved more fine-tuned analysis of customers and personalized offer letters based on this microsegment. This EDM approach generated a 17 percent response rate compared to the less than 1 percent in previous marketing approaches—a 2,000 percent increase.

### *No Comparison Shopping, More Sales*

Besides better targeting, you can also gain revenue at the point of sale simply by pushing decisions to the point of contact and reducing the decision time to zero. Most people aren't ruthless comparison shoppers; they like instant gratification and are generally in a hurry. Pushing decisions to the point of contact and reducing the decision time to an acceptable wait can mean closing the transaction at once. Unlike manual decision making, the automated decision happens fast enough that customers don't need to wait or return later. This practice avoids the risk that customers will find someone else to offer them what they want while they wait for your response. For instance, an insurer using an EDM approach to automating underwriting decisions found that more prospects accepted a policy at a given price when it was offered immediately, while they were still on the phone, than if the same price was offered later by e-mail.

### *More Marketing Opportunities, More Sales*

As you learned in "Hidden Decisions" earlier in this chapter, many opportunities to boost revenue through cross-sell and up-sell offers are missed because no one is there to make the offers. How can you make cross-sell offers for customers who use only your ATMs, the automated check-in terminal, or the Web-based shipping kiosk? Pushing decisions to the point of contact enables these systems to make cross-sell or up-sell offers. Taking advantage of every interaction with a customer or prospect, regardless of channel or device, can increase revenue in new ways.

### *Better Customer Experience, More Sales*

Improving the customer experience is a hot topic in many businesses today. Often it's discussed only in terms of hiring and training staff to act a certain way, but this training isn't enough. Your customers think any action you take toward them is deliberate and reflects the value you place on them. Sadly, in many companies, the way the Web site or call center responds and the way marketing generates offer letters are all disconnected from each other. In addition, customers often get wildly different responses, depending on the channel they use. They get a good response in a branch and a poor response by e-mail, for instance—and the responses have nothing to do with how good a customer they are.

## $30 Billion Global Retailer: Drive Basket Size and Cross-Category Sales

### Old Way

This retailer designed its direct-mail campaigns by hand. These campaigns were designed to get customers who had purchased in only one product category to expand into another product category by making an offer for a product in a category they hadn't purchased from previously. Each campaign had creative elements combined with specific marketing offers, all derived subjectively. The resulting letter was sent to a subset of customers selected by using criteria designed to maximize the likelihood that the offer would be attractive. An industry-standard response rate of less than 1 percent was achieved.

### EDM Way

A decision service generates direct-mail letters and automates the decision on what letter content to use with each customer. Data from the data warehouse produces extensive predictive analytic models that forecast which products specific customers might buy and which products are effective as first-in-category purchases. Business rules on marketing policies, objectives, target categories, and more are combined with these analytics. Each letter the decision service generates contains personalized customer information, specific recommendations based on analytics, and information localized to the customer's usual store derived by using more business rules. The result is a targeted, personalized piece of direct mail aimed at getting a specific customer to buy in an additional category.

### Benefits

- An increase of 2,000 percent in response rates to 17 percent
- Larger basket sizes (more products purchased per trip) for targeted customers
- More purchases from new categories

In fact, all your customer interactions should be based on who they are, how valuable they are to you, and what you know about them. In many ways, customer experience is the sum of customers' perceptions of interactions with your brand. Interactions are what affect the experience, so you need to achieve better interactions with your customers. A recent survey[6] identified four steps you can take to improve customers' perception of critical interactions:

- **Offer high-quality goods and services**—Obviously, this issue is critical for a good customer experience. If you have information-based goods and services, using enterprise decision management to manage critical decisions about configuring and delivering those goods and services can help improve their quality. Physical goods can be improved by using enterprise decision management to manage quality control and diagnostic checks so that you detect problems more quickly. Using enterprise decision management allows all your production facilities, no matter how geographically dispersed, to benefit from the expertise of your best staff, thanks to the ability to embed expertise in decision services that check and control production.

- **Give personal attention**—Not only does enterprise decision management allow automated decisions to be better targeted to smaller segments, some rules in a decision can be owned by customers, which allows them to personalize their interactions. Systems can also use enterprise decision management to improve interactions with customers by using the customer information you have gathered to change how a call is routed or handled, what offer or price customers get, and so on.

- **Reward loyalty**—Enterprise decision management is perfect for making decisions about loyalty programs. Using dynamic business rules to manage awards makes your loyalty program more flexible and responsive yet still consistent across channels and employees. Using analytics to target special bonuses to those who will be positively affected can improve the effectiveness of loyalty programs, too. For example, you can use analytics to predict which customers will respond to a "travel once more to make Gold" offer.

- **Employ well-trained, friendly, helpful, caring people**—Using an EDM approach to eliminate the need for employees to refer decisions for approval lets them act more readily on behalf of customers and, to some extent, seem more caring as a result. Nice employees don't matter much if they can't actually do what needs to be done for customers. Automating data analysis can also help workers who interact with customers focus on the interaction, not on wading through reports on their screen, trying to figure out what a customer might need.

---

[6] CRMGuru.com—survey conducted May 2006.

A major challenge in using information effectively in the context of smaller customer segments, more distribution channels, more store formats, and more products is capitalizing on the insight you can gain from all this extra data. A study published in *McKinsey Quarterly*[7] introduced the concept of "cell-level insight," which is insight into the behavior of very specific segments or cells. Gaining this insight is a complicated problem, but it's just the beginning. After you have "cell-level insight," you must turn it into actions in high-volume operational systems—which is where an EDM approach comes in.

Customer service includes customer self-service, which is increasingly important in today's 24x7 world. Complex decisions are more common in self-service. No longer is it enough for a self-service portal to deliver a PDF of the instruction manual; now customers want some kind of guided interaction to help them find the problem. You need to automate these decisions so that your customers can serve themselves, even when the decision is a complex one. Using enterprise decision management means automating and managing decisions so that they can be used to provide great customer service or great customer *self*-service.

## Strategic Control

The third way in which enterprise decision management can show a return is in strategic control. Although putting a monetary value on this control can be hard, organizations adopting this approach can gain a measure of strategic control over their information systems that can offer increased value.

### Resource Scalability and Focus

Growing organizations are always looking for ways to increase business without having to add staff in an effort to be more scalable. Being able to acquire new business or new customers without having to scale staff proportionately is helpful. Automating decisions with enterprise decision management can be a key ingredient in this kind of scalability. For instance, an insurance company adopting an EDM approach to underwriting increased its business by 35 percent without hiring more underwriters, thanks to automating key underwriting and renewal decisions.

---

[7] John Forsythe, Nicolo Galante, and Todd Guild, "Capitalizing on Customer Insights," *McKinsey Quarterly* No. 3, 2006.

### Leading Computing Hardware Supplier: Preventive Maintenance

#### Old Way

The company had established a group to help customers improve system uptime and availability and reduce incident volume and cost. When known system problems arose, the group issued static documents to its customers that documented the symptoms of specific hardware and software configuration issues. The company had built its own engine for managing the rules that prompted these alerts. As the number of products and product versions increased, maintaining this system became increasingly difficult. In particular, the hardware experts who established the rules couldn't create or maintain them, programmers had to interpret the rules for them, and managing the many rules required for the company's broader product base and more complex customer environments was more difficult.

#### EDM Way

An Enterprise Information Integration (EII) environment brings together data from the company's systems and customers' systems. This information feeds into a decision service that applies the business rules that associate classes of knowledge and symptoms. The service handles hardware, software, and patch-level assessment and examines a variety of other critical systems' data to identify potential problems. It also combines information on symptoms, issues, diagnostics, and configuration to recommend software and hardware versions based on maintenance releases and compatibility. The service also manages event conditions and actions and detection of failovers and failures.

More than 9,000 employees and customers use the decision service to identify and mediate potential problems before they cause downtime. In addition, the patch release management process uses the service to identify specific patches that apply to a customer's software or hardware. All business rules are entered and managed directly by engineers who understand the symptoms, problems, and products. No IT resources are required to make updates, so changes and improvements are made quickly and inexpensively.

*continues*

*Continued*

### Benefits

- The new system took five months to build rather than the two-and-a-half years the old system required.
- The system is readily accessible to engineers to keep rules current.
- The ROI is estimated at 10 to 20 times better than hard-coding rules.

Delivering this kind of result means refocusing what your expert staff actually does. Instead of using their expertise to rubber stamp large numbers of ordinary transactions, they can focus their time on exceptions, new products, and business growth. If you automate the underwriting decision, underwriters can spend more time on the complicated cases, and the company's risk managers—the actuaries—can focus on the overall book of business (the set of all policies written by the company and the corresponding loss reserves and assets backing them), agents' effectiveness, geographic anomalies in results, and emerging trends. They can finally use all those expensive business intelligence tools you bought them. Although this benefit is a qualitative one, it can be important.

Enterprise decision management can also improve focus. Many companies today are trying to outsource some business processes. Manual decision making can make outsourcing hard and reduce its value. You probably don't want to outsource decisions about creditworthiness, risk underwriting, or lifetime profitability potential; they are simply too important. However, you do want to outsource the process that wraps around these decisions, such as the process of printing and sending an offer, collecting paperwork for a loan, and so on. If you focus on automating key decisions in a process, you can decide who should run the process without having to worry about decisions. If you know your team controls the escalation decision for customer complaints, for example, you can outsource the process with less risk and more control.

## Re-creating the Corner Store

Corner or mom-and-pop stores of old knew their customers, could predict their creditworthiness and interests, reminded them if they forgot something they usually ordered, never suggested products that made no sense, and generally interacted with their customers as though they knew them well because they did, in fact, know them well. They knew a lot about their customers' shopping habits, had a small enough number of customers to keep this information in their heads, dealt with customers as individuals whether they came in person or called on the phone, and were deeply aware of the need to repay a customer's investment in coming to their store with better service.

Modern businesses often don't have these options. They simply have too many customers. There's no way to make sure a customer talks to the same CSR each time or to keep the number of customers small enough for the representative to remember them. However, as Richard Hackathorn pointed out,[8] it's possible to use data, decision-making technologies, and an EDM approach to re-create this feeling, even for a large customer base.

As John Hagel, a well-known business consultant, said in his blog,[9] "Too many companies have concentrated their IT investment on initiatives to automate processes—removing people wherever possible—rather than exploring how IT might be better used to amplify the talent of the people left." Although EDM *can* remove people from a process, it can also "amplify" your employees' value by letting them treat customers as though they know them personally. This approach has an additional benefit: Good customer service comes not from one person but from the company as a whole.

---

[8] Richard Hackathorn, "Forward to the Past," *DM Review*, November 2002.
[9] http://edgeperspectives.typepad.com/

**Staffing Reductions**

Although many organizations adopting enterprise decision management find that they get value from reassigning professional staff to qualitative decisions, some prefer to reduce their costs. Clearly, automating decisions that originally required staff to make them manually can justify reducing the number of employees.

Many processes are the same for every organization, except for how key decisions are made. For instance, the process of paying medical claims is essentially identical for all healthcare insurers, but the decisions each insurer makes about paying claims can vary. One insurer might be focused on low cost and decline any claim that's not completely clear; another prefers to focus on customer satisfaction, so it pays even when a claim is in the gray area. Insurers might assess fraud risk differently and make different decisions about who to refer to the fraud department. Automating these decisions means more options for outsourcing. You don't have to be concerned about where or how a process takes place; you control it by controlling the decisions that drive it. Figure 2.9, for instance, shows a process for a claims-processing organization; the process steps are the same for clients. Each client needs to define different rules for the "Assess Claim" decision. If the decision is controlled independently, the process seems customized, even though the steps are common for everyone, because each organization controls which claims are routed to which activity.

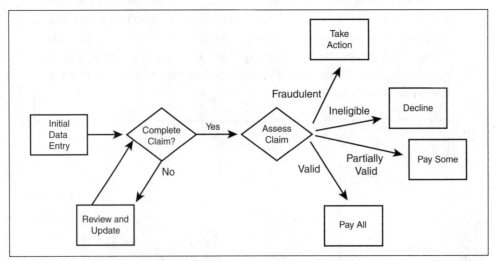

**Figure 2.9    A simplified claims payment process showing key decisions**

## Fast-Growing Eastern European Banking Group: Collections and Recovery

### Old Way

Banks in each country handled their processes differently, with variations in customer acquisition strategies, manual processes and collections procedures, and subjective recovery approaches devised locally. The banking group had rapidly changing objectives that had to be passed on to local offices manually, with no central management or monitoring of policies.

### EDM Way

A decision service handles collection and recovery decisions for banks throughout the group. This service applies centrally managed business rules as well as local customization that's both integrated and controlled. The group changes rules as its business changes or new regulations come into force, and these rules are immediately applied consistently across local offices. The group monitors and improves decision making as it learns what works best. The service handles all decisions in the collections and recovery process—asset management and disposal, recovery, early- and late-stage collections, litigation, and local agency management—and business managers, not IT, control the decisions. Decisions are based on policy and risk level, not just local judgment calls.

### Benefits

- The group now manages and monitors 35 distinct strategies.
- The system handles a 150 percent increase in early-stage collections.
- The number of collection agents expected in one country has been cut in half, as shown in Figure 2.10.
- Bad debt reserves have been lowered.

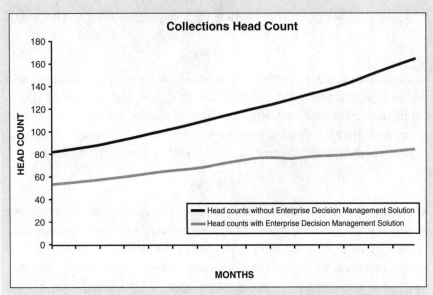

**Figure 2.10    The reduced head count after applying an EDM approach
to collections**

*Strategic Alignment*

As stated in a *Harvard Business Review* study,[10] "Most devastating, 95 percent of employees in most organizations do not understand their [organization's] strategy."

One of the advantages of an EDM approach is the opportunity for real strategic alignment, top to bottom. At first sight, this advantage might seem contradictory with the focus on operational, high-volume decisions discussed earlier. If enterprise decision management is focused on operational decisions, how can it contribute to strategic alignment? Many organizations are challenged to keep their operational activities—the way front-line workers operate and the way self-service applications behave—synchronized with their strategic plans. This synchronization can have results such as the following:

- You might want to treat all gold customers a certain way but have a self-service application that doesn't differentiate between customers.

---

[10] Robert S. Kaplan and David P. Norton, "The Office of Strategy Management," *Harvard Business Review OnPoint*, October 2005.

- You might want to get more aggressive about retaining certain customers but have call center representatives who have too many campaigns to remember, so they treat everyone the same.

- You might want to offer demand-based pricing, but your Web site is disconnected from the demand algorithms sales representatives use.

Divergent agendas and miscommunication between those working on an organization's strategy and those carrying it out it operationally are chronic problems. These disconnects can hinder executive leadership's access to information about what's really going on and their ability to effect change in organizational behavior when needed. No performance management infrastructure in the world can solve this problem; you just have a real-time, accurate view of how badly it's going.

Using enterprise decision management to align strategy and operational decisions can help you reduce inefficiencies and improve effectiveness. For example, an EDM system can help brand managers assess and improve the alignment between promotional campaigns used in the call center, mailing house, and Web site and the overall marketing strategy. An EDM application that manages customer retention decisions could make sure that the right retention offers are made to the right customers regardless of channel (call center, store, agent, and Web site). It also ensures that these offers change as quickly as the strategy does. By focusing on operational decisions that implement the strategy on the front line, automating those decisions, and giving business leaders control over how to make these decisions, you can dramatically improve the alignment between strategic intent and operational reality. Figure 2.11 shows how separating out the decision logic in a decision service allows frequent changes to support a changing strategy without the need for repeated programming projects.

Another basic issue in strategic alignment is secrecy. The top levels of organizations, where strategy is concocted, often hold information close to the vest, with the idea that it's confidential, proprietary, and a competitive advantage. Some strategies, such as being aggressive about raising prices, are kept quiet because they might cause bad public relations. Although you can criticize this thinking, it's understandable. The problem is how to keep strategy confidential yet let it influence the way every employee (or system) interacts with your associates.

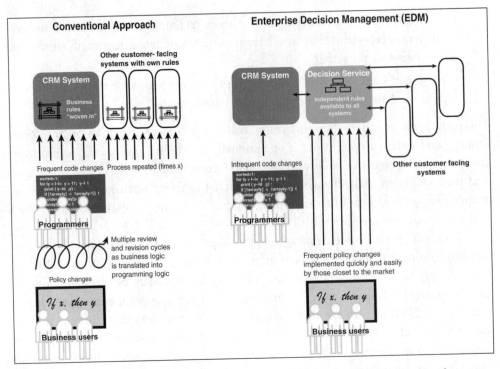

**Figure 2.11**    **Enterprise decision management ensures that decisions affecting interactions remain in sync with market and other changes**

Taking an EDM approach to focusing on key operational decisions—those made by the most junior staff (the ones furthest from the company's strategic heart) or by information systems—allows those who understand the strategy to control how decisions are made without having to tell everyone the strategy. For instance, if retaining profitable customers is a critical issue, you can devise a model to estimate customer retention risk and embed the prediction into rules that handle making retention offers. When data suggests a change is needed, business managers can decide on a new strategy ("get more aggressive about customer retention") and turn it into rules to "make it so." With this method, you have front-line workers who still don't know the strategy, but the strategy drives their interactions with customers. Their interactions are informed by the same analysis of the business yet are agile enough to respond to changes as they are made.

### Risk Management

Many interactions with customers involve risk assessment as part of deciding how to treat them. If you're going to offer customers credit, you have to assess the risk of them becoming a bad debt and going into collections. If you're about to target delinquent customers with an attempt to recover money they owe you, you risk them ceasing to be profitable customers in another product line. When you're pricing auto insurance for customers, you must assess the risk that they will have an accident. When you submit orders to suppliers, you must consider the likelihood of on-time delivery. When you schedule a package on a truck, you're assessing the risk that the truck will arrive when the package is promised.

The precision with which you can calculate risk and apply it to pricing, scheduling, and marketing has a direct impact on the effectiveness of your business. In pricing, if you underestimate risk, you charge too little and risk incurring more expense than you could justify; if you overestimate risk, you might lose a customer to a competitor offering a better price. In general, organizations that can segment types of risk more accurately and precisely than their competitors have better control over risk in their business. This control might result in better on-time deliveries, fewer product quality problems, or just more revenue.

Risk is normally managed by using tiers—levels of risk corresponding to different prices. Having fewer, less-specific risk tiers than competitors can result in what's called being "adversely selected against." Say you have three segments and your competitors have six. Their two highest risk segments compete with your single highest risk segment. Assuming similar pricing models, your price for this segment is likely to be around the average of your competitors' two segments. This pricing tends to mean that prospects in the lower risk half of your segment get a better price from your competitors, and prospects in the higher risk half of your segment get a better price from you. The result is that your customer portfolio is more risky and less profitable than your competitors'.

More pricing tiers or customer segments means that your actual price matches the theoretical "best price" curve more closely, as shown in Figure 2.12. This translates into prices that accurately reflect your risk and allows you to attract customers at a price that meets your risk profile.

In theory, risk-based pricing can be done by hand. In practice, however, people do a good job of discriminating between segments only when there are a few—fewer than seven, say. If you need dozens or hundreds of risk segments, you'll find that people have some favorites and use them if they can. People do a poor job of handling the large number of variables required to segment very specifically. Only by applying automation to this decision can you take advantage of precision in risk assessment.

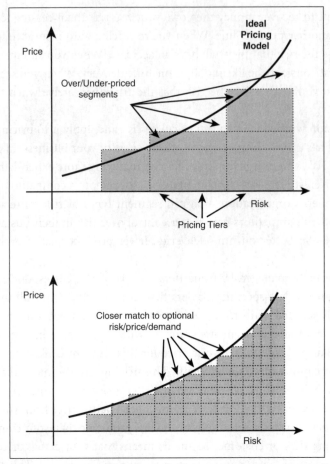

**Figure 2.12    More customer segments allows a closer match to an ideal risk-based pricing model** ©*Fair Isaac Corporation, reproduced with permission*

### Too Many Segments

Remember that a key component of risk modeling is pooling similar risks. If you make your segments too small, you might find that you no longer have enough members in each segment to consider them a "pool." In general, most organizations are far from this point, but it's worth noting and something your analysts should consider.

A focus on risk management can also be applied to considering opportunities. Precision in maximizing opportunities can be achieved in a similar way to risk management. Instead of considering the risks involved in a decision, you can consider the opportunity of a decision. If attracting a new customer is worth a certain amount of revenue, you should invest only a comparable amount in acquiring that customer. Targeting prospects correctly generates more revenue, decreases waste, and manages your opportunity risk.

### Knowledge Retention

Although knowledge retention isn't related directly to the impact of automating decisions, it might turn out to be one of the longest-term strategic benefits of using enterprise decision management. As companies watch experienced professionals retire and face new, younger workers unwilling to take on some traditional roles, they need a new solution. Capturing expertise as rules, generating formal risk and other models from historical data, and using these rules and models to automate decisions helps keep that knowledge in the organization and makes the remaining job (absent the rote approvals) more interesting and desirable. The retirement of expert staff has long been an issue, but the baby boomers will make the problem more noticeable than ever. Although capturing expert knowledge as documents or guidelines can help somewhat, only automating it addresses the issue that incoming workers might not want the same jobs the retiring workers had.

### Costs of Enterprise Decision Management

You should never consider benefits without some matching discussion of costs. Costs for enterprise decision management can be for software, people, or organizational change.

Most companies implementing enterprise decision management need to buy additional software. Although building an infrastructure to manage decisions with an EDM approach is possible, purchasing a business rules management system is more realistic. Even companies with a major investment in an "analytic" infrastructure might find they need to buy additional software. Many business intelligence and business analytic platforms don't have the algorithms needed to build sophisticated models or the technology to deploy these models. They focus on reporting and supporting manual analysis. In addition, they build on a data warehouse infrastructure that's too latent and designed for reporting, not insight. Some products in this category are add-ons to more traditional business intelligence software; others are stand-alone environments designed to turn existing data into executable models.

Building systems with the adaptive control and learning infrastructure an EDM approach requires also means new code, new components, and new software infrastructure in addition to analytic and business rules components. Although none of these approaches is a dramatic departure from traditional software development practices, making them part of the standard IT operating environment incurs extra costs. Chapter 4, "Core Concepts," discusses the technologies typically required to implement enterprise decision management.

### National Bank: Controlling Risk While Doubling Customer Base

#### Old Way

As the bank expanded by acquiring other institutions, integrating a new institution took 12 months. Data was stored in many databases, and the different institutions used different approaches.

Many decisions were account-level, not customer-centered, and as a result they were manual and inconsistent. Competing products within the bank often were sold to the same customer, and many customers were customers of both the main bank and an acquired one. The bank needed to increase its share of its customers' wallets, so approval rates needed to increase. However, collections and risk management remained issues that the bank couldn't ignore.

#### EDM Way

A Customer Data Integration (CDI) initiative brought customer data together, and this single coherent customer view was the basis of decisions. Business rules and predictive analytics aligned product offers around both predicted customer needs and ability to pay.

#### Benefits

- A single integration point on the EDM backbone reduced integration time for new institutions by 75 percent (from 12 months to 3 months).

- Delinquency rates dropped by 30 percent.

- Improvements in collections and delinquencies meant the bank could lower its bad-debt provision by 60 percent, as shown in Figure 2.13.

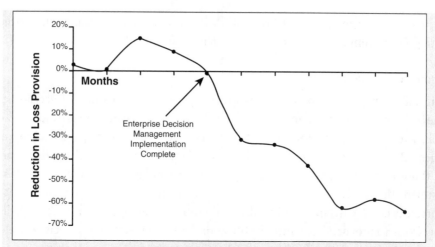

**Figure 2.13    The accumulated reduction in provision for loss, thanks to a risk management EDM solution**

As with any new products, you must also consider training and support costs. Developers need training in how to think about business rules, manage them separately from requirements, and develop and test them. Some business analysts will benefit from similar training. Business managers also need training on how to think about more formal logic and on interacting with programmers. Some organizations find they need additional business resources to manage rules when programmers stop doing so; they still save on the number of programmers needed, but there is to some extent a transfer of head count from IT to the business. Business rules are a new approach for many organizations, so support and mentoring can increase the chance of success at an additional short-term cost.

Similarly, on the analytic front, companies might need to hire analysts as staff or consultants. Even organizations with experienced analysts often incur training costs. The focus on deploying executable models is likely to be new, even for those experienced in analytics, and supporting analysts to make this change in approach matters a great deal to overall EDM success.

More sophisticated analytics might impose additional costs for data. The use of external data, often available at a fee, can dramatically improve the ability to model some customer characteristics, for example. These costs might be incurred once but are more likely to become a regular transactional cost, because data is used in each decision made.

Last, organizational change always costs time and money. Assuming that change can simply be imposed instantaneously without a change management process leads to problems. Time and money must be devoted to getting IT people, analytics people, and businesspeople to change their mind-set and approach to an EDM one. It's best to adopt enterprise decision management in phases, with each showing a clear ROI. Chapter 9, "Getting There from Here," covers this topic in more detail.

### Introducing Decision Yield

If you can't manage what you can't measure, you need a new measure for decision effectiveness so that you can manage decisions. Sometimes organizations find that their established cost/benefit analysis doesn't show the true value of enterprise decision management. By comparing organizations that have adopted enterprise decision management with those that haven't, you can identify some clear differences in the way they make investment decisions. In particular, there's more focus on revenue improvement and opportunity costs (costs implicit in a delayed response to an opportunity). The challenge is how to turn a broader focus into a justification for EDM investments. Decision yield is a new approach that can be effective.

**Decision yield** is a broad evaluation metric that reveals the quality of your current decisions and decision processes and helps you plan, justify, and measure improvements to decision processes. Frank Rohde first described the need for it:[11]

> "We judge leaders by how well they make big, strategic decisions. But corporate success also depends on how well rank-and-file employees make thousands of small decisions. Do I give this customer a special price? How do I handle this customer's complaint? Should I offer a seat upgrade to this customer? By themselves, such daily calls—increasingly made with the help of enterprise decision management technology—have little impact on business performance. Taken together, they influence everything from profitability to reputation."

What constitutes a good decision? Is it the outcome alone? The cost of carrying out that decision? The speed of making the decision? How about coordinating several decisions across different parts of your organization? In reality, all these aspects are likely to be important. Without a consistent method for measuring the performance of high-volume, operational decisions, you might make plans for vital improvements based on metrics that focus on only one dimension of the decision process, such as cost savings. Organizations with such a narrow focus often miss the potential value of an EDM approach.

To determine what constitutes a "good" decision process and measure the current state of your decision process, you must understand the different facets of an operational decision that contribute to business performance. Decision yield is a holistic way of evaluating decisions specifically designed to evaluate automated decisions suitable for automation and management using an EDM approach. Decision yield, then, can be an effective tool for those evaluating enterprise decision management and trying to decide where best to apply it.

---

[11] Frank Rohde, "Little Decisions Add Up," *Harvard Business Review*, June 2005.

Decision yield's holistic approach involves comparing the following five dimensions of decision effectiveness to make a comprehensive assessment of an operational decision:

- **Precision**—How targeted and profitable is the decision?
- **Consistency**—How consistent across divisions, channels, and time is the decision?
- **Agility**—How quickly can you effectively change how the decision is made when you need to?
- **Speed**—How quickly can you make the decision?
- **Cost**—How much does it cost you to make the decision?

Plotting these dimensions for current state, competitive average, and best practice on a "radar" graphic like the one shown in Figure 2.14 can be informative. This graphic shows that the company has real strength in cost (offering lower cost than its competitors) and reasonably competitive speed, but its precision and, to some extent, consistency leave it vulnerable.

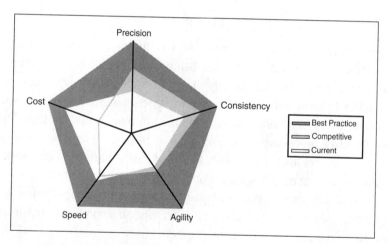

**Figure 2.14    Radar graphic showing a decision yield for a specific decision**

There are many ways to use decision yield to measure decision ROI. You can conduct a decision audit to see how well you perform in relation to competitors or the overall market. You can measure decision yield over time to monitor and optimize performance. You can consider the potential gain in decision yield from different opportunities as part of evaluating which ones to consider. Each is explained in more detail in the appendix, "Decision Yield as a Way to Measure ROI," which includes more information on the approach in general.

## Large Multiline Insurer: International Mid-market Trade Credit

### Old Way

The company's Web site offered trade credit products and credit information to mid-size companies in many of the 130 countries in which it did business. This combination of insurance products and real-time access to customer credit information allowed these mid-size companies to manage their risk and credit exposure. Although the system worked, it required custom coding for each new country added. This coding was complex because it involved international law, risk models, and business conditions that weren't easy for programmers to understand. Adding a country took several months and many IT resources, which slowed the rollout to new countries. Policy updates could take several weeks, increasing the risk to the organization when there were sudden changes in an industry's creditworthiness.

### EDM Way

A decision service provides trade credit calculations, combining business rules and algorithms developed by using predictive analytic techniques. Business experts interact directly with trade credit rules by using rule templates to ensure that rules match the underlying object model, without business users having to understand the object model's technicalities. Effective repository design means the rules for each country share common algorithms yet can be customized easily. Almost all the work in adding a country or changing a policy is carried out directly by business users, and the system doesn't have to be taken offline to bring new countries online. Business users conduct what-if analysis by trying out new rules in a preproduction environment.

### Benefits

- IT cost for new countries and policy updates has been reduced.
- A country can be added in a few weeks rather than months, so the organization went from 2 to 16 covered countries in just 3 months.
- Most ongoing changes can be made in hours rather than weeks.
- The system allows immediate changes to rules in a crisis, preventing the possibility of liability or other legal exposure for the organization.

To see how decision yield can be effective, take a look at Figure 2.15, which shows two examples of a decision yield audit for U.S. insurance companies that resulted in very different recommendations. The two decision yield charts were developed based on their responses. Company 1, on the left, shows generally weak results on all five dimensions of decision effectiveness. This result isn't surprising, because the company had historically competed with a small group of insurers who were equally weak. Comparing decision making against national competitors clarifies obvious weaknesses. Company 2 (a nationally competitive insurer), on the right, has much better results. However, its weakness in precision compared to competitors might make it vulnerable to competitors who manage risk-based underwriting decisions better, and its lack of agility exposes it to risks in a fast-changing market.

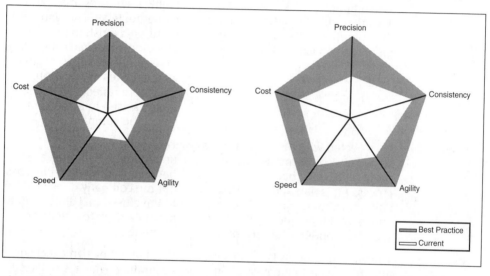

**Figure 2.15** **Decision yields for two insurance companies' underwriting process**

You can also consider specific notes and suggestions made to these companies based on their decision yield assessments, as shown in Table 2.3.

**Table 2.3** **Results for Each Dimension for Two Companies**

| Dimension | Company 1 | Company 2 |
|---|---|---|
| Precision | Its reliance on manual underwriting by agents without widespread use of predictive analytics means its precision was only average compared with national competitors. It has few pricing tiers, for instance. | It rates strongly in precision, although behind industry leaders. This dimension is a major focus, and its weakness comes from its inability to learn and adapt its risk models over time. |

*continues*

**Table 2.3   Continued**

| Dimension | Company 1 | Company 2 |
|---|---|---|
| Consistency | Manual underwriting weakens its consistency scores. Although the company sells a standard set of well-established products, introducing new products and managing them consistently are difficult, especially if the company introduces new channels. | Company 2's consistency is nearly perfect, with only a few problems with agents repricing policies before issuing them. Consistency is clearly a strength. |
| Agility | Agility is low as a deliberate policy; this company prides itself on not chasing trends. Sometimes decision yield simply clarifies underlying approaches, such as this policy. | Company 2 rates agility very highly but scores at a moderate level. This gap represents a risk to its precision score because failing to respond quickly to change would decrease precision. This score reflects the legacy systems used to achieve the speed the company has. |
| Speed | As expected with a manual process, Company 1 performs poorly on speed, especially because processing is handled in batch. With more competitors offering online, real-time quotes, this lack of speed is a potential source of risk. | The speed with which underwriting decisions are handled is almost best in class, but the company doesn't seem to have used this dimension to promote itself to agents or customers. |
| Cost | The manual process is expensive, and this cost is being passed on to the company's agents. It isn't clear how long agents would tolerate this practice or how easily a competitor could use it to attack their agent network. | Company 2 has an excellent cost rating, which is reflected in a very low expense ratio. Being low cost isn't a specific strategy, however, so the decision yield review made it clear the company could sacrifice some of its cost rating to improve other dimensions, such as agility. |

The appendix has more information on how to measure and interpret decision yield results. This technique is just starting to be used in a formal sense but early results, such as those described here, show great potential.

Before you learn more about the business benefits of enterprise decision management and the technologies and implementation approach it takes, understanding how we got here is worthwhile. Read on to find out why your systems, on which you have spent a lot of money and effort, aren't smart enough already.

# CHAPTER THREE

# Why Aren't My Systems Smart Enough Already?

The cost of information technology in today's organizations is substantial and is growing as a percentage of total operating cost—but today's systems still aren't smart enough. Why this is the case can only be understood by taking a historical perspective on business computing and how information technology (IT) developed as a discipline. In the past, IT departments were thought leaders in their organizations, setting the pace for the application of technology. Today, the needs and sophistication of the people who work in organizations are colored by an outside influence—the Internet—and IT organizations struggle to keep pace, burdened by accelerating demands and the drag of maintaining legacy systems. The tools, technology, and techniques for enterprise decision management (EDM) are ready, but impediments are rooted in the history of business computing and the resultant IT cultures. To understand why, after years of spending on information technology, so many of your systems aren't already smart enough, you need to take a walk back through the evolution of business computing in practice. With that in mind, this chapter is a brief look at the history of a typical IT infrastructure. It's not a general-purpose history but a brief outline of how we ended up in this mess.

## How Did We Get Here?

A history of business computing would require volumes. However, a brief overview of the evolution of information technology (IT) in business decision making is useful in understanding why certain aspects of information management are still misaligned. Certain approaches that are taken for granted today are based on situations that disappeared long ago; certain disciplines that are considered unrelated are actually quite similar and synergistic. Some approaches aren't being used in a comprehensive enough way. Only through understanding the basis of these inefficiencies and, often, dysfunctions can you construct a rational remedy.

Computing in business is roughly 60 years old, although the deployment of computers for processing business information didn't start to catch on until the late 1950s. There were many computer manufacturers at that time, and each one developed its own proprietary operating systems and application software, although software was usually limited to a language compiler or two. Some manufacturers developed a reputation for general-purpose computing based on their programming languages (Assembler originally, but expanding to higher-level languages such as COBOL and FORTRAN); others came to specialize in certain applications, such as back-office work for banks (Burroughs, for example). At the time, general-purpose computing was what was needed for computing to take hold across industries.

Because general-purpose computing took hold, subsequent development of the technology proceeded rapidly, which created a constant lag between optimistic expectations and delayed delivery of useful output. Applying technology upgrades and innovations took considerably longer than producing them, a phenomenon that has only gotten worse over time. In the early days, the delivery of a new model meant reprogramming everything, because there was no upward compatibility. Today, that amount of effort seems almost ridiculous, yet according to a survey[1] by Forrester Research, 75 percent of the IT budget is spent on maintenance of existing software and infrastructure. Organizations' ability to absorb new technology and put it to work is just as constrained today as it was at the dawn of computing. Unlike many other industries, the rate of change has neither slowed nor been adapted to.

People responsible for computers have been a unique breed in business. Their skills with abstract concepts or mysterious codes are in stark contrast to the formal, businesslike demeanor of accountants, salespeople, and executives. From the beginning, they were a separate group, in a career that had little or no trajectory into the "real" parts of business. This chasm between IT and the rest of the organization exists to this day and is still a major cause of dissonance between IT efforts and business requirements. In fact, in the past, IT managers had all they could do to manage IT software, hardware, and staff. They had no time to worry about the business itself, which was left to business professionals. Today, the stereotypes of the computer wizard in the basement with the pocket protector and the florid, cigar-smoking CEO are cartoonish and dated, but in reality, the gap is still severe.

---

[1] Phil Murphy, "APM Tools Will Reach $500 Million to $700 Million by 2008." Forrester Research, July 22, 2005.

**Note** *There was no academic path for computer specialists, either. The first PhD in computer science was awarded in 1965. Today's colleges and universities are addressing this gap between IT and the rest of an organization, leading to a new kind of IT professional and offering new majors that are combinations of marketing and IT or finance and IT.*

In general, the issues discussed in this chapter are related to problems with data, problems with programs, and problems with people. Data first.

## Problems with Data

For a long time, computers were used strictly as calculating machines. Data was fed into them manually from punch cards, a holdover from tabulating machinery. The computer crunched the numbers and generated, with limited flexibility, reams of reports on the familiar "greenbar." Data in computers was typically lost because there was nowhere to store it. Storage wasn't considered important anyway, as punch cards and paper reports, usually retyped into forms with a typewriter, were considered the official system of record. The computer and its programs and data were merely tools to speed up some work.

Both greenbar and official reports were stored for recordkeeping. This is how it had always been done, and the appearance of a "big calculator" didn't change anything right away. In fact, many firms, well into the 1990s, kept paper records long after the appearance of magnetic tape and later nonsequential storage devices, such as magnetic disk drives. Perhaps the tradition of keeping important records, such as legal documents, on paper contributed to this habit. It wasn't until total quality management (TQM) and business process reengineering (BPR) took hold that the inefficiencies of large organizations were exposed. Unfortunately, the attitude that computing was just a calculator and not to be trusted for real work would take much longer to break down than it took to get started.

### The Reporting Gap

With the introduction of permanent storage devices, however, computers began to take on a role as archival devices as well as number crunchers and report generators. Although paper was king at the time, the economy of microfiche was easily understood and accepted because it didn't alter the concept of computers outputting information in a format understood by businesspeople. Microfiche just compressed information and made it more durable. However, magnetic storage devices, especially tape, ushered in a completely new way of thinking about computers in business. Tapes stored everything—data, report streams, and programs. The tapes even substituted for core memory, allowing programmers the luxury of writing programs that used more resources than were actually available. Computers gradually became bona fide business tools.

Computers gained speed and flexibility through the advancements of disk drives, solid-state memory, and virtual memory operating systems. Eventually, interfaces or "transaction monitors," such as IBM's CICS, opened a new discipline: online systems. Instead of batch machines that ran serial scheduled jobs, transaction monitors allowed programmers to create applications for real-time, instantaneous processing of multiple processes (although most small "transactions" were stored for later batch processing). Soon, transaction processing was born, the polar opposite of batch computing. Online transaction processing (OLTP) emerged as the next big thing and never really faded. The bulk of corporate computing, even as it moves through generations of technology, is still transaction-oriented.

The advent of formal data methodologies and software (Chen, Codd, Computer-Aided Software Engineering [CASE] tools, and relational databases) also led to better appreciation and use of the information stored in computing technology. So we moved from computers for processing to computers for information. One thing was missing from these transactions, however—decision making. All the "brainpower" in transactions came from people. The computer's role was to capture and store the data needed to record the transaction. If a judgment had to be made, a person made it. If the transaction had to be approved, the system waited for someone to approve it. These transactions were increasingly fast and essential to business operations, but they remained unintelligent.

Additionally, the more transaction-oriented corporate computing became, the more alienated it became from its original purpose: reporting. As a result, a new industry emerged in the late 1970s that was designed to address this gap. At the time, this industry was called decision support systems (DSSs) or sometimes fourth-generation languages (4GLs), but its goal was to enable users, mostly businesspeople, to create models and generate reports without the IT department's involvement. This industry later became known as business intelligence, but almost all the early providers of these products fell by the wayside before then.

Mainstream systems evolved from batch to OLTP to client/server and finally, by 2000, to Y2K/enterprise applications, as shown in Figure 3.1. Business intelligence and analytics developed separately, supported by functional areas, particularly finance and marketing. As computing in general became more advanced and complicated, it ended up back in IT. It was called "data warehousing" and "business intelligence," but it was still a separate discipline. The original motivation for this separation was mostly IT's neglect of reporting and analysis, but as the need for and volume of business intelligence grew, IT took control to protect its existing resources. The gap has continued to grow and is, with today's technology, largely artificial and unnecessary.

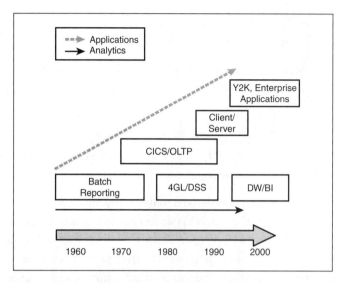

**Figure 3.1  The divergence of applications and analytics as computing evolved**

Many of the early DSS tools were quite ingenious, with features that current analytical tools would envy, such as nonprocedural modeling, multidimensional orientation, goal seeking, statistical and stochastic routines, graphics, and tools for development and collaboration. Their weakness was data. Without the data in transactional systems, these tools were limited to whatever data businesspeople could generate on their own, such as budget, planning, and forecasting data. In many cases, getting existing data required reentering data from printed reports, a time-consuming and tedious process. Nevertheless, these tools flourished, especially in planning and budgeting roles where the need for external data was low.

The IT department wasn't supportive of these tools. There was a constant refrain that they would "bring the mainframe to its knees," but in practice that rarely happened. What did happen was that for the first time, "power users" emerged—non-IT people who could actually develop applications and generate reports from computers, a privileged group that endures to this day. In fact, there are so many of them, and their output is so important, that this group has a name of its own: shadow IT.[2]

Early DSS vendors met their Waterloo in the early 1980s when a small product was launched: Lotus 1-2-3. It turned out that a PC with a Lotus 1-2-3 spreadsheet was capable of doing much, if not all, of the functions of mainframe- or mini-based DSS tools. Connectivity was actually worse, because PCs weren't connected to the mainframe, but the freedom and novelty was so great that, within a few years, most DSS vendors disappeared.

---

[2] "Shining the Light on Shadow Staff: Booz Allen Hamilton," *CIO*, January 2, 2004.

A bigger drain on IT was the constant flood of requests for data extracted from operational systems, both decision support systems and PCs. Many alternatives were tried:

- Formal programming requests with highly specific requirements
- Generic abstracts to flat files that could be shared by more than one request
- Nonprocedural programming languages, such as A Programming Language (APL), that allowed a less programmer-centered approach
- Ad hoc query tools, such as Query Management Facility (QMF), so that users could create their own abstracts

In the end, none of these approaches worked well because, for the most part, they couldn't be maintained. The number of extracts expanded geometrically, as shown in simplified form in Figure 3.2, and changes in programs, requirements, and tools overwhelmed IT's ability to respond to requests. There were no standards or best practices for non-IT people to develop libraries of extraction and importation routines, so the "self-service" aspect suffered, too. The sheer number of extracts was also a burden on often heavily used mainframe and minicomputer hosts.

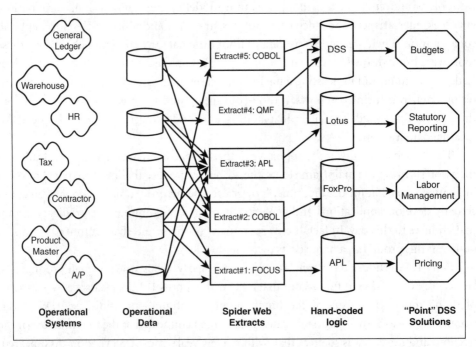

**Figure 3.2    Simplified representation of extracts from various systems for diverse reporting needs**

## Enter the Data Warehouse

Originally, the data warehouse (or information warehouse, as IBM called it) was designed to solve a problem for IT departments, not end users. The goal was to build a database to provide in-place access to physically distributed databases and serve as a repository for satisfying report requests from end users (because individual silo databases couldn't do so), not to support self-service or direct access. This key point explains why even current data warehouse approaches often use a layered, after-the-fact batch architecture with a substantial investment in an enterprise data warehouse that knowledge workers never, or rarely, query directly.

The term "data warehouse" has an uncertain provenance. The most influential person who shaped the concept's development is probably Bill Inmon. For more than 20 years, he has dominated as a thought leader, with dozens of books and countless appearances and publications. However, the practice of data warehousing has surged ahead on many fronts, with broad adoption of Inmon's original work, Ralph Kimball's architecture and methodology, and the contributions of many others. Data warehousing has become a well-established and vibrant strand in the IT mainstream.

However, in the early to mid-1980s, a typical organization owned an IBM mainframe that struggled to perform all scheduled jobs. The computer often simply ran out of computing cycles to do all the work, necessitating an upgrade to a newer, more powerful machine. This solution was expensive and temporary, because new requests were already lined up to absorb all the new computing cycles. This management-from-scarcity approach resulted in a sort of triage process in which requests for new applications were evaluated. Most were put into a queue, the so-called backlog, where they languished sometimes indefinitely. This backlog was largely made up of business departments' requests for reports, because preference was given to operational programs.

The original concept of data warehousing was quite simple: Buy another mainframe, install a more "friendly" operating system (such as IBM's VM/CMS), and provide a set of utilities to build a relational database of data culled from various operational systems. This solution would relieve the other mainframe's load of numerous and overlapping extracts and allow IT to service users' reporting needs with tools of its choosing. How reporting needs were met took different forms. At the simplest level, the new machine simply took copies of data from various systems, in whole or in part. From these files or databases, programmers could draw their own extracts for reporting programs without affecting the "main" mainframe's performance.

This method is very different from the current concept of data warehousing. For one thing, there were no business users in the data warehouse; it was designed for IT. Business units, with or without support from IT, developed their own reporting and analysis solutions to compensate for the weak reporting operational systems offered. None of these solutions, however, was completely effective, and all were expensive and tedious to build and maintain. Eventually, power users of DSS tools and PCs got access to the early data warehouse, and it became apparent that the current arrangement wasn't satisfactory. Combining information from multiple extracts, the data simply did not line up. Whether the problem was caused by coding errors, sloppy data entry, or timing errors, merging information across the various disconnected source systems or "stovepipes" was impossible. Solving this problem was the beginning of data warehousing as it is known today: the integration of disparate data into a common logical model. In time, data warehousing became a structured solution to address these intractable reporting and analysis problems:

- **Performance**—Systems designed for transaction processing performance, especially in an era of expensive, proprietary hardware, were unable to tolerate the added load of query and report processing.
- **Data quality**—OLTP system data integrity was limited to the application's needs, so integrating data across systems was difficult to impossible.
- **Access**—Initially, connectivity issues were paramount, but security, licensing, and organizational boundary disputes also restricted access to information.
- **Stewardship of historical data**—OLTP systems didn't maintain the historical analysis needed for variance reporting, trend analysis, and even statutory and regulatory requirements.

In the 20 or so years since this concept emerged, the data warehouse has taken on far more responsibility, some of which it still hasn't met completely. For instance, many see the "enterprise" data warehouse as the "single version of the truth," a comprehensive repository of the one true set of data and semantics that everyone can get behind. Having absorbed the role of business intelligence, it's also the architecture for all forms of end-user reporting, query, and analysis. It's the plug that fills the gap between operational and analytical processing, a gap that has been steadily widening since the advent of online processing. As Figure 3.3 shows, a data warehouse is the hub for spokes that lead to operational systems, analysts, customers, performance management, and more.

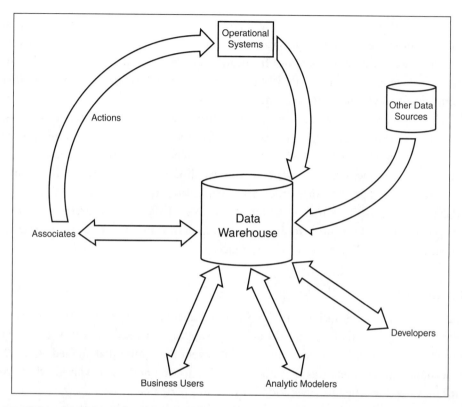

**Figure 3.3 A modern data warehouse plays a more central role in information systems (teradata)**

A functioning data warehouse is a collection of data, models, metadata, processes, practices, standards, and services. At the most fundamental level, a data warehouse gathers data from other systems and transforms it into a merged model of sorts. This process can range from preserving almost all the original data at the most detailed level to compressing and summarizing at a much higher level of aggregation or, in most cases, both. What's most important is finding a way to preserve as much of the data's original intent as possible yet fit it into a single schema, at least initially. This process often involves "cleaning" the data because data in various source systems might be of poor quality, especially historical data. Another unique characteristic of data warehouses is the extent of historical data they retain. This data provides the basis for tasks such as trend analysis, statutory and regulatory reporting, and variance reporting.

Keeping historical data presents a new set of challenges, however. In today's fast-changing world, shoehorning three-year-old data into current data models can be exceedingly difficult. Data warehousing has developed some ingenious methods for pulling off this process, but keep in mind that these innovations were added to the original concept.

Data warehouses have also prolonged and extended the gap between operational and analytical processes. Because data warehouses and the business intelligence tools used with them were separate disciplines from other enterprise applications, even the small amount of reporting and analysis that occurred in operational systems gradually migrated to data warehouse/business intelligence systems.

The data warehouse was a simple idea, but in practice, its implementation caused, and still is causing, problems. Extracting data from source systems and transforming it into an integrated whole is a monumental effort. The latency caused by the load and refresh cycle devalues data. The scale of data warehouses grew exponentially, leading to spiraling costs and performance problems. The industry divided over polarizing issues of database design, architecture, and methodology. Most of all, the data warehouse's purpose changed dramatically from a tool for programmers to an analytical environment for knowledge workers. Enter business intelligence.

### Business Intelligence

The terms "data warehousing" and "business intelligence" are like binary star systems: They orbit each other, but from a distance, they appear to be a single entity. Because the subjects of data warehousing and business intelligence are somewhat aligned with EDM, understanding the differences is important, as is knowing how each evolved, what problems they were designed to solve, and how well they performed.

In its purest form, business intelligence is supposed to be part of decision making in an organization. Phrases such as "better data for improved decision making," "getting the right information to the right person at the right time," and "the single version of the truth" are common. The focus is on informing people with data, who then go about making decisions. Business intelligence is designed to inform people and provide a way for them for evaluate information in retrospect. A branch of business intelligence now called performance management also has provisions for forecasting and planning, but in practice, most of performance management is still retrospective analysis and reporting.

Some people refer to the process of people getting and using information as business intelligence, but the term was coined when many providers, concepts, and methods for today's business intelligence didn't exist. Some fuzziness in the definition of business intelligence is unavoidable. In fact, the term "business intelligence" has more or less subsumed the practice of data warehousing and has become synonymous with a range of functionality that business intelligence vendors offer.

Of all the types of business intelligence, reporting, ad hoc query, online analytical processing (OLAP), dashboards, scorecards, visualization, and even data mining, one common thread is delivering information to people. With transaction systems still relying on human intelligence for decision making and judgment, business intelligence has sold itself to a new group of users by promising to improve decisions. If people must make a decision because the system can't, at least they should make one informed by all the facts or data in the data warehouse. Even business activity monitoring (BAM), which catches data on the fly and applies some simple rules to process data or let it go, ultimately alerts people through visual devices. Some BAM products are capable of bypassing people in the loop and alerting applications, services, or processes directly, but this feature is unusual. Most implementations update digital dashboards for people to view and navigate.

### Operational Business Intelligence

As the gap between operational and analytical processes closes, thinking about the role of business intelligence in this new landscape is natural. Latency in business intelligence is an issue because data warehouses are updated monthly, weekly, and often daily, but rarely within a business day. Operational reporting or monitoring that requires fresher data is a problem. The concept of a data warehouse is based on layers of schema that are updated in batch offline and then conformed, indexed, preaggregated, and otherwise tuned and dispatched. Trickling in new data in real time disrupts this model.

Another problem is that after data is culled from its source and integrated into the data warehouse, the connection to its source can be lost. Although vendors have invested heavily in maintaining these links, persistent connectivity problems make data warehouses a poor candidate for single-source reporting. The solution was a sort of kludge called the operational data store. It violated many data warehouse principles, even though it was still considered part of the data warehouse. In time, operational data stores were also integrated, so they lost their capability to tie back to the original systems. Because of the transformation that happens with integration, they inherited much of the same latency as data warehouses.

The need for more timely analysis of data is strong and growing, however. The business intelligence industry is working toward solutions of operational business intelligence, but that definition is typically limited to daily or "intraday" data.[3] So for the time being, operational business intelligence is characterized as having the same output (to people) and using the same data model (the data warehouse) but taking place a little more often than daily. True real-time data monitoring has been scaled back in business intelligence to a watery concept called "right time," which means as fast as the data warehouse can handle it. Some vendors can trickle data into a data warehouse, but the answer to operational business intelligence clearly lies in the ability to get closer to business

---

[3] Colin White, "The Next Generation of Business Intelligence: Operational Business Intelligence." *DMReview*, May 2005.

processes as composite applications or from message queues. In any case, the lingering shadow of the data warehouse plus people-based delivery of business intelligence will keep business intelligence from participating in making your systems smarter, but it can be a valuable contributor.

### Data Mining, Predictive Reporting, and Operations Research

To improve the value of reporting and analysis tools for knowledge workers, some organizations have adopted data-mining technologies. Data mining involves using powerful mathematical techniques to analyze huge volumes of data, as from a data warehouse, and extract meaningful insight. This insight might mean finding out how two products are related in their sales patterns or what customer characteristics make them susceptible to an offer. Association rules, likelihood scores, and trending are possible outcomes of these insights.

Although much data mining is aimed at understanding historical data, some is focused on predictive analysis. What customer actions predict whether they will cancel a contract? What kinds of customers are likely to respond well to a store redesign? Which suppliers will have credit issues in the future? This kind of predictive reporting can increase the value of analysis by giving knowledge workers a sense of data's future implications. Generally, it doesn't prescribe actions or lend itself to causing change in systems. Most organizations have applied it only to making reporting and analysis more sophisticated. Predictive reporting improves the value of your data but doesn't make your systems smarter.

Operations research grew out of work in the United Kingdom during World War II and has been applied to business problems more over the years. Using a mix of statistical and mathematical techniques to find solutions to problems, operations research is more focused on finding the right action to take, given current constraints and historical data. Using mathematical techniques and optimization and simulation tools, it allows a modeler to set up a problem and then "solve" it to find the best outcomes, given existing constraints. Although some models can be embedded into systems to make them smarter, the range of solutions for which it's sufficient is limited. Therefore, operations research has focused on making people understand possible solutions instead. Many problems have been targeted and solved with operations research, but it hasn't generally been used in programs that run organizations day to day.

Although data mining and operations research have roles to play in solving these problems, problems with data aren't the only ones organizations have. You need to consider problems with programs as well, as discussed in the following section.

## Problems with Programs

The gap between analytics and operational or transactional systems explored in the previous section explains why organizations have such a hard time deriving insight from data and applying that insight to their operational systems. A second major flaw with current approaches is problems with programs. Fundamentally, the programs used to run most organizations today are built without any embedded intelligence. The "peopleware" of an organization, not the software, is what makes decisions.

The inherent inefficiency of these programs has long been obvious to those working with information systems. Attempts have been made to address this limitation. All these attempts, from handwritten code to failed attempts at artificial intelligence, from enterprise applications to business process management and service-oriented architecture, have made little difference. Most organizations have software programs that just aren't smart enough.

### The Weight of Legacy Code

As more custom code is written, organizations find that it lives longer than they intended. Code that's 20 or even 30 years old is still in use in many organizations—still running core business processes and processing vital transactions. Companies have discovered the hard way that they can't code their way into the future. This deadweight of legacy applications has created two problems.

Part of the problem comes from a mind-set that systems, like other enterprise assets, should be built to last. This focus results in detailed but largely static requirements and huge investments in system architecture and design. However, it also buries critical code in complex systems. To make applications robust and complete, a huge amount of business expertise must be embedded in the system, but there are problems with this approach:

- Embedding business expertise in the system is hard because those who understand the business can't code, and those who understand the code don't run the business. Business users can't explain to programmers what they need, and the result is systems that don't quite work the way they were intended.

- Generally, custom code isn't well documented, or the documentation is allowed to get out of date rapidly. The promises of "self-documenting" code notwithstanding, new generations of programmers struggle to amend code to face new challenges.

- Showing a regulator or auditor how custom code works is nearly impossible, and demonstrating compliance with policies or regulations is extremely difficult, costly, and time consuming.

- New challenges and requirements emerge constantly because the world doesn't stop changing, and organizations can't afford to stand still. Therefore, changing and managing custom code is difficult.

All these factors contribute to another aspect of the problem: the maintenance backlog. The maintenance backlog is the list of projects not progressing because of a lack of time and resources or other projects having higher priorities. Most projects don't even make it to the backlog unless they have a positive potential—that is, the project's business value exceeds its cost. An organization that could magically complete all projects in its backlog would add tremendous value to the business. For most organizations, this backlog represents a sink of resources and time that could add significant value.

Organizations have a maintenance backlog for many reasons, but one of the most persistent is that a huge percentage of IT resources is spent on systems maintenance—75 percent or more, as noted at the beginning of the chapter. So much old code is used to run businesses and must be constantly updated (to reflect new regulations, competitors, and products) that this work dominates the IT department's responsibilities. The systems were originally built to specification but no longer do what the business needs. Perhaps the specification was wrong, or perhaps the business has changed. Maintenance takes so long and uses so many resources that little or nothing else can be done.

Even if maintenance work isn't consuming a large percentage of your IT resources, traditional approaches to embedding logic in systems create rigid and unwieldy systems. This lack of agility causes problems if you need to respond quickly and cost-effectively to a competitive issue, new regulations, a new channel, or another major change. Coding business logic into legacy systems perpetuates the separation between those who know the business and those who run the systems and makes it hard to update systems as business needs change. Expert systems and 4GLs were two programming approaches intended to address these issues.

## Artificial Intelligence and Expert Systems

In the 1980s, the IT industry and organizations made a major investment in various forms of artificial intelligence (AI), which was designed to bring the power of human intelligence to computers. Expert systems vendors promised that their software would perform tasks just like the company's most experienced employees. These vendors used intelligence and best practices painstakingly collected from industry experts to power their systems, but most expert systems didn't succeed in practical application.

Expert systems were typically designed as "closed systems," designed to solve a problem on their own. They didn't support or integrate with the programming models prevalent in OLTP systems. Specialized hardware and software were required. At the time, most corporate computer systems were written in COBOL and ran on IBM mainframes, but many expert systems packages required high-end workstations using artificial intelligence languages, such as Lisp or PROLOG. Organizations couldn't easily integrate these systems into their production environments and had no personnel trained in maintenance or programming techniques for them. They had to rely on special training and support from software vendors. Generally, expert systems came with predefined rules for accomplishing specific tasks. Specialist programmers at vendors, working from interpretations of interviews with industry experts, crafted these rules as compromises between the different methods their sources used.

Organizations purchasing expert systems software usually needed to go through laborious tuning sessions to understand how the rules functioned and to modify them for their business preferences. Organizations found it impossible to use expert systems to automate other tasks because they couldn't modify their underlying processing flow and structure. In the end, the organizations that experimented with expert systems became wary of computer software promising "intelligent processing."

In addition, AI software consumed huge amounts of computing resources at a time when these resources were still at a premium. Other factors prevailed as well, especially rampant paranoia that Japan's burgeoning economy would overwhelm the United States and that Japan's government-funded "fifth-generation computing" initiative, largely about developing AI, would pose a bigger threat to the U.S. economy than all the Toyotas it could produce. This mentality created a rush among small AI entrepreneurs to market immature and nonperforming products. Ultimately, the Japanese fifth-generation initiative failed to produce much more than factory (and toy) robots, and many AI vendors returned to the university labs and defense contracts from whence they came. To be fair, some firms survived and, having learned a painful lesson, transformed their products into more commercially useful offerings, such as business rules management systems, data-mining tools, logistics optimization software, and embedded intelligence, such as fraud detection.

Ultimately, even though the outcome was less than desirable, everyone learned from the experience. Lessons included the value of keeping knowledge (rules) in a repository where it could be managed and the power of a declarative approach, compared to procedural programming, to simplify some problems. Expectations for AI were rolled back to more reasonable levels, the buying community became more careful about the next big trend, and AI entrepreneurs learned that they have to embed their inventions in useful applications as well as cooperative architectures. In the meantime, the power and relative cost of processing is dramatically more favorable, and open standards and ubiquitous communication provided the basis for AI-like technologies to have a second chance.

## 4GLs and Other User-Friendly Tools

If business know-how is hard to embed into information systems, even with an expert system, can you make maintaining the code easier? To bring a higher level of abstraction to programming problems, 4GLs were developed. In theory, abstraction makes it easier to see what's happening in code, engages businesspeople in the process more effectively, and makes IT development and modification of sophisticated processes easier and quicker. Many 4GLs came and went, and not much changed in the problems of application maintenance.

Although 4GLs do offer some productivity gains and many are easy for less technical staff to use, they fail to address the core "build to last" problems. Code representing core business logic is still procedural and embedded in code that's "plumbing" or otherwise highly technical. Few business users become fluent enough to write code themselves, and those who do often create programs and scripts that aren't managed or controlled well enough for a company to rely on.

Stretching the metaphor, you could consider a spreadsheet a 4GL (at least its scripting or macro creation capabilities). The problem of maintaining spreadsheet applications is well documented and pervasive. Names such as shadow IT, spreadmarts, and spreadsheet hell are used. The problem is that spreadsheets are helpful tools for composing a piece of analysis, but as shared applications, they are a disaster. They lack version control, a repository, and collaboration features. They are consistently applied to problems for which they were never intended, which is their biggest weakness—in fact, the biggest weakness of almost any piece of technology.

## Business Rules

The use of business rules as a way to specify how an organization behaves began to gain ground in the mid-1990s and was popularized by Ron Ross[4] and Barbara von Halle,[5] among others. Many early adopters regarded business rules primarily as a tool for describing and understanding how an organization wants to act. In one sense, business rules were a way to design an organization. As technology support for this approach increased, business rules

---

[4] Ronald G. Ross. *Principles of the Business Rule Approach*. Addison-Wesley Professional, 2003.
[5] Barbara von Halle. *Business Rules Applied: Building Better Systems Using the Business Rules Approach.* Wiley, 2001.

began to separate into a business-design approach and a higher-level, more declarative way to develop code. Declarative approaches allow managing each piece of code or logic separately instead of in the procedural sequence typical of regular code.

Another major impetus for the business rules approach was to bring the idea of business rule management to problems that didn't involve extremely complex decisions (such as diagnosing cancer). Instead, this approach was used with everyday operational transactions that occur in high volume and involve decisions with low to medium complexity. Instead of using an expert system to handle very complex problems, organizations could use business rules to automate 80 percent of less complex cases and, therefore, improve throughput. Additionally, this approach enabled nontechnical businesspeople to state business rules rather than provide fuzzy requirements that IT translates into the system's real logic—sometimes without enough business input and often with a lot of confusion.

Despite the early and repeated proof of the effectiveness of business rules, their use has been somewhat limited. Most organizations using this approach at a strategic level do so only to describe and understand their business. Organizations using it to make specific systems smarter often do so only in a localized way. The rules are extracted from limited sources and largely ignore the insight that can be gained from an organization's data. Without an overall approach, few organizations have become proactive at finding decisions and automating them with business rules, although this approach is clearly possible. Business rules, as you'll see, are a critical component of a solution to the problem of making systems smart enough, but their potential has been untapped so far.

### Buying Solutions

In the past, IT departments had no alternative but to build their own software. As the industry matured, however, more packaged applications became available that offered quicker time to market and less need for specialist programmers. In theory, you could buy a package for inventory control, for example, and install it and be up and running quickly.

In fact, many packages were overly rigid, based on a single interpretation of how a certain business process might run. Configuring and installing these packages, especially as they grew into today's enterprise applications, were time consuming and costly. In addition, enterprise applications still assumed that people were the motivating force behind systems. They had a data model, captured data through various generations of user interface technology, and stored it in an operational database. They provided reporting or integrated with business intelligence/data warehouse products so that data could be transferred to an analytic environment and used to help people make decisions. Attempts to customize or extend these applications resulted in custom code with all the problems described previously. IT departments still spent a lot of money and time on maintenance, organizations still had backlogs, and systems still didn't do what businesses needed them to do .

### Processes and Services

At the end of the twentieth century, a new class of software became perceived as a way to solve many problems with IT: workflow or business process management (BPM) software. These products generated high initial ROI because they integrated many disparate systems, linked people in different departments into a coherent process, and made management and reporting of an overall business process possible, often for the first time.

BPM systems, however, still assumed that intelligence and decision making in processes come from people or are embedded in systems. The use of worklists, alerts, and the paraphernalia of integrating people into processes is widespread. Most BPM systems allow limited replacement of human decision making with automated decision making. Those that do tend to focus on routing and other kinds of simple decision making, not making decisions about operational transactions.

In parallel with the growth of business process management, service-oriented architecture (SOA) started making inroads in IT departments. SOA promised a new level of agility and flexibility and reduced maintenance backlogs. To some extent, it's delivering on these promises. However, an SOA approach doesn't change how business expertise is turned into computer code, nor does it address the issues in delivering analytic data discussed previously.

Although BPM systems and SOA don't offer a way to make systems (or even processes) smart enough for today's business environment, they do offer a framework for using the approaches and technologies discussed in this book. Integrating business rules engines and analytics with the process automation and orchestration capabilities they offer can make smart enough systems more possible.

One common factor in problems with different approaches to programs is people. Relying on people to make decisions has a consequence: You can move only at the speed of people.

## Moving at the Speed of People

The third major problem with the prevailing attitude toward information systems involves people. Because of the reliance on people to provide the "intelligence" in a system and the lag between data analysis and operational processes, new ideas move only at the speed of people. You can see this problem in the training and adoption lag, the use of policy manuals and intranets, and the prevailing focus of knowledge management on supporting people.

## The Training and Adoption Lag

When new approaches, techniques, and policies must influence people's behavior, typically there's a noticeable lag. Explaining to people how a new process should work takes time, and they must take time out from their jobs to attend training. These formal processes take time and can also create an adoption lag. Adopting a new policy is hard until everyone has been trained, for instance.

For example, suppose your company is concerned about customer retention, so you develop a new policy for making retention offers. You might put it in writing, e-mail it to all your customer service representatives (CSRs), and arrange for training sessions for them. If you have CSRs in a number of locations (to provide 24x7 coverage, for instance) or have outsourced them, training might require several separate training events. In addition, you might not want the new policy followed until everyone can follow it consistently. Eventually you have trained everyone, given notes on the new policy to everyone, updated the new CSR training, and can roll out the new policy. How long might this process take? Days or weeks—perhaps months.

## Procedure Manuals and Intranets

A consequence of using people to make decisions in information systems is the widespread use of procedure manuals, often made available on an intranet. Policies and procedures are in writing to ensure that a manual process is carried out in a consistent and compliant way. This information is widely distributed, often in electronic as well as written form. Incentives for using the policy or punishments for failing to might be developed to increase adoption.

In practice, however much those who understand the regulations try to write a manual explaining how to make a decision, adoption is limited by the extent to which experts can explain what must be done and by the typical problem that not everyone will follow the manuals every time or perhaps even read them. In addition, relying on auditing and random checks to enforce compliance is an expensive and inefficient way to ensure consistency of operation. Attempting to make sure a decision is made consistently and accurately by publishing a manual is an uphill struggle, no matter how good the distribution mechanism is.

### Knowledge Management

The final consideration for the challenges of moving at the speed of people is knowledge management. It's often proposed as a way to capture an organization's knowledge to make it accessible to others and increase the predictability and quality of decision making. The challenge with knowledge management is twofold. First, it still assumes a manual decision-making process, which might not be practical for many decisions in a fast-moving world. If you need to deliver a decision in seconds, no amount of knowledge management or training will help. You must automate the decision. Second, it focuses on managing documents electronically to automate and improve a process designed around paper. Like the obsession with using reports, managing knowledge as though it belongs in documents is limiting. Breaking down large blocks of knowledge into pieces is hard, so linking them to systems that need them, regulations that drive them, and circumstances that might affect them are also difficult.

Knowledge management is not useless in an enterprise decision management approach. Many knowledge management techniques can help capture the information you need to adopt enterprise decision management. The problem is focusing on capturing and managing knowledge, not on operationalizing knowledge in the information systems and processes that make your business function.

Unfortunately, an organization can invest heavily in IT and yet still find that it doesn't have systems smart enough to support it as it moves into the future. The lack of focus on decisions, especially operational decisions, and IT's focus on reporting for managers might be the primary culprits, but the characteristics of most application development have a role, too.

## SmartEnough's Experience

So far, you have learned about the general history of computing, but in this section, we consider a specific example. Instead of picking a familiar organization to illustrate the problems, the imaginary company SmartEnough Logistics is used again. Like most companies, SmartEnough Logistics bought into the major IT trends of the past couple of decades. Like most, it got some return from these investments but found that its systems infrastructure wasn't smart enough. In no particular order, then:

- **Enterprise applications**—SmartEnough bought both enterprise resource planning (ERP) and CRM software but found the systems had overly rigid processes when used as is. Any time SmartEnough wanted to add functionality, it had to write custom code, which turned out to be hard to maintain and update. Some modules were modified so much that they couldn't even be upgraded. When SmartEnough eventually gave up on modified code and replaced some modules with new versions (which was painful), it found that it no longer had any differentiation from other companies using the software. If only 5% of its business was unique,[6] clearly that 5% wouldn't come "off the shelf."

- **Business intelligence**—SmartEnough was an early adopter of data warehousing, reporting, OLAP, and indeed the whole business intelligence stack. Status meetings were enhanced with colorful, detailed reports. Executives got pretty dashboards. Management got a grip on what was actually happening. However, being better informed about where packages and shipments were didn't improve SmartEnough's on-time delivery much. Managers went from complaining about no data to complaining about too much data. Dashboards, it turned out, were requested and developed but often not used. All the reporting gave analytically minded people the power to manipulate and understand the data but offered little improvement in operations.

When "Operational BI" was tried, pushing reports and analytical tools down to front-line workers, SmartEnough found that perhaps only 20 percent of those workers could use the tools. Even the ones who could often didn't have time to review a report or graph before deciding how to treat a customer. Customers wanted answers, not just information, and even the best graphs couldn't be displayed well on drivers' handheld devices. Simply having more data didn't help.

- **Custom applications**—SmartEnough recognized early that IT and custom systems matched to its business could offer a competitive advantage. It focused on marketing systems (both direct and to distributors) and the pricing engine. SmartEnough discovered that each channel needed its own technology stack and built several engines: one for the call center, one to support the ERP system, and so on. This code was hard to update and suffered from rampant inconsistencies that upset customers when prices varied inexplicably. Ultimately, the maintenance difficulties caused delays in introducing new products and pricing policies and made it hard to offer custom services to more demanding customers.

When the Internet took off, SmartEnough added a Web site so that customers could track packages. Nevertheless, customers ended up calling constantly because they could track packages but do nothing to influence delivery. On top of that,

---

[6] Comment attributed to Shai Agassi, formerly head of the product and technology group and on the executive board of SAP AG.

alerting and tracking were fine for customers with a few packages but overwhelmed those with many (SmartEnough's best customers). In the end, multiple platforms and expensive maintenance used up so much of the IT budget that they prevented new development.

- **Customer experience**—At the time SmartEnough bought the CRM system, its focus was on using technology to improve the customer experience. Most of the technology had the opposite effect—acting as a barrier to good customer service. Customers hated the interactive voice response (IVR) system because it never remembered them and gave the same mindless options to everyone. Most customers learned how to jump past it and speak to an actual person. Wait times increased, and customer satisfaction fell. The Web site, kiosks, and call center software failed to make customers feel known or appreciated.

Deciding that the problem was a lack of best practices and high turnover in the call center, SmartEnough tried outsourcing some call center work, but it found the resulting lack of control over decision making unacceptable. Focusing back on its internal staff, SmartEnough initiated a major knowledge management exercise to capture policies, procedures, and best practices. Many documents were produced and stored; many were e-mailed to drivers and call center staff. Little changed, however; employees had too many e-mails to read and too little time to read them.

- **Automated package scanning**—Realizing that packages were at the heart of its business, SmartEnough has continually invested in package scanning and tracking technology. It has bought everything from handheld computers and barcode scanners to radio frequency identification (RFID) and global positioning system (GPS)-enabled trucks. Despite major improvements in visibility and tracking, SmartEnough still found that drivers couldn't act for their customers; they couldn't cross-sell or up-sell effectively by offering higher-value services when a customer wanted urgent delivery, for instance. The drivers didn't understand the trade-offs and were moving too fast to spend time reviewing detailed analysis graphics on their handheld devices.

Meanwhile, the managers tracking overall results appreciated the data they got but still found that everything hinged on people responding to the alerts and reports the system generated. As staff became inundated with reports and notifications, alert fatigue set in, and more alerts were ignored. Simple decisions were held up until someone in another time zone got to work, and the whole edifice relied on a few experts juggling data and analysis.

- **SOA, BPM, and BAM**—Most recently, SmartEnough has tried to upgrade its IT infrastructure to become more agile, which has helped. SOA has made composite applications easier to develop, but many services are still hard to change, and reuse of services has been slower than expected. SmartEnough worries that it has JABOWS (just a bunch of Web services), not a real architecture at all. Making legacy applications available as services seemed to help, but the same number of maintenance requests come in, and legacy systems are no easier to change than before.

  BPM has helped control and monitor some processes and given SmartEnough more flexibility in some dynamic processes. Problems have arisen, however, in processes customized for major customers. Managing all these different processes is complex, even though almost everything in a process is the same. SmartEnough also found that the benefits, which were published in a major IT magazine, wore off quickly after major inefficiencies were eliminated, because there were still too many manual referrals and too much waiting for decisions. Adopting BAM solved some of these problems, but too many people were still responding to too many alerts, and critical activities were often held up until the next morning.

Perhaps SmartEnough Logistics sounds like an artificial nightmare to you. Perhaps it sounds like your company. Probably your company falls somewhere in between—no one has tried everything and had it all go wrong, but most organizations have had at least some of these experiences. If, like SmartEnough Logistics, your systems aren't smart enough, you probably want to know how enterprise decision management will help and how you actually go about it. The next few chapters introduce the core concepts you need to understand, describe an easy path for adopting enterprise decision management, and show you how it might affect your IT environment. Read on.

# CHAPTER FOUR

# Core Concepts

**B**uilding smart enough systems using enterprise decision management requires understanding a number of core concepts about data, analytics, business rules, and adaptive control. This chapter gives you an overview of these concepts without attempting to get into details. Subsequent chapters provide more detail on data and analytics, business rules, and adaptive control, respectively.

## Introduction

Enterprise decision management involves a series of connected steps that include the following:

1. Identifying areas where enterprise decision management can be used effectively in your organization

2. Gathering and preparing the data needed

3. Defining analytics to understand the data and to form and test hypotheses

4. Building and continuously refining rules

5. Analyzing, optimizing, and adapting the way decisions are made

What makes the EDM approach effective is its focus on micro or operational decisions as a separate class of problem and the application of technology to automate and improve those decisions. To implement enterprise decision management effectively, you need to do the following:

- Understand and have access to the data or information that supports your business.

- Understand the ways in which new insights can be gained from looking at your data analytically.

- Have people with the most complete understanding of the business be responsible for the rules that drive and control the business.
- Build learning and improvement into your systems.
- Integrate the end result into existing applications and the application architecture.

Before starting, it's important to know what decisions you're going to tackle—where you're going to apply enterprise decision management.

## Finding the Right Decisions

As discussed in the section "Finding Hidden Decisions" in Chapter 2, "Enterprise Decision Management," not every decision is suitable for enterprise decision management. Before you apply the steps outlined in the rest of this chapter, you should spend some time reviewing the decisions that might repay an EDM investment.

Chapter 9, "Getting There from Here," explains a step-by-step approach to adopting enterprise decision management that focuses on showing a return on investment (ROI) at each phase. Without going into detail now, the basic steps are as follows:

- **Phase 1: Piecemeal approach**—This phase uses the elements of enterprise decision management separately for simplicity. Most organizations find that they pick an initial business rules project and then a first analytic project. In parallel, organizations need to build some critical foundations for future EDM projects.
- **Phase 2: Local decision management**—In phase 2, organizations begin integrating business rules and analytics and start developing the skills and technology they need for adaptive control of decisions.
- **Phase 3: Expansion**—This phase is about improving the foundations for enterprise decision management and using overlapping and adjacent problems to broaden the analytic base. Organizations also begin to develop responses to possible future scenarios to improve their responsiveness.
- **Steady state: Enterprise decision management for real**—In the final phase, all aspects of enterprise decision management are in use throughout your organization.

This chapter is an overview of critical EDM concepts rather than this adoption process. The first concept to understand is decision services, explained in the following section.

## Decision Services

The most effective way to apply enterprise decision management to operational decisions is to design what's called decision services—applications in your application portfolio or services in your service-oriented architecture (SOA) that automate and manage highly targeted decisions that are part of your organization's day-to-day operation.

A **decision service** can be defined as a self-contained, callable component with a view of all conditions and actions that need to be considered to make an operational business decision. More simply, it's a component or service that answers a business question for other services.

> **Note**   The term "decision service" is used throughout this book. This use doesn't imply that only an SOA works; it just keeps the terminology simple. Later chapters cover how decision services can be deployed in a variety of architectures.

Decision services use your data and the insight derived from it for automated decision making. They also isolate the logic behind your operational decisions, separating it from business processes and the mechanical operations of procedural application code. A decision service represents a single point of decision making throughout all your systems and processes, so it allows you to focus resources on improving and even optimizing that decision.

You can reuse decision services in multiple applications in many different operational environments. Decision services can also eliminate the time, cost, and technical risk of trying to reprogram many systems simultaneously to keep up with changing business requirements. For instance, the decision of whether to pay an insurance claim can be removed from the definition of the claims-processing business process. The legislative change cycle (that changes the decision) is different from the business cycle that drives process change, which allows these two update cycles to run separately. The business rules in this decision service could also be reused, such as for helping customers tell whether they have a valid claim before submitting it or for supporting third-party agents.

A decision service can be used to provide a "brain" for your composite applications. Composite applications are an effective way to assemble existing, working functionality to serve a new business purpose. You can put together purchased, built, or legacy components and create new applications more quickly. With decision services plugged into this approach, you can make these composite applications "smarter" and less reliant on people for decision making. Sometimes this approach makes it easier to connect existing services, and sometimes it lets you take more advantage of the services you have.

**Legacy Modernization**  *A focus on decisions lets you make advanced deci-sion making available as a service to legacy applications. For many legacy appli-cations, decision-making elements are responsible for almost all maintenance work. The basic system might not have changed in years, but regulations, poli-cies, and pricing models change all the time. Providing a decision service makes it possible to replace the one high-maintenance component of a legacy system. This legacy modernization approach can have a very high ROI.*

---

### Vehicle Registration Department in a Large U.S. State: Vehicle Fees

#### Old Way

With both a centralized batch computer system and online systems at each local office, the complex task of calculating registration fees for a huge population of cars, trucks, and other vehicles was a problem. The systems were 30 years old, hard to maintain, and often out of synchro-nization with each other. Changes and updates required two separate development efforts, which made coordinating changes and ensuring consistency between the two systems difficult. Because of the complexity of programs and duplication of effort, the vehicle registration department was challenged to meet legislatively mandated deadlines for fee changes. Any change to systems required a major IT project and ran the risk that the change would introduce unintended side effects. Risk was unaccept-able because the systems handled more than $4 billion in annual registra-tion fees, revenue the state needed. There were many rules for each kind of vehicle and regular legislative changes to those rules.

#### EDM Way

A decision service calculates vehicle fees for both systems, batch and online. The service uses more than 2,000 business rules to process sev-eral hundred thousand transactions per day. Nontechnical analysts who are responsible for overseeing legislative compliance can ensure correct implementation of policy rules throughout the systems without having to become programmers. These analysts develop and test problems with existing and newly mandated rules without involving IT, resulting in rapid turnaround and better accuracy in rule changes. The decision ser-vice complements existing systems, and by modernizing legacy systems, it reduces risk and expense.

**Benefits**

- Consistent rules could be made available rapidly to the new external-facing self-service Web site and telephone response systems.

- The decision service enhanced existing systems without requiring replacing or rewriting the majority of legacy applications and systems.

- In the first year alone, 13,000 hours of IT work was saved.

- The time to make a change in response to a transaction error was reduced 97 percent—from 8 hours to 15 minutes.

Building decision services involves data, analytics, business rules, and adaptive control. First, data and analytics.

## Data and Analytics

Preparing data for use in enterprise decision management can require a substantial effort, even if your organization has a data warehouse. Because enterprise decision management is most effective at the operational level, having access to the raw operational data is necessary for building and testing analytical models. "Operational business intelligence," an emerging trend in data warehousing, is applying business intelligence (BI) technology to operational systems and processes instead of using aggregate analysis. Even though the term is generally used for applying existing BI techniques to more timely, detailed data culled from source systems, it's still subject to the single-model, integrated data warehouse view. In other words, some or many original data attributes are lost in the process. In those cases, the data in data warehouses isn't adequate to mine for analysis or to train and simulate models.

Data can be roughly categorized into these groups:

- Structured relational data (stored in typical relational databases)
- Structured nonrelational data, such as XML documents (text files with a strong structure controlling their content)
- Unstructured data, such as documents, graphics, and video

In addition, data might be controlled by your organization (internal data, such as customer and order information) or available from a third-party data provider (external data, such as demographics of a zip code or a credit score). Enterprise decision management uses this data in two ways: to make decisions and to develop analytic insight.

---

### Data Quality and Integration

The EDM approach takes full advantage of the data you have. Data in most organizations suffers from two main problems: The data is poorly integrated (data from different systems doesn't match up well), and the data quality is poor.

Integrating data, such as linking all customer accounts to a master customer record (sometimes called customer data integration, or CDI), improves the quality of decision making in enterprise decision management. It results in more robust decisions and more sophisticated models. Data integration isn't essential, however; you can automate decisions at a more granular level if you can't integrate your data or haven't yet done so.

Improving data quality helps improve the quality of analytic models developed in enterprise decision management and makes it easier to generate reliable answers from decision services. Many analytic techniques, however, do compensate for poor data quality. You can generally produce a good-quality model despite missing, incorrect, or invalid data. Understanding this distinction can save you a lot of time. Precision is needed for audit, compliance, and reporting purposes, but for finding cause-and-effect relationships, complementarity, dependencies, and predictors, absolute precision isn't necessary. The more you know about your data's quality problems, the easier it is to produce good models. However, the point of an analytical model is to understand the relationships of underlying phenomena the data represents, not to assemble a perfect rendering for reporting, which requires much higher data precision.

If your data has quality issues or isn't integrated, and you're adopting an EDM approach, you should certainly invest resources in fixes for these problems. That said, you don't need to put enterprise decision management on hold while you correct these problems. You can use EDM projects to decide which data integration or quality projects to prioritize.

---

### Data Requirements for Decision Making

The requirements for data and data sources in decision making as opposed to analytic insight are quite different. When making a decision, you need rapid access to the right information, which is typically structured data. Response times are critical, especially in real-time decision making. If external data is used, the data provider must guarantee the

> ### Credit Card Issuer: Customer Management
>
> #### Old Way
>
> With more than 50 million customers and 100 million accounts, keeping track of customers and developing customer management approaches was almost impossible. In particular, when customers called to ask about a specific account, customer service representatives (CSRs) had trouble responding to them based on their overall customer profiles. Generally good customers might be treated like defaulters because they were calling about the one account they had forgotten to pay, for instance.
>
> #### EDM Way
>
> Instead of trying to integrate all the data, a decision service uses business rules to perform calculations and assessments on each account. These rules generate a full picture of each account in terms of how often the customer is late, the largest unpaid balance in any month, and more. The service uses additional rules to collate summaries of accounts to create an overall profile of customers. For instance, what's the latest a customer has ever been on any account? The final set of rules determines the most profitable approach to dealing with customers and records this information in the customer record attached to each account. When CSRs pull up account records, they don't just see more data; they see a set of specific decisions about how to treat account holders most profitably.
>
> #### Benefits
>
> - Implications of complete account history are accessible to all CSRs.
> - CSRs treat customers better.

service levels and interfaces you need. The decision also needs to be structured to cope with failures in any data service. Unstructured data usually provides merely context for a decision; you might retrieve a document in support of a decision, for instance. Technologies that make it practical to use unstructured data in decision making, such as text analytics or text-mining tools, are constantly improving, so unstructured text data is likely to become more integrated into operational decisions.

## Data Requirements for Analytic Insight

The requirements for data used to derive analytic insight are different. What matters is access to information for a statistically significant group of customers, products, or suppliers and reliable access to potentially large volumes of data. Most analytic models don't change in real time, so response time is less of an issue. The accuracy and reliability of data are important to understand, as they influence the model's quality. Most analytic modeling tools and analytic modelers don't get their data directly from operational systems; instead, they need to work with an IT department to extract the data they need in a format that lets them work on it. This process, too, must be established and performed reliably.

Analytic approaches in enterprise decision management fall into two broad categories: descriptive analytics and predictive analytics. **Descriptive analytics** use various techniques to improve understanding of the data, such as clustering, grouping, or segmenting information into useful categories. This can be used to segment (or microsegment) customers to treat each segment differently, to group products or suppliers based on reliability, or to identify products that are crossover purchases between categories, for example. The most common way to "operationalize" these models is to turn them into a set of business rules and then manage and implement them as described later in this chapter. In many cases, this method is sufficient for enterprise decision management.

The clustering shown in Figure 4.1 uses age, education, and income to group a set of customers into meaningful clusters. The customers can then be treated distinctly, according to the cluster in which they fall. This clustering could be operationalized by being turned into business rules, such as "If customer's income is low and his age is middle-aged and his education is moderate, then…."

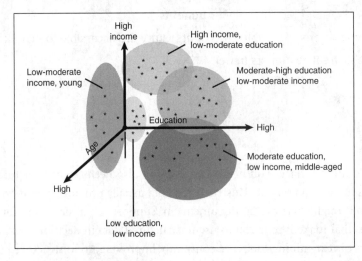

**Figure 4.1    Descriptive analytics group like items** *©Fair Isaac Corporation, reproduced with permission*

> **Note**   *"Operationalize" is a somewhat awkward shorthand term for "embed in an operational system so that it can be used in high-volume, real-time or near-real-time decisions."*

**Predictive analytic models,** on the other hand, are designed to make predictions about a specific customer, product, or transaction, such as the likelihood of a transaction being fraudulent, a customer accepting an offer, or a delivery being late. Represented as mathematical models or equations, they are combined with business rules to make a decision.

For instance, if certain types of transactions are predicted to have a high likelihood of fraud, what's needed in an EDM approach are models that calculate the likelihood of fraud combined with rules about how to interact with customers, such as the risk of annoying a good customer or the risk of overlooking a fraudulent transaction. Figure 4.2, for example, shows the ratio of good customers to bad ones for a range of scores a model produces. Rank-ordering customers to group them by likelihood of a specific behavior is a typical use for a predictive model.

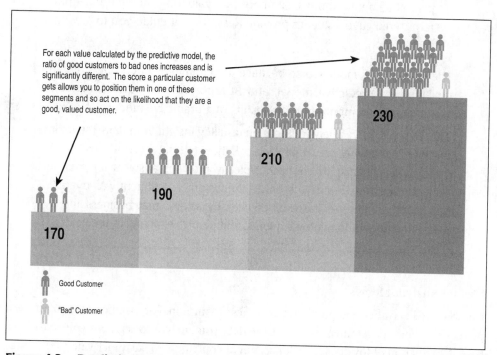

**Figure 4.2    Predictive analytics rank-order customers, products, and transactions**
*©Fair Isaac Corporation, reproduced with permission*

## Business Intelligence, Data Mining, and Predictive Analytics

These three terms are often used and abused in combination. All three use the same data, more or less, and seemingly similar techniques. However, they are different:

- Traditional BI tools extract, aggregate, and summarize data and present it in formats such as dashboards and reports. BI tools are exploratory and informational rather than action-oriented. Business intelligence helps you understand past performance and trends—in other words, what happened.

- Data mining uses sophisticated mathematics to solve business problems. Data-mining tools typically search for useful patterns in large data sets. They help you search for clues in your data and understand it better.

- Predictive analytics use data patterns to make predictions or complex statements about customers by evaluating multiple data patterns. Predictive analytics provide answers that guide you to a "what next" action.

The confusion is made worse because data mining is often one stage in developing a predictive model, and BI reporting and dashboard tools are invaluable in monitoring the results of a predictive model.

Although predictive analytics focus on distilling insight from data, the main purpose is to advise individual decisions (how to treat a certain customer). Business intelligence, in contrast, typically provides answers for a large body of data (how effective a particular customer treatment was overall). You might summarize these differences by saying that business intelligence analyzes, data mining explores, and predictive analytics predict.

### Uses for Analytic Models

Combining descriptive and predictive analytics is common. For instance, you might use a prediction about a customer as part of the data you analyze to segment your customer base. A prediction of loyalty, for instance, might contribute to customer value segmentation. You can also build different predictive models for each segment to describe your segments better. For instance, you might predict the likelihood of failure differently for various product segments.

Predictive models are most useful when you have a sizable population to analyze. For example, predicting which mortgages are most likely to default in a portfolio of 100,000 loans requires a model, unless you have the luxury of thousands of analysts to keep an eye on them. This prediction is especially crucial when the residential housing market is in a slump, and many homeowners find themselves owing more than the home's value yet facing major increases in monthly payments as adjustable rates increase. Some lenders use predictive models to pinpoint homeowners most likely to default.

This example brings up another important point: There's no point in making predictions unless actions can be taken. For example, mortgage lenders have little interest in becoming property managers of foreclosed properties in a weak market, so they might contact borrowers with adjustable-rate mortgages by phone and mail months before the rate on their loan resets. The goal is to make borrowers aware of upcoming payment increases and apprise them of their options in an effort to prevent loan defaults. Lenders might offer a number of solutions, including forgiving a monthly payment or rolling it into the principal, delaying interest rate adjustments for a few more months, or selling borrowers' homes at a loss and then forgiving the debt (a strategy called a "short sale").

The point is that predictive modeling by itself is insufficient for achieving business value. It must be followed by actions that take advantage of the knowledge and insight gained. Because predictive models are most useful with a large population, which implies that the volume of decisions is also large, closing the loop with enterprise decision management in an integrated environment is both logical and efficient.

Both descriptive and predictive analytics can be built automatically with software, manually by an analytic modeler, or with some combination of automation and expertise. Automated analytics can be built more quickly and updated more often but typically are less powerful than those incorporating a specialist's business *and* analytic expertise. The technical term is **lift**—how much lift a model gives over the random approach is a measure of its power and usefulness. Manually constructed analytics have lots of expertise embedded but can be time-consuming to develop and update when things change. A combined approach often works well—automating most of the repetitive work followed by injecting expertise and judgment manually to finalize the model.

Chapter 5, "Data and Analytics," goes into more detail on the concepts, technologies, and steps in assembling data and developing analytic models. The next stage is to turn your business policies and know-how into business rules.

## Business Rules

Conceptually, business rules are the rules by which you do business. More practically, **business rules** can be considered statements of the actions you should take when certain business conditions are true. For example, a business rule might be "If a customer is high risk and has good profit potential, make a retention offer" or "If the applicant's age is lower than 25 and the application doesn't have a guarantor, schedule an interview."

Today's organizations have a lot of business rules—regulations to conform to, policies in policy manuals, rules of thumb from experts, code in legacy systems. The trouble is that these rules aren't always accessible, can't be managed and checked easily, and are hard to enforce consistently and effectively in information systems.

---

### Rules and Models

A potentially confusing aspect of rules and models is that many models can be represented as a set of rules. For instance, a predictive scorecard might be designed and built as a model and then implemented as a set of business rules—or at least carried out as a set of rules. A decision tree can also be represented as a set of business rules, with each branch representing one.

For the purposes of this book, a distinction has been made between analytically derived models and explicitly written rules. This distinction doesn't mean implementing some models with business rules is bad; it just blurs a necessary distinction. If a model has been built analytically, it should be maintained and modified analytically. Transforming it into rules increases the risk of having it be maintained subjectively, and typically, that's a mistake.

---

The business rules that need to be used in your information systems, especially when automating decisions, are the key point on which business and IT professionals must agree. IT is responsible for systems and their behavior, upkeep, and performance. However, only the business staff knows what the rules should be. They understand the regulations, they wrote the policies, and they have the expertise. Managing these business rules collaboratively and deploying them into operational systems effectively are crucial to enterprise decision management.

> ### Government Department: Work Permits
>
> #### Old Way
>
> This government department was responsible for work permits for foreign nationals. Government employees had to check each request manually to qualify the applicant, causing delays and increased expenses. When applications were numerous, employees were unable to focus on other tasks.
>
> #### EDM Way
>
> A decision service supports an online form. As applicants enter data into the form, the rules for eligibility run automatically and, in most cases, an answer is given immediately. When an answer can't be given or an appeal is made, the decision service includes information on why the application was referred and/or denied to help with the manual review.
>
> #### Benefits
>
> * Quick turnaround for work permit approval and disapproval
> * Employees' ability to focus on other tasks increased
> * Decreased employee head count and expenses

To manage and deploy business rules in an EDM approach, you need to adopt technologies that support the approach and new procedures. For business rules to be manageable

- You need to be able to state them in a declarative way so that each rule is independent of the others and distinct so that it can be managed.

- You must be able to manage potentially very large numbers of rules. Managing large numbers means being able to version them, control access to them, and track changes so that you know how you got the rules you have.

- They must be represented so that both business and technical users can interact with the representation. Both groups must be able to read, edit, create, and delete rules so that business and IT can collaborate on rule management effectively.

Figure 4.3 shows some representations of business rules suitable for both business and technical users: straightforward rules written in a formal syntax, a decision tree, a template-based editor, and a decision table. These representations are easier for business-people to use than traditional code, and the graphical representations are particularly accessible.

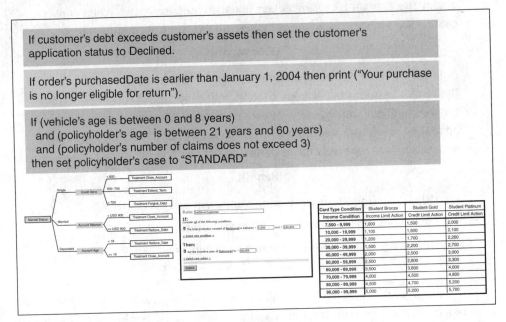

**Figure 4.3**    **Representations of business rules**

To deploy business rules, your IT department needs technology to turn these rules into executable code that runs in your application architecture. They also need support for testing, release management, data integration, and the rest of their standard application development process. The most effective approach is adopting what's commonly called a **business rules management system (BRMS)**. This has a repository to store and manage business rules, rule-editing tools designed for business and technical users, a rule engine to execute rules in a system context. It also has pieces of technology to handle integration with data, deployment into different systems, and other essential functions.

## High-Technology Manufacturer: Ensuring Product Quality

### Old Way

Global production was increasing in several facilities, and product design was constantly improving. Ensuring product quality at every location was difficult, given the high rate of product change. Each location handled quality assurance and failure analysis independently, which meant local employees were often following written rules developed by experts in another country (and another time zone). These rules had to change constantly to reflect new products as well as new information about what should be tested. As production volume increased, the volume of needed diagnostics rose. Ensuring that testing was done and done correctly became more difficult.

### EDM Way

A decision service automates monitoring and testing products. The business rules in the decision service come from technical experts at the R&D facility, who capture rules for each new product quickly and accurately without IT involvement. Local instances of the decision service support each location, and new rules can be transmitted around the world rapidly to update the diagnostic process at every location. Each location is therefore using the same expert-driven set of rules to test products, thus ensuring consistency and quality.

### Benefits

- Experts in one location drive quality checks worldwide.
- Tests are done accurately and rapidly in every location.

Chapter 6, "Business Rules," goes into more detail on the concepts, technologies, and steps in developing and managing business rules. The final stage is to ensure that all rules and analytics can be modified, improved, and optimized over time.

---

### Decisions Are Different

An important difference in automating decisions is that, unlike other aspects of information systems, decisions change continually. Most IT departments consider code that must be constantly revisited to be suspect or "broken" in some way. Decisions, however, aren't static. The best way to make a decision should be expected to change. Organizations learn, new data is collected, and regulations change, and all these events change how you should make a decision.

This change of mind-set is an important to adopting enterprise decision management. IT departments and their business customers must plan for decisions to change and evolve over time. Subsequent chapters go into the technology and approaches that support this mindset.

---

## Adaptive Control

Regardless of the combination of rules and analytics you need for a specific decision, you also need a way to learn about that decision in terms of what works, what does not, and how you can improve it over time. To learn about a decision, you must create an environment where you can track the results of decisions to see which ones were effective and which ones were not. Sometimes the result can be seen immediately (Did the customer accept a cross-sell offer?), but sometimes there's a major lag. A model that predicts how likely a product is to fail during its usual lifetime, for instance, might require a wait of many months. Regardless, to improve decisions over time, you must capture this information and be able to show how close your models were to reality and how effective your rules were. This process is called **adaptive control.**

Improvements in decisions, like building models, can be manual or automated. Automated learning has the advantage of being responsive and adapting rapidly. When a decision is regulated, however, or has many facets that contribute to its being a good decision or a bad one, reviewing results and updating the decision manually might be more effective. A manual method requires reporting and analysis tools, such as those common in business intelligence and performance management systems.

The most basic element of adaptive control is the **champion/challenger approach,** which involves developing a "challenger" approach to a decision that's different from the current or "champion" approach. The system implementing the decision runs a small percentage of transactions through one or more challenger approaches instead of through

**National Bank: Credit Processing**

**Old Way**

After a merger, credit processing was inefficient, with 22 percent of transactions needing to be rekeyed. Six distinct origination systems were being used, with no coherent customer view. All changes to these systems were IT projects that took time and cost money. In addition, the multiple platforms were inconsistent. Any change had to be phased to show benefit at each stage and keep systems up and running.

**EDM Way**

A decision service processes existing customers regularly to identify good credit risks. Existing customers looking for more credit (extensions or new unsecured loans) are now fast-tracked safely, resulting in 60 percent more credit granted. Fast-tracking uses preapproval decisions stored in the customer management system and updated regularly by a batch process using predictive analytics and business rules. An adaptive control infrastructure constantly refines approaches for issuing credit, resulting in a 30 percent increase in approval rates.

**Benefits**

- Increased straight-through processing rate
- Consistent lending decisions
- Better provision for credit loss

the champion approach. The approach that was used is recorded for comparison purposes, the consequences of the decision play out, and the data is captured.

If a challenger approach shows better results (in whatever timeframe is appropriate for the decision), you can promote it to be the new champion. You can then design new challengers and test them ad infinitum. This process allows constant improvement in decisions with minimal risk. Some mechanism for constantly monitoring and improving the way a decision is made is critical because decisions are unlike other parts of an operational process.

Designing good challenger approaches is important in adaptive control, and various techniques for good experimental design can be applied. These techniques help ensure that challengers cover a wide range of scenarios so that an organization can learn about the decisions it's making as rapidly as possible.

Additionally, offline modeling and analysis are possible to see how other decisions might improve or degrade performance. You can build models to see what might have worked better in the past and to estimate what might work in the future. With decisions that have a direct impact, you can often model responses to different approaches with reasonable accuracy. This method is obviously preferable to running trials, when possible, as it doesn't actually affect your associates. This kind of optimization and simulation uses what are sometimes known as decision models or influence diagrams and involve managing and optimizing trade-offs.

Decision models also help handle complexity. As you get more sophisticated in analytic modeling, you often end up with several models for each transaction. For instance, if you're offering customers a new credit line, you might have models that do the following:

- Predict the likelihood of customers using the new credit line.
- Predict the likelihood that they will pay off the whole balance every month and therefore pay no fees.
- Predict the likelihood that they will fail to pay part of the balance and end up in collections.
- Predict the likelihood that the credit line will improve their loyalty (measured by their willingness to buy other, more profitable, products).

The trade-offs between these models to find, say, ideal targets for a marketing offer get complex quickly. A **decision model** is a mathematical model of these trade-offs that calculates the best outcome, given your business constraints. The result of these models is typically a set of rules that use predictive models to make an optimal decision, based on the current assumptions under which you're operating.

Figure 4.4 shows a decision model for pharmaceutical marketing. The inputs are data or the results of predictive models for a transaction. They drive actions, shown in the center box, and have an impact on reactions. These reactions are chained together before resulting in an impact on the objective—in this case, profit. Each relationship is described mathematically. Some relationships are simple, such as the total sample cost reducing profit dollar for dollar. Others are more complex, such as the impact of census data on prescription volume. This model can be used to simulate a decision, allowing you to try different approaches and select the best one.

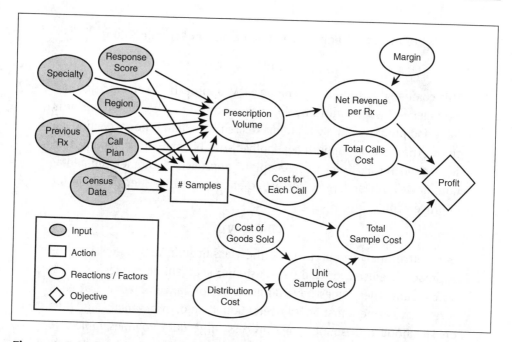

**Figure 4.4    Decision models optimize rules based on constraints** ©*Fair Isaac Corporation, reproduced with permission*

Chapter 7, "Adaptive Control," goes into more detail on the concepts, technologies, and steps in optimizing decisions and developing and using adaptive control.

## Deployment

After all the business rules, models, and learning infrastructure have been built, the result must be deployed. Unless the operational systems that run the business and interact with customers and support staff can access these decisions effectively, you won't gain any value. For the decision service to have any impact on your operations, you must deploy a decision service that can plug into your IT system. You must consider many issues and options for this process. Integrating decision services into the rest of the application portfolio is possible, although not always straightforward. The good news is that centrally managed decision services, taking advantage of emerging design patterns and standards, can be plugged into multiple systems so that constant improvement of decisions doesn't require large-scale IT projects.

Figure 4.5 shows how business rules and analytic models are brought together in decision services. These services handle requests for decisions from operational systems and return precise, consistent decisions. Decision analysis seeks to constantly check and improve a decision's performance over time, using data from operational systems as well

## European Credit Card Issuer: Customer Segmentation

### Old Way

This company was already using an EDM approach. Credit card account management was handled by a decision service that combined business rules and predictive analytics to make credit line and other account decisions. The service supported adaptive control, and the company had seen good results from its "champion" approach. Customer segmentation, however, was largely subjective and seemed to offer potential for improvement.

### EDM Way

Descriptive analytics, particularly the classification and regression tree approach, are used to build new customer segmentation rules from historical data. These trees have different performance objectives at each level; they segment first on, say, retention, then on profitability, and then on likelihood to respond. They process large data volumes rapidly to develop new models on a regular basis. They develop and profile new trees, compare differences offline, and ultimately transfer new rules (in the form of a decision tree) to production by using the adaptive control infrastructure.

### Benefits

- The whole project took just three months from start to finish, thanks to the existing adaptive control infrastructure.
- More specific segmentation where it adds the most value
- Segmentation that's closer to optimal for the company's goals
- Growth in revenue of 8 percent per account in six months

as new decision designs. Deployed decision services are dynamic and require continuous monitoring to ensure they remain effective tools for the success of your business. This closed-loop process of devising, deploying, and measuring is crucial.

Chapter 10, "EDM and the IT Department," goes into more detail on the concepts, technologies, and steps in deploying decision services and the impact on an IT department.

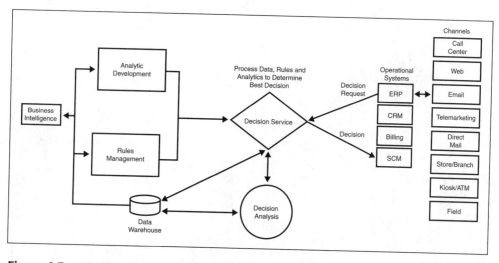

**Figure 4.5** **All the pieces come together in deployed decision services that support operational systems** ©*Fair Isaac Corporation, reproduced with permission*

## More Information

You have seen an overview of everything that goes into an EDM approach to building smart enough systems. Some technical and implementation details have been glossed over, but they are covered in subsequent chapters. If you only need an overview of the technology, you might want to skip to Chapter 8, "Readiness Assessment," which explains how you can tell whether you're ready to adopt enterprise decision management. If you'll be involved in implementing smart enough systems, the following chapters explore the concepts introduced in this chapter in more detail. Although these chapters don't include code samples or installation instructions, they do assume you have basic knowledge of IT terminology.

If you're already familiar with one or more of the core concepts, you might be tempted to skip over the corresponding chapter. However, these chapters offer EDM-specific notes and comments that are useful if you'll be working on the details of EDM systems in any capacity. Similarly, you shouldn't expect these chapters to teach you everything you need to know about these concepts. Data mining, analytic techniques, business rules, and optimization are well-established fields with much to learn and many sources of education and advice. Exploring these topics in depth is beyond the scope of this book, so the chapters focus on applying these technologies and approaches to enterprise decision management.

# CHAPTER FIVE

# Data and Analytics

**W**hen developing smart enough systems by using enterprise decision management, the use and management of data and the production of analytic models are essential to creating usable insight. This chapter covers the concepts, technology, and process for managing data and producing analytic models. The concepts and technology are presented first and the process second. If you prefer to get a sense of the steps first, however, you can skip ahead to that part and refer back to concepts and technology as necessary.

## Architectural Overview of Data and Analytics

Figure 5.1 shows how data and analytic modeling relate to other EDM elements. The diagram is not formal—it mixes architectural concepts with process flow—but it does show how the elements come together:

- Decision services are identified and designed.
- Data is used to build analytic models and determine outcomes in decision services.
- The modeling process can result in rules or models for deployment into decision services.
- Rules are developed, mined from data, built to use other models, and maintained by business users.
- Optimization and simulation maximize the value of rules and models by building optimal decision logic.
- The infrastructure for adaptive control links these design environments to the deployment environment for the decision service and manages the feedback loop.
- The decision service is the point of contact with the rest of the ecosystem.

This diagram is repeated at the start of subsequent chapters to establish a context for the discussion. This chapter focuses on the data and analytic modeling aspects of the architecture, shown with the oval in Figure 5.1. Most organizations have made substantial investments in data management tools and skills for initiatives such as enterprise resource planning, enterprise application integration, data warehousing, and customer/master data integration. Much of this effort can be reused when implementing EDM, but some data requirements for EDM are unique. This chapter focuses on those unique requirements and ways to use data effectively.

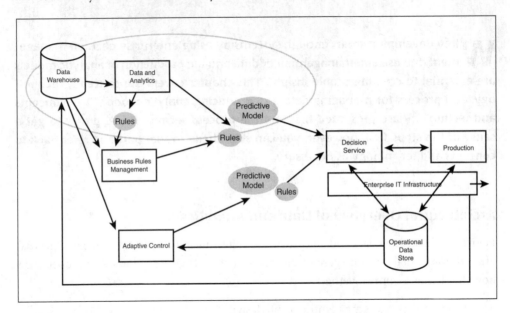

**Figure 5.1    An EDM architecture**

Applying an analytic model to an operational decision requires modeling something that's known (or at least presumed to be known). A simple rule such as "If there is no PO number on the invoice, notify the vendor" is based on policy or procedure. Policy isn't always so clear-cut, but in general, it's something the business decides and agrees on. Policy can be and often is ambiguous, but it isn't generally meant to be. Typically, it has just been described poorly. Policy is determined by design, negotiation, or just management prerogative. Ascertaining a policy doesn't require scanning a database to see how certain decisions were made in the past. You wouldn't ask a database to "Scan all invoices submitted in the past three years and give me the percentage returned to the vendor because there was no PO number," unless you were checking to see whether the policy was followed. Policy isn't usually discovered through data; it should be explicit externally.

In general, the need for analytics in enterprise decision management is derived from one of more of these conditions:

- There's uncertainty in the information available for making decisions. When not all the data available for a decision is exact and defined, or when something that might affect your decision isn't known when you need to make the decision, analytics can be used to estimate or predict the missing data.

- The outcome is poorly defined or unconstrained. When a variety of outcomes is possible, analytics can help you choose between them.

- The responses you can anticipate to your decision influence the decision itself. When and how the recipient responds, or is likely to respond, affects how you decide to act, analytics can help estimate that response and, therefore, improve the decision.

If these conditions apply and there's uncertainty, a need to model reactions, or a balancing of risk and reward, analytic models and techniques are often useful.

In analytics, data mining, also known as knowledge discovery in databases (KDD), is useful in building a rules model when there's no policy, there's uncertainty, or there are too many variables to discover cause-and-effect relationships manually. It's also a preliminary step in producing many kinds of predictive models. For example, suppose the simple decision to reject or pay an invoice depended on many other factors, such as the following:

- The trade-off between a discount not taken and rejecting the invoice
- Penalties for late payment
- The type of contract or invoice
- Whether previous invoices for this vendor had a purchase order
- The relationship with the vendor
- The likely result of not paying the invoice

In this example, using analytics to help estimate impact and resolve uncertainty might be critical to automating the decision.

In addition, the decision might not be dichotomous—to accept or reject—but might have values along a sliding scale. Perhaps there are many outcomes, and a decision is needed on which one to follow. Trade-off analysis is a good example of this situation: Produce more DVDs and sell them at a lower price, or limit production to maintain profit margin? Sell more airline seats to maximize revenue yield, at the risk of upsetting travelers? Target previously rejected customers to increase your portfolio, and risk more bad debts? You can imagine dozens of examples in your own business.

---

**Rules and Models**

One complicating factor is that many predictive models can be represented as a set of business rules for deployment. Continuing to think of this collection of business rules as a model is useful, however, because it should be edited, monitored, and managed as though it's a model.

---

One consideration, however, is that the shape of the curve of possible outcomes in trade-off analysis, even though each variable might be linear, is like the one in Figure 5.2. An undeniable point about curves is that when you're on the slippery side of the slope, your velocity *away* from the optimum point increases. In other words, it takes more effort to climb back up the curve than it does to slide farther. That's why it's imperative to have experts who can see through the possibilities and be ready to evaluate every decision—or good models to automate reasoning for you.

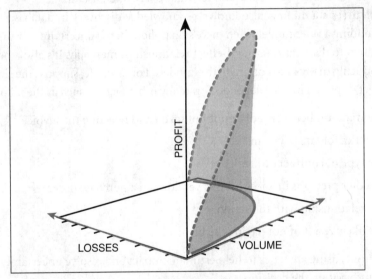

**Figure 5.2    Representing the cumulative outcome of many decisions as a curve with at least one maximum point of value**

To get the full value of your data in an EDM approach, you must be able to turn that data into analytic insight. Although a wide range of tools are available for this purpose, there's little consensus on what to call them. Some are called predictive analytic workbenches, data-mining tools, or statistics workbenches. These tools support techniques for gaining knowledge culled from statistics, artificial intelligence, operations research, and

---

**Mature Mall-Based Retailer: Attracting Customers Back to the Store**

### Old Way

This retailer, with more than 600 stores, had conditioned consumers to shop with discounts, especially for seasonal offers, and had no way to tell whether offer selection was optimal. It had limited customer understanding and many internal opinions (but no insight) about shopper frequency, lifetime value, and demographics. With the addition of Web and phone channels, it also suffered from poorly integrated data and channel-by-channel decisions.

### EDM Way

Transactional data is integrated with external demographic data to develop descriptive analytic models that match all customers with those covered in qualitative research projects. These models explain the demographics of different channels and product ranges. Trials of different offers support developing predictive analytic models for marketing response and future revenue. Trade-off analysis between these models affects offer rules. For instance, different offers are made to high responders who generate low revenue and low responders who generate high revenue. An adaptive control infrastructure supports decisions that are integrated across channels and use heavily segmented discount promotions.

### Benefits

- Store traffic increased 200 percent over the control group.
- Sales went up $3.4 million and increased profit net of offers.
- Understanding of customers increased, including how few multiple purchasers existed and how many visits per purchase were required.

---

other fields, such as neural networks, Bayesian networks, and graph theory. Some techniques are designed to discover "knowledge," others to prove or disprove hunches or hypotheses, and others to inform about possibly interesting phenomena through clustering, segmentation, classification, estimation, or prediction.

For example, you scan your cell phone bill and see lots of calls from 1 to 2 minutes, but a few stand out that are 20, 30, or even 45 minutes. You notice they're all to the same phone number, but different days or times of day. Your brain was data mining; it caught a pattern in the data. The fact that the pattern was interesting isn't data mining; that conclusion depends on your own knowledge and judgment. If you're specifically looking for longer calls, that's directed knowledge discovery. If you just scan the page without a particular variable in mind, that's undirected knowledge discovery. If you believe your minutes have been historically escalated by this one caller, you would retrieve bills for the past year and search them for records confirming or disproving this idea. This process is hypothesis testing.

### Different Approaches

*Knowledge discovery is a bottom-up process.*

*Directed knowledge discovery is trying to discover specific information about a target; undirected knowledge discovery is finding patterns or groupings.*

*Hypothesis testing is a top-down process.*

*Hypothesis testing is reviewing historical data to validate or refute a theory.*

You could take the results of this data mining and turn them into a set of rules that establish which kinds of calls are worth highlighting. These rules could then be automated. You could go further and develop predictive analytic models that assess the likelihood of going over your plan's limits, based on the patterns of calls seen early in the month. In EDM, simply knowing something is true isn't the focus; being able to do something in response to that knowledge is.

Data mining and predictive analytics have wide application in areas such as planning and asset evaluation, cash-flow analysis, contingent claim analysis, financial ratio calculations, trend analysis, resource planning, competitor and market direction monitoring, and pricing strategies in highly competitive markets, to name a few.

## Concepts in Applying Analytics

Before learning the process of applying analytics, you need to consider a number of concepts, explained in the following section, as a background for this process.

### Different Types of Data

Until recently, the term "data" referred to information stored in databases or other highly structured formats, created and maintained by computer programs. However, the definition of data has expanded to include unstructured data, as you learned in Chapter 4, "Core Concepts." In practice, the universe of data is divided between structured data and everything else. Including XML documents in most definitions of "unstructured" proves that the term is misleading, given how structured some XML documents are. Few documents are truly unstructured. Technologies such as text mining and text analytics are improving rapidly to render these unstructured data sources into information that can be used reliably in enterprise decision management.

A more useful distinction is between relational and nonrelational data. Relational data is stored in a relational database and can be accessed by using Structured Query Language (SQL) and standard database functions. Nonrelational data is stored in a content management or file management system and is usually harder to access from an operational perspective or in volume.

Structured information is generally the most useful in decision making because it's more amenable to analysis for building analytic models and easier to access as part of an operational system. IT departments have invested heavily in making sure structured data can be used in high-performance and real-time environments. Unstructured information, however, can be useful in deciding how to build analytic models and for decision making in less typical situations. Sometimes, it's simply a matter of pulling together unstructured data with structured data to pass on to someone when an exception is found. Sometimes you can analyze the content of unstructured data to help automate more complex decisions that couldn't be automated with only structured data. Increasingly, unstructured text is becoming an important aspect of data for decision making.

### Internal and External Data

As explained in Chapter 4, data might be internal or external. In general, privacy and use rules apply to both types, but they are different and are enforced by different regulatory bodies. Both kinds of data also have costs. Internal data has a cost in terms of hardware, software, and staff required to make it available to decision services. It also has a potential opportunity cost if the data must be made unavailable to other systems while a decision service is using it. External data has an actual business cost—you must pay for it. Important principles include using only the data you need and checking that additional data can repay its costs by improving decisions.

### Event-Based and Stored Data

In most organizations, available data is stored in a database or data warehouse. However, the messages associated with events flowing through message queues or an enterprise application integration bus, for example, can also be considered data because they often have encoded XML information. Engines that allow analyzing event-based data as it's received rather than after it's stored allow rapid updates of analytic models and decisions based on that data. They can often manage running totals and rolling averages and even rework information hierarchies. For some data sources, the volume might be so high that storing data isn't practical, so processing events as they arrive could be the only way to derive useful analytic insight.

Characteristics of Predictive Analytic Models

An analytic model in EDM has four main characteristics that differentiate between types of models, and you should be clear about the characteristics you want before you develop a model. The following list describes these characteristics:

- **Business purpose**—With any predictive model, you should establish its business purpose first—what you hope to predict and why. For example, you should know that one model is intended to predict the likelihood of customers canceling their subscriptions in the next 90 days, and another is designed to predict the best approach (of many) for dealing with an overdue tax bill. To do anything useful, you must understand the model's purpose. As noted previously, the purpose must enable you to achieve a business objective more effectively; otherwise, the model is merely interesting rather than useful.

- **Quantification of outcome**—After you have established how a model should be used to meet a business purpose, you must choose how to quantify the target outcome in the training data. The outcome might be binary (such as "claims that should be paid without review/claims requiring review"), multivalued discrete states (to which of these seven groups should a customer be assigned), or continuously varying (estimated profit from a customer in the next 12 months). Understanding the model's expected results helps clarify its purpose, defines how it can be used in decision services, and influences subsequent decisions about how to develop the model.

- **Mathematical representation**—Depending on the kind of outcome you want to predict, you must choose an appropriate model structure or formula. This choice establishes how the predicted result is actually calculated and frequently influences the method of solving for unknowns in that formula. You might use scorecards (see "Scorecards" later in this chapter), regression formulas, neural net formulas, or decision trees representing a set of rules (see Chapter 6, "Business Rules"). These representations have clear differences. Scorecards are easy to explain, for instance, but neural nets usually aren't. This characteristic is often defined with the next one—algorithms.

- **Algorithms for training the model**—The mathematical techniques used to build a model fall into various categories, as discussed in the next section, "Modeling Techniques." Some types of prediction imply certain techniques (continuously varying predictions require linear rather than logistic regression, for instance). Some types of representations also lend themselves to certain techniques; some are useful for deriving decision trees, for instance.

---

### Role: Analytic Modeler

Analytic modelers have a number of key skills:

- A statistical/mathematical background to understand and use data-mining and modeling techniques

- An understanding of business domains so that they can apply statistical techniques appropriately

- An ability to understand and interpret data

- Communication skills and an ability to work with both technical and less technical people

Analytic modelers can be hard to find and train because of the need to combine technical and mathematical skills with business know-how and communication ability.

---

This list of model characteristics isn't comprehensive, nor is the list of modeling techniques in the next section. Selecting and building models is a complex business and should be undertaken in that light.

### Modeling Techniques

Data mining and developing predictive analytic models are broad subjects. This discussion is meant to give you an overview but is by no means complete. Data mining and analytic modeling draw on the fields of mathematics, statistics, cognitive science, and artificial intelligence, and the conceptual foundations are beyond the scope of this book. As the field has matured, tools, techniques, and applications have become accessible to business. You shouldn't underestimate the value of analytic modelers' experience and skills in building and understanding models or the effort involved in this process. Just the process of provisioning data for analysis, building, training, and testing requires substantial work.

Data-mining techniques often overlap in function and output, but skilled analytic modelers know when to use several techniques to achieve the best result. Some common data-mining techniques are defined in the following list:

- **Regression**—Regression is a general term for a variety of statistical techniques that attempt to predict dependent values from independent values. The least squares method of linear best fit is a common regression technique. Linear regression is useful for estimating and predicting continuous numerical values. A variation, logistic regression, is used for predicting dichotomous variables (yes/no, for example).

---

### The Semantic Web

The emergence of the semantic Web is powering the use of link analysis. This is because ontology is also an application of graph theory, and technology providers are beginning to offer data management and storage tools more aligned to following a graph's links. Relational databases aren't optimized for this purpose.

---

- **Case-based reasoning (CBR)**—CBR techniques use existing data to "reason" about new cases. Mathematically, they apply distance and confidence functions to determine relevant cases. Training a CBR model requires experience and skill. CBR models are useful in predicting which new cases are likely to have desired (or undesired) outcomes.

- **Link analysis**—Link analysis uses the techniques of graph theory, a branch of mathematics that deals with relationships. Unlike hierarchical taxonomies, a node in a graph can be related to many other nodes in a variety of direct or indirect ways. In the Dewey Decimal System, for example, a book can be placed in one and only one slot on a shelf, even if its content is relevant to more than one topic. It can have multiple entries in a card file, such as for author and subject, but it can't be shelved in more than one place. In graph theory, several relationships can exist simultaneously and bidirectionally.

- **Neural and Kohonen networks**—Neural nets accept incoming data and create a general model of the patterns. Training a neural net involves working backward from a known outcome and having the neural net adjust "weights" to arrive at the right conclusion. Neural nets are weak at explaining the models they create, however. Kohonen nets, a form of self-organizing maps, are useful for finding unknown patterns in data, doing unsupervised learning, and clustering. Some people refer to Kohonen nets as "winner takes all" neural nets. Neural nets are often used for estimation and prediction or continuously variable outcomes.

- **Classification**—Classification techniques make use of collections of preexisting, well-defined classes or groupings. The techniques are designed to establish what variables and values of a new, unclassified datum can be used to assign it to an existing class. These techniques are considered directed or supervised (see the sidebar "Supervised Versus Unsupervised Techniques").

- **Clustering**—Clustering is another technique for grouping similar things. Unlike classification techniques, which examine attributes to determine where to place

---

**Supervised Versus Unsupervised Techniques**

Supervised or directed modeling techniques are often contrasted with unsupervised or undirected techniques. The terms might sound daunting, but the distinction is straightforward:

- In supervised techniques, a set of data exists that exemplifies the desired results. For instance, you might have a set of customers for whom you have behavior data and information about whether they renewed their contracts. A supervised technique uses this information to train a model so that new data can be processed correctly.

- In unsupervised techniques, you have no target. You're applying a technique in the hope and expectation that you find new and interesting characteristics of or relationships between your data.

Both techniques are useful.

---

things in predefined "buckets" or classes, clustering creates buckets dynamically. A common technique is the K-Means algorithm, which creates clusters by measuring the "distance" between things and the space between the boundaries of clusters and hierarchical clustering. Because most data isn't in spatial coordinates, analytic modelers have to convert attributes to numeric values, a particularly refined skill.

- **Affinity grouping or market-basket analysis**—An undirected form of data mining is affinity grouping. This technique is used to understand what things occur together, such as what events follow other events in time or what products are purchased together (market basket analysis) or in sequence (complementarity). Self-organizing maps (SOMs) and Kohonen nets are typically used for these models. One advantage of affinity grouping in enterprise decision management is that the output of these models can often be used directly to create rules.

- **Genetic algorithms**—Genetic algorithms mimic the idea of evolutionary adaptation, mostly for problems of optimization and prediction. They can be applied when a single best solution is desired (pricing, for example) or for finding a good solution in a large population of good solutions (network design).

Each technique has different strengths and weaknesses. Sometimes deciding which one should be applied is easy, but more often, you need to try several to see which one best meets your business objectives. Understanding this point is one of the most critical skills for an analytic modeler.

### Electronic Commerce Solutions Provider: Risk Management

#### Old Way

More than four million merchants process transactions with this company, and each one must be assessed for the risk of fraud. Disparate systems contain a wide range of both internal and external data on merchants, including transactions, demographics, payment information, and more. Implementing a new risk management approach in all these disparate systems was slow and expensive. Heavy IT involvement in updates increased costs and separated those who understood risk models from those who implemented them. The high-volume processing environment made it hard to replace these systems without a lot of risk.

#### EDM Way

A decision service combines predictive risk models and business rules to calculate the likelihood of fraud. This service uses information from multiple sources, supports regular updating of the service to reflect new rules and models, and provides consistent, up-to-date decisions across systems. Business users create and maintain the business rules and risk models that drive the decision by using graphical metaphors, such as decision trees, decision tables, and scorecards. The decision service generates a rich set of information about how decisions are made, allowing the current risk management approach to be monitored effectively.

#### Benefits

- Monitoring allows a closed feedback loop for improving risk decisions. By keeping a tight connection between the decision service and the effects of the actions taken, it is possible to refine the decision service through experience.

- Risk management approaches previously too complex to attempt are now routinely and rapidly implemented.

- Business users control decisions in a high-volume environment.

## Training Models

When discussing directed or supervised techniques, you often hear the phrase "training a model." It refers to the process of using existing historical data that includes the information you want to predict. This process of training a model involves taking historical data with known outcomes (such as which records turned out to be fraudulent) and analyzing data that will be known about new records to see which elements of the data, or combinations of elements, are good predictors of the outcome. You can then apply the model you devise to new records to create an approximation or a prediction of the outcome. The details of the process vary depending on the modeling technique.

### Large North American Card Issuer: Risk Model Deteriorating

#### Old Way

This credit card issuer had an expanding customer base and was using a single model for predicting risk for all customers. The risk model was showing signs of increased losses and incorrect actions for customers, although it was rank-ordering customers (by risk) accurately.

#### EDM Way

Descriptive analytics divide customers into multiple segments, each with a distinct risk model. These risk models are more specific because they handle only a subset of all customers.

#### Benefits

- Improved accuracy in risk modeling
- More than $1 million in loss savings

## Lift

As mentioned in Chapter 4, "Core Concepts," **lift** is a measure of how much better the results from using a model to predict an outcome are than by chance alone. For example, suppose 9.5 percent of the customers receiving a retention offer are actually retained by using a subjective approach. If introducing a model increases retention to 12.6 percent, the model's lift is 1.33—the ratio between 12.6 and 9.5.

Lift is often used to compare predictive analytic models. In Figure 5.3's lift graph, the straight line is the graph for random declines of applications. When 100 percent of applications are rejected, 100 percent of "bad" customers are also rejected, and the percentages match exactly along the graph. In contrast, when an analytic model (Model B) is used, far more of the "bad" customers are identified sooner. This graph enables an organization to decide what percentage of "bad" customers it wants to reject (shown by a "1" in the graphic). Model A, shown with the other curved line, has better lift, so it's separated from the first model line; the gap between the lines for both models widens as the difference in lift increases. With Model A, more bad customers can be rejected without increasing the rejection rate, or fewer applications can be rejected without increasing the number of bad customers accepted. Both options deliver better value to the organization. Because the extra value gained is often applied to many transactions, the gain from improved lift is often significant.

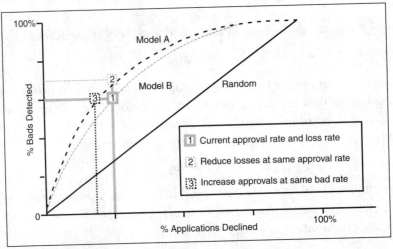

**Figure 5.3    A small increase in model performance yields high payback by allowing more effective decision making**

## Scorecards

One of the most effective ways to represent predictive models in EDM is the use of scorecards. The term "scorecard" in EDM is quite different from uses in business intelligence or performance management. In EDM, a **scorecard** is a way of creating a score that reflects a prediction about a customer, product, or supplier. As you can see in Figure 5.4, you arrive at the total score by summing the scores found by matching an object's attributes or calculated variables (see the next section, "Variables") to various ranges or "bins" the analytic technique has established as significant. Each attribute has a contribution to the total score that represents its relative predictive power for the model's purpose.

| YEARS AT EMPLOYMENT | |
|---|---|
| 0 | 30 |
| 1 | 40 |
| 2 or more | 50 |
| No information | 42 |
| NUMBER OF BOUNCED CHECKS | |
| None | 50 |
| 1 | 40 |
| 2 or more | 30 |
| No information | 39 |
| YEARS AT CURRENT ADDRESS | |
| 0-3 | 15 |
| 4-7 | 20 |
| 8-9 | 25 |
| 10 or more | 35 |
| No information | 26 |
| **Score** | **105** |

**Figure 5.4    A scorecard showing how different attributes contribute to a predictive score**

For instance, in Figure 5.4, the score might reflect risk of defaulting on a loan. The person being considered has two or more years at her current job, resulting in a partial score of 50, and two or more bounced checks, producing an additional 30 points. The nine years spent at her current address equates to another 25 points. These attribute scores add up to a total score of 105. In this case a higher score represents a higher risk of default. The ranges and contribution to the total score for each attribute or "bin" are derived analytically.

Scorecards are particularly effective for representing models in EDM for a number of reasons:

- They are easily represented by rules or a simple equation, so they can be implemented rapidly at runtime.

- They can return the most important reasons for a score, which helps explain it to those affected by the score. This feature is often critical when automating decisions because simply saying "the machine said so" isn't generally acceptable.

- They are simple to use and explain, if sometimes complex to build correctly.

- They can easily be made to conform to the many rules regulators often impose on using analytics in decision making, such as not using certain attributes (ethnicity, for instance) or not penalizing someone for age, for example.

## Variables

Most analytic models require you to develop additional **variables** (sometimes called characteristics or predictors). They might represent a summary of transaction data or the transformation of raw data to a more useful form for modeling and scoring. For instance, knowing the maximum late period or how often a customer was late with a payment might be more useful to a model than knowing dates of payments or their value. Much of the transactional data so important to developing good models is summarized into these kinds of variables. Establishing which summaries are most predictive and then specifying how the value is calculated are critical steps in developing a highly predictive model.

Although the development of variables is often considered part of developing a model, considering them separately can be useful. Some variables might be used in many models (because they are core to your business), and calculating them can be the hardest part of implementing a model.

## Standards

A number of formal standards are relevant to analytics in EDM. They help you use predictive models with different analytical modeling tools and provide a standard framework for analytic modelers. A widely used method, Cross-Industry Standard Process for Data Mining (CRISP-DM),[1] is available for managing data-mining and predictive analytic model development projects. Its steps cover business understanding, data understanding, data preparation, modeling, evaluation, and deployment. The process is defined as highly iterative—a necessity for analytic modeling, because having many steps can create circumstances that require returning to a previous step. A consortium of companies interested in data mining defined this process, which is under active revision, with a 2.0 version planned to focus more on scalability and ease of deployment.

In addition, you can use Predictive Modeling Markup Language (PMML) for models. PMML is an XML standard designed to describe data mining and predictive models and provide a vendor-independent definition of models so that they can be exchanged between applications. With PMML, you can develop models in one application and use another application to visualize, analyze, evaluate, or deploy them. PMML has limited support for the variables entered into models and none for reason codes (the justification a model gives for a calculated score) but helps enable model interchange between products.

There are also standards for calling analytic models and analytic model development algorithms, particularly in the Java world. JSR 73 is a pure Java application programming

---

[1] Links to find informatipon on CRISP-DM and the other standards listed can be found in the EDM wiki at www.smartenoughsystems.com.

interface (API) that supports building data-mining models, scoring data by using models, and managing data and metadata that support data-mining results. The impact of this standard in allowing vendors to use each others' algorithms in modeling or allowing applications to access models without having to know how they were created isn't clear yet.

**Note** *Like all JSRs, JSR 73 is managed through the Java Community Process. JSR 73 is currently being replaced by JSR 247, or JDM 2.0.*

More standards work is to be expected, and a gradual coalescing around core approaches is likely. Both PMML and CRISP-DM seem well positioned to be part of this solution, and organizations adopting EDM should consider both.

## Technology for Managing Data and Analytic Models

For most organizations, managing data and analytic models requires a mixture of existing and new technology. Figure 5.5 shows how the elements of these management technologies interact. Most analytic modeling software runs against data stored in a data warehouse or an analytic **data mart**—a subset of a data warehouse intended solely for developing analytics in a particular area of the business—although decision services run mostly against operational databases.

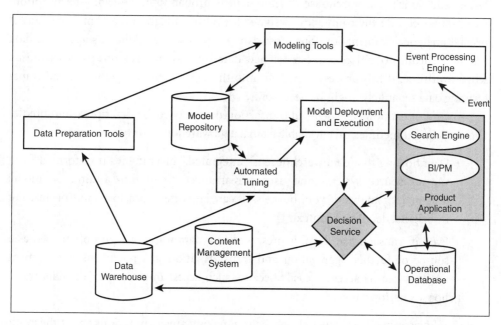

**Figure 5.5   Components of data and analytic model management technology**

## Operational Databases

The source for internal structured data is usually operational databases based on relational technology. In some cases, specialized databases, such as multidimensional databases, are the source for certain information. Quite a few nonrelational databases are still in production, particularly IBM's IMS, and they require special expertise to understand and navigate. SQL, however, is the universal data query language, and the preponderance of relational databases makes the physical and logical (but not semantic) effort of accessing data straightforward.

**Operational Data Stores** *An **operational data store (ODS)** is an integrated and detailed collection of data on a single subject designed to deliver up-to-date, operational information. This database integrates data from multiple sources and handles some data cleaning. It's designed to contain specific, detailed data, such as transactions, that can be used for analysis and reporting. Broad-based, aggregated data is stored in a data warehouse.*

## Data Warehouses

Data warehouses can be the source of the bulk of structured information used to develop analytic models. If some of the data needed for EDM hasn't been mapped to a data warehouse, additional data warehouse development is probably the best long-term option. The data warehouse environment is designed for robust integration and management of needed analytical information, but most data warehouses are built in stages. The data warehouse team prioritizes requests for new data sources and expands the warehouse's scope over time. If this process doesn't fit into the EDM schedule, gathering and transforming data separately might be necessary.

A word of caution: The detailed transaction data needed for descriptive and predictive modeling sometimes isn't available from a data warehouse for two reasons:

- Data flowing to a data warehouse is "integrated," meaning it's transformed from various source systems and usually rearranged to fit into a common model designed for analyzing your business. It can, and often does, lose some or much of its original detail and context.
- Even if transactional detail is preserved in a data warehouse, it's often used as a source of further aggregation and transformation. It's not in an environment where it can be accessed easily because such access might impair the data warehouse's performance.

You should examine these issues closely before making any assumptions about the availability of data for analytic model development.

## Content Management Systems

Most nonrelational data should be stored in some kind of content management system if you intend to use it in decision making. Both structured XML documents and unstructured documents can be stored. You might use both for model development, especially to understand the context or absence of historical information. Most likely, your only access to these documents at decision time is for retrieving supporting information, unless you use text analytic tools to mine the information first and render it in structured form.

Any unstructured information used in the decision is almost certain to have been passed in directly from the application that needs a decision. For instance, the content of a text field on a form an applicant uses to enter information for which no structured field exists could be passed to the application-processing system.

## Search Engines

Search engine technology is being used more to access structured and unstructured information. Because a search engine tends to return a variety of information in different formats and levels of detail, it's not that useful for making automated decisions. However, search technology can be effective in supporting decisions by delivering additional information, such as all information about a customer who falls into the exception category.

Search technology can also be useful in developing models as a way of exploring and understanding transactions. For instance, you could use it to help find records of customer complaints by searching through free-text fields. Additionally, mathematical results from searches can also be used in decision making and developing analytics; for example, you could search for the absence of reports of problems with a specific product model number.

## Business Intelligence and Performance Management

Although traditional business intelligence (BI) and performance management (PM) technology don't play a direct role in developing analytics, they do play a role in EDM. Most production applications are monitored through dashboards and reports or other BI/PM infrastructure. These technologies provide a way to get feedback on the behavior of production applications and, indeed, of the decision services supporting those applications. In addition, many of the query and visualization tools that are part of a typical BI/PM software solution are useful in understanding data before building analytic models.

For instance, a dashboard might be used to monitor key performance indicators for a loan origination process. One indicator might be the offer acceptance rate, which is a useful measure for considering how aggressive the loan decision is. A rising acceptance rate might imply that the rules have been loosened; if this trend wasn't the intent, some investigation would be called for. Similarly, throughput and acceptance rates over time could be used to track the effectiveness of decisions in the process.

### Stream-Processing Engines

Although most data used to develop models or carry out decisions is stored, a growing range of products are available for processing information attached to events without storing all the data first. Processing events and messages before storage allows generating data for analytic models that isn't yet stored (or is never stored) and making decisions for these events, much like analyzing transactions in real time. Data is analyzed continuously as a stream, typically by capturing events with XML structures attached. The analysis engine handles calculations, rules, aggregation in various time windows, and so on. This kind of analysis enhances EDM systems because real-time data can be processed without having to bring the data warehouse infrastructure up to real time.

For instance, data from RFID chips might be collected in such high volumes and at such high speeds that it makes no sense to store and then analyze the data. Real-time analysis of the data as it streams in—to predict out-of-stock situations, for instance—might be the only practical option.

### Repositories

Unlike the technology for business rules, analytic modeling technology has only recently begun to embrace using a **repository**—a controlled environment for storing and managing information—for models and modeling artifacts. Although most models in the past were developed using scripts and files, the trend is clearly toward a more managed environment. Collaboration as well as versioning and control are important for models. As models become more sophisticated, several analytic modelers often need to work together on the same model, so the value of a model repository increases. Similarly, as organizations model a wider range of problems and consider the trade-offs between them, being able to share parts of a model or the process for creating a model is more important.

Analytic teams also benefit from access to past models and models created by other teams, because they establish a baseline for new models and can help determine whether they're good enough to be put into production. More-established teams would have an increasing variety of historical models to review. A repository supports these activities in a way files do not. An analytic model repository must allow managing variable definitions as well as models. It should also provide reporting on which variables support which models and manage the data sets used to produce each model.

### Data Preparation Tools

Many data preparation tools are used in producing analytic models. They include data integration and extract-transform-load (ETL) tools, tools for bringing together data from different sources, and tools for managing metadata. Additional tools for data cleansing

---

**Data Sets in Analytic Modeling**

When developing analytic models, generally you need three sets of data:

- **Training data**—This data is used to train or estimate the model and create the initial model.

- **Validation data**—This data is independent of the training data and is used to fine-tune the results and make sure you aren't overfitting the model to the training data.

- **Test data**—This data confirms that your model is usefully predictive for data not used to train or validate the model. It's independent of the other data sets and is run through the model to see how well the model would have done in the past compared with actual results.

The details of these data sets depend on the model-building techniques, but you should be aware of the need to have multiple sets of data when building models.

---

and data enrichment are often used to improve the quality of data used in producing models, while master data management and customer data integration (CDI) technologies help ensure that all data about the same customer or topic can be integrated into a coherent whole.

These data preparation tools are used to prepare a set of training data for developing a model, a validation data set for tuning it, and a final test data set to make sure the model isn't "overfitted" to development or validation data. "Overfitting" means creating a model that works far better for your training and validation data than it does for other data. Your validation data gives you an estimate of how well the model *should* work, and the test data tells you how well it *really* works.

## Modeling Tools

Modeling tools range from exploratory analysis tools that help you understand your existing data to those that process data to produce a deployable model. Many commercial offerings combine these types of tools in a single workbench and/or scripting language to support all stages of model development. These tools include but aren't limited to the following:

- Variable creation and calculation of meaningful "bins" for values

- Data and probability analysis

- Correlation and visual analysis
- Variable selection
- Model development

Many data-mining tools offer a "point-and-click" approach to building models, but being successful at data mining requires the efforts of a skilled analytic modeler who can design models as well as understand the results in the context of your business. The mathematical algorithms of techniques such as logistic regression or classification and regression trees can churn through reams of data and produce great output, but data mining isn't a crystal ball or a substitute for real know-how.

Model validation tools, typically combined with model development tools, include the following:

- Performance analysis and charting
- Model explanation
- Model comparison and selection
- Calculation of lift and other statistical measures of effectiveness

Modeling tools include academic and open-source offerings and commercial products with support and training. Some are focused on a specific set of models, and others support many different kinds of models.

### Model Deployment

For EDM purposes, all models must be deployed. This procedure involves generating rules or code that implements the model and its variables or executing the model's definition and supporting variables in a model production environment. Deployment requires mapping the model's inputs to the data available at runtime, testing the deployed model for performance and stability, and other steps an IT department needs to perform to be comfortable with running the model in the production environment.

### Automated Tuning

After a model is deployed, it must be tuned periodically to reflect changes in data and requirements. Manual tuning uses the standard tools described previously, but automated tuning requires additional software with access to the model definition, the results of deploying the model, and new data fed to the model. Automated tuning software uses all these inputs to see how relevant the model's variables and design are at any moment and can change the deployed model to make it more relevant as circumstances change.

### When to Use Automated Tuning

Automated tuning is suitable for some models. It involves tailoring an existing model's weights on the fly to adjust for shifts in population over time. Some models respond well to automated tuning, and others don't. To respond well to automated tuning, the following must be true:

- The performance variable or result must be captured and immediately available for the feedback loop. If finding out whether a decision was a good one takes a long time, automated tuning doesn't work. For instance, seeing whether customers are retained after their initial 12-month subscription takes a long time; seeing whether they accept a Web-based cross-sell offer doesn't. The first variable isn't suitable for automated tuning, but the second one might be.

- The decision's potential upside or downside can't have a major impact. Most organizations are unwilling to allow a machine to change the way it decides something with a big impact without some kind of expert supervision. (Remember, EDM is about making use of experts, not eliminating them.) Similarly, a model with a smaller value might not be worth manual retuning, which takes time and money that might not be justified.

- The data used in the model must have some variability; otherwise, there's no reason to adapt the model. However, that variability shouldn't be controlled by the organization. For example, you probably don't want a response model to tune itself when you run a promotion during the Super Bowl. For this kind of variation, you should be conducting more formal "what-if" analysis and developing several models that can be put into production for a suitable period to cope with this kind of known and expected variation.

If automated tuning isn't suitable, you need to assess the model regularly to see how well it performs and set a threshold for manual updating.

---

**Expanding Asian Bank: Managing Credit Card Growth**

**Old Way**

The bank used a manual application process and assigned all customers the same initial credit limit. Subsequent manual decisions increased this credit limit in response to customer use and requests. The lack of consistency and control meant that estimating the potential impact of any change in credit policy or regulation was hard. In the face of growing competition, this manual approach was increasingly unacceptable.

**EDM Way**

Predictive analytics create application scores used to set initial credit lines. Account management uses business rules and additional predictive analytics to target specific customer types yet control acceptable loss levels and approval rates. The same approach is used to automate credit line increases and authorizations. Performance-based pricing generates attractive offers to customers. An adaptive control infrastructure gives the bank more control because it can experiment and assess what will and won't work.

**Benefits**

- Retention rates for good customers increased, and these customers have and use more credit.

- Balances have had a 15 percent growth, and the activation rate for new cards has increased.

---

## The Model Development Process

The model development process, shown in Figure 5.6, has eight steps (described in more detail in the following sections): Determine the desired outcome, determine data requirements, prepare the data, conduct data mining and analysis, develop the model, validate the model, deploy the model, and tune the model.

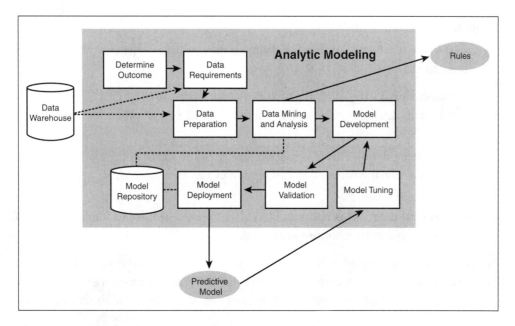

**Figure 5.6    Developing an analytic model in EDM**

## Determine the Desired Outcome

This step is the most important one in model development. Analytic models aren't crystal balls. Building them requires skilled analytic modelers who not only grasp modeling tools and concepts, but also understand the business issues involved. Without understanding why and how the model will be used, little or no useful work can be done. For example, if the number of click-throughs on a commerce Web site shows a gradual deterioration over time, knowing the time of day and the URL from which users are lost is useful but not prescriptive; this information doesn't provide advice on how to solve the problem. What's needed are more appealing offers to customers, which requires analyzing the data to form a hypothesis and a solution that can be deployed in a decision service. The modelers have to know what problem to solve, so the outcome must be defined and stated specifically.

> **Stating Outcomes**    *Wrong: We need to increase the click-through rate on our Web site.*
>
> *Right: We need a new model for creating dynamic offers that doesn't degrade through repeat use.*

### Determine Data Requirements

You must know what data you need to diagnose the problem. In general, three types of data are needed:

- **Transactional data**—Records of events at the lowest level of detail, such as ATM transactions, cash register tickets, inbound calls to a call center, or "clicks" on a Web site.
- **Supporting data**—This information describes and explains the markers for axes of transactional data, such as demographics tied to a zip code or account status tied to a caller.
- **Historical data**—This information adds a time perspective to transactional and supporting data to enable trend analysis.

Supporting data means your modeling tools can "mine" the transactional data. The more information you have about events, the more likely it is that patterns will emerge that are useful for understanding phenomena such as causation, association, and complementarity.

> **Sequence for Determining Necessary Data**   *Wrong: Catalog everything you have, and decide what data is important.*
>
> *Right: Work backward from the solution, define the problem explicitly, and map out the data needed to populate the investigation and models.*

### Prepare the Data

Preparing the data that's needed involves integrating data from a number of sources and then cleaning the integrated data to ensure consistent use of field codes, precision in numeric fields, and so on. A data warehouse and supporting processes might deliver data this way, but as noted previously and in Chapter 3, "Why Aren't My Systems Smart Enough Already?" the data might not be sufficient. In that case, you must build the integration/cleansing process independently of the data warehouse or add the process to the existing environment. Missing data—data that isn't known for every record—must be handled with dummy values or some other approach. The whole data set must then be flattened to make it usable for modeling and split into training, test, and validation data sets suitable for the modeling technique.

Although many organizations have substantial data warehouses and a wide range of data, these assets might not help with developing analytic models. The process of assembling the right data for developing analytic models requires a focus on getting historical data, both internal and external. Well-designed data warehouses can be useful in assembling this data in the correct time sequences. However, data often needs to be date/time normalized in relation to an event such as customer acquisition or product launch. Consider a statement such as "Show sales increases or decreases within the first 90 days of an in-store promotion, regardless of when the promotion occurred, in the past five years." The absolute date on which events happened might be less important than the number of days before or after an event. These kinds of time transformations aren't actually performed by data warehouses. Hand-coded SQL or BI or statistical tools are needed to query a data warehouse and reassemble the results as needed.

Figure 5.7 shows records of calls from customers, which are typically summarized by reporting and data warehouse processes. However, for retention prediction, the sequence of events and the time between events might be more significant. This information is impossible to calculate from the summary data typically kept (shown on the right in Figure 5.7). It must be derived directly from raw data.

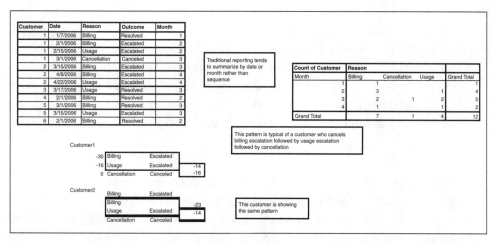

**Figure 5.7    Different time perspectives in building predictive models and reporting**

Finding the right data to develop models and accessing it in a way that supports the model development process are iterative steps and require understanding the analytic models. In general, starting with the desired model is best. Perhaps you want to segment delivery routes into different groups with increasing risk of delays, and then work backward to see what data you might need to develop this model. The data you need could be available internally in a form usable for model development, available internally but requiring a lot of manipulation, or available only from an external data provider.

## Conduct Data Mining and Analysis

Before building a model, you must understand and explore the data set, which involves using profiling and exploratory analytics and visualization tools. Analysts must understand the data set and its relationships, cardinalities, data quality, and possibilities for model development. You might also produce new rules and rule sets from the data based on this analysis and data mining. You can do this informally—by identifying significant thresholds, for instance—or more formally by creating a set of rules mathematically, as with the CART algorithm. These formal rule sets are often represented as decision trees (covered in more detail in Chapter 6, "Business Rules").

> **Note** *You can implement and execute these derived rule sets like any other business rules. However, they were derived analytically and reflect your data, not policy or expertise, so they should be managed differently.*

## Develop the Model

Techniques such as classification, regression analysis, neural nets, and genetic algorithms are used to develop a model. They require an analytic modeler with the experience and skill to understand the concepts and tools and interpret and communicate the findings. Building an effective model usually involves trying several different techniques to see which generates the best lift. Sometimes several techniques are used together to build the final model, and sometimes one technique works best for the model under development.

## Validate the Model

Model validation consists of using metrics such as **model correctness**—analogous to software quality assurance; **model evaluation**—statistical metrics and comparisons of abstract R-squared measures; and **model valuation**—what you expect the model will yield in terms of business results. Valuation metrics and best estimates of the model's incremental business value *must* be part of the validation. Statistically savvy analysts tend to become enamored with their models and the process to the exclusion of sound business judgment. This tendency should be resisted. Another consideration is your organization's ability to absorb and act on these findings. If there are structural, cultural, or other impediments to acting on the findings, pursuing a particular model might not be worthwhile.

## Deploy the Model

Model deployment involves turning the model and its calculated variables into something usable. This process might mean translating it into rules that can be deployed, deploying it to a model production environment, or generating code that carries out the equation at the heart of the model.

## Tune the Model

After they're deployed, models start to age, or become less predictive, immediately. Automatic and/or ongoing tuning of a model is critical to keeping it productive. Tuning might be automated and run continuously, done periodically by an analyst, or some combination of these two methods.

Having analyzed your data and derived the insight you can from it, whether as business rules, general insight into your business, or predictive models, you need to combine this insight with the policies and procedures that drive your organization. This step brings you to business rules, discussed in the next chapter.

---

**The EDM Wiki**

You can find more information on data and analytics technology and approaches in the EDM wiki at www.smartenoughsystems.com.

---

# CHAPTER SIX

# Business Rules

The next core concept is the definition, management, and execution of business rules. Business rules are the component of an enterprise decision management approach that ensures your policies, regulations, and business know-how power your systems. This chapter covers the concepts, technology, and process for managing business rules. The concepts and technology are presented first and the process second. If you prefer to get a sense of the steps first, however, you can skip ahead to that part of the chapter and refer back to concepts and technology as necessary.

## Architectural Overview

Figure 6.1 repeats the overview of how the core technologies fit together. This chapter focuses on business rules management. Automating operational decisions by using an EDM approach involves bringing a new measure of control to the business logic or business rules that make up those decisions. Although there are many ways to manage business logic, by far the most effective is a business rules management system (BRMS). A BRMS is a complete software platform for defining, managing, and executing business rules in an information systems environment. A number of advantages can be gained by expressing business logic in business rules and using the processing and management facilities in a BRMS, including the following:

- Separating decision logic from mechanical implementation gives you more flexibility to make changes. Business rules "describe" each unit of logic independently, making it easier to focus on the "correctness" of each atomic piece of logic and on changing it without unintended consequences.

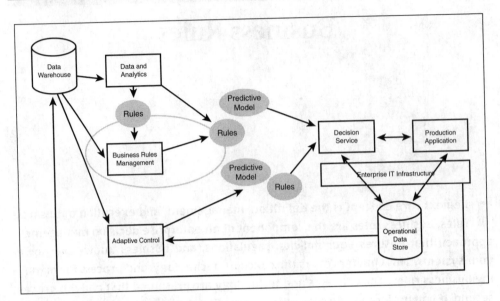

**Figure 6.1    An EDM architecture**

- Business rules are more understandable to business-level people, leading to better business-technical cooperation. Business rules syntax offers a lot of flexibility that you can't replicate in traditional programming languages. Rules use English-like phrases, such as "If customer's age exceeds 65, then set customer's discount to .05." This familiar structure helps business policymakers work side by side with the implementation team.

- A BRMS has many capabilities for managing and developing business rules. They enable you to retain control and management of business rules, which are essential for regulatory compliance and corporate oversight. You can develop and change them aggressively to meet business needs.

## Concepts in Business Rules

Business rules aren't a new concept; they are well established in certain areas such as loan origination and insurance underwriting. To use them effectively, you should understand a number of concepts first, but none of them are terribly complex.

## Truck Manufacturer: Truck Design

### Old Way

Every truck this company makes is custom-designed to meet unique customer requirements. The options customers request have to be matched against tens of thousands of parts and components to decide how to place equipment on the chassis. This company had developed a then-revolutionary software application capable of automatically determining chassis placement for 35 to 40 percent of components, based on the customer order. About 60 percent couldn't be placed automatically, which required costly manual intervention. The system also couldn't cross-check the design for incorrect or conflicting placements, so errors and omissions sometimes weren't spotted until post-assembly testing, which resulted in redesign and reassembly costs.

### EDM Way

A decision service determines which components from the original customer order are required and places them on the chassis according to each component's unique rules. The company's engineers have developed more than 17,000 rules for automatically placing nearly 90 percent of components. For instance, if the decision service is working on a truck with a total fuel capacity of 120 gallons, it considers other specifications, such as the number of axles or truck length, to see whether the fuel capacity should be split between two 60-gallon tanks or three 40-gallon tanks. It also locates these tanks on the best place on the chassis and specifies the assembly order. The service can also generate a 3-D model in a CAD/CAM system. The company's engineers can add or modify rules at any time, based on engineering best practices and new or changed parts from suppliers.

### Benefits

- Design, preproduction, and manufacturing processes are faster.
- Manufacturing costs are lower, and there are savings in work in progress and scrap.
- Rules can be changed quickly and implemented immediately when internal procedures, design parameters, or safety requirements are changed.

---

## Role: Business Analysts

Business analysts have a role as part of enabling IT and business collaboration and need the following:

- A basic understanding of core development techniques, such as object or data modeling, service orientation, and testing
- Business domain knowledge so that they can be primary authors for many of the business rules needed
- An ability to understand and interpret data
- Communication skills and an ability to work with both technical and less technical people

Business analysts often play a role in managing business rules and choosing analytic options when making them available to business users directly is inappropriate or overly complex.

---

## Business Rules

Business rules are the rules by which you conduct business. The specific use of business rules in EDM is just one of the formal ways in which business rules are used. Some organizations use a formal business rules approach as a way to specify how their business should operate or what the requirements should be for a system. Some use them to define constraints on data or in processes. For the purposes of this book, however, business rules are used to represent the logic of business decisions.

More formally, a business rule is a statement of business logic that specifies performing one or more actions in the case that its conditions are satisfied. A business rule is usually presented in this format:

```
if [condition] then [action-list]
```

Some implementations extend this definition to include an "else" construct, as in this example:

```
if [condition] then [action-list] else [alternative-action-list]
```

Others reverse the order of elements in the rule:

```
do [action-list] if [condition]
```

Business rules are typically grouped into **rule sets,** which provide a means of collecting rules as a functional unit and act as a runtime unit of execution in a BRMS. The rules in a rule set operate on a set of objects or facts made available to the BRMS (see "Rule Sets" later in this chapter for more details).

The impact of a rule set can depend on the implementation order of its rules. This order might be set explicitly or determined by an algorithm that's part of the BRMS (as explained in "Implementation Modes" later in this chapter).

### Rule Syntax

The syntax for business rules has certain characteristics, such as the following:

- **Declarative**—A declarative syntax supports the definition of independent rules and ensures that the rules specify *what* should happen, not *how* it should happen.
- **Understandable by business experts**—Given the need for businesspeople and IT people to collaborate on editing business rules, the syntax must be easy for business users to understand so that they can read and write rules quickly and accurately.
- **Protected from technical object names**—Using labels for the objects and properties being manipulated must be possible, as many of them have technical names that business users don't understand.

In addition, the richer the syntax, the less likely codelike constructs will be required. You want a syntax that handles common rules and allows simpler construction than equivalent code, as in these examples:

If at least one of the customer's departments has an order where the total is greater than $40,000, then...

If the customer's status is unknown, then `getCustomerInformation()`.

A bad customer is any customer where payment history is poor and order volume is low.

If a customer is a bad customer and this order has a total less than $1,000, then...

**Note** *No syntax can handle 100 percent of your rules, so you also need easy ways to extend it and access existing system components with it.*

In addition to a rule syntax, a BRMS has different rule artifacts, such as decision flows, rule sets, and patterns. A decision service typically requires all these artifacts along with access to other services or data, some procedural logic, temporary variables, and other programming structures.

### Decision Flows

Decision flows have a lot in common with the flow normally associated with process definitions. Essentially, a **decision flow** (sometimes called a rule flow) lays out the steps and branches (both parallel and conditional) in a decision and makes it possible to run a series of independent steps as a set. Most BRMSs execute a rule set as a unit (see "Implementation Modes" later in this chapter), and a decision flow allows assembling and implementing these units to solve a business decision problem. A decision flow is sometimes referred to as a decision process flow.

In Figure 6.2, you can see how each step contributes to the decision. The decision first branches into two distinct paths based on a value. The upper branch has a loop that runs until some condition is met and has another branch within that loop. The lower branch, in contrast, has a number of tasks that are performed simultaneously. Therefore, some of these tasks are carried out one at a time, some in parallel, and some only if specific conditions are met.

Tasks in a decision flow can be rule sets, calls to other system components, other decision flows (to allow drilling down into more detail), analytically derived rule sets, or predictive analytic models.

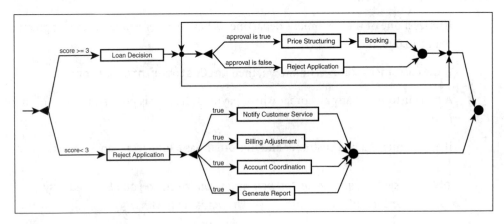

**Figure 6.2    A decision flow showing branching, parallel implementation, and loops**

## Auto Manufacturer: Warranty Claims

### Old Way

The manufacturer's warranty claims processing system was outdated and difficult to modify or update. Warranty rules are notoriously complex, with date of repair, date of purchase, model, year, part, circumstances, and previous maintenance work all playing a part in determining what is and isn't covered. Ensuring that the code in the legacy system was up to date was time-consuming and costly, particularly because the programmers didn't understand the complex warranty process. In addition, when claims were rejected, the legacy system provided only a minimal amount of information on the reason for rejection.

### EDM Way

A decision service processes all warranty claims for validity. Applying a complex set of business rules maintained by warranty employees who understand the process, the decision service processes valid claims and reconciles these claims with the invoicing system. Rejected claims are accompanied by a comprehensive description of which rules caused them to be rejected.

### Benefits

- Higher rate of automatic processing
- Rules controlled by warranty experts rather than programmers
- Lower maintenance costs

## Patterns

An important construct in managing business rules, a **pattern** defines a set of instances of a class of objects, typically a set that matches a condition, such as "all old customers" or "all former employees." These patterns are used to run rules against a subset of all instances or to check whether an instance is part of a pattern. Because patterns make it easy and effective for a rule to operate on subsets of objects in your systems, they produce a definition that's more flexible in implementation. Writing a rule against a pattern means that at runtime, the rule is performed for every instance that meets the pattern's condition, as in this example:

The pattern "Old_Customer is any Customer where Customer's Age is greater than 65" is defined.

A rule "If Customer is Old_Customer and income is greater than $50,000, then…" is created.

At runtime, this rule checks every customer whose age is greater than 65 to see whether the income is greater than $50,000 and performs the actions for the rule if it is. This process might involve checking zero, one, or many customers, depending on the number matching the pattern.

## Rule Sets

Rule sets are the typical unit of execution for rules. Executing a rule explicitly defeats the point of managing them, because a considerable amount of code might be written to coordinate execution. As a result, most BRMSs instead focus on rule sets, which represent the execution scope of a set of rules. The rules are executed sequentially or by using another mechanism described in "Execution Modes" later in this chapter. Rule sets are often parameterized so that different instances of an object can have the same rules performed against them and are highly reusable. The rule set that validates an object or determines a price, for example, might be used in many decisions.

Many rule sets are simply represented by a list of rules—the default representation, as shown in Figure 6.3. Others, however, lend themselves to display in visual representations or metaphors, as described in the next section.

The rules in a rule set also have an editing style—how the rules' details are represented and modified. Some rules, such as those presented in graphical metaphors, can be manipulated graphically. Some business rule approaches also build graphical models of rules and allow users to manipulate these diagrams. Graphical models of individual rules can be effective for complex rules but cumbersome when many rules are required.

| Adjust Income Rule Set (new Applicant) |
| --- |
| Name: Six months or less on the job<br><br>if new Applicant's months In Current Job is less than or equal to 6<br><br>then decrement new Applicant's income by 5600. |
| Name: About 1 year<br><br>if new Applicant's months In Current Job is between 6 and 13<br><br>then increment new Applicant's  income by 1000. |
| Name: Greater than 1 year<br><br>if new Applicant's months In Current Job is greater than 12<br><br>then increment  new Applicant's income by 2500. |
| Name: Compute Total income<br><br>if new Applicant is married<br><br>and new Applicant's spousal Income is greater than 0<br><br>then new Applicant's total Income is equal to new Applicant's income plus new Applicant's  spousal Income.<br><br>else new Applicant's total Income is equal to new Applicant's income. |
| Name: Minimum income<br><br>if new Applicant's total Income is less than 40000<br><br>then new Applicant is not eligible. |

**Figure 6.3    A list of rules representing a rule set**

Most tools provide a structured syntax for editing rules. These syntax definitions are like a programming language, in that they have strict rules about how the syntax is written. However, they're usually designed to be user-friendly—allowing natural names for objects and standard verbs for actions, for example. Some tools offer rule templates (see "Rule Templates" later in this chapter) to provide a rule design pattern. These patterns restrict how a rule can be edited and make it possible to offer a point-and-click interface that business users can use to view and change rule parameters.

Alternatively, a natural language, such as English, can be used to edit rules. With this approach, a tool limits the facts and syntax that can be used, at least somewhat, and then interprets written statements for execution. A third approach is using a technical language, such as Lisp or another artificial intelligence (AI) language. These languages are the traditional representations of declarative logic, but reading and writing them usually require specialized skills. Some tools combine using a technical language with a rule template to hide the syntax from users.

An important characteristic that sets a BRMS apart from traditional coding is the richness of the language used to define rules. Although atomic, declarative rules and rule metaphors have huge advantages, a powerful syntax reduces the number of rules and makes them more likely to match the way business users think. At some level, business rules are all about organizational thinking.

## Rule Set Metaphors

Although many rule sets are displayed as a list of rules, some can be represented more graphically. Two main metaphors are used: decision tables and decision trees. In both, a single graphical element represents many, possibly hundreds or even thousands, of rules.

Some rule sets can and should be represented as decision tables, such as the one in Figure 6.4. For example, when business rules are based on a few conditions, with each rule corresponding to a combination of data values or value ranges, a **decision table** is effective. Common examples include rate tables, pricing charts, discount schedules, and so on. The postage chart on the wall of your local post office is a decision table, based on shipping method, weight, and destination. Rules in a decision table are usually exclusive or unique—any combination of data maps to only a single rule—and often exhaustive—a rule covers every possible combination of data.

| Income | 25,000 - 34,999 | 25,000 - 34,999 | 25,000 - 34,999 | 35,000 - 44,999 | 35,000 - 44,999 |
|---|---|---|---|---|---|
| Card Type | Poor | Good | Excellent | Poor | Good |
| Credit Limit | 2,500 | 3,000 | 4,000 | 3,000 | 3,500 |

| Income | Card Type | Credit Limit |
|---|---|---|
| 25,001 - 35,000 | Student Bronze | 2,500 |
| 25,001 - 35,000 | Student Gold | 3,000 |
| 25,001 - 35,000 | Student Platinum | 4,000 |
| 35,001 - 45,000 | Student Bronze | 3,000 |
| 35,001 - 45,000 | Student Gold | 3,500 |
| 35,001 - 45,000 | Student Platinum | 4,500 |
| > 45,000 | Student Bronze | 4,200 |
| > 45,000 | Student Gold | 4,700 |
| > 45,000 | Student Platinum | 5,200 |

← 1-Axis Vertical     1-Axis Horizontal     2-Axis Grid

| Card Type | Student Bronze | Student Gold | Student Platinum |
|---|---|---|---|
| Credit Rating | Poor | Good | Excellent |
| Home Owner? | false | true | true |
| Income | Credit Limit | Credit Limit | Credit Limit |
| 25,001 - 35,000 | 2,500 | 3,000 | 4,000 |
| 35,001 - 45,000 | 3,000 | 3,500 | 4,500 |
| >45,000 | 4,200 | 4,700 | 5,200 |

**Figure 6.4    A selection of decision table layouts**

With **decision trees,** such as the one in Figure 6.5, you can trace a chain of conditions to a single appropriate action. By looking at branches coming from a decision point (or node) in the tree, you can quickly confirm that all applicable possibilities have been accounted for. A rule set with rules that share many initial conditions and result in a single outcome can be represented effectively as a decision tree, such as a diagnostic tree. As in decision tables, the rules in decision trees are usually exclusive and exhaustive.

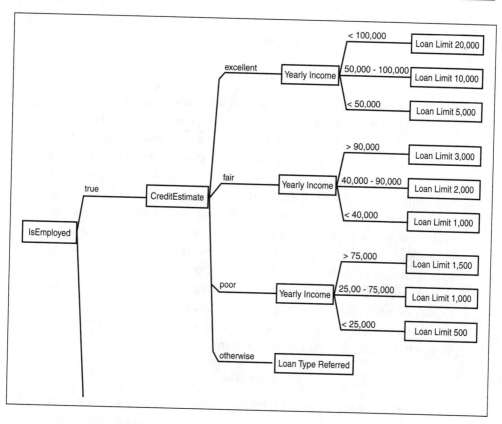

**Figure 6.5    A decision tree**

### Execution Modes

Business rules are declarative rather than procedural, as noted previously. Therefore, rule authors don't specify the full details of the sequence in which rules are to be executed. Instead, a variety of execution modes, available in most BRMSs, determine the order in which rules are executed at runtime.

A number of widely used execution approaches are available for business rules, but the most common are inferencing (sometimes called forward-chaining) and sequential execution (noninferencing). Some rules are executed in a backward-chaining approach, although this is usually associated with expert systems, so it's less relevant in enterprise decision management. What makes the three approaches different is how the engine chooses which rules to execute next.

## TV Network: Ad Slotting

### Old Way

Companies advertising on the network had specific events, event types, or time slots for which they chose to purchase broadcast time. For example, a basketball shoe company might purchase a contract for commercials that specifies the ads must run during the first and last quarter of certain basketball games and no other shoe companies can advertise in the same quarters. With thousands of advertising contracts, the network's scheduling coordinators had the impossible task of assigning each commercial to a "slot" by hand. This task was compounded when scheduling changes occurred at the last minute, which is common in sports, because commercial slots need to be rearranged. Even without changes, the process of putting ads into the right slots might take weeks. Customers were anxious to know during what events their ads would be aired, and the network's sales team didn't have an accurate, current picture of the available commercial inventory.

### EDM Way

Objects representing advertising contracts and their properties and stipulations are stored in a database. A decision service evaluates that information against slotting rules created by the network's best commercial schedulers. The decision service then books a commercial with a specific event in the system that manages commercial inventory. The decision service is always checking for new or updated advertising contracts, and slotting rules are applied automatically and immediately to determine placement of new commercials whenever new or changed contracts are detected. The rules handle exclusivity and rotation (advertiser's commercials spread out over one month) and many other contract terms and customer preferences. Slotting analysts no longer need to assign commercials by hand and can focus on other tasks. If the programming for a night changes, the decision service reassigns commercials automatically. The decision service takes advantage of inferencing to ensure that rules are reapplied to all contracts when data is changed by the rules executing for a given contract.

> **Benefits**
>
> - The advertiser's commercials can be scheduled in minutes instead of the previous time frame of as much as two weeks.
>
> - The sales team has an accurate, up-to-the-minute picture of the commercial inventory.
>
> - Automatic rescheduling can be done when the program lineup changes.

**Sequential execution** is used when executing all rules is quicker than figuring out which rules are eligible and when rule ordering is irrelevant (all rules are mutually exclusive) or explicit (the rule author explicitly orders, or sequences, rules for execution). This approach is the simplest; the engine simply follows the designer's instructions and executes the rules once, and only once, in the specified order. If the rules change information in the system, subsequent rules use the new information. If changed information means that previously executed rules should be executed differently, the engine executes them in the new way only if the designer explicitly directs the system to do so. For instance, if a rule didn't execute previously because a condition was false and then data is changed by a subsequent rule so that the condition is true, the rule is reevaluated and executed only if the designer specifies that it should be.

**Inferencing** is used when rules might depend on other rules or when only a few rules are expected to run from a large number in the rule set. It might also be used so that the rule author can write rules in any order without risking that this might result in a less than optimal execution sequence. Inferencing engines use an efficient rule selection algorithm, such as Rete[1] or its derivatives, to schedule a set of rules by determining which ones are worth considering, given the data available, and then beginning to execute them. Each rule is evaluated and, if true, executed. Any rule that's executed can change the data being used at that time, which causes the engine to reschedule a new set of rules based on the changed data and then work through the newly scheduled rules. The upshot is that rules are considered only if there's a reason to believe they might execute, and rules are constantly reevaluated in the light of changed data. Therefore, designers need not worry about the impact of placing one rule before another rule whereby the first rule might change the data the second rule relies on. Essentially, the engine handles rule scheduling.

---

[1] Charles L. Forgy, "RETE: A Fast Algorithm for the Many Pattern/Many Object Pattern Matching Problem." *Artificial Intelligence* 19:17–37, 1982.

---

### Some Business Rules Definitions

When discussing business rules, the following phrases are often confused, so they are defined here:

- **Business rules engine**—A piece of software that takes business rules defined in a rule syntax and executes them by using one or more of the standard rule execution modes.

- **Business rules management system**—A complete set of software products for managing and executing business rules. A BRMS includes a business rules engine, a rule repository, and rule design and testing tools.

- **Decision service**—A service designed to answer a question about the business—to make a decision, in other words. It uses business rules and analytic models to come up with a precise and consistent answer.

- **Rules service**—A service that can run a collection of business rules against business data and be called by other services and applications.

Therefore, a rules service is a kind of decision service, and a business rules engine is a critical component of a BRMS. For historical reasons, "business rules engine" is sometimes used to describe a business rules management system. "Business rules management system" and "decision service" are used throughout this book, but when reading other materials, you might need to substitute business rules engine and rules service, respectively.

---

**Backward-chaining** is used in expert systems when rules are designed to be goal seeking. In this approach, the engine sets an objective. It then searches for rules that have a consequence (a THEN clause) meeting the objective and establishes which rules must fire to meet its goal. It then tries to fire those rules, firing additional rules as necessary to establish the facts the rules need. It works backward from its goal, in other words, to see which rules must fire.

### Semantics and Business Rules

The field of semantics (as it applies to data, not natural language) is undergoing a lot of innovation as the result of several factors. Tim Berners-Lee, the creator of the World Wide

Web, envisions a "semantic Web," in which the Web becomes more than a collection of Web pages and is an active, searchable database. Achieving a semantic Web requires more than search engines, because the Web is too vast and relationships are too difficult to ascertain with just keywords. Instead, the semantic Web would have "tags" on every unique piece of information that could be searched for pattern matching as well as semantic content—in other words, what does the tag actually mean in relation to everything else?

The semantic Web, if it's ever realized, is years away, but in the meantime, many exciting and creative technologies are appearing in support of this effort. They are loosely called **semantic technology**, and almost all use what's called ontology. Most systems used to organize information are hierarchical in nature, such as the Dewey Decimal System for books or the nomenclature for classifying living organisms into species and phyla. Object-oriented design is hierarchical, as is a chart of accounts. **Ontologies**, however, are graphs or networks. This endows them with unique and powerful qualities, such as the ability to reason about relationships between things and capture ambiguity and double meanings without the need to create artifacts that don't really exist.

A semantic model can be a useful first step in building a rule base. By eliciting the relationships between terms first and providing an ongoing process to refine them, as well as drawing on an ontology's inferencing capabilities, you can develop rules faster and with more certainty of completeness and consistency. Because rules are arranged in classes hierarchically, their underlying model is a semantic model, at least implicitly. Surfacing this model in an ontology offers additional benefits, such as rule-firing sequences, optimization, and runtime efficiencies. In general, semantic models don't contain all the decision rules you need, but business rules are a viable way of effectively managing some semantic content.

## Metadata and Business Rules

Metadata is an amorphous term with many meanings. For example, if a database contains an entry "Size of Crater" to indicate that is the name of a column in another table that contains sizes of craters, this entry is considered reporting or user metadata. A database entry with the number 3 representing the number of password entry tries before a user is blocked is considered system metadata. However, metadata can be data from another perspective. For example, in the query "What is the average number of tries before blocking all users in the application?" the number 3 is now data for a query. The point is that metadata can't be identified merely by its location. Context matters, too.

What metadata does is control, inform, and abstract. System metadata can be queried at runtime to find a parameter, such as the number 3, or to gather terms dynamically to build an SQL query. Metadata also informs by providing at least descriptions and definitions of data elements. Where metadata gathers momentum, however, is in providing abstraction. For example, developing an application for a single use or client takes much less time than developing package software for a broad audience. The reason is that the package has to consider the variations in use and customizations of processes and models that a large number of clients require. This process requires abstraction—removing the specificity of a single application and developing more general routines and models that can be directed and modified, not by recoding but by substituting values at runtime that are maintained in a repository. Business rules can represent some but not all of this metadata.

### Model-Driven Design and Business Rules

A model is a description or an abstraction of something—in EDM, an information system. With models of information systems, designers and developers can focus on critical aspects of the design without having to consider potentially distracting details. Using models to design or document code is fairly common, but model-driven design takes it one step farther by having the model contain enough information that the application can be generated from the model. Essentially, the model becomes primary, and the code secondary.

Model-driven design involves a number of model types that use the Object Management Group (OMG)[2] framework:

- **Computation-independent model (CIM)**—A model of the required behavior that's independent of any consideration for automating it in an information system
- **Platform-independent model (PIM)**—A model of an information system that specifies how it should work and what it should do but is independent of any implementation platform
- **Platform-specific model (PSM)**—A model that's specific to an implementation platform so that a working application can be generated that's optimized for that platform

The basic approach is to define a CIM to establish what should be done and then a PIM of the system you need. The PIM can then be transformed, ideally in a reversible and standard way, to a PSM for the deployment platform you've chosen. This process requires defined and ideally reusable definitions of the transformations.

In this approach, you can consider business rules, which don't contain platform-specific information, to be platform-independent and a way of representing elements of a PIM. Business rules, in an EDM sense, aren't computation-independent because they relate to the actual data or objects in information systems and are intended to be implemented in a system.

---

[2] Links to find information on OMG and the other standards listed can be found in the EDM wiki at www.smartenoughsystems.com

**Use of Business Rules in CIMs**   *Note that the term "business rule" is sometimes used to describe a more generic, computation-independent concept. These business rules might be implemented in an information system or represent a policy manual's contents, for instance.*

*For the purposes of EDM, these rules are considered useful ways to specify system requirements and track what a PIM does and doesn't do, but they aren't as important to the process as implementable business rules in a PIM.*

Some modeling approaches use a domain-specific language to handle the description of platform-independent logic, but business rules can usually be considered a substitute for a domain-specific language, as far as business logic is concerned. Indeed, you could argue that typical business rule syntax is a domain-specific language in which the domain is "business logic." Most, if not all, of the benefits claimed for domain-specific languages can be attained with business rules and rule templates.

## Rule Standards

The adoption of rules technology has been growing rapidly, which has led to a number of standards. The first on the scene was JSR 94, a standard managed through the Java Community Process. This lightweight standard makes it easy to identify and call a BRMS in a standard way, such as the Java Database Connectivity (JDBC) standard used to access databases with the Java language, but it's simpler and lacks an equivalent for SQL. Although JSR 94 is a standard way to call a BRMS, there's no such standard for the syntax of rules. Syntax is where other standards come in, because JSR 94 can't be developed further without some definition of operational semantics.

Operational semantics for business rules are being developed in a couple of other standards, however. The OMG has the Production Rules Representation (PRR) standard, which outlines a basic structure for sharing production rules—those that run in a BRMS. It's essentially a PIM in OMG terms, in that it's focused on being executable without being tied to syntax for a specific BRMS. The PRR standard handles forward-chaining and sequential rules and has an optional extension that uses Object Constraint Language (OCL) to define rules' semantic content.

In addition, the World Wide Web Consortium (W3C) has a standard called the Rule Interchange Format for describing rules for interchange in a wide variety of areas. This standard's charter is to produce a core rule language plus extensions that allow translating rules to other rule languages and, therefore, using them in other rule systems. PRR and the Rule Interchange Format are expected to become interoperable.

---

**Another OMG Standard**

Another OMG standard is Semantics of Business Vocabularies and Rules (SBVR), focused on developing business rules as a way to describe a business, not necessarily to implement a business rules-based solution. This specification defines the vocabulary and rules for documenting the semantics of business vocabulary, business facts, and business rules. From a BRMS point of view, it's mostly a standard to help manage business rules as requirements and allow production rules to be mapped to them systematically for traceability and impact analysis. In OMG terms, SBVR can be considered a CIM.

---

Progress on these standards is good. Publication and adoption should result in much more interoperability between business rules technologies from different vendors and BRMSs and other tools for analyzing and designing services, such as model-driven design and requirements management.

## Business Rules Technology

Figure 6.6 shows how the technology elements needed for business rules management interact. Business rules are created by IT staff in an integrated development environment (IDE) or by business users using rule management applications. All rules are stored in a single, structured repository, usually appropriate for a specific BRMS. A BRMS allows deploying these rules to a decision service so that other applications can use the service to answer questions and provide services to associates. Each element has certain key characteristics and functions, as described in the following sections.

### Repositories

A **repository** is a database or file system that manages the set of artifacts that all other components use. It should be independent of the production and development environments so that implementation scenarios aren't hardwired to storage arrangements. In other words, the specific rules and rule artifacts needed for a decision are accessible in the repository but are not limited to a specific decision service. A repository should do the following:

- Contain multiple projects, whether or not those projects share rules.
- Support versioning so that multiple versions of a rule or rule set can be maintained.

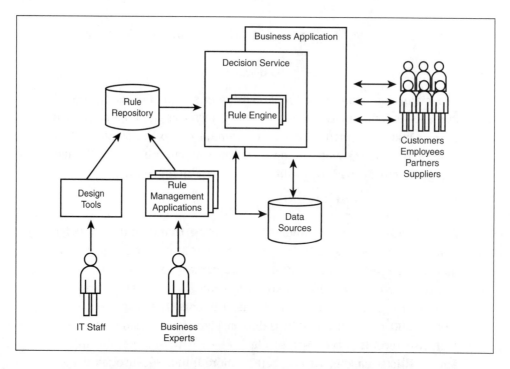

**Figure 6.6   Elements of business rules management technology**

- Allow production rules to be rolled back to a previous version if a new version turns out to have problems.

- Provide an audit trail for tracking all changes and associate changes with a person for review and approval. The value of business rules in compliance is severely affected if the audit trail for rule changes is inadequate.

- Support the concept of "effective dates" or periods of time during which a rule is enforced or not. This feature makes it possible to have rules that are in effect only at certain times of day, until a certain date, or after a piece of legislation is passed.

- Allow effective management of rules and other artifacts in a way that matches how the company thinks about its rules. Generally, this management means having content structured into specific projects or directories, assembling these groupings in various ways, and effective cross-referencing and domain management.

- Support traceability. As noted previously, there's a difference between rules that run as part of an information infrastructure (often known as production rules) and rules managed at a high level or defined in response to regulations. Impact analysis, tracing which production rules need to be reconsidered when a policy or regulation changes, allows effective management of production rules as well as

## Large European Tax Authority

### Old Way

At a major European tax authority, customer service, efficiency, flexibility, and accountability were becoming increasingly important. The agency had responded to a major overhaul of tax legislation with a renewal of its IT systems. The new systems still had problems with managing and processing the new tax code's many changed rules.

### EDM Way

A set of decision services handle tax processing, claims, and fraud detection. These services give the agency flexibility in defining logic to validate tax claims, for instance, and support easy plug-in of new data sources. The decision services are flexible and scalable enough to support other application domains and departments. The core service runs some 1,500 rules on 200,000 claims in eight hours, using millions of database records. Because the rules are easy to change, the agency applies stricter validations and detects more fraud. Because tax experts can manage the rules, the agency has flexibility in adapting systems to legislation changes and spends less time and money updating systems to respond to these changes. The tax experts can make changes to the system logic and try what-if scenarios to test their impact. The decision service has also allowed the agency to include predictive analytic models that score fraud risk, so it can detect more fraud.

### Benefits

- Changes to systems are handled in days instead of months.
- The decision service's additive nature means only one year between project start and the system installed in production.
- Stricter validations are applied, so both fraud detection and tax revenue have increased.

higher-level rules. Similarly, being able to trace which rules implement decisions in a business process or the impact of a change on an object model is necessary to achieve agility of business rules.

- Support approval and review cycles so that the people who need to interact with rules can do so effectively.

- Be extensible so that additional artifacts or properties for existing artifacts can be defined. Extensibility allows effective integration of a rule repository into a company's software development life cycle and processes. Indeed, a growing trend is for repositories to support federation—linking related repositories so that they can query each other for more information. With this support, a rule repository could reach into a modeling repository and extract information about models for use when writing rules. Federation often works better than trying to develop a single complete repository for everything.

## Design Tools

An advantage of a BRMS is the ability to engage business users in managing and developing business rules, but designing and integrating decision services are still largely IT responsibilities. To this end, a BRMS needs a robust set of decision design tools.

To manage decisions, defining coherent decision services that other applications can use for decision making is necessary. The design tools in a BRMS need to make defining input and output data for decision services easy and manage a decision service as a coherent object in the repository. Whether or not an enterprise is using service-oriented architecture (SOA), other applications must have a clear interface for calling and using a decision service. Ideally, BRMS design tools allow the same logic components (rules, rule sets, decision flows) to be deployed in a variety of technical implementations to make using a decision service as easy as possible for an application or service.

Information management should be supported by BRMS design tools. Business rules need to be able to access other data sources and services as part of execution. A decision service might require additional data besides its inputs, want to use another service (potentially but not exclusively another decision service), or otherwise need to be integrated with the existing systems portfolio. Having design tools that allow easy access from the rules environment to source data and other services and systems makes this process more straightforward.

Decision services typically aren't a system of record. They don't normally maintain the data that defines the organization's current state. It's more common for them to use information from systems of record, process that data by using rules and models, and

> ### Service-Oriented Architecture
>
> A company committed to SOA might choose to always wrap decision services as formal Web services. If all the systems that might need access to a decision service are service-enabled, multiplatform deployment of decision services might not be necessary. It should be noted, however, that rule sets are often reused in decision services, so all decision services need to be deployed on the same platform, or rule sets have to be deployed as component services that can be called from decision services. Either method might be unacceptable, so even a "pure" SOA implementation could require a BRMS that can be deployed to multiple platforms.

return data representing the best action to take to another system or service for implementation. For instance, a decision service might read customer information from the customer database, run rules and models to decide whether a customer is a retention risk, decide what retention offer is most compelling, and then return the customer's identifiers and the offer for an e-mail marketing system to dispatch the offer. One of the most important aspects of decision services is how often they can be additive and add value to existing systems and processes. Design tools must make designing this integration easy.

### Business User Rule Maintenance Applications

Although having business users maintain rules is a major factor in agility and cost savings when using a BRMS, generally business users don't want to maintain rules any more than they want to write code. They want to run their business better by doing the following, for example:

- Relax underwriting policies
- Reduce risk exposure
- Retain more customers, even if it costs more
- Promote slow-moving products
- Catch a new kind of fraud
- Enforce new regulations

These goals are all ways of saying business users want to be able to specify which rules are to be implemented in their systems or at least in the decision services within those systems, but that's not how most business users think. Therefore, to get business users to

---

### Role: Business Users

In an EDM environment, business users have a number of key roles:

- A willingness to share responsibility for the business logic within information systems, not just pass it off to IT

- An understanding of their business and its "numbers" and a desire to run their part of the business by the numbers

- A basic familiarity with their organization's technology

- A willingness and ability to move from mechanical decision making to a focus on activities that increase value

Business users have a critical role to play in EDM. They need not become technology gurus, but they must be willing to share responsibility with IT for the pure business logic within systems that is needed to achieve maximum effectiveness or at least measurable effectiveness.

---

maintain rules in their systems without them feeling as though you're trying to turn them into programmers, you need to do several things:

- Make rule maintenance a business function. Businesspeople shouldn't feel as though they're maintaining code, nor should rule maintenance seem too technical. It must look, in fact, as though business users are doing what they want to do—changing the way their business runs.

- Make the environment for rule maintenance familiar and easy to understand. It should use the same layout and style as other systems business users use routinely. It should use their terminology and expectations, not that of the BRMS or programmers, and the process of rule maintenance must be integrated with the other systems they use. Going from a task to changing the rules should seem like a seamless process that lets business users do rule editing when it makes sense for them.

- Make the whole environment secure and controlled. Doing so means providing audit trails, user-friendly testing and what-if tools, release management, security, and authentication to prevent unauthorized changes. Most important, this environment prevents business users from making errors in editing rules.

- Provide guidance in how businesspeople can identify business metrics that will measure the rules business performance so that incremental improvement through rules becomes possible (and the new norm).

One of the best ways to encourage business users to maintain rules is to use templates, as explained in the next section.

## Rule Templates

**Rule templates** are structural definitions of a class of rules—what attributes should be used when evaluating conditions, what kinds of checks are allowed, what range of actions rule writers can choose from, and so on. A well-designed template prevents unwanted editing to provide the control and security you need. A template also allows you to use a user interface that business users find compelling.

As shown in Figure 6.7, templates keep much of the complexity of rules away from end users and ensure that rules conform to the template's definitions.

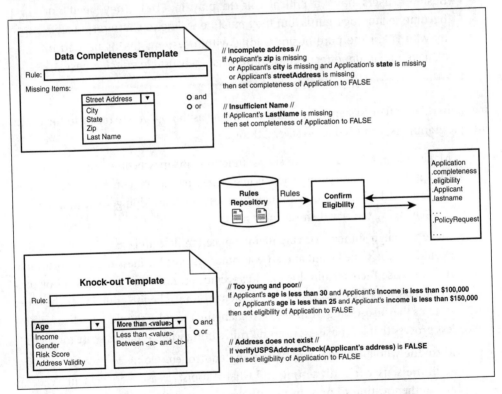

**Figure 6.7   Rule templates control how rules are created and make maintenance simple for business users**

---

| **Pharmacy Benefits Manager: Drug Interaction Management** |
|---|

**Old Way**

A third party provided drug-interaction information to patients. The company had no control over this process and couldn't expand how it was used. Frequent changes created problems and resulted in information from the third party being out of date. The information was provided to pharmacists, who had to consult it to find drug interactions so that they could pass it on to patients.

**EDM Way**

A decision service uses business rules to determine which drugs might interact with each other. Drug-interaction rules can be based on patient age, other drugs being taken, length of dosage, time between dosages, and so on. This information is looked up in patient records, and the decision service uses it to warn about potential drug-interaction problems. Pharmacists can create and maintain their own conflict rules in an easy-to-use environment with little or no IT involvement.

**Benefits**

- Pharmacists with medical know-how control rules without IT involvement.
- Patients get up-to-date information.

Realistically, no business users would maintain code such as this example:

```
public class Application {
  private Customer customers[];
  private Customer goldCustomers[];
  ...
  public void checkOrder() {
  for (int i = 0; i < numCustomers; i++) {
    Customer aCustomer = customers[i];
    if (aCustomer.checkIfGold()) {
      numGoldCustomers++;
      goldCustomers[numGoldCustomers] = aCustomer;
      if (aCustomer.getCurrentOrder().getAmount() > 100000)
        aCustomer.setSpecialDiscount (0.05);
    }
  }
}
```

They might maintain code that looks like this:

```
If customer is GoldCustomer
    and Home_Equity_Loan_Value is more than $100,000
    then college_loan_discount = 0.5%
```

However, what business users want to see is something like Figure 6.8.

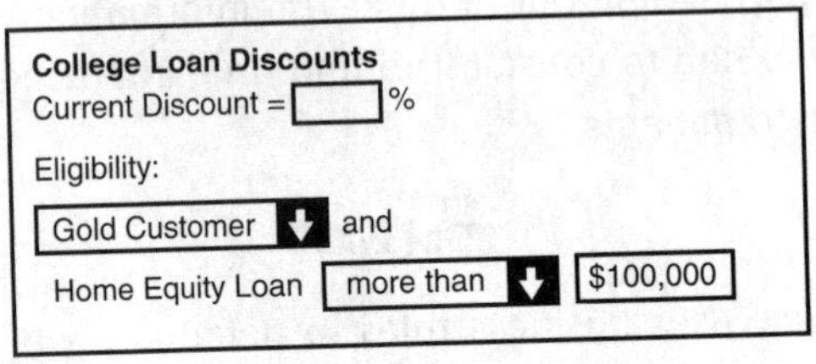

**Figure 6.8    An interface for business user rule management**

As organizations move to support highly personalized products and services, the need to have consumers, employees, or people at other organizations participate in managing the rules becomes more important. Indeed, many organizations already allow customers to do a limited amount of rule management; think about frequent-flyer programs that allow you to specify your preferred seating choices, for instance. Most of these choices are very simple ("window or aisle") or overly complex, requiring an understanding of how the underlying systems work. For instance, the minimal choices for seat selection on most travel-booking sites don't meet a frequent traveler's requirements, who would prioritize certain row-seat combinations, such as "any exit row seat" over "any aisle seat." A BRMS can make templates available for customers and other associates that allow this flexibility. Allowing people to manage some rules that affect their transactions can personalize the service you give them, make them feel as though they have more control in their interactions with you, and reduce customer service calls and problems.

**Thousands of Rule Editors**    *If you allow consumers to manage their own business rules, you must take serious note of the performance implications. You will have many thousands of people creating their own small rule sets, which has different performance and scalability issues than a single very large set of rules has. In addition, guidelines for making the user interface accessible and integrated are even more important when large numbers of people are involved.*

Deployment Management

Any BRMS must be capable of managing deployment of rules into decision services. This capability requires the following features:

- **Release management in terms of collecting and grouping rule artifacts**—The repository should contain artifacts for many projects and many decision services, all at different levels of completeness and usability. To deploy well-defined and coherent decision services, a BRMS must be able to manage releases to the next level of deployment (development to test, test to production, and so forth).

- **Deployment to other platforms as well-defined components and decision services**—Many organizations adopting EDM have legacy systems and platforms or purchased components that can't easily use a decision service if it's deployed only as a Web service. Effective deployment of a decision service to other platforms in a way that allows easy access to the service is crucial to meeting the "write once, use everywhere" principle of business rules. This feature might be less important in organizations that effectively implement an SOA everywhere.

- **Live updates on demand or scheduled updates after deployment**—As rules change, decision services that have already been deployed must be able to pick up the new rules. Some services need to make updates on a regular schedule, and some need to do it on demand, and a BRMS must support both methods.

- **Scalability through threading and agents**—Like any high-level approach to developing systems, using business rules can have a performance implication. Essentially, you're trading some maintainability and ease of change for initial performance. Making sure this trade-off is viable means having a BRMS that can deploy decision services that support multithreading, multiple **agents**—instances of a decision service that can handle transactions in parallel, grid computing, application servers, and so on. This support allows the decision service to take advantage of the underlying platform's scalability and performance.

- **Reliability through uninterrupted deployment of new rules into running agents**—This feature is required for any decision service running in real time. It must be possible to force decision services to update rules (restarting any in-flight decisions so that they use the new rules) or queue rule changes so that all new transactions use the new rules, and in-flight ones are completed using the old rules.

Deployment management is critical, because without it, business rules simply fill up the repository without supporting any production applications. Taken together, the combination of deployment management and the repository support the process of putting business rules into decision services.

## The Rule Development Process

The rule development process shown in Figure 6.9 has four key steps, as described in the following sections.

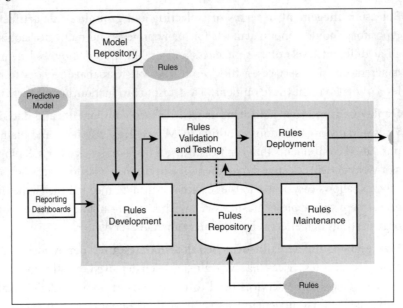

**Figure 6.9    The rule development process in an EDM architecture**

### Rule Development

The first step in developing business rules for a decision service is to develop an initial set of rules and templates or rule types. As shown in Figure 6.10, business rules come from five key sources:

- **Regulations**—Many decision services support a process that has strict compliance guidelines, so regulations are often an essential source. Identifying the regulations that must be enforced is easy, and most legal requirements are tracked closely for relevance and timeliness. However, regulations contain much information that shouldn't be implemented. For example, regulations for how to carry out inspections or for data storage requirements aren't decision rules. Capturing these rules can be useful but should be separate from the process of capturing decision rules. The main problems with regulations are the "legalese" in which they're written and trying to interpret the business rules from the guidance and process information in regulations.

**Note** *Going back to check the original regulations' wording is often easier than trying to read the code or manuals that are interpretations of those regulations.*

- **Policy manuals**—Policy and procedure manuals are a rich source for business rules, especially if an automated decision is replacing a manual decision. Policy manuals sometimes (but not often enough) state rules explicitly and aim for readability. However, the rules in the manual might not be in use—they might be documented but no longer enforced, and they may be vague enough to vary in interpretation. You need to invest some time in watching how people use the manuals and comparing what they do in practice with the manual. You should also plan time to resolve likely inconsistencies in the policies and their practices. You may need a formal conflict resolution process.

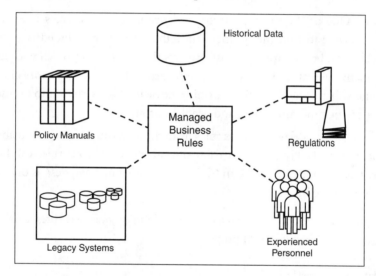

**Figure 6.10** **Business rules can be extracted from a variety of sources and then managed effectively**

- **Business experts**—Many of the rules in decision services come from business users. You can gather rules from them by using many of the same techniques for gathering requirements: focus groups, direct observation, interviews, and workshops. Disagreements among business users are likely, so identifying and resolving them are important. More often than not, business experts, although they are the most knowledgeable, may not know how to express their expertise.

**Note** *Very few EDM projects don't need to extract some rules from experts or validate rules with those experts.*

> ### Code as the Only Source of Rules
>
> When code is the only source, use some of the many available code-analysis tools to find out where your decisions are made, determine what data elements are used, and get a sense of what the code does. Then try to build rules to mimic the results without getting distracted by details of how the old code worked. Try refactoring the code to make it easier to compare results, and be prepared to invest heavily in testing. Be sure to review the rules with business experts who can identify rules that are irrelevant or even harmful.

- **Code**—One of the most common and overused rule sources is existing code. Mining code to find the business rules that were implemented is tempting but rarely is the best approach. Most projects that try this approach end up with far too many rules at far too low a level. Business rules must map more closely to the business than code does. Transforming extracted legacy rules into useful business rules can be time consuming and problem prone.

- **Data**—You can derive business rules from the data you have captured about how a process runs. Data mining for rules and thresholds in your rules can be productive. This technique, covered in Chapter 5, "Data and Analytics," is one way to use analytics in EDM.

Being thoughtful and thorough in collecting and defining business rules is an important prerequisite for success in an EDM project.

### Rule Validation and Testing

Testing business rules to maximize their benefits consists of traditional software testing and more business-centered testing. Most IT departments rightly insist on a rigorous testing regimen. Testing tools should also be available to business users who have access to rules so that they can do their own testing. These testing functions might be similar for both business users and IT, but the implementation needs to reflect their different perspectives. You need testing capabilities in four broad areas:

- Performance testing is required for business rules in decision services, just as for any code. The time from invocation to completion must meet the design objectives. This testing differs for business rules in the ability to analyze each business rule to see which rules take the most time.

## Top Five U.S. Consumer Magazine: Ad Pricing

### Old Way

The volume of requests and complexity of ad pricing meant that advertising customers weren't getting immediate and accurate quotes. Thousands of requests for ad prices needed to be processed each year, and they were often complex, with many factors affecting pricing, such as placement, use of color, creative development, time of year, and time of distribution. Analysts with specialist knowledge used spreadsheets of pricing information and a lot of experience to come up with prices. Salespeople couldn't generate quotes for customers; they had to wait for an analyst to be available. Pricing updates from corporate policies, cross-magazine discounts, and special arrangements were difficult to integrate, resulting in slow turnaround for price quotes.

### EDM Way

A decision service was created to calculate ad prices, and rule templates were developed so that analysts and others in the organization could create and manage all the pricing rules. Those with domain expertise could use the templates to manage pricing rules without any new technical knowledge. Most pricing requests are handled by the decision service after data entry by salespeople. Salespeople can now handle typical pricing, leaving analysts to handle custom and complex pricing.

### Benefits

- Analysts have freed up 30 percent of their time to spend on high-value, nonpricing issues, such as account management, yet the number of ads purchased has increased.

- Salespeople can give immediate quotes and do what-if analysis with customers, which maximizes customers' perceived value of ads they buy. As a result, revenue and customer loyalty have increased.

---

- Black-box testing—testing the whole decision service without concern for its internals—isn't usually any different from the way other services or components are tested. Problems might be debugged differently, but the testing is identical.

### Knowledge Management

Knowledge management, the process and techniques of managing intellectual capital in an organization, has many overlaps with using business rules to automate decisions. As the baby-boom generation retires, capturing knowledge of experienced staff is more important than ever. Traditional IT solutions, including those built with business rules, focus on planned responses to anticipated stimuli. Most knowledge management processes focus on expert or tacit decisions. Nevertheless, there's overlap, and the approaches can be complementary.

When you use EDM, the range of decisions you can automate expands. As Frappaolo[2] notes, "In some cases, knowledge believed to be tacit is only so labeled because no one has ever taken the time or energy to codify the knowledge." Using a BRMS to manage and deliver codified knowledge enables you to automate decisions that you might otherwise have handled manually. Using knowledge management techniques to take control of these rules and using business rules to automate decisions can be effective.

Companies often think they can't automate a decision because it's handled personally or inconsistently, but in reality, as Frappaolo says, "... it is a logical, methodical thinking process that simply is not recognized as such." Using knowledge management techniques to take control of and automate these rules can bring them into the realm of planned, automated responses and EDM.

• White-box testing—testing specific scenarios in which you analyze the decision service's actual performance—is quite different with business rules. The atomic nature of business rules makes it easy to walk through the implementation and see what's happening and makes business users' participation in testing practical. They can see and understand the rules in a way they can't understand traditional coding environments. Their involvement can reduce test cycle times and improve quality.

---

[2] Carl Frappaolo, *Knowledge Management*, Wiley, 2006.

---

### Referential Rule Integrity

Referential integrity testing includes static analysis of rules, based on their structure, and dynamic testing performed by running rules. Static analysis can find missing or overlapping rules, rules that contradict each other, and other structural issues. Logical inconsistencies at runtime and compliance with regulations can be assessed for test or real transactions. Referential integrity testing should check for these factors:

- Completeness testing can be about checking for all values in a range and not omitting values, for example. Rules might be correct but incomplete, in which case some situations won't be handled correctly.

- Consistency is about identifying rules that contradict each other and flagging them for editing and correction.

- Coherence and correctness are measures of how well the problem domain is represented in the rules—how close to the user intent do they get?

Checking all three factors makes for better decision services and fewer problems.

---

- You must also test completeness and correctness—what some call "referential rule integrity."[3] Because business rules are declarative, atomic, and defined to make applying business expertise easy, testing a set of rules for completeness and correctness is possible; testing most programming languages in this way isn't possible (or at least isn't reasonable).

## Rule Maintenance

Maintaining business rules—modifying them in response to changing needs and new feedback on their effectiveness—is critical to their value and is one of their key advantages over code. Some rules in a decision service are certainly "owned" by IT staff. You can also engage business users in ongoing maintenance of decision services. The main value of business users participating in maintenance is business agility—making it possible for those who understand the business to change the way information systems behave and,

---

[3] Steve Hendrick, group vice president of IDC, invented this term, deriving it from the concept of referential integrity in relational database design.

---

## Governance, Management, and Maintenance

Although these three terms are often used interchangeably, they differ, so they are defined here:

- Governance is business-centered. Making sure business rules align with defined business objectives or actual regulations is an example of governance.

- Management is about controlling and analyzing business rules. Being able to do impact analysis to see which stakeholders, processes, and even customers will be affected before making a change is an example of management.

- Maintenance is the mechanics of making a change, as in maintenance programming.

In the end, someone must make a change (business rules maintenance), but before that change is made, someone should check its potential impact (business rules management), which is affected by someone with governance authority who came up with the idea for the change. All three functions are important, and they intersect.

---

therefore, keep the business strategy and information systems synchronized. Structured correctly, business rules can provide this agility yet reduce maintenance costs. Most systems have increasing maintenance costs, thanks to a constantly changing business environment, and IT expenditures on maintenance can be excessive.

### Rule Deployment

Although rule development, testing, and maintenance are necessary to get the right rules into a rule repository, these steps don't allow rules to support a decision service. Any BRMS you use must support the process of collecting current, tested rules and packaging them, along with any models, for deployment to a decision service. One characteristic of decision services is that they change more often than many other kinds of services. Good deployment and redeployment skills and technologies are required to keep everything up to date. Having the right rules in a repository is only part of the solution; you must also be able to deploy them rapidly and accurately to decision services.

After decision services are deployed, they rarely remain static for long. The way you make decisions changes constantly, so the ability to adapt and optimize decision services is critical to long-term success.

---

### The EDM Wiki

You can find more information on business rules and business rules technology in the EDM wiki at www.smartenoughsystems.com.

---

# CHAPTER SEVEN

# Adaptive Control

The final core concept is adaptive control of decision services. Adaptive control is how the management aspect of enterprise decision management is applied to decision services. Over time, decision services must be improved and revised to make sure they continue to make the best possible decisions. Eventually, they can and should be optimized to maximize their value to the organization. This chapter covers the concepts, technology, and process for adaptive control. As before, the concepts and technology are presented first and the process second. If you prefer to get a sense of the steps first, you can skip ahead to that part of the chapter and refer back to concepts and technology as necessary.

## Architectural Overview

Figure 7.1 repeats the overview of how the core technologies fit together. This chapter focuses on adaptive control. Enterprise decision management requires constantly improving decisions over time. Building decision services so that they can be improved or adapted over time requires a mix of approaches called adaptive control. Adaptive control involves setting up champion/challenger strategies, designing learning strategies, and using optimization and simulation to find the best decisions.

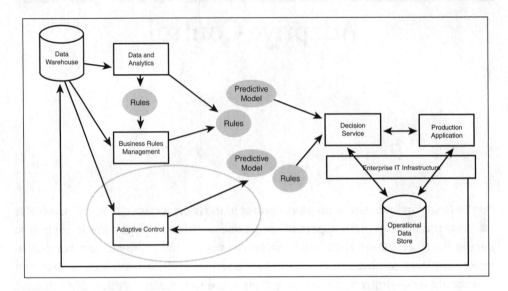

**Figure 7.1    An EDM architecture**

The first consideration, however, is why you should invest in the necessary infrastructure to improve your decisions over time. This infrastructure requires applying software assets and staffing not to building new decision services, but to improving old ones. Although this goal might seem to contradict one of the key benefits of EDM, reducing maintenance costs, it doesn't. You can consider this kind of adaptive control or continuous improvement as maintenance, but the comparison isn't fair. Some improvement work comes from changing business conditions that *force* a change in the approach to the decision. Mostly, however, this work involves making a decision better over time to boost profits, reduce losses, or improve retention. You constantly learn more about your customers and gather more information about their behavior. New insights and market trends come from you, your competitors, and third parties. With a process for continual review and improvement of how you make a decision, you can detect and respond to changes in customer behavior without having to start a special project *and* show a return on investment (ROI) for the data you collect and analyze.

An important reason for building an adaptive control environment for decisions is that at the point of decision, you don't know the long-term outcomes. Figure 7.2 shows how actions taken today influence profitability over time in different ways. One causes a steady growth in profitability, one has good profitability but only after some time, and the third has a rapid growth in profit followed by a falling off.

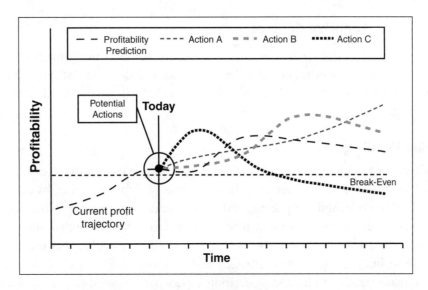

**Figure 7.2    Actions influence profitability in different ways** ©*Fair Isaac Corporation, reproduced with permission*

If you use a single strategy for every decision, you can plot only one of these curves, and you have no data on how other actions might have had better (or worse) results. By building an adaptive control environment into your decision services, you can create a learning environment in which you gather data about many possible actions and their impact.

As you gain more understanding of a decision, you can begin to optimize and simulate the way it's made. In **optimization,** you model the problem with some constraints and an objective function, and the optimization engine or solver searches for the best possible solution that satisfies the constraints by using an algorithm suited to the problem. **Simulation** involves running many scenarios through an engine to see how different sets of constraints, rules, assumptions, or data might influence the results. This method is often combined with optimization so that each scenario is optimized. The process can be described simply—designing the model, running the simulations and optimization, and then tuning the results—but the mathematics and technology are fairly advanced.

Complexity increases gradually as you move from implementing adaptive control for a decision by using a champion/challenger approach to experimental design to being able to optimize and simulate the entire decision. Underlying this range of approaches is a set of core concepts, explained in the following section.

## Concepts in Adaptive Control

Adaptive control involves a number of key concepts. Some complex mathematics are used, especially in optimization, and there are critical differences between how most systems are developed and how decision services should be developed to allow for adaptive control.

### Champion/Challenger Approach

The champion/challenger approach is the main technique in adaptive control. As you learned in Chapter 4, "Core Concepts," the idea is to identify a "champion" by documenting the business rules and analytic models that represent the organization's best approach to date. Challenger approaches are then developed that differ from the champion in some measurable and defined way and, therefore, produce different results. They might be better or worse, but only by testing challengers with real transactions in a live environment can you make this determination. A decision service is configured to push a small percentage of transactions through each challenger approach and push the majority through the champion. Results from these different approaches can then be measured and compared over time. If a challenger does better than the champion, it can be made the new champion, and the process of identifying and testing new challengers is repeated to continue improving the decision.

Figure 7.3 shows the advantage of considering several approaches in parallel. If you have a current approach and a target but unknown, optimal approach, your objective is to move toward the optimal approach over time. With a single current approach, you gain experience in only a limited area, so you can move toward the optimal approach only in that area of experience. Therefore, you might have to make many attempts at an approach before you reach the optimal one. When seeing the full impact of an action could take months or years, this approach might be too slow to be acceptable. In contrast, if a number of challenger approaches are defined, you increase the "decision space" considered dramatically and can move toward the optimal approach more quickly. This increased speed of improvement is enhanced by champion/challenger's more systematic approach to comparing approaches.

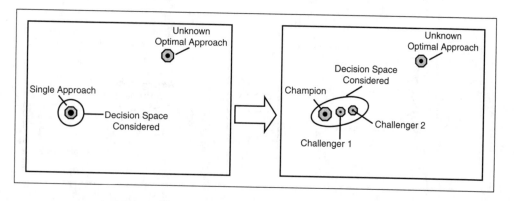

**Figure 7.3** **Comparing the opportunity for optimizing a decision rapidly with a single strategy and multiple challengers** *©Fair Isaac Corporation, reproduced with permission*

## Experimental Design

Experimental design is a mature and extremely successful science dating back to R. A. Fisher's pioneering work in the 1930s.[1] It's designed to generate efficient experiments that yield results suitable for accurate analysis, including understanding causes of variation, predicting how changes in operating conditions would influence the outcome, and determining the possibility of optimization to achieve a desired outcome.

To apply this technique to adaptive control, you must design challengers in a systematic way. By adding a pair of challenger strategies, you gain experience in a wider range of decision strategies. However, you might not pick the best areas for challengers. You might choose to vary aspects of the strategy that aren't the most important. Even so, you're likely to move toward the optimal strategy in fewer steps. Good design for challengers is critical, however.

Figure 7.4 shows a danger with poorly defined challengers: The best challenger (Challenger 2) becomes the new champion, but there's no guarantee it represents a move *directly* toward the optimal approach. In this case, it implies improvement in a direction that will result in new, less optimal challengers. Good challenger design involves constant movement toward the optimal approach.

---

[1] Ronald A. Fisher, *Design of Experiments*, 9th Edition, Macmillan Pub. Co., 1971.

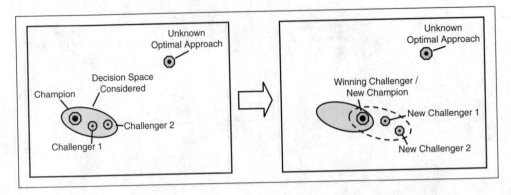

**Figure 7.4    Poorly designed challengers might not move toward the optimal approach quickly or directly** *©Fair Isaac Corporation, reproduced with permission*

In contrast, if you do a good job of designing challenger strategies (by using good experimental design), you can expand challengers around your champion in a way that maximizes the likelihood of reaching an optimal strategy quickly. This method requires careful design and specific control over your challengers so that you can infer likely results for challengers and cover a wide range of variations. Figure 7.5 shows how to model a range of challengers around the current champion by using experimental design to ensure that the new champion moves directly and rapidly toward the optimal approach.

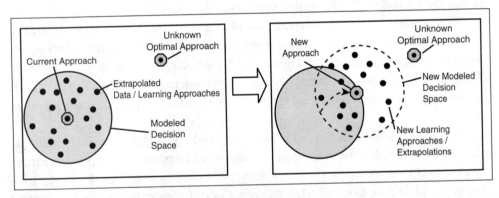

**Figure 7.5    Experimental design of challenger strategies allows you to find the optimal approach quickly** *©Fair Isaac Corporation, reproduced with permission*

Experimental design requires having a general idea of the predictive models used in the decision and plausible ranges for control factors. Data is then collected in the most efficient manner to provide sufficient coverage of potential approaches throughout the decision's operating range so that the model yields accurate predictions and optimization results. Prior experience and theoretical insight into a problem help with the task of designing the best experiments for efficient, systematic data acquisition. When experiments are designed correctly, the number of challengers or experiments you need is minimized.

## Optimization Techniques

Optimization contrasts with a rules-based or case-based approach, in which you model the problem as a set of rules specifying the actions to take when certain conditions are satisfied. Optimization includes fixed constraints (often prioritized) and degrees of preference. The goal for optimization engines tends to be finding the best among many possible solutions. Optimization involves these components:

- **Choices**—A decision must be made, and multiple choices are possible.
- **Constraints**—Not all decisions are acceptable; some limits can't be exceeded (such as the maximum number of calls that can be made), and some thresholds must be met and preferably exceeded (such as profit for a marketing campaign).
- **Target function**—Not all decisions are equal, and a measurable target differentiates between good and less-good decisions.
- **Trade-offs**—A number of alternative goals must be weighed against one another to find the optimal balance between them.
- **Data**—Information is required to create target measurements, establish limits, and understand relationships.

A suitable problem for an optimization engine would be "Given certain facts about demand elasticity, available supply, and competitors' pricing, what offering price for a commodity would be likely to generate the highest profit?" Another suitable problem is "Given that I'm willing to trade four percent of the anticipated profit for the increased customer satisfaction to be derived from same-day delivery time can be reduced, which merchant would be the optimal source for a line item?"

The use of optimization models is well established. Using these models in real-time systems and using optimization and simulation technology and methods to manage trade-offs in predictive models and generate optimal business rules are fairly advanced and recent concepts, however. In this context, optimization and simulation share a vision of constant improvement in a decision service's behavior.

**Rules Versus Optimization**   *When a rule system is used, the essence of the decision comes from outside the rule system. Someone has to know the rules; the rule engine then implements the rules mechanically but inexpensively (in terms of implementation cost) and safely.*

*When an optimization engine is used, the essence of the decision comes from inside the optimization engine. Business personnel need only define the problem domain and goals, and developers need only translate those definitions into software objects. The optimization engine is then turned loose to perform its mathematics (which might look like magic) and produce its recommendations. The optimization engine is more expensive (in terms of resources used) and less simple and safe to implement in a production system.*

*Optimization and related simulation techniques can be used to develop the right set of rules. This combination of approaches balances the strengths of an optimization engine to find the optimal solution with the implementation and ease of explanation of business rules.*

In optimization, variables represent decisions (choices), and constraints (limits) are relationships between variables. Each constraint can also be an algorithm that reduces variables' domains. The model responds to changes in variables, propagates these changes to other variables, and has a procedure that can backtrack to find solutions in a group of possible solutions (called the "search space").

Optimization techniques tend to find the best solution among many possible solutions, which makes them useful for generating such things as counteroffers and product configurations in which being as close as possible to the optimal solution is valuable. Optimization engines are based on mathematical algorithms with support for forward-looking heuristics, backtracking, and partial solution building.

What's critical is that a decision isn't formulated in advance; it's derived by applying a mathematical algorithm to a specified model, constraints, and objectives. Optimization engines are better suited when you need to search a large and complex set of solutions efficiently, especially when the steps for generating a solution can't be expressed easily. To solve a specific problem, you need to select the appropriate algorithm from among the available ones.

Constraints are more compact than rules, more easily maintained, and adapted for problems in which you need to describe a solution's structure instead of how it's derived. Constraints are nondirectional, and the problem is expressed as a feasible domain with the benefit of reducing the search space efficiently. Some constraints are "soft" and add preferences. Constraint propagation ensures that impossible values are eliminated from

---

### Operations Research

Operations research (OR) uses mathematical modeling, statistics, and algorithms to tackle complex real-world problems and try to come up with a best possible solution scientifically. OR focuses on a complete system and works toward specific goals for improvement within defined constraints. OR and EDM overlap a lot in techniques and tools, especially between OR and EDM's analytic aspects.

EDM differs from OR in its focus on ongoing management of decisions, not just point-in-time solutions, and in embedding analytic insight into operational systems driven by business rules. Organizations already using OR will find taking advantage of that experience for EDM projects easy.

---

variable domains. By using an appropriate search procedure, you can explore possible solutions efficiently and do the following

- Complete a partial solution.
- Generate a good first feasible solution.
- Generate a number of feasible solutions.

**Which Techniques to Use**   *Both rules and optimization have practical limits. Given these limits, one technology is generally favored over another, although there's a gray area where either might apply. A key characteristic is the decision alternative size. When the number of alternatives in a decision is high, optimization tends to be more useful.*

*For example, suppose you're trying to control the temperature on a milk evaporator. The temperature is represented by a real number, with infinite (or a very high number of) alternatives during the period of time the evaporator is used. Using rules to make the decision might be prohibitively complex, but optimization would be fairly easy.*

*The complexity of a decision that lends itself to optimization might also come from a need to consider many decisions as a set, even though each decision has only a few alternatives. Conversely, a complex problem might not lend itself to optimization if no mathematical model can be constructed to measure the decision's impact.*

## Decision Models

Decision models, introduced in Chapter 4, "Core Concepts," show the underlying dynamics of expected outcomes, given a set of different actions. For instance, they show the forecasted profit if you take action A, B, or C. This information then feeds an optimization algorithm, which solves for the best action given your constraints. Models can contain inputs (data or the results of predictive models), actions that must be selected, and reactions. These reactions are chained together to show the impact on an objective. Each relationship is described mathematically; some are simply proportional or inversely proportional links, and others are more complex formulas.

Decision models can be simple. For example, if the criterion to buy a pencil is strictly lowest price, no computation is required to evaluate the decision. This decision model is simple, with no predictions (prices for a set of pencil products), and the optimization algorithm is simply to find the lowest price. Bigger, more complex problems require predictive models to reduce uncertainty in variables and increase precision. For analytic modelers, building a decision model of this kind is complex and rather advanced.

Figure 7.6 shows an example of a moderately complex decision model. It shows how different measures and models (utilization, behavior score) affect a credit line increase that in turn influences factors such as attrition, revenue, bad debt, and ultimately profit. The inputs on the left have an effect on the credit line increase offered and on actions and reactions, such as attrition and revenue. For instance, the current use of a credit card is one of the factors influencing the additional credit line offered and the likelihood of attrition. Both relationships need to be modeled by using historical data and expert judgment. Similarly, attrition has an impact on revenue and loss. Clearly, revenue and loss combine to determine profit. Building this kind of model and deriving relationships between the elements make it possible to simulate and optimize the decision.

## Efficient Frontier

A single objective is unusual for optimization problems; more commonly, they have several conflicting objectives. Optimizing in these circumstances requires managing trade-offs between objectives effectively. Explicit management of trade-offs is limited, however, because a trade-off might change in some circumstances (the cost you're willing to incur to acquire 1,000 more customers might well be different if it moves you from 1,000 to 2,000 rather than from 9,000 to 10,000, for instance), and objectives might influence each other if they interact.

### Large U.S. Retail Bank: Improve Retention

#### Old Way

The bank analyzed data each month to create a set of rules for retention offers. This largely subjective approach was used to indicate what each agent did in response to a particular retention-related call. Those doing analysis couldn't try what-if scenarios, and managing trade-offs between profitability and attrition was hard. Balancing transactions with portfolio-level constraints on resources, such as the amount of new credit available or the overall tolerance for bad debt, was also difficult.

#### EDM Way

A decision model was developed that included the factors, actions, and reactions in the retention process. Overall constraints were applied to the model, and simulation was used to find the optimal decision for each customer, given these overall constraints. Business users could use what-if analysis to understand the trade-offs in retaining customers who might not be immediately profitable, for instance. The best set of outcomes for the current constraints can be established, and optimal rules can be generated.

#### Benefits

- Retention offer acceptance rate increased by 33 percent.
- Voluntary attrition was reduced by 13 percent.
- Profitability of retained accounts increased.

An **efficient frontier** is the set of best outcomes given the values being traded off between objectives. In Figure 7.7, for instance, you're trading off increases in projected profit per account against a projected increase in losses. The efficient frontier in this example represents the largest gain in profit per account possible for a given change in losses. An organization can maximize its return by operating anywhere along the efficient frontier. Business users must choose where to operate. In this case, what level of additional losses they would tolerate to gain additional profit per account? Operating below the efficient frontier implies a suboptimal set of decisions.

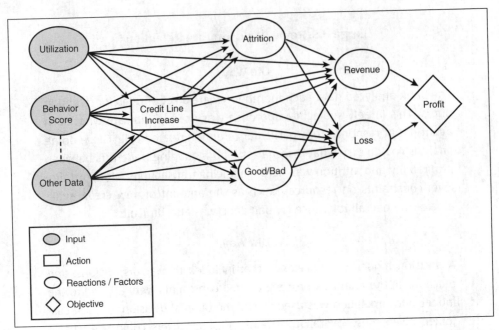

**Figure 7.6    A mathematical model of trade-offs between analytic models and constraints**
©*Fair Isaac Corporation, reproduced with permission*

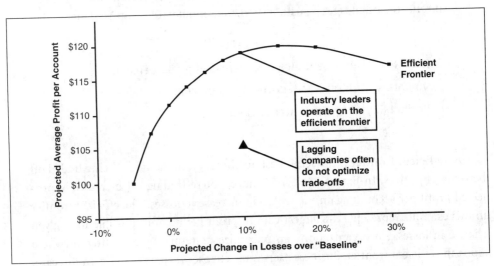

**Figure 7.7    An efficient frontier between profit per account and increased losses.**

The purpose of decision modeling, optimization, and simulation at the portfolio level—within a set of similar decisions—is to find the efficient frontier and establish the rules for a decision that enable the organization to operate on it.

## Business Simulation

In **business simulation,** business users run multiple scenarios through a simulation engine to see how different assumptions, market conditions, or constraints affect the recommended outcome. This simulation uses a model of the business, such as a decision model, but simplifies the interface to the model so that business users can use it. Simulation is often combined with optimization to find a set of optimal solutions.

Business simulation can be conducted without a complex mathematical model of the underlying business just to evaluate results from different sets of rules. It can also be used with models that don't require optimization, when a simple model of the decision can be used to simulate the value of different approaches. Your ability to derive *optimal* solutions is affected, however, unless you have both a simulation environment and a robust mathematical model. The better the model of the underlying business, the more realistic the simulation is.

Simulation is particularly useful when decisions must be considered as a set to manage them effectively. Suitable problems might include how to allocate a finite amount of new credit to an existing customer portfolio to maximize profit, given an acceptable level of risk, or how to allocate a finite inventory of retention offers to maximize profitable retention.

## Adaptive Control Technology

Figure 7.8 shows the technology components necessary for adaptive control and decision optimization. The production environment needs to support deploying multiple challenger approaches to the existing champion, business users need access to simulation tools, and analytic modelers must be able to design decision models.

The five main areas of technology to consider in adaptive control are explained in the following sections: modeling tools, an optimization engine or solver, a suitable production environment, a suitable simulation/ testing environment, and business user tools to control experimentation, testing, and analysis.

### Modeling Tools

With modeling tools, you can define optimization and simulation problems in terms of decision models or linear/nonlinear regression models. Setting up and verifying a model are complex tasks for experts, and modeling tools are usually robust but designed for mathematically sophisticated users. Modeling tools are used to construct predictive models and models to show the impact of actions (action-effect models) and to set up optimization and decision models. They are similar to the tools used to build predictive models, described in Chapter 5, "Data and Analytics," but they focus on optimization problems. They aren't required for developing basic adaptive control but are essential for adding optimization and simulation.

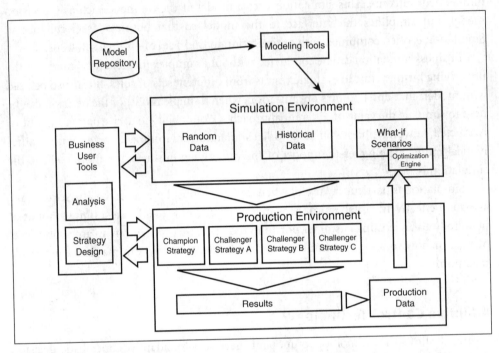

**Figure 7.8    Elements of adaptive control technology** ©*Fair Isaac Corporation, reproduced with permission*

### Optimization Engine or Solver

An **optimization engine** is a software library that implements optimization algorithms, which are based on mathematical optimization. It computes or searches for the best solution to maximize an objective (such as profit), typically within specific constraints. There are different optimization algorithms for specific problem structures or types.

> **Using Inline Solvers**    *Using optimization technology to generate an optimal set of business rules and implementing those rules in real time is one way to get real-time, optimized decisions. Deploying solvers directly into an operational system is possible, however. In this case, the solver engine is run not offline, but inline with the rest of the application, which also provides optimization in real time.*

*Organizations shouldn't underestimate the risks and issues in running an inline solver engine in an operational system, however. Solving a linear or nonlinear programming problem during a transaction imposes a high processing cost and could cause a failed transaction unless it's done right. Offline optimization and simulation offer lower-risk, high-value options. Offline analysis also allows more sophisticated trade-off analysis of decisions.*

---

### Linear and Nonlinear Programming

Optimization using forms of linear and nonlinear programming (LP and NLP) builds an optimal solution for a problem defined in terms of what you can change, such as how much product to make, and limits (constraints) on your decisions, such as speed and maximum payload.

This optimization process tries to produce decisions that make better use of resources by increasing production with the same resources, for instance. Optimization can be used to increase business revenue or reduce costs. It gives you insight into situations where decisions are involved, can be used to benchmark performance, and provides information about costs of limitations and implied costs of policy decisions or arbitrary rules. An optimization model can be used for what-if and sensitivity analysis.

Optimization can be used offline to generate rules in much the same way as data mining, or it can be used in an operational system to provide answers or actions that can be enforced by using rules.

---

## Production Environment

The production environment must allow a decision service to have its current or champion approach as well as a number of potentially better strategies—challengers. Selecting some transactions randomly and running them through a challenger approach should be possible, instead of running them through the rules and analytics currently defined as the champion.

You need to capture both immediate and long-term results in a way that lets you know which decisions were made in which way (champion versus challenger) when you begin analysis. Performance management dashboards and key performance indicators need to show the overall average for all approaches, the champion's results, and the challenger results when the measures for them differ. Therefore, if a challenger approach sacrifices retention for profitability by dropping unprofitable customers more aggressively, measurement reports and dashboards showing retention need to show the results appropriately so that they don't mislead those managing the decision.

In general, only a small percentage of decisions are made with one of the challenger strategies; more than 90 percent are likely to be made with the champion.

### Simulation/Testing Environment

You need a simulation/testing environment with access to both historical data and randomly generated data. For example, if you can analyze customers rejected in the past to predict what they might have looked like as customers, this kind of data can be useful. If you change your customer acquisition or origination strategy, you can then do some analysis to see how this change might affect your customer base. In this simulation environment, you need to be able to test how different rules and analytics could affect results in various what-if scenarios. This procedure might be simple, such as running a test decision service against the data and seeing what results you get, or complex, such as running formal simulation and optimization technologies.

### Tools for Business Users

Business users, those who understand how the business operates and what its measures and objectives are, must be able to interact with production and simulation/testing environments and analyze the results of both production challengers and simulations. They should be able to design and run simulations for new scenarios and be able to design new challengers and push them to the IT department for final testing and production deployment. These tasks require a combination of reporting and dashboard technology with rule management applications.

> **Note**   *Business users who already have dashboards and other analysis tools might think this type of adaptive control infrastructure is overkill. After all, they can examine their results to determine what aspects of a decision are working well and which aren't and then redesign the decision to move closer to the optimal decision. This method might work for less complex situations, but it's not repeatable or rigorous. For important decisions, an adaptive control infrastructure yields good dividends.*

## The Adaptive Control Process

The tasks in adaptive control are straightforward, as shown in Figure 7.9. You must design the environment for champion/challenger testing, design your experiments or challengers effectively, capture data about your results, and perform ongoing decision analysis. To move toward optimization, you must define an optimization model that's deployed directly or used to power a simulation. This simulation can then tune the model until it produces an optimal set of rules, given the constraints, for a certain situation.

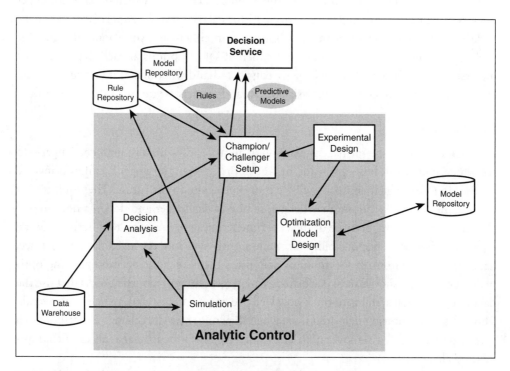

**Figure 7.9    Adaptive control in an EDM architecture**

### Champion/Challenger Setup

Each decision service needs a different, albeit similar, champion/challenger setup. Some transactions are sensitive, so you'll probably pass only a few transactions to a single carefully designed challenger. Others might not have a clear champion, at least at first, so you should spread the transactions evenly among several different challengers.

Over time, an organization adopting EDM should develop a standard champion/challenger infrastructure, but initially each decision service is likely to have its own arrangements. You must make sure you can replace the champion strategy with a challenger and add and remove challengers without affecting the decision service. The decision service must also record the approach used for each transaction, either as part of the transaction or separately. All this infrastructure must be established before useful adaptive control can take place.

### Experimental Design

With some decision services, you have little or no experience on which to base challenger designs. With others, you might have strong historical data or vivid experiences that make it clear what kinds of changes make a difference. In either case, you should design your challenger strategy to test a sensible and coherent set of options at each step. You must understand why each challenger is being considered and what makes it different, so you should perform as much static analysis of rules and models as you can.

### Decision Analysis

**Decision analysis** is the formal comparison of approaches—champion or challenger—to see which ones work best, given the organization's current strategy. It can also involve analysis to assess which approach will be more successful in the future. The result of this analysis might be to promote a challenger, remove a challenger and design a new one, or change the underlying premise of the experimental design. Ensuring that business users, especially those with responsibility for maintaining rules in a deployed decision service, have the right environment to monitor data helps them keep the decision running optimally. These users should have performance management and reporting tools that use the data in operational systems to track how well processes and systems are behaving overall. This kind of monitoring helps them see when they might need to change a threshold in a rule or perhaps add or remove rules. The results feed into the formal analysis of champions and challengers.

> **Informal Decision Analysis**   *Many decision services, especially those containing many rules and few models, can be tuned by using a less formal process. Business users with access to their regular dashboards and reports might have enough of a view into how well rules are performing that they can make changes to the rules based only on these reports.*

You can compare actual results with predicted results or the results of two alternatives. These comparisons can be made at a specific point or over a more extended period. Statistical analysis and standard reporting tools are used to understand how well deployed rules and models are working, see how champions and challengers compare, and formulate strategies for improvement. Figure 7.10 shows an example of this kind of analysis—swapset analysis. The two approaches are compared, and the number of transactions or customers that move from one treatment segment to another are documented. In this case, many customers who were previously "aggressively defended" are now simply "maintained."

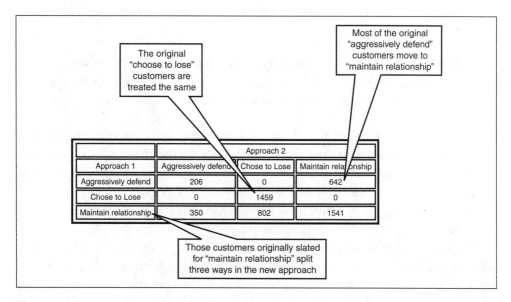

The original "choose to lose" customers are treated the same

Most of the original "aggressively defend" customers move to "maintain relationship"

| Approach 1 | Approach 2 | | |
|---|---|---|---|
| | Aggressively defend | Chose to Lose | Maintain relationship |
| Aggressively defend | 206 | 0 | 642 |
| Chose to Lose | 0 | 1459 | 0 |
| Maintain relationship | 350 | 802 | 1541 |

Those customers originally slated for "maintain relationship" split three ways in the new approach

**Figure 7.10    A swapset analysis showing change in treatment of customers with different approaches**

### Optimization Model Design

Designing an optimization model can be difficult, but it's essential if optimization and simulation are to yield useful results. You must identify the attributes and predictive models that are relevant to the decision and then determine the influence they have on each other. In other words, an increase in the value of this implies what for the value of that? Typically, each link has a mathematical description—a formula that shows how one value varies with another. You can test the model with historical data and develop it until it generates results that match your data. At this point, you should have an LP or NLP model, a decision model, or an influence diagram that describes the mathematical relationships affecting your decision. You'll probably also have constraints on possible solutions, such as resources or time limits .

## Simulation

The next step is to simulate your data—a sample or the complete data set—which involves running the model against each record to see what the model implies for that record. Typically, you try to maximize an outcome such as revenue or profit by assigning actions to each record based on your decision model. The simulation tests scenarios against each record, using the decision model, and identifies the most successful. At the end of this process, you have a set of actions for your records that result in the best possible outcomes.

> **Simulation of Rules** *Running simulations and developing scenarios with less sophisticated models is possible. The advantage of a formal model is that the simulation handles interactions between models and rules more effectively.*

In reality, the optimal solution is rarely useful. Most decisions are constrained by resource availability or because another value (besides the one for which the decision is being optimized) must stay in a certain range. For instance, you might try to maximize profit while retaining a minimum number of customers, which could reduce your theoretical profit by forcing you to retain some unprofitable customers. In fact, most situations have a number of potentially conflicting constraints.

Tuning and refinement involve running and rerunning a simulation under slightly different circumstances to see which constraints might be worth changing, such as accepting more risk. The process is finished when you have the best possible outcome given your current constraints (including any changes to constraints justified by the simulation) or when you have the best possible outcome for a set of possible *future* constraints. In this second situation, you can see what actions work best in a theoretical situation and develop responses to what-if scenarios in advance.

In many situations, you simulate a sample rather than a complete set of records. To apply your optimal actions to records not in your sample or new records created after running your simulation, you need to turn action assignments into rules. You can do this easily by using data-mining techniques to segment records so that each segment has the same assigned action. The rules for this segmentation can then be deployed or stored for use in the future. Figure 7.11 shows the cycle for adaptive control after you have moved to using decision optimization and simulation. New data is used to find new optimal approaches, which are then deployed to the adaptive control infrastructure and adopted if the results are satisfactory. New decisions generate new data, new actions, and new reactions, which all feed back into further modeling and optimization.

**Actions or Rules**

At the end of optimization and simulation, you have an optimal set of actions to take for your input data. If the data is complete—you used all your orders or customers, for instance—and you don't need to create actions for unknown circumstances, you might be able to generate actions directly. For instance, you can create a list of optimal production sequences or retention offers that cover every possible situation.

Alternatively, you might want to use your optimal outcomes to control situations you didn't consider as inputs. In this case, you want to develop rules that match your actions, because these rules can be injected into your decision services, and then handle transactions you didn't model. You might also choose to convert to rules so that the resulting decisions in your operational environment can be interpreted.

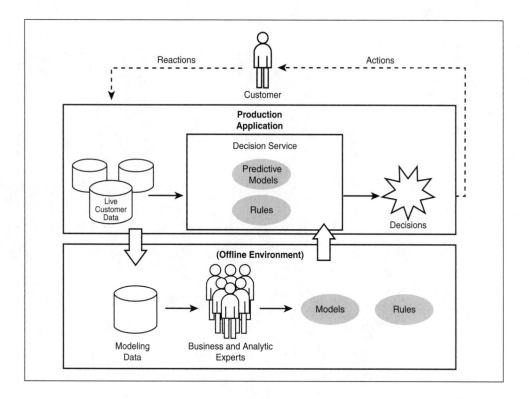

**Figure 7.11    The adaptive control cycle when using decision optimization and simulation**

Whether you use champion/challenger testing for adaptive control or have developed formal models for deriving optimal decision approaches, you must be able to constantly improve your decisions. As you will see in Chapter 9, "Getting There from Here," these technologies and approaches are adopted incrementally. Before you adopt them, however, you should consider your general state of readiness, as covered in Chapter 8, "Readiness Assessment."

---

**The EDM Wiki**

You can find more information on adaptive control and optimization and simulation technology in the EDM wiki at www.smartenoughsystems.com.

---

# CHAPTER EIGHT

# Readiness Assessment

**B**efore adopting enterprise decision management, having a sense of your organization's readiness is important. IT and business departments' ability to collaborate, the quality of data and how well you understand it, analytic strength, willingness to change, and a focus on operations matter and should be assessed. You might find decision yield particularly useful as a tool for understanding your strength in specific decisions.

## Overview of Readiness Assessment

How can you tell whether your organization is ready for EDM? If it is, how do you figure out an effective approach for adopting it? If it isn't, what can you do to start laying the groundwork for adopting EDM? Many characteristics of an organization might identify it as a good or poor candidate for EDM, but none of them prevents progress. Each organization needs to understand the different areas of readiness and decide how to leverage what it does well and mitigate what it does poorly. The five key areas of readiness are

- Business and IT collaboration
- Data readiness
- Analytic understanding
- Willingness to change
- Management focus on operations

Each section of this chapter has a checklist designed to help you measure your organization's readiness. These checklists have a number of criteria for assessing readiness and some possible actions to take if you think you aren't ready.

## Business and IT Collaboration

Decision services are perhaps the point where IT and business users come together most closely. Business decisions are, by their nature, intensely important to business users and management. These decisions are often regulated in ways only certain businesspeople understand. They must conform to policies business users write, and they must take into account fluctuations in the market—small and large, long-term and rapid. Insight from data, another key ingredient in decision services, also depends heavily on the business context. No predictive model is worthwhile if it doesn't predict an outcome of interest to the business at a level of accuracy useful to the business and early enough for some business response.

Decision services must also manipulate corporate data, integrate with high-volume systems, and be on the critical path for applications that interact with customers. IT departments have invested a lot of time and money in making sure applications meet performance and scalability requirements, privacy rules, and so on.

Building effective decision services, therefore, requires business and IT to collaborate more than ever. Although the technologies needed for EDM address collaboration, at least in part, this issue still has a cultural aspect. Some business departments simply don't trust IT departments, and some IT departments return this suspicion. Part of any plan to move to EDM must be resolving this issue.

One possible approach is to pair business analysts and programmers (similar to pairing programming approaches) and have them work on the same problem. With a rules-based approach that allows both to understand the core logic being coded, this pairing can be effective. Even if you don't go quite this far, keeping business analysts and users involved in the design process is important. It's easy to design a service that business users can't maintain, even if that was the intent. The way programmers and business users or analysts look at a problem is often very different.

Table 8.1 lists five areas in which you should assess your readiness in terms of business and IT collaboration, along with actions you can take where you find issues.

## Data Readiness

To derive insight from data, you must have data available first. The accuracy, completeness, and integration of the data you have determine the quality of insight you can derive. Building predictive analytic models from inaccurate data or mining inaccurate data for business rules could be fatal, because the results build on inaccuracies in the data and produce inaccurate predictions.

**Table 8.1    Checklist for Business and IT Collaboration Readiness**

| Readiness Criterion | Actions |
| --- | --- |
| Trust between business and IT | If there's a lack of trust between these departments, you must take specific, deliberate steps to rebuild it. Rebuilding trust is best done as part of a small initial rules project. |
| Proof for collaboration | If there's proof that collaboration results in better systems or more productive projects, you need to emphasize it. Using a previously successful group for the first project also helps. |
| Business users' involvement in systems development | Ensuring that business users have management practices that allow and reward them for participation helps keep them involved. Most business users know they need to participate in systems development that affects them, but they often lack time in their schedules and management support to do so. You need to work with management and perhaps human resources to address this problem. |
| Work habits | When business users are assigned to IT projects, how do they work with IT staff? Would pairing a business user with a programmer work? Can business and IT resources be located in the same place? |
| Maintenance projects | How maintenance work is specified for systems and handled by IT is important. If the approach is adversarial, with IT defending the system and business users complaining, you need to try a different approach. In particular, business users must become part of the maintenance-budgeting process. |

You can get analytic insight from accurate data, even if it's limited in scope or completeness. Clearly, however, the more complete the data, the more robust your analytic models are likely to be. Similarly, customer-based data provides more opportunities for interesting analytics than account-level data does.

Projects to improve data quality and completeness are, therefore, synergistic with EDM projects. By focusing data integration and quality efforts on projects for which analytics are being developed, you can apply resources more effectively. Knowing what kind of insight you need can help prevent wasted effort by focusing on areas where more or better data means better business results.

Constantly evaluating data that can help make a decision more effectively should become part of the organization's culture. This cultural change might result in projects to enhance data capture, capture new information about customers or products, or find data outside the organization. Some organizations are sophisticated consumers of external data, such as geographic data, consumer data, or demographic/census data. Others are not. This kind of external data, if it's integrated with internal records and applied to specific problems, can improve analytic models. As EDM projects progress, teams should periodically ask whether external data is available to improve the quality of insight or derive new insight. Although privacy issues—such as ensuring that individual consumers' social security numbers cannot be compromised—must be considered, external data can enrich analytic models.

Table 8.2 lists five areas in which you should assess your readiness for EDM in terms of data, along with actions you can take where you find issues.

## Analytic Understanding

Delivering EDM solutions, especially more advanced ones, requires analytic skills. You should consider several aspects of readiness to determine whether your organization has these analytic skills.

Some organizations lack the necessary analytic skills. Organizations without a history of analyzing data and using mathematical models are unlikely to have any analytical staff. Although you can build a department of people with these skills, starting by hiring external consultants with these skills is probably easier. Fortunately, many companies offer services for turning data into analytic models. For EDM projects, you should conduct due diligence to ensure that an analytic provider can deliver a deployable analytic model suitable for use in a decision service, not just develop a report explaining the model. Over time, as analytic models prove their value, hiring in-house analysts could be worthwhile. If you lack analytic skills in house, the first few projects should be focused on rules (regulations, policies, expert judgment) rather than data-driven insight.

Some companies have analytic skills but find them focused on reporting and analysis—business intelligence (BI) analytics. Although these skills are useful in an EDM context, a change in focus and an upgrading of skills are required. People who can use a regression analysis tool to understand data trends have many of the skills for building a

**Table 8.2    Checklist for Data Readiness**

| Readiness Criterion | Actions |
| --- | --- |
| Data management | Organizations without formal data management processes find it hard to build good models without introducing a more formal approach. Although EDM shouldn't be delayed during this process, it should be used initially on projects with more of a rules focus. |
| Data sourcing | A lack of external data might show a general lack of focus on finding new data sources to solve problems. Developing a review procedure to consider what data would be useful for a project, instead of just what's available, can help with this problem. |
| Reporting | How are new reports requested? If the focus is on the decision being made with them, EDM is easier to adopt than if the focus is on content only. Reviewing report requests to find out what decisions are influenced by these reports can identify opportunities for EDM. |
| Metadata | Managing metadata improves model building and provides an infrastructure for considering rules as metadata. Organizations already making progress in managing metadata and semantic information find adopting EDM easier. |
| Customer data integration (CDI) and master data management (MDM) | Projects to improve CDI and MDM materially improve the quality of models you develop and offer new opportunities for models. |

predictive model that uses regression analysis, but they need to learn how to apply them differently. If you have a BI competency center or other concentration of analysts, you might find suitable people to work with you on EDM projects, but you might not. Either way, make sure you involve these analysts early in a project so that they can see how upgrading their skills and changing their focus help produce a better ROI from business intelligence and data warehouse investments.

The last option is a center of modeling excellence in the organization with a narrow focus, such as a group focused on risk modeling or an actuarial group. These groups are ideal resources for projects dealing with their specialty, but getting access to them for projects in other areas could prove difficult. Even if they can participate, they might have problems applying their skills to operational systems and new domains. On the plus side, you should be able to use them as proof of the value of modeling and analytics, which makes hiring or contracting with the necessary resources easier.

In general, unless you have an existing group developing models for your domain area, you'll probably need to look for outside help at first. If the internal or external analysts you use aren't used to the EDM approach and expect to deliver a report describing a model rather than work with you to deploy a model into a decision service, you have a change management task ahead of you. Fortunately, the data-mining/analytic-modeling community is increasingly aware that a model is no good unless you deploy it.

Table 8.3 lists four areas of analytic readiness that you should assess, along with actions you can take where you find issues.

**Table 8.3    Checklist for Analytic Understanding Readiness**

| Readiness Criterion | Actions |
| --- | --- |
| BI competency center | If the organization hasn't yet established a BI competency center, a new group is necessary to "store" the analytic expertise being developed. If one does exist, it needs to be adapted, but this process is less painful. Although most sophisticated organizations have a centralized analytic group, it's more effect than cause, so don't plan on creating a single central group until you have demonstrated success in several areas. |
| Data-mining experience | Organizations already using data-mining techniques to extract value from their data find adopting EDM's analytic component easier. A first project focus should be wrapping an EDM approach around existing data-mining tools and processes. |
| Operations research (OR) or decision science group | Organizations with an OR, or a decision science group, should work with these groups to use their experience in EDM projects. Their skills and existing knowledge of the organization's operations are invaluable. |
| Risk or other modeling group | Organizations with a narrowly focused analytic group should work with this group and consider selecting EDM projects within its scope of experience. |

## Willingness to Change

Automating operational decisions can cause organizational change. Sometimes roles change—people go from making many simple decisions to considering the overall patterns of decisions. For example, underwriters might go from spending most of their time reviewing policies to spending most of their time analyzing agents' success. Advertising managers might spend more time on account management than on calculating ad prices.

This change in roles means some people go from being good at their jobs to being less good, and vice versa. Someone who was adept at processing many simple transactions rapidly could find this skill less in demand, and people able to use their knowledge to assess overall trends and effectiveness find this skill more useful. You must explain this new focus to employees and manage the implications.

If you don't plan staff reductions, you need to reassure people that the computer won't replace them. If staff reductions are expected, you have to manage this change. Organizations that have a hard time managing this kind of change might want to start with projects that automate decisions not made at all in the past (adding a cross-sell engine, for example) or that have been automated poorly (a generic cross-sell embedded in the Web site, for example).

If the proposed decision service will provide decisions employees must pass on to customers, such as a call center representative using a pricing engine, employees might be reluctant to trust the computer's judgment, especially if bonuses or reviews are tied to the decision's effectiveness. One way to manage this reluctance is to implement the new decision service incrementally and make it available to only a small group (those more willing to change) to show it works. You can also use retrospective analysis to show how much more successful the organization would have been if employees had used the new service rather than the old subjective process. If you can tie this analysis to statements such as "You would have made X more money," so much the better. Nothing succeeds like success, so try to demonstrate success with a few employees or show that the new approach would have been more successful than the existing one. Be prepared for initial concern no matter what you do; you'll see a spike in complaints or appeals at first, but if the decisions are sound, negative responses will be reduced.

Customers getting automated decisions might be glad they can do more in a self-service way but will probably feel aggrieved if they don't get what they want because "the computer said so." Managing this outcome requires decision services that explain decisions at least to staff, if not to customers. Decisions that say "No, but …" rather than just "no" also do better. For instance, "You can't have that product, but you can have this one" works better than "You can't have that product."

Be sure to have your legal department review any decisions covered by regulations or that have resulted in lawsuits because of employee bias. Making sure in advance that the rules and analytics you use can be defended is easier than dealing with lawsuits. Again, introducing decisions incrementally and with explanation, especially when the decision is important to customers (loan approval is, cross-sell is not), is important and should be planned for.

Finally, beware of counterproductive incentives. Sometimes the sophistication possible in an EDM solution overwhelms the performance and reward structure. For example, your marketing department might have objectives for volume and response rate. A decision service that improves the response rate dramatically could reduce the volume of offers mailed, which could cause people to miss bonuses and, therefore, make them unwilling to use the decision service. When decision services affect employees' behavior, simulate the impact you hope for from the decision service and see whether it increases or decreases their pay. If they lose out but the decision service is making decisions that are better for the organization, make sure you address this result as part of the rollout.

Table 8.4 lists five areas in which you should assess your willingness to change, along with actions you can take where you find issues.

**Table 8.4    Checklist for Readiness in Willingness to Change**

| Readiness Criterion | Actions |
| --- | --- |
| Self-service focus | Organizations already focused on helping associates self-serve find adopting EDM easier than those who find self-service difficult. If you can't let your associates do things for themselves, you're unlikely to be comfortable with automating decisions. |
| Decreased authority | EDM is about giving your information systems some decision-making authority. Yes, decisions are still controlled and managed, but some decisions are made without a person reviewing them. Organizations with a history of central control and micromanagement need to address this issue. |
| Organizational change program | Many EDM systems cause organizational realignment and job changes. If your organization lacks a program or expertise for this outcome, you need to allow extra time for EDM adoption. |
| Regulatory environment | A complex regulatory environment is often viewed as an inhibitor of change. Organizations should find EDM unique in that it's a change that can make regulatory compliance easier. Nevertheless, organizations worried about regulations need to allow for review time. |
| Incentive management program | EDM systems affect employees' and customers' behavior and will be accepted only if the incentives for those affected are positively impacted by the system's behavior. If your organization has a hard time changing incentive programs, you might want to start with a project that doesn't affect salespeople, for instance. |

## Management Focus on Operations

A key facet of EDM is its focus on operational decisions. For EDM projects to be success-ful, you need to get management to consider operational decisions as worth improving and amenable to improvement. This task might not sound hard, but it can be. Some man-agers are focused on "being strategic" or on "big picture" issues. Working on improving the small, incremental decisions that drive business operations might not seem worth their time and energy. Considering these decisions takes a certain focus, too; you have to stop thinking about macro decisions, such as "campaign design," and start thinking about micro decisions, such as "offer for this customer." Old habits can die hard and make mas-tering this new focus difficult.

One effective way to get management attention is to focus on decisions—specifically, operational decisions—that support a particular business strategy. If an organization is trying to retain more customers, for example, many operational decisions, from routing calls to retention offers to self-service pricing, might contribute to customer retention problems. Showing executives that improving these operational decisions can have a direct impact on their strategic goals is a good way to get their attention.

Perhaps even more effective is asking managers how long they think the organiza-tion's changing to respond to a new strategy would take. Given how unresponsive to change many information systems are and how often decisions are duplicated in many systems, the answer could be distressing. Focusing on automating the contributing opera-tional decisions can improve alignment of operational systems with the business and make changing and managing strategies more realistic.

Another issue that comes up when you start using analytics in decision making is management's tendency to trust instinct over data. Generally, this attitude isn't helpful for anyone trying to introduce analytically driven decisions, but you can overcome it more easily for an operational decision than for a strategic one. Think about it: Whose "gut" makes an operational decision? Not the CEO's, not senior management's, probably not even a highly trained professional's—usually frontline workers are the ones making oper-ational decisions. Why would management want these employees to make operational decisions affecting customers based on their instincts? Most managers prefer having some degree of analytic support for these kinds of decisions. Relating examples of how incor-rect operational decisions upset important customers can help focus management's attention on the need to automate and improve these decisions and overcome a reluc-tance to trust data.

In general, you do need management support, so try to focus on projects that have an impact on business areas with managers who understand the benefits of EDM.

Table 8.5 lists three areas to assess management's readiness to focus on operations and some actions you can take where you find issues.

**Table 8.5    Checklist for Management Focus on Operations Readiness**

| Readiness Criterion | Actions |
|---|---|
| Business by the numbers | Organizations in which management tries to run business by the numbers—using reporting and measurement to assess how well projects succeed and compare new strategies, for example—find adopting EDM easier than those relying on "gut" feelings. Focus first on areas of the business where data about operations is considered important for early EDM success. |
| Strategic planning in detail | Organizations with a strategic-planning process that fails to develop detailed plans, that delivers only "make it so" plans, find EDM a challenge. Those trying to delve into implementation details find it a more natural fit. |
| Constant training and improvement | EDM changes the way frontline staff work and interact with associates. Organizations committed to constant training and improvement of these workers have a ready-made infrastructure for adopting EDM. Others do not. |

---

### The EDM Wiki

You can find more information on readiness assessment in the EDM wiki at www.smartenoughsystems.com.

# CHAPTER NINE

# Getting There from Here

Organizations trying to develop the processes and infrastructure to build smart enough systems need to adopt some new technologies, adapt their existing infrastructure and processes, and manage the resulting changes. EDM can and should be adopted incrementally, and different organizations will take different paths. This chapter gives you an overview of EDM elements, how they fit together, and how they can be adopted effectively.

## Themes in EDM Adoption

EDM is an additive approach for most organizations and can be incorporated gradually into an existing business and IT structure. The approach includes activities that fall into six distinct areas:

- **Deployment infrastructure**—You must develop an enterprise architecture that incorporates decisions as a component. This activity means considering decision services part of the application portfolio, making sure the IT infrastructure allows effective deployment of decision services in online and batch systems, and adapting the software development life cycle.

- **Business rules management**—You need to adopt technologies and approaches that make managing business rules possible. You must also move from a procedural to a declarative approach to business rules and involve business users in maintaining these rules.

- **Analytic modeling**—You should consider data in terms of how it can be used to improve operational systems, which means applying new techniques and applying established techniques in new ways. It means bringing the analytic process into the system development process.

- **Adaptive control**—Your organization needs to reassess how it maintains and modifies applications. You must regard constant change and evolution in your systems as normal, and you need to adopt formal techniques to ensure that decision making continues to improve over time.

- **Optimization and simulation**—You must develop the ability to build and run models that simulate critical decisions in your organization. Simulating decisions without affecting your associates and optimizing the way you act in these decisions improve your ability to respond.

- **Organizational change**—Your business and IT departments must work out new ways to collaborate and balance responsibilities for systems development and maintenance. Similarly, analytic staff are involved in operational systems in a new way and have to become part of the IT process. All this organizational change must be managed.

In each phase of EDM adoption (explained in subsequent sections), you consider the relative importance of these areas, ranging from not relevant (the phase doesn't require much improvement in that area) or low-through high-impact (the phase causes or requires a change in that area).

---

### Note for Analytically Sophisticated Companies

Some organizations already make use of sophisticated analytics in operational systems. In particular, marketing organizations often use sophisticated models to manage promotions and design campaigns, and many banks and insurers use advanced scores and models to manage fraud and credit risk. Therefore, these companies might think some steps in the early part of the EDM adoption process seem overly simple.

Perhaps, but consider the rest of the systems in your portfolio, and you might rethink that position. Although systems that have already been integrated with sophisticated decision-making systems, such as fraud detection or automated loan origination, might not need to work through the whole process, the organization as a whole probably does. Even companies with one or two areas applying decision automation effectively aren't likely to be using EDM fully, because they're not treating decisions as an enterprise asset or applying EDM in all the places it would make a difference.

## Adopting EDM

The rest of this chapter describes the steps for going from a typical current state, with largely "dumb" systems, toward a future with smart enough systems. Not every organization needs to go through every step, and some find different rates of adoption in each area of their business. You should consider assessing your overall readiness for EDM before beginning to adopt it to help identify potential problem areas or opportunities. Some methods for assessing readiness were outlined in Chapter 8, "Readiness Assessment."

The steps build on one another, and each step focuses on how to generate a return on investment (ROI) for that step. Figure 9.1 shows you how the steps in adopting EDM interact and build on each other. The steps are divided into four main phases, each containing several projects or elements:

- Phase 1: Piecemeal approach
- Phase 2: Local decision management
- Phase 3: Expansion
- Steady state EDM

These phases are designed to enable you to adopt EDM in easy-to-digest pieces while moving toward a true enterprise-wide decision-making platform.

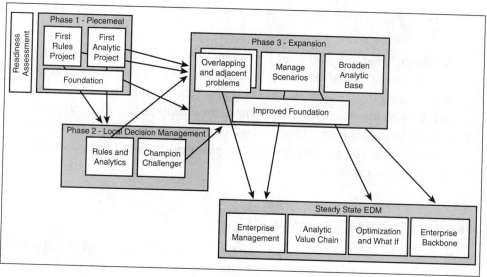

**Figure 9.1    An overview of traversing the steps in EDM**

## A Methodology for EDM

This chapter doesn't describe a formal methodology for EDM, partly because doing so would take an entire book. However, most organizations already have a method for building information systems. What matters to most IT organizations when they adopt EDM is how it affects existing approaches and what steps to take to integrate it. This information is discussed throughout this chapter, as well as in "Extending Your Software Development Life Cycle to support EDM" in Chapter 10, "EDM and the IT Department." Most business organizations adopting EDM are concerned with how to show an ROI and manage the organizational change issues that come with automating decisions. Therefore, each section includes notes on generating and proving an ROI.

Companies implementing EDM for others and organizations well on the way to developing an EDM environment should have a more formal EDM methodology that includes how to find the right opportunities, how to manage the business and technical infrastructure required, and how to bring data, rules, and analytics together in an operational environment that supports ongoing improvement.

**Decision Yield**   *Regardless of your organization's readiness characteristics and the pace of change you attempt, decision yield is strongly recommended as a way to identify high-value areas. Knowing which characteristics of a decision are worth improving, which give you a competitive advantage, and which are holding your organization back help focus resources and effort on the right problems and in the right way. See the appendix, "Decision Yield as a Way to Measure ROI," for more information.*

## Phase 1: Piecemeal Approach

For most organizations, the best place to start is with piecemeal adoption of technologies and approaches to improve specific applications or services. This piecemeal adoption usually means finding a first project involving business rules and another first project where you can use predictive analytics. This is what we call Phase 1.

In this phase, laying some foundations for EDM is also important. It's not a separate project but a set of considerations for early projects. You can carry out more than one business rule or analytic project in this phase, and as long as they remain independent of each other, an organization remains in phase 1. When you start to integrate these projects, you move into phase 2. Table 9.1 shows that business rules management and organizational change, two of the areas listed previously, are particularly important in phase 1, and analytic skills make a significant contribution.

**Table 9.1   Phase 1 Overview**

| Area | Importance | Key Issues |
| --- | --- | --- |
| Deployment infrastructure | Low | Integration of decision services |
| Business rules management | High | Structuring rules management for long-term success |
| | | Proof of business user involvement and ownership of rules |
| | | Changes to the requirements management process to include rules |
| Analytic modeling | Medium | Focusing on predicting the future, not analyzing the past |
| | | Data availability and quality |
| | | Analytic skills |
| Adaptive control | Low | |
| Optimization and simulation | Low | |
| Organizational change | High | Business and IT collaboration |
| | | Business involvement in IT projects |
| | | Analytic involvement in IT projects |

## A First Business Rules Project

Most organizations adopting EDM start by using a business rules management system (BRMS) and a business rules approach to develop specific decision services. This phase involves identifying projects suitable for business rules, architecting a suitable decision service, capturing relevant business rules, and deploying and maintaining these rules.

---

### Portfolio Assessment

Sometimes you can identify a suitable project immediately, but conducting a portfolio assessment with the following steps can be useful:

1. Identify potential decision services in your enterprise.

2. Identify enough business processes to find the high-value decision services, the experts who understand them, and the legacy systems that are affected.

3. Establish knowledge management processes to capture and engineer business rules.

4. Find the highest-value/lowest-risk decision service for your first project, potentially using decision yield as an assessment tool.

It's helpful to find the right first project and start as you mean to go on—considering decisions a corporate asset.

---

### *Identify the First Project*

Selecting a first project is important when you're implementing EDM. Without early successes, initiatives can't develop momentum. There are two ways to approach selecting a project: Review the portfolio of development and maintenance projects to find candidates, and review existing systems to see which one might repay adding a project with business rules. Regardless of the approach, you want to find systems that can show a positive ROI for using a rules-based decision service as part of the application functionality.

Business rules offer a strong ROI for systems meeting these five basic criteria, any one of which can be enough to justify using them (although a combination of criteria is even better):

- **The system has many rules**—If the system implements a business decision with hundreds or thousands of business rules, it's likely to offer a high ROI based on business rules management. For example, when a data transformation requires 100,000 accounting rules, or when processing a medical insurance claim is governed by 250,000 state and federal rules, the challenge for the system is management. Coding thousands of rules as conditional logic in a traditional programming language becomes unmanageable rapidly, with "spaghetti" code as the consequence. Checking conformance to rules and ongoing maintenance are also problems.

  A system that must implement lengthy regulations or handle huge numbers of slightly different kinds of transactions is likely to meet this criterion.

## Credit Card Issuer: Dispute Resolution

### Old Way

When a customer disputed a credit card charge, a formal process was used to follow up with the vendor before considering the dispute to be one that the credit card issuer could handle. Verifying that online disputes card members entered were truly bad charges was a time-consuming and expensive process, resulting in customer service representatives (CSRs) talking to customers when they should have been working on the problem with the vendor who made the charge. This problem increased call wait times and took CSRs away from trying to resolve legitimate disputes.

### EDM Way

A decision service initiates an interactive dialogue with customers who are entering disputes. The business rules control the questions and select them dynamically, depending on a customer's previous responses. The decision service identifies valid disputes and schedules a CSR to contact those customers. It also informs customers who don't yet have a valid dispute what their next steps should be.

### Benefits

- Charge disputes are verified automatically.
- Service representatives talk only with customers who have a valid argument.

- **The system has rules that change often**—If a system has some rules that are never stable—that change weekly, daily, or even hourly—using business rules can offer a great return. By externalizing business rules, you can manage and change them independently of the rest of the system. The atomic, declarative nature of business rules also makes it possible to change them independently of each other more easily than equivalent code.

A system is a good candidate to meet this criterion if stabilizing some requirements seems impossible because they change constantly or some component is designed to be table-driven or highly parameterized. Similarly, systems with many maintenance projects assigned or that users complain are always out of date are also likely to meet it.

- **The system has rules that are complex or interact in complex ways**—Some systems contain complex rules, in that they have many clauses and conditions, or rules that interact in a complex way, as in changing the state of a condition that has already been checked, thus forcing a reevaluation. This complexity makes coding them in traditional languages difficult and extremely error-prone. Large blocks of code match a single complex rule, and the implementation sequence of those rules must be considered in every circumstance to make sure no transaction causes unintended consequences.

  A system that has been through several design approaches because previous ones failed or has a number of failed implementations might be a candidate for this criterion. A system for which users have many notes about sequencing or how to "trick" the system might also be showing signs that its rules are too complex for the coding environment.

- **The system has rules that require domain expertise to understand**—Some systems must implement logic that requires sophisticated experience or knowledge. For instance, programmers might not be able to turn complex financial regulations into specifications without years of working in the banking industry. Sometimes rules aren't that complicated, but there's real value in having business users control them. For instance, with medical rules, such as for drug dosages or interactions, errors are more visible to medical professionals than to programmers. Using business rules brings business users into the process more fully so that they can collaborate with the IT people building the system to reduce errors and risk.

  A system in which programmers struggle to understand requirements or business users have insisted on having a full-time team member to check something might meet this criterion.

- **Business users need or want to maintain the system**—This fifth criterion combines the second, rules that change often, with the fourth, rules requiring domain expertise. Business users (who see the need for a change first) being able to make changes without IT involvement can dramatically reduce an organization's response time. Having rules configured by business users also involves business users more in maintaining the system, which reduces the IT workload.

  A system designed to replace something business users coded is a good candidate to meet this criterion. Implementing logic in the new system with rules configured by business users enables IT to have a more managed, integrated system without forcing users to give up control. The need for business user control might also be a specific requirement.

## Community Healthcare Network: Hospital Care

### Old Way

Medical decisions were made using paper-based medical records kept at the department level, so patients who moved between departments had to have copies made and sent around manually. Guidelines on care and best practices were also distributed by hand, because no electronic system existed. Enforcing these guidelines was a manual process, too. Finally, paperwork flow through some processes, such as admissions, was time consuming and confusing. All these problems created extra work, delays, and the potential for errors.

### EDM Way

An electronic medical record contains all information about a patient from all departments. Decision services support the main paperwork processes and contain business rules to ensure that work flow and paperwork are handled correctly and the right information is collected at each point, such as admissions. Another decision service operates at the point of care to implement business rules that monitor critical states in patients, lab results, and drug doses and interactions. The service provides alerts and guidance for medical professionals at the point of care. Medical professionals create and review these rules, which helps ensure their accuracy and improve their acceptance.

### Benefits

- Improved patient safety and quality of care
- Reduced costs and delays in processing paperwork

A system can exhibit more than one of these criteria, making it an even better candidate. Similarly, a system might not change that often or have that many rules, but having a moderate number of rules that change regularly could make it a good candidate. The best candidate systems are those that everyone agrees meet one or more of these criteria, but even if there's disagreement, you can use these criteria to help you find the right candidate for a first business rules project.

*Design a Decision Service*

The next step is designing a decision service into the system. It need not be an actual service in the sense of a service-oriented architecture (SOA), although it could be. Examples of implementations include the following:

- A Web service
- A COBOL subprogram
- A Windows DLL
- A .NET assembly
- A J2EE Message-Driven Bean (MDB)

You can use any of these implementations or many others. All you need is the ability to define an interface to the service (data in, data out) and encapsulate the rules in that service. An interface might mean a pair of COBOL Copybooks and a program or Web Services Description Language (WSDL) and a service implementation. You should pick the implementation that works best with the platform you have selected.

To decide how many services you might need, consider the business decisions you're automating. Each decision service should implement a single, coherent business decision. If you have some variations within the business decision, you should consider them as separate entry points to the service. The key design concerns are

- Independence, so the decision can evolve separately from the application
- Coherence, so the decision is self-contained and complete
- Statelessness, so the decision can be reused and integrated into different systems and processes

Finally, you should consider the technical implications of your preferred decision service deployment. If you need to run additional infrastructure software or connect the system to a new environment (a mainframe to a UNIX service, for example), make sure you understand these technical needs and have included them in your plans.

*Capture Rules*

In almost all circumstances, you have to capture rules from various sources. One of the first decisions is what sources should be considered, and then whether each source results in largely stable rules or more variable ones. When a source provides stable rules, the purpose of analyzing it is to write actual rules for your BRMS to implement the decision. When a source provides highly variable rules, the purpose of the analysis is to design templates for the rules.

**Rules and Rule Templates** *Although rules can be defined by writing each one separately, having many rules with a similar structure is common. One of the most effective ways to manage them is with a rule template. Consisting of a series of characteristics, requirements, and restrictions, a rule template constrains the rules based on it so that they conform to the template's definition.*

*Using a template speeds up development, because the template can be defined and integrated, and the project can move on while you're defining the rules. This approach also enables iterative development by IT and business users, as templates provide stability yet allow rapid iteration of rules.*

There are five main sources for rules, as discussed in Chapter 6, "Business Rules": policy manuals, regulations, business users, code, and data. Each of these sources should be considered, although any given project is likely to only require that a subset of them be analyzed in detail. By far the most common are policy manuals, regulations, and business users who understand how the decision is made today. In contrast, analyzing existing code for rules is the most overused.

---

### Rules Are Not Requirements

When developing business rules, mistaking business rules for requirements and vice versa is one of the main sources of confusion. Making this mistake results in managing business rules as though they are design requirements, when they're not. As Kulak and Guiney say:

> "The requirements list must be replaced by something with more structure and more relevance to users and designers alike. We suggest that use cases, use case diagrams, and business rules replace the traditional requirements list." [1]

Requirements are the design constraints on the solution. Use cases are the scenarios you need to support. Business rules are the statements of how the business should run. Managing them as separate, equal, and linked aspects of the design can make the change cycle for business rules shorter than for other elements of the system, resulting in improved business agility and more business user control.

---

[1] Daryl Kulak and Eamonn Guiney, *Use Cases—Requirements in Context*, Second Edition, Addison-Wesley, 2005.

*Deploy and Maintain Rules*

Given the value of business rules in supporting change and ongoing application mainte-nance, deploying and maintaining rules are even more important than the equivalent steps in traditional approaches. Deployment involves the usual test, quality assurance, and production environments you have already established.

Using business rules doesn't mean you can short-circuit good development practices; release management and version tracking through different systems, for instance, are as important as always. In addition, you need to establish maintenance processes for rules that enable business users and programmers to collaborate, if needed, on new and updated rules and then redeploy and retest them before pushing them into production. You don't normally have to synchronize rule changes with other updates; no code changes, model changes, or business process changes must be done at the same time. Making independent rule changes work is critical to getting the full benefit from business rules.

When you do need to synchronize changes to both business rules and business processes, an update looks more like a traditional software update. Figure 9.2 shows what it might look like when a pricing decision changes regularly but the process that uses it doesn't. In this example, pricing rules change three times before a synchronized process and decision change is needed.

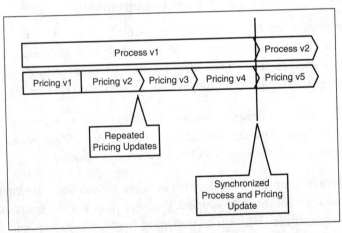

**Figure 9.2    Making pricing updates without changing the process requires rule updates without any other change**

### Loyalty Program Management

#### Old Way

The company had applications written in code (as well as some home-made rule engines) to implement loyalty programs and rewards. Maintaining rules for these programs involved changing multiple systems and scheduling an IT project. The IT maintenance budget was high, and the systems weren't handling the complexity of modern loyalty programs well. For instance, rewards often change monthly, and many transactions could potentially apply to several reward programs.

#### EDM Way

Account information is passed to a decision service that assigns points to each account transaction by using a wide range of business rules. The service then returns the correct points for the account. Business users maintain all business rules, so they can add and remove loyalty programs and rewards quickly and effectively. Only a single easy-to-maintain decision service must be altered to make a change to all the reward programs.

#### Benefits

- The maintenance budget for existing systems has been reduced.
- Business users can direct new loyalty programs and rewards.

### Calculate ROI

You should generate an ROI for every project, and the first business rules project is no different. The simplest method is focusing on the cost to develop and implement the system, which includes prices for hardware and software, along with costs for programmers and consultants and training and familiarization programs. ROI also includes maintenance costs, which must incorporate the frequency and difficulty of making changes and the cost of opportunities lost because resources were committed to maintenance work. Remember, most business systems outlast their initial implementation and must be modified over time. For ROI calculations, you should consider a system's total cost over the first few years of its life.

In addition, some costs can be described as "inconvenience factors," such as staff costs to manually adjust transactions or ordering reports when they aren't needed. Sometimes problems with systems can lead to fines and legal action. Table 9.2 lists the types of costs worth considering. When you're replacing or upgrading a system and creating a new one, the ROI calculation differs slightly.

**Table 9.2    ROI Elements in a Rules-Based Approach**

| Cost | Calculation | Notes |
| --- | --- | --- |
| Development costs | The total cost of hardware, software, and staff to develop and implement the system | Even though a BRMS requires additional software and training costs for the first project, a well-selected project typically takes less time to develop. You can assess this time by comparison with original estimates or previous development projects for the same problem. Some projects show up to a 33% reduction in development time. |
| Maintenance costs | The cost to maintain the system, making needed changes over time, for the period used to calculate the ROI | Gartner has reported 5% to 40% savings for maintenance work on systems developed by using business rules. In highly volatile systems, this savings can be significant compared to development costs. Examples of savings include 80 to 90 hours saved per rules change and application maintenance staff reduced from 50 to 5. |
| Opportunity costs | The value of business opportunities missed because the system hasn't been changed to take advantage of them | When system changes are to respond to competitive actions or launch new products, the opportunity costs saved can be important. Rules-based systems show major reductions in time to change—for example, from 42 days to less than 2. When opportunity costs can be measured in thousands of dollars a day, this saving is significant. |

| Cost | Calculation | Notes |
|------|-------------|-------|
| Operating costs | Costs incurred in running the system, such as staffing and external reports | Beyond the obvious reduction in staffing, a business rules approach can eliminate unnecessary report and data costs. For instance, not always paying for a house inspection can represent major savings. Increases in transactions handled for the same number of staff are also common ways to reduce operating costs. One organization handled 35% more transactions with the same staff, for instance. |
| Business penalty costs | Fines or penalties incurred because of delays or problems | Regulated industries sometimes find that the cost savings from eliminating fines can be high. If delays incur fines or transactions can result in fines if they don't meet certain criteria, a rules-based approach can generate a positive ROI by eliminating or reducing those fines. |

Experience with rules-based development shows some benefits that often contribute to a positive ROI:

- Faster development offsets the cost of a BRMS and initial training.
- Considering a system's total cost, including maintenance, shows the value of reduced maintenance costs.
- More transactions per staff member and fewer unnecessary reports or fines can make a big difference when the transaction previously required manual approval.
- With legacy modernization projects, in which a decision service is the core upgrade to a large legacy system, you can renovate a system by upgrading one component rather than replacing the whole system, which results in a high ROI.

Showing a positive ROI for a first rules project usually isn't complicated. You should go through the process of documenting it, even if everyone is enthusiastic about the project, because proof of the project's value can be useful later.

---

### Methodology Change

One of the changes that a business rules approach requires is the IT department's development methodology. Most development methodologies—agile or formal, model-driven or not, iterative or waterfall—don't explicitly manage business rules. So any standard approach needs at least a little change.

The changes are usually minor. For example, you should catalog or list business rules separately and include them by reference in other models or specification documents (use cases, requirements documents, and so on). Business rules should be captured at the source level—readable statements in a form close to the original policy or regulation, for example—and at the production level in a BRMS. Using templates to manage classes or types of rules should also be encouraged.

For most organizations using a formal development approach, these changes are obvious and easy to adopt. In subsequent rule projects, you'll do a better job of managing rules separately. In early projects, you might find some rules hidden in requirements or specifications, but adding rules to the process is rarely difficult. You'll learn more about this topic in "Extending Your Software Development Life Cycle to support EDM" in Chapter 10.

---

### A First Analytic Project

Organizations adopting EDM also need to develop analytic competency. Many organizations find adopting business rules before analytics easier, but you should start some analytic development sooner rather than later to focus on making use of data as well as knowledge. Some organizations, however, find adopting analytics before business rules easier, especially if they're already using optimization or predictive analytics or have a highly developed data-mining capability.

#### Identify the First Project

If you have never embedded predictive analytics in an operational system, you should look for a simple first project. One of the best choices is using your data to generate a prediction that can be used to improve an interaction. To quote Isaac Asimov:

> *"No sensible decision can be made any longer without taking into account not only the world as it is,*
>
> *but the world as it will be."*
>
> *—Isaac Asimov*

Giving your people predictions about how the world "will be" can improve their decision making.

For instance, a credit score is nothing more than a prediction of how likely someone is to make credit payments on time. In the early days of credit scores, they were simply displayed onscreen as a "grovel index" for customer service representatives (CSRs). If the score was high, they knew to grovel; if it was low, they knew not to.

More seriously, making a prediction available as a simple score rather than a report can make using data easier for employees. Figure 9.3 shows a graph of cell phone use that might show a pattern implying that a customer is a retention risk, but only an attentive and experienced CSR would spot the pattern. In fact, the customer bought a new plan from a competitor over the weekend (days 20 and 21). The increase in minutes shown in the monthly graph made the customer's current plan more expensive. The daily graph shows the regular weekday versus weekend pattern ending suddenly when the customer gets a new phone with a competitor. Showing retention risk as a score would be clearer and could be used to improve service more readily.

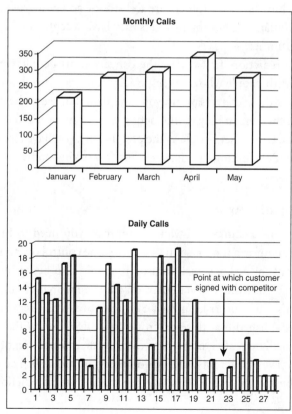

**Figure 9.3    Even graphically appealing reports might not show implications clearly**

> ## Optimization
>
> An alternative to a first analytic project is the straightforward use of optimization to show the value of analytic techniques on operational decisions. With a problem in which you can test all the transactions where you need an action (for instance, only existing customers need to be considered), optimization can result in a specific set of actions, such as customer retention actions for all existing customers, rather than rules or a model. These actions can affect operational systems directly, often without a need to integrate rules or analytics with the operational system.

This score should be *predictive* rather than retrospective, however. Most reporting presents historical data in the hope that the viewer can make a useful prediction from it. A score that predicts how likely customers are to leave or accept a cross-sell offer is more useful than one summarizing how many offers they have accepted in the past or how long they have been a customer.

To generate a prediction, first review the conversations people who work for your organization have with people who don't, especially conversations that influence revenue or costs. For some of these conversations, you have data that seems helpful to those conversing: data about the person they're interacting with or historical data about how conversations have gone with other people in the past. Ideally, you have already been working on reporting and understanding this data and have a working knowledge of the data and its implications.

### Identify the Integration Point

Having found the conversations you want to improve, you need to find an integration point. It should be an information system you have some control over and that your organization's participant in the conversation uses. It should also be visible early enough in the conversation that someone can act differently if given a prediction. For instance, displaying a customer's retention risk on the CSR's retention offers screen isn't helpful; the CSR has already established that this person is a retention risk by that time. Displaying retention risk immediately after customers identify themselves might be more useful, because CSRs can have a different conversation based on the risk. The employees you're helping must be able to change the decisions they make, or the prediction isn't helpful.

*Develop the Model*

The next step is analyzing your data to see how you can turn it into a prediction. Without going into too many details, you should consider the following:

- The data probably isn't organized the way you need it, especially in terms of how time is handled. Say you're trying to predict retention. You need data about customers who canceled their service, organized by number of days before they left, so that you can detect patterns in the days and weeks before customers leave. Your data is probably organized by date, however, so it needs to be processed before you can use it. Similarly, your data warehouse and reporting infrastructure might have aggregated data in a way that makes it less useful. You might have easy access to usage by month, for instance, but find you need usage by day to predict retention.

- You need to make a useful prediction from the data you have, which means finding a correlation or causal relationship in your data. If the decision you're trying to improve is a regulated one that must be justified to a legal authority or an auditor, you probably need a causal relationship. Showing a correlation you can't explain might not be enough. For example, there's a famous correlation between buying brown bread and income, but no one can say that buying brown bread makes you wealthier—there's no causal relationship. If you're simply trying to improve a marketing decision, correlation might be fine. Having different cross-sell offers for buyers of brown bread and white bread (because buyers of brown bread tend to be wealthier) wouldn't attract regulatory attention. On the other hand, denying people a store credit card because they're buyers of white bread would.

- Selecting a suitable time horizon makes a big difference in a prediction's usefulness. For instance, predicting that a customer is a retention risk in the next few days isn't helpful if she has already signed up with another service. Predicting that a customer won't renew a contract 30 or 60 days before it ends makes intervention possible, however. A longer time horizon is often more useful, even if the prediction's accuracy drops as a result; perfect accuracy isn't useful if the prediction is too short term to be useful.

- Be reasonable about precision. Don't overstate how accurate your model is, as it could mislead users of the model. A "soft" prediction—not highly accurate—might still be useful, but only if users of the model understand its limitations. One of the dangers with models is that they assign numbers to something, so they seem official. Using a red/yellow/green rating based on a score might be more useful than displaying the actual score.

### Leading Asian Bank: Control Rates of Bad Loans During Expansion

#### Old Way

A mostly manual auto and mortgage loan approval process depended on local loan officers to make many small loans. No data on rejected customers was captured, and acceptance rates were high (implying that offers were perhaps too competitive). Additionally, bad loan rates were high—more than 13 percent in some cases.

#### EDM Way

A central credit decision service enforces consistent decision making throughout the bank and its branches. The bank's business staff controls rules in the decisions, which ensures that they reflect the portfolios and customers being targeted for growth. Predictive analytic models based on application data estimate risk consistently across regions and products and run as part of the central decision-making process. Local loan officers can override decisions, but guidelines and support from automated decisions ensure that overrides are done correctly and consistently.

#### Benefits

- Control of risk across regions and product lines
- Consistent decision making across branches
- Confidence to increase loan volume, thanks to improved risk management

### Deploy the Model

After you build a model, you have the specification for an equation—something that calculates a score from your data. Some mechanisms for deploying a model into your information systems are shown in Figure 9.4 and are described in the following list:

- The simplest mechanism is adding a field to your database to store the score that represents the prediction and then running the model's equation against all records in the database and populating the score field. You can then display this score onscreen with the technology used to retrieve other read-only data. You need to decide how often to rerun the calculation, but for many scores, weekly or monthly is fine.

**Predictive Reporting**

In some reporting environments, you can bring predictive models into a report. You could import a model that conforms to the Predictive Model Markup Language (PMML) standard, for example, or use a proprietary approach. If a report is already displayed to proposed users of the model, or they have ready access to a suitable report, incorporating predictive models in reports might be a cost-effective way to give users a prediction.

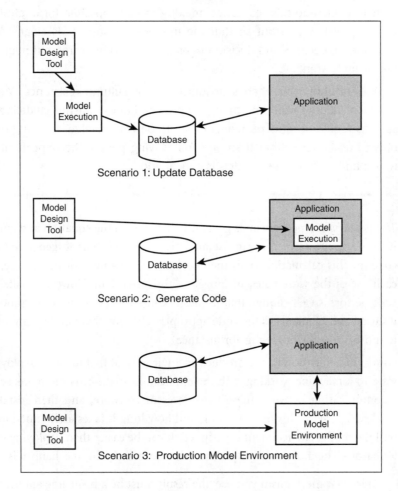

**Figure 9.4    Mechanisms for deploying an analytic model into an information system**

---

### Cultural Resistance to Models

One challenge in adopting any analytic approach to driving the business, including EDM, is cultural resistance. Many people and organizations have a hard time taking action "because the model says so" or having their judgment "criticized" by the data. For instance, if a model suggests making an offer to a subset of the customer base that differs from the marketing department's usual target, the department might resist adopting the model because this implies criticism of its previous actions.

To help overcome this resistance, making models possible for analysts to interpret is important so that the model's "reasoning" is clear. For example, scorecards and decision trees are easy to interpret, but neural nets usually aren't.

In the end, however, there's no quick fix for cultural resistance. You need a solid organizational change approach that establishes guidelines such as requiring retrospective criticism to be constructive—focusing on how to do better—rather than personal. Giving people the opportunity to test and learn to trust models is critical, too.

---

- The next easiest mechanism is generating code from the equation and embedding it in the application. You can use analytic modeling tools to generate C or Java code for this calculation. This method has the advantage of being "live," in that each use of the score takes advantage of the latest data. However, make sure the code performs well enough that it doesn't cause delays in the conversation where it's used and IT manages the code appropriately (not changing it without talking to those doing the modeling, for instance).

- Some modeling tools have a production environment that involves deploying software to a machine working with the application that needs the score, setting up communication between these two pieces of software, and then installing the model. How hard this mechanism is and how long it takes are a function of how well the model environment is designed. It can be easier than deploying code or a lot harder. The more models you have, the more likely this mechanism is feasible.

No matter what mechanism you use, the result must be a front-line application that displays the results of a model calculation in a way that enables better decisions without causing delays or inconveniences to application users.

*Calculate ROI*

Calculating the ROI of a first analytic project is more about results and improvement in results and is less mechanical than calculating the ROI of a first rules project. The costs are easy to calculate: data preparation time and software, model development time and software, and IT costs to handle deployment, testing, and so on. The return might come in a number of ways, but the core factor is the value the organization places on improved results from using the model. Table 9.3 shows potential returns, notes on how to calculate the benefit, and some possible measures.

**Table 9.3    Potential Returns for a First Analytic Project**

| Return | Calculation | Possible Measures |
|---|---|---|
| Time not spent | If incorporating the model can make a conversation go faster or more efficiently (avoiding the need for users to open and analyze a report, for instance), the conversation's cost is reduced. | Call wait times<br><br>Call volume handled |
| Activities eliminated | If using a prediction can prevent the need for an inspection or a report purchase, the cost of these activities can be eliminated. | External reports ordered<br><br>Site visits |
| Risk management | If the conversation has a risk of loss of revenue or reduction in profit, reducing the risk can increase the model's value. For instance, a conversation with a customer about renewing a contract carries the risk of losing that customer's business. | Retention rate |
| Fraud avoidance | Predicting risk of fraud before a transaction is completed can reduce total fraud and prevent "pay and chase," in which fraud is discovered only after the payment is made. | Fraud percentage |

*continues*

**Table 9.3    Continued**

| Return | Calculation | Possible Measures |
|---|---|---|
| Better targeting | If the conversation has a potential upside (making a successful cross-sell or up-sell, for instance), tracking success rates can show if the targeting of those conversations has improved | Sign-up rates<br><br>Cross-sell value |

Benefits of a project can come from one or more of these returns. To see whether the project generated a positive ROI, assign a value to each measure (such as value per customer retained, second reduction in average wait time, sale of a specific offer). If assigning a value isn't possible, track results for a few months and see what the value of each measure needs to be to show a positive ROI. For example, if your benefit comes from improved cross-sell rates, but you can't put a value on a specific offer, you could count the number of offers accepted, compare it to historical norms, and calculate the increase caused by the change. You can then divide the project's cost by the number of new offers accepted to find the break-even value. Even if a value is hard to assign, you might be able to get management to agree it must be more than a certain threshold and still show that the project has a positive ROI.

### Building Critical Foundations for EDM

Unlike a first rules or analytic project, building critical foundations for EDM in phase 1 isn't necessarily a specific project. Instead, this step is a set of tasks you should complete while you're working on first projects in rules and analytics. You can combine these tasks with a first rules or analytic project or group them into a specific project. You might have a group that focuses on methodology and tool adoption complete these tasks as part of its ongoing work. Whatever works for you is fine, as long as you don't neglect these tasks. Neglecting them makes it harder to move toward taking control of decisions and treating them as a corporate asset in the full EDM way.

#### Design a Repository for Rules and Models

Although the first projects use a repository, they don't require a repository designed for enterprise use. Making local decisions about repository design might help you complete a first project on time, but this approach is shortsighted. Long experience with databases, data warehouses, and metadata makes it clear that failing to consider enterprise implications in repository design leads to problems in the future.

---

### Using Commercial Scores

One way to short-circuit the process of developing a model is to see if you can buy a commercial model or score from someone that might help. You may find a vendor with a score that predicts something clearly useful—creditworthiness of an individual or financial stability of a supplier for instance—and be able to purchase that score. Most suppliers of scores have published APIs and ways to integrate the results into your systems. As scores have a price per score, it should be easy to assess your ROI.

Even if you can't find a score that's exactly what you need, you might find one that has a good correlation for your organization. For instance, you might find that you can buy a score that measures how timely an organization is at paying its bills and that this is a good predictor of how long it takes to sign contracts. You can then use this score as an indicator of how likely an organization is to sign this quarter even though that was not its original intent.

---

You must balance overdesigning the repository (resulting in long delays and perhaps unnecessary work and performance implications for the first few projects) and underdesigning it (making it hard to reuse and manage pieces of the process when you have many projects). No upfront design is likely to be perfect—some refactoring of rules and models is required when subsequent projects reuse them—but some attention in this phase of EDM adoption can help prevent future problems.

General organizational guidelines for repository design specify four main components:

- **Business library**—Contains the business rules and analytic model elements that business users maintain. It' organized to make navigation easy for business users.

- **Technical library**—Contains the technical "infrastructure" entities that technical users create and maintain, such as object definitions, overall decision flow, models, and templates that control what business users can edit. Groups of related services have common object models and templates.

- **Decision services library**—Contain everything deployed in the decision service, including the external interface definition and the repository entities that make up the service. Typically, it assembles all or part of the technical library and some business library folders.

- **Testing library**—Contains the rule services to be unit tested, test data, a mechanism for loading test data from a data warehouse, and other test artifacts.

### Data Quality and Integration

Depending on the data warehouse's current state and related data quality and integration efforts in your organization, you need to invest in ongoing improvement of the quality and integration of available data. As noted in Chapter 5, "Data and Analytics," building models has quality and integration requirements different from those for data reporting. So even existing programs to ensure data quality and integration might need to be changed or updated to include the activities needed to support model development.

In particular, making historical data available in a format suitable for modeling needs work. As data formats change and new information is collected, integrating and ensuring the quality of data over a long enough period to build good models can be challenging, and existing programs might not manage this effort well.

Most organizations, however, already make efforts to integrate data, such as around customers, and improve data quality, so these efforts just need to be reviewed and updated to reflect new EDM activities.

### New Tools

Adopting EDM is almost certain to require using new tools in business rules management and analytic model development. Organizations that already have a BRMS and analytic model development tools might have adopted them without considering how they will work in an EDM environment. No matter how powerful a tool is or how well designed or well suited to an organization it is, some kind of adoption plan is necessary.

At this point, the issue is to support first projects while preparing for wider EDM adoption. If you have groups that focus on adopting new tools and making standard decisions for projects, you should involve them in the process. If not, you need to recruit internal champions and early adopters.

In general, the process of adopting EDM tools should follow these guidelines:

- A BRMS is part of the standard tool set available to developers.
- The tools for capturing and managing requirements include explicit capture and management of business rules.
- Statistical analysts have tools designed for understanding data as well as creating models that can be used in information systems.

*Development Methodology*

Most IT organizations have a formal systems development methodology, even if it's not always followed strictly. Most past methodologies don't include business rules as part of the development process, so they need to be amended. Similarly, an organization's analytic process is unlikely to be connected to its IT methodology, making it difficult to include analytic models in information systems. Both problems need solutions if you're to adopt EDM successfully.

What process works best depends largely on how your organization regards methodology. Organizations with a strong attachment to formal planning and development often have an official process for changing or extending the methodology that you should use. In organizations with a more relaxed approach, developing a methodology might be as simple as collecting some best practices (see the "Best Practices" section) and having a meeting to explain to others what worked and what didn't. Chapter 10 provides additional information on the impact of EDM on systems development methodology.

*Decision Services*

As in most organizations, if you're moving to an SOA, you should include the definition of decision services in your approach. Decision services are business services that deliver an answer to a specific question but generally don't update information or make any permanent change to the organization's state. Decision services are, among other things, built to change, not built to last.

You should plan to use a BRMS to implement a decision service and your usual SOA infrastructure to access the service. The decision service can access enterprise resources and other services (by using the same SOA infrastructure) and can make business-level interfaces available for other services to use.

A definition of the behavior of the decision service's behavior needs to be integrated with your standard service repository. The mechanisms you give developers for finding existing services also need to include decision services and make it clear how they can be adapted. Impact analysis and other tools for assessing the service infrastructure should also consider how rules are shared between decision services.

*Best Practices*

An important side effect of the first few projects should be collecting best practices in using rules and analytics to build decision services, but many projects fail to gather this information. Therefore, in subsequent projects, you must relearn these lessons unless someone from the first project is on the team. Most organizations have some kind of knowledge management or best-practices approach you can use to collect this information. Failing that, adopt an approach of your own for capturing best practices so that you can use them in your internal promotion (as explained in the next section). Here are some tips to consider when collecting best practices:

- Best practices should come from your own experience and research into what others have said on the subject. Many vendors and consulting firms publish guidelines or hints you can use.
- Something might be a best practice for others but not work for you.
- You might come up with some insight that's not generally available.
- Your environment and tool choices might lead you to some unique conclusions.

Regardless of where best practices come from, you should collect and organize them so that others can learn from them. You can categorize what you learn into the areas of data, predictive analytics, business rules, adaptive control, and optimization.

### Internal Promotion

When you adopt a new approach, such as EDM, you need to invest some effort in internal promotion of your successes if you're to move beyond a single project. Merely being successful isn't enough; you must show others that they can be successful, and how. Many organizations have a successful first project and then revert to their old ways on the next project. This is likely to undermine the first project's success, because subsequent maintenance and extension don't build on it. For instance, suppose a business rules project is successful, but when a new module is needed, there's no organizational incentive to use the business rules approach. Over time, the business rules project becomes the "odd man out" and risks being replaced with code—not because it didn't work, but because the project was never promoted and because the use of business rules was never made part of the organizational culture.

You can promote projects through any existing mechanisms—best-practice sharing events, brown-bag lunches—or your own activities. Vendors whose products you use are often willing to help you run an internal promotion event or get external publicity for your project (although you probably need permission from your PR department). You can informally promote the project with your peers, too, as a group or one-on-one. If you have an architecture or standards group, you can write a white paper or guideline document for the group.

Whatever approach you take, don't neglect this step. Without it, you'll struggle to move beyond isolated projects.

## Phase 2: Local Decision Management

Phase 2 is developing the first decision service that includes rules and analytics as an integrated whole. Even though the service focuses only on a tactical problem and on one system, the rules and analytics are complementary and reinforcing. Additionally, you should begin using a formal champion/challenger strategy. When projects start to overlap and intersect, the organization has reached phase 3. Table 9.4 shows that analytic modeling and adaptive control are particularly important in phase 2, while deployment issues and organizational change make a significant contribution.

**Table 9.4    Phase 2 Overview**

| Area | Importance | Key Issues |
|---|---|---|
| Deployment infrastructure | Medium | Deployment of analytics into rule-based decision services |
| Business rules management | Low | |
| Analytic modeling | High | Focus on operational systems and their behavior |
| | | Integration with rule development process |
| | | Performance of analytic models in production |
| Optimization and simulation | Low | Possible generation of optimal rules |
| Adaptive control | High | Reporting to allow comparison of approaches |
| | | Infrastructure to allow selecting an approach at runtime |
| | | Proof of the value of the approach |
| Organizational change | Medium | Willingness to experiment to improve results |
| | | Change management for operational systems and processes |
| | | Tighter integration of analytic and IT staff |

> ## Using a Champion/Challenger Strategy
>
> It might not be obvious why you need a champion/challenger strategy at this point. After all, a project can include rules and analytics but not a champion/challenger infrastructure. Such a project could be attempted, but experience suggests that including champion/challenger is more effective.
>
> An interesting aspect of developing analytics is that you add new and predictive information about a customer, product, or prospect. Understanding how to act in response to this new information is a challenge, so you're unlikely to get it right the first time. Not only that, you probably won't know whether you got it right or even what "getting it right" involves.
>
> Using a champion/challenger strategy at this point solves these problems. It forces you to create a measurement environment to see how well you're doing and a testing environment where you can try different approaches to see what works best. Without this strategy, your first use of rules and analytics won't be as successful as it could be. Managing and improving decisions are as important as, if not more important than, the initial configuration of those decisions.

## Integrating Rules and Analytics

Phase 2's most crucial activity is using rules and analytics together to automate a decision. You can approach this activity in a number of ways, depending on the project. First, you need to find a suitable project and then determine what combination of rules and models works best.

Predictive analytics improve precision by expanding the data and depth of analysis you can use for automated decisions. When business people make a decision, typically they refer to reports and outside sources of information as well as their own experience and official policies. Increasingly, business intelligence tools give them sophisticated insight into operations to assist in their decision-making process. Embedding predictive analytic models into a decision service is the equivalent—using insight derived from data to improve an automated decision.

### Find a Suitable Project

To begin integrating rules and analytics, you must find a suitable project. You have three main options:

- Add analytics to an existing rule project.
- Add rules to an existing project that displays scores derived analytically.
- Find a new project in which both rules and analytics are relevant.

Adding analytics to an existing rule project is perhaps most common. Improving the results of a rule-based decision service requires integrating analytics and making a small change to rules but not much architectural change, so you can easily show a positive ROI for using analytics. A rule project is a good candidate if it has decision trees or decision tables for dividing transactions into different segments so that you can treat them differently. Most of the steps discussed in this phase are about this option—introducing analytics to improve rule-based decision making in a project.

Adding rules to a project that displays an analytically derived score works but is more complex. Essentially, you're replacing a manual decision related to the score with an automated one, which can result in a large-scale new project if you aren't careful. If such a large project has a clear ROI, this method might be worthwhile if the decision can be shared between an internal system and a self-service system. If not, a better approach might be tackling the part of the decision that depends most on the score and leaving much of the decision manual. This way, you can show rules and analytics working together more quickly. You might use some of the steps outlined in this phase, but you should certainly use the last one, writing new rules that take advantage of the score.

With the third option, finding a new project, you should look for one with the potential to automate the underlying decision with business rules and the potential to produce a useful and predictive model with the data you have. The best candidate for a combined rules/analytics project is one in which segmentation and treatment of customers, prospects, suppliers, or transactions is an issue.

### A Combined Rules/Analytics Project Obscures ROI Contributions

*A combined project shows an ROI only for the use of business rules and analytics in combination, while the other two project options might show both an overall ROI and an incremental ROI for adding rules or analytics. Not having a clear ROI for rules and analytics separately isn't necessarily a problem, but you should be aware that you might not be able to address how much the rules or analytics are worth individually.*

If you use a new project, almost all the steps listed in this phase might be useful as you develop it, although these steps are interleaved with steps from the first rules and analytic projects in phase 1.

## Mid-Tier U.S. Property and Casualty Insurer: Auto Insurance Underwriting

### Old Way

Quoting and underwriting auto policies were manual processes. For new policies, prospective customers went to see an agent, who answered their questions and gave them a quote. After customers had several quotes, they returned and worked with an agent to fill in information for a policy request. This request was transmitted to the insurance company and queued for an underwriter. When the underwriter reached that policy request, she consulted the policy manual, ordered additional reports, asked the agent for more information, and eventually assembled the data she needed to make a decision and underwrite the policy for a specific price. This price might not match the quote given the customer, however, which could mean several conversations with the agent to gather all the right information.

Almost all the underwriters' time was spent on this policy-by-policy decision making. Underwriters also spent time reviewing renewals going through the system; however, their workload meant that 80 percent of renewals were never reviewed.

### EDM Way

An underwriting decision service that combines business rules and predictive analytics was added to the application portfolio. The business rules ensure that decisions meet requirements for regulatory compliance (with federal and state regulations), knock-out rules (which reject applicants for specific reasons), and company policies. Predictive analytics make it possible to embed risk models (scorecards that use information about prospects to predict their future claims risk) into this decision. This decision service worked smoothly behind the scenes to enable consistent, real-time decisions.

The decision service underwrites 99 percent of policies without referrals to underwriters, so agents can write policies while customers are waiting. In addition, the company has been able to sign up three times as many agents without adding underwriting staff. Customer service is improved and business has increased, with customers signing up more readily because of immediate decisions. Underwriting staff can focus more time on managing the overall business and on agency performance, resulting in better overall management of auto policies. Decisions are consistent across channels and more closely managed throughout the business. In addition, 100 percent of renewals are processed by using the same rules and models, and demonstrating regulatory compliance has been straightforward.

### Benefits

- The same number of underwriters can process 35 more applications.

- Agents and the company have a clear understanding of risk management policies.

- The company can profitably win the good business it wants and lose the bad business it doesn't want.

### Analyze Existing Rules with Data

Next in integrating analytics and rules is analyzing existing rules, especially decision trees, using the data you have about results. Often a rule set, such as a decision tree, assigns a record to some kind of action or treatment. For instance, a rule set might use a customer record to decide what retention offer to make or use an equipment record to decide whether proactive servicing is called for to reduce the likelihood of failure. A rule set essentially segments records you have for customers, products, or equipment so that each segment can be treated differently. The expert who designed the rules can describe each segment—for example, high-risk/high-value customers or unreliable/critical equipment—and the rules show what action is being taken.

There are two main ways to compare rule sets, especially those that segment records so that a specific action or treatment can be applied. The first is **swapset analysis,** comparing segments resulting from the first rule set to segments resulting from the second rule set. The analysis identifies the records that went from a given segment in the first instance to a given segment in the second. These records were "swapped" from one to another. If 100 percent of the records in segment A in the first rule set go to segment 1 in the second, the segments are identical. More likely, most of the records go to one segment, and others are distributed. The movement of records from one segment to another is a good indicator of differences between two rule sets. Figure 7.10 in Chapter 7, "Adaptive Control," shows an example of this kind of report.

The second way to compare rule sets is **segment profiling,** analyzing records in each segment to see how attributes vary within that segment. What are the mean and distribution? How are values distributed? How statistically coherent are the records put into each segment? Changes and differences in the kinds of results and graphs shown in Figure 9.5

can be very informative and help clarify the makeup of various segments. For a more robust approach to this analysis, see "Using Champion/Challenger" later in this chapter.

You can use analytic approaches to evaluate how effective rules are at segmenting your records and taking the right action. A sample set of records, large enough to result in a significant number of records in each segment, is assembled, and the rules are applied to each record. The segment in which a record falls is recorded, and analytical techniques are then applied to see how coherent the segment actually is. In other words, how statistically alike are the records in each segment?

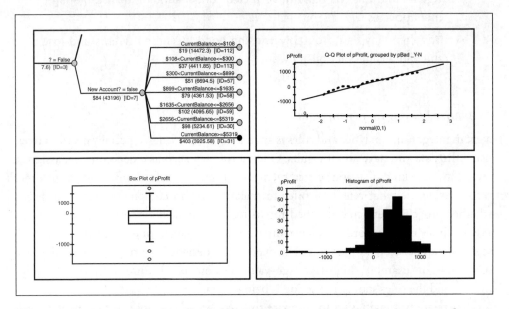

**Figure 9.5    Graphs showing distributions within segments and coherence of segments**

Having established how alike the records are, similar approaches then assess how well these segments worked. If a segment is a high-risk one and the assigned action mitigates that risk, how did this mitigation perform? How does this segment compare with others? Clearly, the fact that an action was taken means you never know whether the result you feared, such as customer attrition, would have occurred if the action wasn't taken (one of the reasons champion/challenger testing is so important). However, you can at least compare the results to results in other segments. Similarly, you can analytically derive the records that turned out to belong to a certain segment but didn't fall in the segment when you first applied the rules to each record.

*Mine Data for Rules*

Statistical analysis of subjective rules often establishes some rules that don't seem to match their intent—a high-risk segment that doesn't contain many of the customers who subsequently canceled their subscriptions, for instance. The next step is to replace these subjective rules with rules derived from historical data you have.

The simplest way to mine data for business rules is to use a classification or segmentation algorithm, such as Classification and Regression Trees. These algorithms run through large numbers of records to identify attributes and values for attributes that represent statistically significant groups or segments, given a performance variable. For instance, you might "know" that the age of a piece of equipment is significant in predicting its reliability. These algorithms would tell you what values for age divide records into statistically coherent groups with similar reliability. Perhaps some equipment is unreliable (it fails almost immediately), and there's an age above which reliability declines rapidly. This information might imply that the first step in your decision tree is to branch based on these values to create three subtrees. Each step in the tree can refine this information, using different attributes and values, to get more coherent groups. With many algorithms and tools, you can also change performance variables at different stages—such as selecting first for reliability and then for maintainability.

> **Performance Variables**   *A performance variable is one you're interested in tracking, such as profit or retention. It's different from decision variables used to make a split and subdivide records into different segments. Typically, decision variables are more readily available than performance variables, which makes predicting performance variables from decision variables useful.*

Data mining can often come up with rules for other rules and rule sets, too. Working with a data-mining expert and tool is ideal, but in some data-mining environments, the process for business users to develop rules from data is quite straightforward.

> **Optimization for Rules**   *Optimization can also be used to generate rules. Although many optimization and simulation problems are complex and shouldn't be attempted this early in your implementation of EDM, some are suitable.*
>
> *If you have a history of using optimization to solve problems or you have a long-term interest in developing optimization skills, this method might work well for you. The process is similar to data mining for rules, except you build an optimization model, run it against a sample data set, and develop rules to reflect the results of your optimization.*

*Decision Trees and Tables That Use Scores*

As you start mining data for rules, wanting additional information to help you make segmentation decisions is common. For instance, predicting future profitability instead of using past profitability usually results in better customer segmentation rules. At this point, you want to develop scores for these predictions and include those scores in the information you use to build decision trees. The sequence for developing more sophisticated decision trees is as follows:

1. Develop a model that generates a score for the prediction. Perhaps it's a customer risk score (likelihood that customers won't renew their contracts) or a future reliability score (likelihood that a piece of equipment will fail in the next 90 days). You can choose from several analytic techniques for this step, from regression analysis to neural networks, as noted in Chapter 5. Different data and predictions work better with different techniques. Picking the right technique and creating a model require some experience and expertise.

2. Apply the model to all records in the data you're using to develop your trees. Essentially, you add a field to your analytic data set and then populate it by calculating the model's value for each record. Each record now has the model result (or possibly results from several models) included.

3. Rebuild your rules with the same data-mining approaches you used before, but with additional information—your predictions. Typically, this rebuilding process results in a new set of rules with different thresholds.

4. Make sure these scores or models are available when rules need them. This means ensuring that the database contains the model's value for any record that might run through the rules or that the rules can call code to calculate the model's value at runtime. The first method works best when the records are fairly stable and the models don't result in different values often; a model predicting future profitability might not change quickly, for instance. The second method is more dynamic and more easily applied to new records (such as a customer signing up during a process for whom no data exists). It's more suitable for models in which the result changes often, but it requires more infrastructure investment to make sure the model can be calculated quickly enough to avoid performance problems in the rules.

**Computer Systems Company: Financing**

### Old Way

Old risk-based pricing was static, failed to consider the profit margin on products, and didn't differentiate enough between high- and low-risk customers. These problems led sales representatives to send a large portion of financing opportunities to competitors. Even basic changes took 6 to 12 months, which further decreased the attractiveness of the company's financing offers. In addition, the company took a brute-force approach to fraud and collections and, as a result, could review only two-thirds of applications for fraud.

### EDM Way

A central decision service or "universal decision engine" uses business rules and predictive analytic risk models to deliver continuous pricing—risk-based pricing with suggested alternatives. The decision service has highly specific risk bands to make sure prices match customers' risk level and the profitability of products being purchased. These prices are delivered consistently to a real-time Web-based process and the call center. Business users can change rules and models in the decision service quickly and easily to ensure rapid time to market for new pricing approaches. The decision service uses information from internal and external services to make sure a broad range of information is used to assess risk, which improves precision.

Figure 9.6 shows a simplified version of the architecture this company used to bring consistent decisions to online and offline offerings, based on thorough risk and fraud assessment.

### Benefits
- 100 percent of transactions reviewed for fraud
- Continuous pricing to maximize profitability of financing with acceptable losses

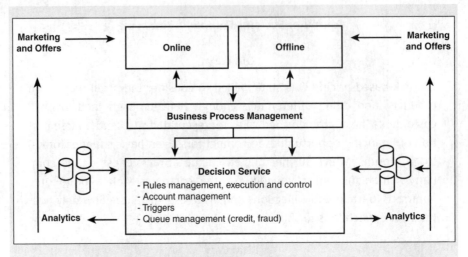

**Figure 9.6     Delivering risk-based pricing decisions to systems through a business process management hub**

*Different Scores for Different Branches*

An interesting side effect of segmenting records by using rules is that the segments might have very different characteristics. Indeed, this side effect is almost a definition of what makes them good segments. When it happens, you might find that the right way to predict something for each segment varies.

For instance, if you use a rule set to segment customers by retention risk, the characteristics of low-risk customers might be radically different from those of high-risk ones. The difference might be so great that the ways you predict what offers they would accept vary widely. In these circumstances, you need to develop different predictive models for each segment, even though the model's purpose is to predict retention for each customer. In Figure 9.7, for instance, the three segments shown on the right have very different ratios of good to bad customers, so models to predict retention might work better if they're developed separately for each segment rather than the whole population, with its mixed set of customers.

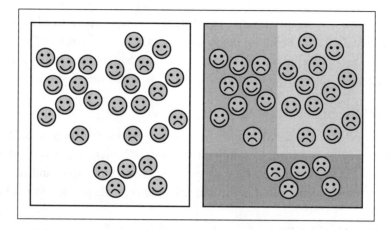

**Figure 9.7    Segmenting a population before scoring to improve models**

If the segmentation is clear and the number of segments isn't too high, you can develop models for each segment the same way you would develop a single model—just repeat the process for each segment. By building several segment models instead of a general model for all segments, you can improve each segment model's accuracy. Sometimes, however, the segments and models are intertwined. Without knowing how much variation is in the segment models, you can't tell how many segments you should have. In this case, you have to use automation to try many segmentation styles and related models to see which ones work best. Genetic algorithms (introduced in Chapter 5), with their capability to modify and mutate models, are effective for this purpose. They can generate segmentation approaches and models for each segment and then modify them, checking a model/segment combination's effectiveness at each stage of model evolution. Merging subtrees into new forms proceeds automatically, and many combinations can be evaluated quickly. You can do it by hand, but trying even a modest subset of all possible model/segment combinations is time-consuming.

### New Rules That Rely on Scores

The final step in integrating rules and analytics is evaluating the possibility of writing new rules that rely on models. For instance, with models that predict future profitability, you might write new rules that route calls in the call center based in part on that prediction. If you can predict failure likelihood, you could write new rules for scheduling engineering visits. The additional information models offer opens new avenues for rules-based decision making.

This step is often combined with developing different scores for different branches. For example, the accuracy of a model aimed at only a single segment might be enough to justify using it in a new way just for that segment, or you might decide to add a new branch to your segmentation rules because a prediction makes it possible to do so. This step is kept separate from that of developing new scores for each segment only because it uses a slightly different mind-set: What can you automate now that you have this prediction?

### Calculate ROI

When adding rules to an analytic project or analytics to a rules project, your ROI comes from incremental improvement in automation (if you add rules) or precision of action (if you add analytics). If you picked a wholly new project to combine rules and analytics, you combine the ways to calculate ROI in the first rules and analytics projects from phase 1.

## Using Champion/Challenger

Champion/challenger, the first step in developing adaptive control, involves software infrastructure and methodology. You must not only design and describe champion and challenger approaches correctly, but also track them in production and be able to change them as results are gathered.

### Define the Champion and Challengers

You should formalize definitions of a champion and challengers first. The champion is easy to find—it's the one in production—but you also need to document and collect rules and models so that they can be described as the champion. Then consider ways to alter a champion to develop challengers. Perhaps the segmentation rules can prioritize records differently. Perhaps new models can be introduced or existing models changed to use different approaches. Based on analysis of the rules and models, develop a number of challengers and test them, using your analytic and business rules tools, to see which ones seem worthy of testing in a live environment.

Before starting to use challengers in a runtime environment, you need to know your measure of success and the timeframe. Comparing a challenger to the champion is pointless without a good idea of what it is you hope to improve, be it customer retention, reliability, or profitability. The best measures are ones that can be tracked easily by using the existing reporting infrastructure and have the minimum reasonable timeframe. Some decisions simply take a long time to play out, and nothing can be done. Sometimes you have several ways to track success, and some measures show up more quickly than others. Quicker measures are preferred.

### Split Transactions at Runtime

Challengers aren't useful unless you can split transactions between the champion and challenger approaches. While developing challengers, you need to design the champion/challenger infrastructure into your decision service. You can do this for a single decision service, or you can develop a champion/challenger component for reuse in many decision services. Developing a champion/challenger for local use first is probably better so that you have more experience before developing a standard component for reuse.

The infrastructure must be able to generate a random number, use it to decide whether a transaction should go to the champion or a specific challenger, and then carry out the decision based on that choice. The infrastructure should allow varying the number of challengers and provide some dynamic control over the number of transactions being routed each way (although this control should be constrained to ensure that most records go through the challenger). You can easily develop a rules component to handle this dynamic control.

The final step is returning the result. Either the return needs to include information on which approach was used (champion, challenger 1, challenger 2, and so on), or you need to record this information separately (by logging a unique identifier for the transaction and the approach in a separate table). This information is essential to report on comparative values of the champion and its challengers.

### Report Differences

Using the data you stored about the challenger used for each transaction, you can develop reports to show how the approaches compare. They should include results-based comparisons (What is the retention rate difference between various retention approaches?) and unintended consequences. You should track other variations among the approaches that might be significant in assessing their value. Additionally, you should do some general analysis of the distribution in each segment to make sure the random assignment is truly random. For instance, when comparing approaches for customer retention, you could track retention results (the target measure), profitability and subscription use (potential unintended consequences), and demographics.

Knowing the timeframe over which you expect approaches to differ is important. Although a challenger's immediate results might be so much worse than a champion that you decide to stop running any transactions through it, proving a challenger is better needs to wait for the right timeframe. This is especially true in long-running relationships, such as customer subscriptions, or when the periods involved are quite long (mean time between failures on equipment, for example). Allowing challengers to play out is a prerequisite for proper analysis.

Reports should aim to show statistical differences between approaches, not just create attractive graphs. Remember that what happens over time might be quite different for each approach; one might show an immediate spike in customer turnover but offset this result with higher retention rates later, for example.

### Update the Champion/Challenger Strategy

Having tracked and measured the results, it should be clear whether the champion or one of the challengers is stronger. Depending on the outcome, you can do the following:

- If the champion is stronger, run 100 percent of the records through it and retire existing challengers. Develop new challengers based on different assumptions and techniques than those you used previously. The idea is to generate different challengers, not more of the same.

- If one of the challengers is superior to the champion, move the challenger's rules and models into the champion slot. Typically, the remaining challengers are assessed, and most, if not all, are retired, leaving 100 percent running through the new champion. You should then develop new challengers. Some should build on the experience of the successful challenger to see whether the characteristics that led to success can be developed further, and some should take a new approach to see whether it works better.

Although you don't necessarily replace challengers often, it's helpful if it doesn't disrupt operation of the decision service or require a major hardware or software restart. Modern BRMS and analytic tools include functions to make live updates possible, and your champion/challenger infrastructure should take advantage of this capability.

### Calculate ROI

Calculating the ROI for champion/challenger involves assessing the improvement resulting from using a successful challenger. You can show the ROI by projecting the improved results from the challenger to the point at which the champion was introduced. You can calculate the extra value that would have resulted from using the challenger approach for that period, and use it as an estimate for the challenger's likely future value. By comparing this return to the costs of establishing the champion/challenger infrastructure, you can generate an ROI.

If your initial challengers do worse than your first champion, you can't prove a direct ROI. Instead, you make a risk management argument: The champion/challenger infrastructure allows you to be more certain that you don't have a poor approach, especially as the environment in which the approach operates changes. Although your staff has spent additional time developing and comparing the challenger, you can argue that this time investment is part of their regular review and measurement of the business.

# Phase 3: Expansion

Phase 3 is crucial for moving from localized projects to a more integrated department-wide or enterprise-wide implementation. The foundations for a true enterprise decision-making backbone must be developed, and overlapping and intersecting problems must be addressed to justify this investment. In this phase, typically you manage trade-offs between different predictive models more formally because you are automating intersecting decisions.

Building the capacity for what-if analysis is essential to incorporate robustness into the decision-making process, too. Change revolves around moving from a narrow focus to a broad focus, which has implications for simulation and optimization. In addition, organizations become more aggressive about closing the feedback loop from results to models and moving from offline to real-time decision making in both implementation and logic design. Table 9.5 shows that analytic modeling remains important while deployment issues and optimization and simulation are also very important. This phase has all six areas showing at least Medium importance, reflecting the challenging nature of moving to enterprise-wide decision management.

**Table 9.5    Phase 3 Overview**

| Area | Importance | Key Issues |
| --- | --- | --- |
| Deployment infrastructure | High | Enterprise-wide backbone |
| Business rules management | Medium | Focus on enterprise management and reuse of rules |
| | | Adoption of standards |
| Analytic modeling | High | Widespread use of sometimes-sophisticated analytics becomes common |
| | | Adoption of standards |
| Optimization and simulation | High | Better understanding of decisions allows extending adaptive control with optimization and simulation |
| | | What-if analysis formalized |
| Adaptive control | Medium | Adaptive control extended more often with optimization and simulation |
| Organizational change | Medium | Proactive identification and management of decisions |
| | | Competency center or other institutionalization of knowledge |

> ## When to Centralize Analytics
>
> Most organizations that use analytics frequently have a centralized analytics group, but having this group is a *consequence* of widespread use of analytics more than a *necessity* for using analytics widely. Most organizations are better off focusing on developing analytic expertise in specific areas of their business—perhaps not in a specific business process, but certainly in support of a specific group of business processes. An understanding of data, business expertise, and a focus on improvement are easier to develop with a strong focus on a specific area of the business.
>
> The time to focus on a centralized analytics group is when you expand into several areas and start to focus on a standard deployment infrastructure and tools. After multiple groups are using analytics and sharing common deployment infrastructure, a central group can reduce redundancy and make skills more portable between groups. Moving to a centralized group too early could also be dangerous, though, as it separates the modelers from the business they are modeling.

### Improve the Decision Management Foundations

As you move toward enterprise- or department-wide decision management, you must improve the foundations on which you build each decision service. In particular, you must develop a decision-making backbone, improve standards, and become more proactive about identifying decision problems in new projects.

#### Develop a Decision-Making Backbone

An enterprise-class decision-making backbone consists of three main components:

- **Enterprise repository**—An enterprise repository for the rules and models that make up your decisions is critical in this phase. Managing local repositories independently or designing only for projects is no longer adequate. The design elements identified earlier for an enterprise repository must be fully incorporated now. The repository doesn't need to be a single physical repository, but it must be a single logical one. All projects must be able to access this logical repository to manage and modify rules and models they need and to create new ones. The repository should be robust, backed up, and considered by IT as a key element of its infrastructure, in the same way as the e-mail system, Web site, or accounts payable system.

- **Standard deployment infrastructure**—To support enterprise-wide deployment of decision services, you need a standard infrastructure for deployment. Regardless of the number of platforms used in your organization, any project should be able to integrate and deploy a decision service rapidly and effectively. You can make enterprise deployment practical and easy by having the systems management infrastructure connected to decision services, having services monitored and controlled, and having standard ways for projects to use decision services.

- **Standard rule management infrastructure**—One of the most important characteristics of a decision service is its agility. Decision services tend to change more often than other services, and business users are more likely to initiate changes directly. The infrastructure to test and deploy new business rules, manage and audit changes to business rules, and control access to business rules should be standard throughout the organization. Integrating this technology with existing intranets or portals makes it possible for different groups to participate in managing decision services for different projects.

The details of these components depend on the technologies you choose to implement EDM, but you need to create these components with any technology.

**Separate Rules and Models**  *Rules and models commonly have separate repositories and deployment infrastructures, but this separation doesn't need to prevent integrating or deploying and managing effective decision services. The degree of integration between your analytic and business rule environments determines how much work is necessary to make decision services deployable. At a minimum, you should try to pick technologies that support interchange formats and allow well-defined access points.*

### Standardize Tools and Approaches

Enterprise-wide deployment in most organizations means having internal standards. For EDM, you should make sure decision service and business rule development tools are standard ones available to all development projects. Developers of any new project can then define decision services and the rules for those decision services with their standard arsenal of tools. They shouldn't need to write business rules in code simply because they don't have the right tools. Similarly, standards for analytic tools should be enforced. Many analytic techniques are available, so analysts often have different preferred tools. Having different tools isn't a problem, however, if there's a common approach to data preparation, variable development, and model deployment. Reducing the number of tools used might be necessary to bring deployment under control, however, so consider this factor as part of improving standards.

**Changes for Modelers**  *For organizations with analytic modeling staff, a critical change in adopting EDM is the focus on deployment. Traditionally, most analysts are judged by the "lift" or predictive power of their models. The idea that a model must be deployed, and deployable, to be useful is sometimes new to them.*

*Similarly, although most analysts realize that models need to be timely, they sometimes consider only the time to develop the model instead of the total time to develop and deploy the model. It's hard to get modelers who think in these ways to give up their favorite tools in an effort to ease deployment. Managing this organizational change is necessary before you can standardize tools.*

You need to standardize development methodology, too. Most large organizations have a standard for developing new systems or updating existing ones, so they have certain approaches to portfolio and project management and tools and documentation that support these approaches. Training for programmers and others involved in projects might include these approaches. To make EDM adoption work, the concepts of decision services and the technologies outlined in Chapter 4, "Core Concepts," must be integrated with these standard methodologies.

### Identify Decision Problems Proactively

A major challenge in adopting EDM is ensuring that all decision problems are identified. Therefore, you need to identify business services (sometimes called "elemental services"), planned or already under development, that are decision-based. People running these projects need to be taught how to spot decision-based services and then build them appropriately.

You can impart these skills by training, using architectural or other project reviews, running competitions, or another method suitable for your organization. Ensuring that projects become proactive about separating out decision services isn't optional; you must create an environment that seeks out and manages decision services in other projects. Chapter 2, "Enterprise Decision Management," covers finding suitable and hidden decisions in more detail.

### Calculate ROI

The ROI for building an enterprise decision-making backbone is in two main areas:

- **Reduced costs in projects**—Increasing the infrastructure for developing and deploying decision services reduces the cost for single projects to do so. Just as having an enterprise database approach makes identifying, designing, and managing new data more efficient and effective, an enterprise decision-making infrastructure allows better management of decisions. Similarly, an enterprise repository makes it easier to manage and reuse rules and models, which reduces training costs.

- **Improved results**—Because the infrastructure allows reuse and there's a focus on decision problems as a type of project, results also improve. More projects that are best implemented via EDM can be approached that way, and these projects perform better as a result. There's less risk of attempting a project in a suboptimal way, because a decision-making infrastructure exists.

Precise numbers for some of these returns can be hard to come by. You should make an attempt to quantify, or at least qualify, benefits of the infrastructure, even if your calculations aren't perfect.

### Overlapping and Adjacent Problems

An important part of moving toward a true EDM approach is developing decision services that solve overlapping and adjacent problems. These decision services are powerful in showing the value of managing decisions as a corporate asset rather than as part of a project.

> **Keep Doing Stand-Alone Projects** *Although overlapping and adjacent projects are powerful ways to bring true EDM to your organization, you shouldn't neglect stand-alone projects with good ROI. Stand-alone projects don't move you toward enterprise decision management, but they do show the local value of the approach and make it possible for more projects to incorporate the core concepts. Some decision services are local to a single project; others are shared only if you can work through the backlog of applications not being built because of maintenance work on other projects. Building stand-alone projects while thinking about enterprise-level issues improves momentum and experience.*

## Hospital in Multipayer System: Bad Debt for Hospital Bills

### Old Way

Most U.S. hospitals don't assess how or whether patients can pay for their hospital bills, other than to check for insurance coverage. Out-of-pocket expenses and treatments not covered by insurance are simply added to a patient's bill, and then the hospital attempts payment collection after the patient leaves. As a result, as much as 30 percent of patient bills end up being written off as bad debt, which harms the hospital financially and forces it to spend resources on collections and accounting that would be better spent on patient care. The hospital can't refuse care to patients, however, so it needs a way to manage the billing process to reduce bad debt without turning patients away.

### EDM Way

During the admissions process, business rules perform real-time validation of patient-supplied data against medical records and external data sources. By making certain patients are who they say they are and that addresses and other information are complete and correct, hospitals can reduce their financial risk. Predictive analytic models make it possible to predict an optimal initial payment request and payment plan for patients. Guidance on initial payment requests increases revenue upfront and improves the intake staff's effectiveness. Knowing which patients can and will pay enables financial counselors to work with patients who need help, minimizes the number of payments that go to collections, and generates maximum revenue for hospitals.

During a patient's stay, business rules and predictive analytics can also check the patient's information against rules governing eligibility for charity care, Medicaid, and other supplemental funding. Business rules are created and deployed consistently to comply with government and hospital policies on patient payments, and hospitals can monitor staff for compliance with these policies.

Instead of treating all overdue accounts with the same sequence of letters and calls, hospitals can collect more money by doing less. Analytics can identify differences between patients likely to self-correct, those likely to be influenced by collections treatments, and those unlikely to pay under any circumstances. Hospitals can use this segmentation to save money by making fewer outbound calls and referring accounts with a high likelihood of nonpayment to a collections agency earlier.

### Benefits

- Hospitals can collect more money more quickly and remain compliant with their obligation to treat all patients.

- Fewer resources are spent on collections and bad debts, and more resources are spent on patient care.

### Look for Opportunities for Reuse

A high-quality SOA enables reuse of services, but some rules from first projects can often be reused in other systems, usually when rules are the same in different channels or lines of business. Sometimes a whole decision service can be reused (as a service in the SOA sense or by regenerating rules into a new deployment for a different platform). More often, only some rules can be reused, however. For instance, you might have an opportunity to use customer segmentation or dispute-rating rules again. You might need to replace code or add functionality to old systems, but you can often justify doing so by reducing ongoing costs (reducing or eliminating maintenance) or adding value (better-targeted cross-sell offers increasing revenue).

The first opportunities for reuse often require refactoring of the rules you have, unless there's a stable and well-defined object model. Organizations well on the way to a model-driven approach should have object models that are defined well enough to make refactoring straightforward. Others might have to allow refactoring time.

> **Note** *Some problems might clearly overlap when they're first identified. You might see, for example, that automating a decision requires changing several systems that currently automate the decision in separate ways or assume it's being made manually.*

The use of rules in many decision services help ensure that the repository design and deployment infrastructure truly support managing decisions across systems. At first, you'll probably find that sharing rules isn't easy. No theoretical planning prepares you for actual sharing. Good preparation and a focus on decisions make planning more straightforward after you do have examples. As Scott Ambler, a well-known writer on agile methods, said:

> *"You can't call something reusable unless it's been reused at least three times on three separate projects by three separate teams."[2]*

### Manage Change

As you begin to share rules and models in projects, you need to become more adept at managing change to projects. You should think in terms of updating rules or models, not systems as a whole, and you need ways to resolve conflicts when projects or teams want to change rules in different ways or have models judged by different criteria.

Remember that decisions are corporate assets; your associates regard them as deliberate acts on your organization's part. Before you allow two groups to make a decision in slightly different ways, determine whether it makes sense from an external perspective. If it does, perhaps you have two decisions that share many rules or use the same models in different ways. If it doesn't, you should have one decision service, and the groups who use it need to resolve their differences. Getting the business users who are supposed to manage the decision to step up and own the decision service's results, not just the rules behind it, can be effective in improving your results.

### Calculate ROI

Finding overlapping and adjacent projects can have a very high ROI that comes from a combination of the following factors:

- **Valuing consistency and control**—When the same decision service is used in multiple systems or the same rules are used in multiple decision services, consistency and control increase. Organizations that put a value on consistent customer treatment and control of this treatment can put an ROI on this factor.
- **Reducing development time**—Projects that share rules, models, or decision services have reduced costs. Using these reduced costs to offset the expense of identifying and managing overlapping projects can show a positive ROI.
- **Decreasing compliance cost**—Organizations that must pay fines for errors or spend a lot of money on compliance find that compliance is easier and its cost is reduced.

---

[2] Scott Ambler, John Nalbone, Michael J. Vizdos, *The Enterprise Unified Process: Extending the Rational Unified Process*, Prentice Hall, 2005.

- **Reducing maintenance cost**—Because rules and models are maintained once and deployed many times, the cost of maintaining systems that use them is lower. Particularly if a decision must be changed often, making a change in a single place for several uses is less expensive.

### Broaden the Analytic Base

As your use of EDM expands, you need to broaden the base of your analytic approach. You should develop models based on richer, more complete information to increase their value and lift. You also need to develop predictive models and data elements that describe customers or prospects, multiple (sometimes opposing) objectives, possible actions, possible customer reactions (forecast by predictive models), constraints (risk, resources, schedules), and outcomes.

This more thorough analysis of your associates makes it possible to identify the single best (optimal) method for achieving the performance goal, given constraints and objectives. Initially, you might use a manual process for this analysis, but over time, you need to move to a more formal, mathematical approach. When applied to a decision correctly, a mathematical approach to optimizing decisions doesn't increase the automation percentage but quantifiably improves each decision's value. With this improvement, an organization can balance conflicting objectives and constraints and take market and economic uncertainties into account. Last, you need to increase your iteration speed—the time it takes you to develop and release a new model—so that you can improve models more aggressively.

#### Broaden the Information Base for Analytic Models

As you become more sophisticated in the kinds of decision services you build, you need to broaden the base of information you use for analytic models. In particular, you need to increase the scope of data you consider by moving from a specific focus to a broad focus—for example, from account-level to customer-level data. Broadening your focus increases your models' complexity and value. Richer data, such as from customer data integration (CDI) projects, and a broader range of data from several sources—perhaps from wider use of Enterprise Application Integration (EAI) or Enterprise Information Integration (EII) technology—improve the modeling process. In addition, you should become more aggressive about seeking external data to enrich your models. If you already have relationships with data providers, explore other data they have to offer. It not, consider establishing these relationships.

### Consumer-Branded Goods: Increasing Brand Loyalty Directly with Consumers

#### Old Way

Because the company's product is sold entirely through retailers, it has no direct contact with consumers, so its ability to understand or influence customer behavior is limited. The company conducted focus groups and other forms of outreach but was dissatisfied with the results. It had access to consumer databases with demographic data but little data on buying patterns and no way to use this information. In addition, campaigns that did capture consumer information didn't build on one another to create a growing, richer data set; these campaigns remained mostly independent efforts.

The company needed to connect with consumers more directly, collect information from them, and strengthen these relationships over time. In particular, the company wanted to connect with younger consumers and saw the growth in youth-oriented social networking sites, increased participation in entertainment, and time and location shifting of programs as challenges.

#### EDM Way

A sophisticated set of decision services supports a new Web site. When consumers interact with it, predictive and descriptive analytic models in the decision service score and segment customers so that they can be targeted. Business rules in the service control what survey questions are asked, how those answers change the site layout, and what content is displayed. Consumer interests determine what content is displayed, as do their preferences, location, and other data. The decision service creates a completely personalized and targeted Web site for consumers. In addition, consumers earn loyalty points and manage them through the site, exchanging them for rewards. Point-of-sale advertising and separate product sites are integrated so that specific promotional offers are displayed consistently. No blanket messaging is used; everything is tailored to consumers, their interests, and their purchase patterns.

#### Benefits

- Far better rates of involvement by purchasers than any previous loyalty program
- Better understanding of the impact of marketing messages
- First successful relationship-building platform

### Identify Models' Potential Proactively

To maximize the value of analytic models to your organization, you need to become proactive at identifying their potential. Just as you need to seek out decision services, the teams working on these projects should examine available data to see what inferences they can draw and establish what would be useful to know to see whether that knowledge could be inferred from data. You can't always create a model that infers what you need to know, but you might identify the extra pieces of data you should capture or the need for external data to make it possible to make these predictions in the future.

Part of the challenge is that you need to make assessing available data and developing models to enrich data part of the standard process of identifying models' potential. Doing this means integrating your analytic process, especially the early exploratory phase, with your IT development process while the data or model is being developed.

**Many Lower-Value Models** *Another challenge in proactively identifying the potential for models is that it can result in many models, sometimes of only small incremental value. As you build more models, more of them show only a small lift or improvement. This slight improvement doesn't mean you shouldn't build them, just that you must consider how much analysts' time to invest in them. Typically, using more automation to build models and tuning them automatically after deployment helps show a positive ROI for these lower-value models. Lower-value models cannot typically justify a large time investment.*

### Increase Model Iteration and Development Speed

At phase 3 of adopting EDM, you need to increase the ability of your analytic resources to produce more models, more quickly. You need to build models faster, with more automated support for analysts and perhaps automated model development. Having expert analysts involved in model development is valuable, but many tasks in model development are amenable to automation. If you haven't already adopted tools and approaches that focus on streamlining model development, now is a good time to do so.

You should also improve your ability to iterate models faster. Nothing about models developed at this point requires more rapid iteration, but improving and adapting models faster than your competitors is a potential source of competitive advantage. By now, you should have enough of the infrastructure in place and enough experience to focus on faster model development.

### Formalize a Trade-off Approach

As you develop a richer set of models that describe associates' likely future behavior, increasingly you find that more than one model applies to a decision. Indeed, more sophisticated analytic organizations target many models for a decision in an effort to predict several aspects of associates' behavior. This method improves the quality of decision making but also requires making trade-offs. Should you make an offer to someone who's likely to accept it but also at risk of failing to pay on time? Should you use a machine part that has high predicted reliability but is supplied by a company with a high risk of business failure? The review of multiple models in a decision service needs to be formalized, and you should analyze the trade-offs. A few analytic models can be traded off manually against one another, and rules for managing this trade-off can be implemented easily. For instance, Figure 9.8 shows how a risk prediction model and a revenue prediction model can be traded off to create new segments for credit line offers. The intersection of these models is analyzed, and the relative importance of what they tell you about associates is traded off to determine the best action to take.

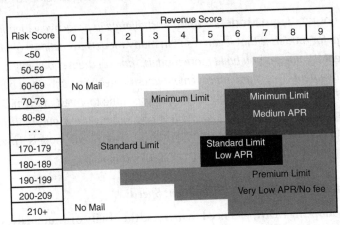

**Figure 9.8** **Predictive models can be traded off to establish the best rules for a decision**

### *Adopt Optimization and Simulation*

Moving up a level in analytic sophistication to build decision models that allow modeling trade-offs mathematically is important in improving the quality of decisions. These decision models can help you find an optimal trade-off that maximizes profit, retention, reliability, or some other measure.

After building a mathematical model of interrelationships between your models, you'll probably discover real-world constraints on your best solution. Perhaps you can't maximize profit if it means dropping your customer retention rate below a certain point; you might have to keep some unprofitable customers to maintain a reasonable retention rate. Perhaps you can't sign up all the new customers you want because you have a limited capacity for handling those customers. Being able to find the optimal decision in these circumstances requires simulation within these constraints. Most organizations have some hard and some soft constraints. Hard constraints must be enforced, but soft ones are usually just standard operating procedures. Simulation can show the cost-benefit analysis of changing soft constraints so that you can consider whether to change them.

**Complement Adaptive Control with Decision Modeling** *A consequence of adopting more formal models and finding interactions between predictions and constraints is the gradual replacement of arbitrary challengers with challengers derived from decision modeling.*

*Decisions continue to need an adaptive control process, but some can use a formal modeling process to replace subjective design of new challengers. Using optimization and simulation also helps you see how different approaches might play out, without having to risk suboptimal treatment of associates.*

### Calculate ROI

The ROI for broadening your analytic base comes in three main areas:

- **Better use of information**—More models, used more widely, increase how well your data is used. Better use of information increases the return on CDI and master data management (MDM) projects and for your data infrastructure in general. Improved development processes reduce the cost of models, so you can build more and gain more lift for the same investment in analytic staff.

- **Lower costs from adaptive control**—Adaptive control is an essential ingredient in making smarter decisions, but it does impose a cost. Some associates get a worse treatment than your current champion, causing a loss of revenue or another negative consequence. There's also an ongoing cost for operating the experimental infrastructure. After you understand a decision well enough to model it formally and run optimization and simulation on it, you can eliminate some of these costs. With simulation, you can try various scenarios to see which one is likely to be better before trying them in real systems, so you get better challengers more quickly.

- **Maximization and potential for profit**—Optimization and simulation techniques allow for the possibility of profit maximization—finding the efficient frontier. All organizations operate under constraints that prevent them from behaving in a truly optimal way. Nevertheless, mathematical modeling and simulating decisions can maximize profits or minimize costs for a decision and a set of constraints. The increased ROI from using these techniques can be dramatic.

Manage Scenarios

A powerful consequence of managing decisions as a corporate asset is being able to conduct what-if analysis to prepare for new opportunities or threats. You might change the model you're using to reflect a more aggressive competitor or a natural disaster. You might try the model under different interest rates or economic constraints. A simulation can give you the best models and the best rules for these circumstances. You can then put these optimal rules and models "on the shelf," ready for use if the situation develops. Having new ways to make decisions ready to go can cut your organization's response time to new situations dramatically and help you respond effectively and quickly.

### Establish a Scenario-Planning Process

The first step is developing a process for considering scenarios that make sense. Typically, a decision's business users need to brainstorm potential changes to the business environment, such as different economic conditions, competitive changes, new or revised regulations, natural disasters—anything that could materially affect how you make this decision. You can't plan for all these changes, however, so you need a process to identify the highest-likelihood/highest-value scenarios. The process should be ongoing so that you can conduct regular reviews to see whether scenarios have changed.

Some organizations use this process for large strategic issues, but few do it for more operational issues. Your organization must continue to operate, even if the scenario happens, so establishing which critical operational decisions should be considered when assessing a scenario's impact is valuable.

### Establish a Monitoring Process

No scenario-planning process is much use unless you also have a process for tracking the environment to tell whether these scenarios are happening. Some scenarios are easy to spot, such as one depending on a bank rate increase, but others might happen more gradually or be harder to spot, such as a tightening of consumer spending.

Any organizations performing scenario planning should make sure they have a process for tracking scenarios and finding indicators that the scenario is happening. With information from these processes, organizations can revise their approach to decisions more quickly. This monitoring should be part of ongoing strategic planning or assigned to a competitive intelligence or market intelligence group.

### Develop What-if Scenarios

For each scenario you identify, you need to develop new models and rules that are suitable for the revised circumstances. This development usually involves simulating a decision under the revised circumstances to see how different models and rules perform. Optimization and formal models help because you can use these techniques to tweak models and generate new values for constraints and assumptions. Then you can rerun simulations to see what changes.

> **Different Objectives**    *An organization might have different objectives as well as different constraints and assumptions in a scenario. Normal operations might focus on maximizing profit for a risk, but operations in some scenarios might focus purely on minimizing risk or maximizing short-term customer retention. When you're analyzing scenarios, make sure objectives match the scenario.*

### Integrate into a Strategic Planning Process

The value of what-if analysis for operational decisions is twofold. First, it improves operational decision making in different scenarios. Second, it allows strategic planning to take into account the cumulative impact of changes on operational decisions. Building a strategic plan to cope with a scenario should include establishing likely changes in the results of key decisions, such as customer retention or supplier selection. Integrating simulation and what-if analysis of an organization's key operational decisions into the overall strategic-planning process maximizes the value of scenarios.

### Calculate ROI

The ROI from managing scenarios comes from risk management and mitigation. If none of the scenarios happen, there's no explicit return from the work. However, most organizations put some value on risk management planning, and managing the impact of scenarios on critical operational decisions improves the precision of this planning. It also enables you to apply what-if scenarios at the operational level instead of just a summary level.

## Steady State: Enterprise Decision Management for Real

Finally, an organization achieves steady state enterprise decision management:

- A complete enterprise backbone for deploying decisions across the application portfolio makes it possible to identify opportunities proactively so that you can inject decisions into applications.
- The rules and analytics that make up these decisions are managed as an enterprise asset.

## European Online Bank: Credit Origination

### Old Way

The bank, operating only through its Web site and a call center, had two systems for credit origination. Ensuring that credit decisions were consistent in these two systems and, therefore, the two channels was time consuming and costly. Any change to the system required a major IT investment. Despite this investment, the systems still generated too many manual referrals. Manual referrals are expensive because they force credit specialists to become involved and are damaging to customers' perceptions because online and phone customers want instant decisions. Long lead times between updates to the credit process also meant that bad debt was higher and acceptance rates were lower than what was required for growth.

### EDM Way

A core decision service that handles credit decisions combines business rules and predictive analytics that the credit risk team developed. Business users manage rules and scorecards directly, and the decision service is integrated with an adaptive control and test infrastructure that allows business users to test new rules and scorecards thoroughly before putting them into production. No IT resources are needed for updates to the production system that take place almost every month. In addition, rules and models are more customized for customers, and automated decisions are made quickly and returned to the point of request, whether it's the call center agent or the customer using the Web site.

Figure 9.9 shows the architecture for this decision service. Rules are developed and tested on a PC and then deployed to a UNIX-based decision service. Extensible Markup Language (XML) and custom middleware are used to pass decisions to front-end applications and to receive requests from them.

**Benefits**

- Average rule change time reduced by 94 percent

- Manual referrals reduced by 75 percent

- Income through raised acceptance rates increased by 1.5 percent

- Provision for bad debt reduced by 1 percent

- A "what-if" facility for trying different scenarios before implementing them identified potential increase in credit risk of 4.5 percent

- ROI in six months, with an ongoing savings of nearly $10 million a year

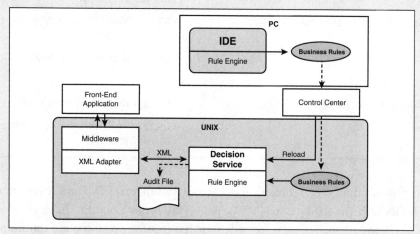

**Figure 9.9    An architecture for changing credit origination decisions rapidly**

- Optimization and what-if analysis are coordinated to ensure that decisions are robust in the face of change.

- Data is captured with an analytic value chain (explained later in this section) in mind.

Table 9.6 shows that organizations need to focus on optimization and simulation in this phase. This is largely because it is the least well established at this point. In contrast, business rules management should be well established and therefore involves less work. Continuing to develop analytic modeling remains somewhat important, as do deployment issues and organizational change.

**Table 9.6    Steady State Overview**

| Area | Importance | Key Issues |
|------|-----------|------------|
| Deployment infrastructure | Medium | Complete rollout of deployment infrastructure |
| Business rules management | Low | |
| Analytic modeling | Medium | Manage increased demand for analytic models |
| | | Automated tuning of deployed models |
| | | Automated support for analytic model development |
| Optimization and simulation | High | More formal models of interactions and decisions |
| | | More focus on what-if scenarios |
| Adaptive control | Low | |
| Organizational change | Medium | Continual adoption in new areas |
| | | Increasing change management as reuse increases |

As part of this phase, an organization develops a **universal decision engine** or **enterprise policy hub.** According to IDC, "The policy hub is that point in a business process at which decisions are made and from which the results of the decision are communicated to the people and business transactional/operational systems that are affected."[3] This engine or hub centralizes an organization's operating policies, procedures, regulations, models, and expertise and delivers them to front-line transactional/operational systems and business processes throughout the extended enterprise. All processes and systems go to this platform to make operational decisions. We refer to this as a **decision service hub.**

A decision service hub can be logical or physical. An organization might have a common set of application programming interfaces (APIs) and calls that handle all decisions, or it might use a standard SOA to manage a set of decision services. A typical heterogeneous IT environment is likely to be a mixture—a single BRMS and rule repository with deployments as services and components in traditional architectures (Java, .NET, or COBOL). As shown in Figure 9.10, a decision service hub delivers precise, consistent, agile decision making to all applications and processes in an enterprise.

---

[3] Henry Morris and Dan Vesset, "Policy Hubs: Progress Toward Decision-Centric BI," IDC, 2004.

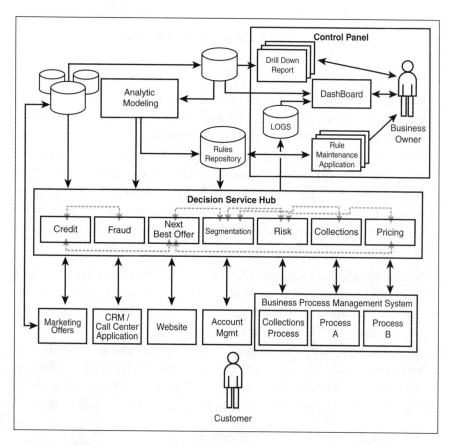

**Figure 9.10    Overview of a decision service hub** ©*Fair Isaac Corporation, reproduced with permission*

A decision service hub has a number of key requirements:

- **A logical or physical service or set of services to deliver decisions to operational systems**—In a pure SOA environment, this component might be an actual decision service or services, but in a more heterogeneous environment, it consists of services, Java or .NET components deployed without a services wrapper, and even COBOL programs. Regardless of the implementation, a decision service hub is responsible for responding to requests for decisions on behalf of the enterprise in a consistent manner, regardless of a request's origin.

- **Capability to answer requests for the core operational decisions other systems require**—These decisions, such as those assessing credit or calculating the best next offer, are often used by many systems. They interact with each other and can share rules. A decision service hub must make sharing rules easy and effective and ensure consistency of response in different systems and implementation environments.

## European Bank: Basel II Compliance

### Old Way

For Basel II, compliance has three pillars: Pillar I requires data models, validation, and documentation; Pillar II requires oversight, stress testing, governance, and functional independence; and Pillar III requires reporting disclosure. In addition, demonstrating compliance requires banks to meet the "use test." Any approach adopted needs to be "proved" to supervisors, so it must be clear and easily replicated. Banks trying to meet the Basel II accord need an automated method for consistent, enterprise-wide, risk-weighted asset calculation that's flexible enough for local variation.

The bank had a major investment in existing infrastructure, software, and processes. To demonstrate compliance, the bank had to process large amounts of data manually and generate reports. However, the Basel II accord isn't static, not even the core calculations, so reports and data extraction and manipulation logic have to be changed periodically at a high cost. In addition, countries are allowed some discretion in adopting the accord, so the bank needed different logic and reports in each country. Passing the use test with this largely manual approach was difficult.

### EDM Way

A decision service takes advantage of existing investments such as scoring systems that measure risk and software that supports origination and account management decisions. It has business rules to extract and match information from disparate systems, segmentation rules developed from customer information, and predictive analytic models to calculate risk and other required elements of the accord. The service contains an operational standard and rules for geographic variations. A structured repository allows shared and local rules, reuse, and overriding in a controlled way. Business users who understand the accord and analysts who understand risk models can access and update rules and models without IT involvement. Figure 9.11 shows how information from various systems affects the development of rules and models that feed decisions back to current systems. The decision service handles these rules and models and generates the necessary Basel II reports.

## Benefits

- Increased speed of implementation and implementation adjustments
- Centralized implementation of Basel II models and support for local variations
- Meets the use test by integrating transaction, account, borrower, and portfolio risk-based decision making

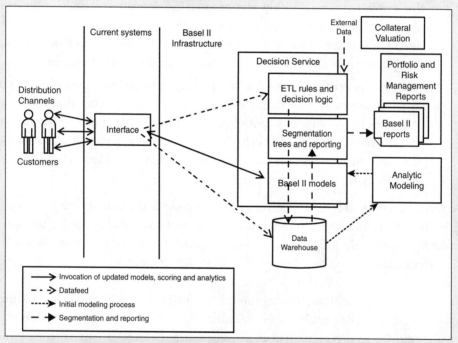

**Figure 9.11    An architecture showing how different rules and models run against existing data to update the data warehouse and generate reports**

- **Operational data available directly**—A decision service hub can rely on information passed with the request, but it should also be able to reach out to operational stores and even external sources for additional data required to make a decision.

- **Decision definitions driven from an enterprise rules repository (physical or logical)**—Business users and IT manage the rules in this repository collaboratively. Business users can use a performance management dashboard to monitor the business, including the decision service hub's behavior in the form of decision logs and corresponding changes to rules. This monitoring might involve adding, changing, or removing rules and taking advantage of the repository's rule authoring, rule versioning, release management, and other features.

- **A deployment infrastructure for predictive analytic models**—Because analysts and business users mine data for business rules or use data to build predictive models, these rules and models are deployed into the decision-making framework that implements the decision service hub. This infrastructure allows deploying analytics to operational systems, allows creating new rules that take advantage of new insight, ensures consistency in model use, and maximizes ROI by guaranteeing that the analytically enhanced decision is reused throughout the enterprise.

- **A control panel for controlling and managing behavior**—Typically, a control panel is integrated with corporate performance management dashboards and other reports. Because this control panel can be used for rule maintenance, the business can go from tracking behavior to controlling and managing it. With these tools, true business intelligence that guides operational decisions is in the hands of business users.

A decision service hub or decision-making backbone is the best vehicle for adopting EDM broadly across the enterprise. It provides control and agility and is the best way to make operationalizing insight from data easy. Figure 9.12, for instance, shows how a decision service hub is used by a European bank to deliver consistent risk decisions across many systems.

For most organizations, moving toward true EDM also requires a more systematic approach to including analytics in information systems. The **analytic value chain** involves moving an organization from a business or operational barrier to creating value by overcoming the barrier. A barrier to meeting business goals might be an identified business problem or an as-yet unmet opportunity for superior business performance. The steps in the value chain are as follows:

1. Establish business objectives.

2. Collect and prepare data.

3. Analyze data to gain predictive insight.

4. Determine the optimal decision.

5. Deploy to a decision service.

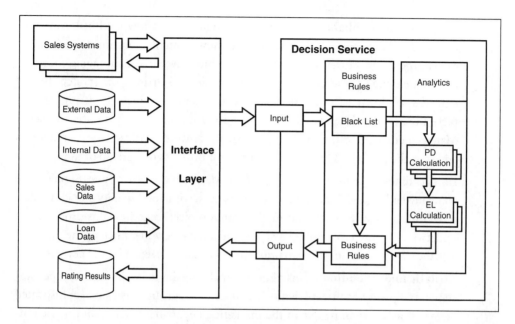

**Figure 9.12　A central decision service uses rules and analytics to deliver batch and online credit decisions for a major European bank**

The quality of decision making in your decision services, especially more sophisticated ones, is only as good as the weakest step in the value chain. Collecting the data you need to work on a problem, handling and understanding the implication of missing or bad data, being able to analyze data effectively to gain insight, and being able to use that insight to make a better decision in a decision service are important.

## What SmartEnough Logistics Did

To see how this sequence might work, take a look at SmartEnough Logistics again. SmartEnough found itself in the same mess that many organizations do today (see Chapter 3, "Why Aren't My Systems Smart Enough Already?"). Having decided to adopt EDM, it has moved in stages to become a decision-centered company with excellent operational implementation (see Chapter 1, "The Need for Smart Enough Systems"). SmartEnough went through the phases you have learned about in this chapter and the readiness assessments described in Chapter 8, "Readiness Assessment."

### Readiness Assessment

When SmartEnough Logistics assessed its readiness, it found, as most organizations do, a mixed level of readiness:

- **Business and IT collaboration**—SmartEnough found a low level of business-IT trust and collaboration. With little proof to show how collaboration helped and no management structures or work habits conducive to encouraging business involvement in IT projects, SmartEnough was clearly starting from scratch. To deal with this problem, it resolved to start with a small business rules project and picked the cross-sell/up-sell decision because it was an entirely additive decision. Management staff in the marketing department were involved to ease schedules and start the process of buying into the idea of business ownership of the system.

- **Data readiness**—Data readiness, in contrast, wasn't a big issue for SmartEnough. The company had a good handle on much of its data, with good quality and cleanliness programs. Its one weakness was in CDI, but a project to address this problem was underway. Because cross-sell/up-sell had been tentatively identified as the first project, the CDI project was asked to prioritize information needed for the new project.

- **Analytic understanding**—SmartEnough had a business intelligence competency center and plenty of BI experience. The operations group was using sophisticated analytics, and several people in the marketing department were doing some limited data mining. No immediate action items were established, although it was clear that this area would need improvement in the longer term.

- **Organizational change**—SmartEnough felt organizational change was a real strength. It had been trying give its customers and agents more decision-making power for some time and was already comfortable allowing pilots, drivers, and distribution center managers to make decisions. The regulatory environment, aside from customs, was straightforward, and the company managed organizational changes effectively. The customs issue was identified as a second candidate for a rules project.

- **Focus on operations**—Similarly, SmartEnough was operationally focused. Most management staff had been promoted from operational roles and knew how important day-to-day operations are to overall profitability.

In the end, SmartEnough's challenges were in business and IT collaboration and, to some extent, expanding its analytic understanding.

## Using Pieces

One of the first steps was measuring the decision yield for SmartEnough's portfolio of potential projects. The company had little experience with decision yield, so it used this technique in only a general way. However, decision yield did emphasize the value of the cross-sell/up-sell project and in solving its problems with customs. Both routing and service configuration/reconfiguration also showed potential for improvement.

As part of its initial adoption of EDM, SmartEnough continued the push to adopt both SOA and business process management (BPM) but focused on separating decisions into decision services. In particular, it worked with the marketing department to develop a rules-based cross-sell and up-sell decision service and integrate it into the Web site, call center, and drivers' handheld devices. Marketing staff often changed the rules in this decision service and quickly saw the value of being able to "own" the system's behavior. At first, they were disconcerted that the IT department provided templates but not rules, because the system wouldn't do anything until they added rules, but they adjusted. Now they change the rules more often than expected for some products and circumstances and less often than expected with others. The ROI from improving cross-sell rates and reducing maintenance (of up-sell code used in the call center) was much higher than expected.

For a first analytic project, SmartEnough turned to operations because that was where analytic expertise seemed to be. It worked with the analytic team to develop a model predicting the likelihood of on-time delivery and integrated a simple red/yellow/green traffic light to update call center staff. This model replaced a potentially long list of transit points and dense information on times and schedules and improved the call center staff's ability to give customers immediate feedback. The model was so successful that it was also integrated into the delivery status display on the Web site.

The final piece was the customs application. Using business rules to manage customs regulations enabled the team who handled this matter to interact more directly with the system that handled customs paperwork and improved the success rate by eliminating coding errors. The number of fines paid was reduced dramatically, generating a positive ROI, and the IT department discovered that rules could be repackaged so that customers could check customs regulations in advance. This feature had been on the wish list but had never been scheduled for development.

## Decision Management

The first integration of rules and analytics came in phase 2 of the up-sell/cross-sell application. SmartEnough was able to apply the marketing department's data-mining skills to the problem of analyzing subjective rules to see how well they were working. It gradually replaced them with rules derived from historical data, especially for customer and package segmentation. For the up-sell part of the process, SmartEnough discovered that it needed to know the likelihood of future business from a customer to make good offers. This information became the focus of its first predictive model; after building it, SmartEnough adapted decision trees mined from data to add the value this insight provided. The ROI was very positive, not least because the decision service was used in several systems, which multiplied the value of improving the service.

Although SmartEnough implemented an adaptive control infrastructure in support of this marketing application, it immediately saw value in using it to manage service experimentation and development. With the adaptive control environment in place, it could develop new rules and models for new services and test them more rigorously. Improvements in development and testing made it possible to address the service configuration problem as a stand-alone decision service, too.

## Expansion

Along with the necessary infrastructure improvements, SmartEnough found that its work on improving cross-sell and up-sell rates shared many rules and models with the service recommendation engine it had been considering. This engine was designed to help customers find the right service based on their needs and preferences. By focusing on these shared components, SmartEnough was able to get the engine to market quickly and validate its enterprise repository design.

SmartEnough was also determined to expand its analytic base so that it could be more proactive about using analytics in information systems. This effort involved increasing analytic staff and integrating them better with the software development process. The company decided to run analytics awareness training for developers and tried to ensure that all data-modeling work on IT projects included discussion of what would be useful to know that could be derived from data. It also started formal trade-off analysis in marketing as part of developing models for response, profitability, and use for customers.

SmartEnough took advantage of its growing use of business rules to hand over some control to customers—specifically, managing some rerouting rules and adding policies about extra paperwork to the customs application. Both changes enabled major customers to be more involved in processes and take more control over them, which improved customer satisfaction and retention.

Finally, SmartEnough started doing scenario planning in scheduling. Focusing on how major storms disrupted transportation, it was able to develop a new set of rules and models to be implemented in this situation. These new rules and models prioritized urgent packages more ruthlessly and made other similar changes.

## EDM Adoption

After SmartEnough Logistics finished its adoption of EDM, it became the company you read about in Chapter 1. It's using models to find optimal outcomes and conducting formal what-if analysis. It has standby rules and models for key scenarios and uses champion/challenger as well as decision analysis to achieve constant improvement in decisions. In fact, it replaces its models and rules with better ones so fast that it's inside the decision cycle of competitors—changing its decisions before competitors can react to the previous change.

## Extending EDM

After an organization has established itself as a mature EDM organization, it still has opportunities for improvement in state-of-the-art analytics and sophisticated approaches that EDM organizations are just beginning to adopt. They can improve the quality and sophistication of decisions, the speed at which decisions can be modified, and the degree to which decisions allow completely automated activity. Possible opportunities include the following, which are described in more detail in subsequent sections:

- Integrated decision models
- Time-sequenced decisions
- Automated evolution of decisions
- Bringing text into the mainstream
- Independent agents

### Integrated Decision Models

Often several decision models should be integrated to reflect shared resources or cross-impacts. For instance, you might have many different decisions about sales approach and marketing channels in which the total budget for marketing and sales is fixed. You might have different models for optimizing offers on a Web site but have a shared, fixed piece of Web real estate for displaying them.

Decision models sometimes influence each other, too. For instance, in multichannel marketing, you might see synergistic effects, such as sales calls that are more effective when TV commercial spending is at a certain level. Sometimes models of how operational decisions work influence each other, but some decision models are also influenced by strategic decisions that aren't modeled as separate operational decisions.

In general, integrating decision models involves a gradual increase in complexity. You might build a decision model to optimize sample configuration and timing for a product, repeat this process for coupons, and then integrate it with the model for samples. Your overall marketing resources are constrained, and you might find that certain coupon approaches improve the effectiveness of certain sample approaches, and you need to be able to optimize the combination. Say you add newsletters and continue to develop a more complex model of how your operational decisions interact. After considering all aspects of marketing a single product, you might consider multiproduct issues, and so on.

Besides this combination of operational decisions that share resources (marketing dollars, customer attention) or influence each other, you might also want to combine operational decisions with nonoperational factors, such as the impact of TV advertising on operational decisions. With simulation, you can bring them together and do something like marketing mix optimization built on separate operational decisions, not an aggregation of those decisions. You're simulating strategic questions, but you can still drill down to specific operational decisions that must be made to support the strategy. Now you're beginning to link your business intelligence/performance management environment, your operational environment, *and* your strategic decisions.

### Time-Sequenced Decisions

More sophisticated modeling can also pay off in time-sequenced decisions. Decision models can optimize a single decision, but optimizing a set of decisions over time is more complex, especially when each decision in the sequence affects subsequent decisions and associates' likely responses to those decisions. Although prioritization of possible options and other "lightweight" time sequencing are often done by using the techniques already described, formal modeling and optimization of these sequences is quite complex.

In Figure 9.13, the impact of an initial decision on profitability is enhanced by considering the impact of a second decision. The choices available at the second decision point are different for each original decision choice. Modeling this environment mirrors real life more closely than the simpler models discussed earlier, in that you make successive decisions that affect the same customers, for example. However, these models are extremely complex to develop and test and even harder to optimize.

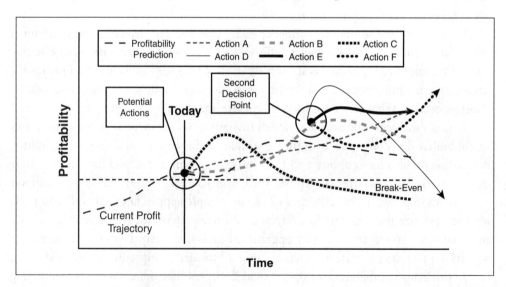

**Figure 9.13    The profitability of a series of decisions can vary widely**

## Automated Modification of Decisions

When decisions are deployed in a high-change environment, automated development and management of champion/challenger adaptive control is valuable. Sophisticated algorithms can automatically generate new challenger rules and models that deliberately vary from an existing champion. They might even be known to be suboptimal, and there's no expectation that they'll do better than the existing champion. They are designed to test an assumption as part of an experimental design.

At runtime, an automated process constantly develops and tests new challengers, puts them into production, and evaluates the results to refine the approach automatically. This combination of automation, experimental design, decision modeling, and adaptive control is definitely leading edge.

## Bringing Text into the Mainstream

EDM currently includes text analytics and the use of text in evaluating business rules, but its use of text couldn't be considered mainstream. Most business users use search technology to help them make decisions and to search the Web or documents in a section of an organization's intranet, for example. Most decision services currently have no such option. Some text analytics might be used to develop predictive models (when patterns in text are used as variables), and some access to text might be used to retrieve explanations, for example.

In the immediate future, technologies such as the following may well achieve mainstream status and will commonly be included in decision services:

- **Named entity recognition**—The process of labeling specified types of entities (such as people's names, company names, locations, financial amounts, or part numbers) in text automatically. This feature helps turn unstructured text into more structured text by identifying and labeling business objects.

- **Entity disambiguation**—This technology decides that two data records deal with the same entity, often by using text analysis. It has many other names in different domains, including deduplication, fuzzy matching, and reference reconciliation.

- **Undirected entity discovery**—This technology processes a volume of text and finds potential entities of interest without any initial specification of what they might be. It's usually iterative at present, so it includes a large manual component. However, the technology is advancing and requiring less training, and the results are becoming easier to deploy.

Ultimately, these tools allow processing text in decision services almost as easily as structured data.

### Independent Agents

Using rules and analytics to build completely independent "intelligent" software agents is just beginning. Combined with technology designed for complex event processing (CEP) or other forms of activity monitoring, an agent built with EDM technology can respond automatically and correctly often enough that some organizations are beginning to eliminate manual response—essentially targeting 100 percent automation.

Other ways to expand EDM are sure to develop as understanding and experience with the approach develop. Regardless of how far you progress toward steady state EDM or whether you try some of these extensions, you need to consider the impact of EDM on your existing and future IT architecture.

# CHAPTER TEN

# EDM and the IT Department

The impact of EDM on the IT department can be profound and positive. EDM builds on some of the most important trends in IT, solves some of IT's most persistent problems, and helps power some of the capabilities most in demand from IT departments. This chapter covers some of these impacts and discusses how decision services are deployed. The impact of EDM on software development life cycles and methodologies is also considered.

## Complementing, Solving, and Enabling

In many ways, the time is right for EDM, and it probably wasn't right until fairly recently. Although some organizations, many used as examples throughout this book, have been using these technologies and their predecessors to build smart enough systems for some time, the widespread adoption of EDM technologies and concepts wouldn't have been possible without today's IT ecosystem. Indeed, a major advantage of EDM is that it complements other technology adoption trends. It's additive rather than competitive.

A typical IT architecture has many components that relate to two aspects of EDM: data infrastructure and operating infrastructure. Some components relate to both.

The data infrastructure contains more data that's better understood, better organized, more timely, and more integrated. Many technologies, from enterprise information integration (EII) and enterprise application integration (EAI) to customer data integration (CDI) and master data management (MDM), contribute to integrating and organizing information. Business intelligence/data warehouse (BI/DW) and corporate performance management (CPM) technologies help manage and understand it.

All these technologies build on an operational infrastructure structured around a backbone of enterprise applications—such as customer relationship management (CRM), enterprise resource planning (ERP), and sales force automation (SFA)—that store, manage, process, and maintain data as part of running the business. These enterprise applications also provide an electronic backbone for delivering information and, therefore, decisions to front-line staff and associates who need them.

Enhancing and supplementing these applications with business process management (BPM) software makes them easier to use in support of complex business processes, and the move toward a service-oriented architecture (SOA) makes building, managing, and reusing components and services easier. Ever-improving Web and client user interfaces, including those labeled "Web 2.0", and their capability to make more systems accessible to a wider audience continue to push this electronic backbone closer to those concerned with these processes.

Meanwhile, IT departments struggle to develop new applications while being submerged in maintenance requests to upgrade and enhance existing systems. Many are asked to deliver business activity monitoring (BAM) and event processing to make businesses more responsive and to mobile-enable their workforce, customers, and associates. Providing more self-service applications that work in multiple channels is a persistent problem, as devices multiply and the Internet changes communication styles. IT departments have legacy platforms of all types, many of which must be coordinated, yet the pressure to introduce new technologies, such as social media, and new approaches, such as model-driven development, continues.

EDM offers opportunities to build on and complement your IT architecture, solve some problems your IT department is facing, and provide some of the most demanding functionality on your to-do list. When you think about a modern IT architecture, you probably do so in one of two ways. Perhaps you're an optimist and a follower of technology trends who sees the new capabilities and technologies revolutionizing enterprise IT or perhaps you are a pessimist who can think only about your organization's hodgepodge of aging technology and the limitations this imposes. Table 10.1 compares these two contrasting views of enterprise IT.

### Table 10.1   Comparing Views on IT Architectures

| Optimistic View | Pessimistic View |
| --- | --- |
| The state of the art is moving to a world that's "digital, mobile, virtual, and personal," as Carly Fiorina, former CEO of Hewlett-Packard, said in 2004. | Most organizations have an IT architecture that's static, complex, messy, and impersonal. |
| All functionality is made available through well-defined services running on a robust SOA platform that provides a strong repository and high performance registry. | Although new projects take an SOA approach, much of the functionality the organization uses isn't available as services. |

| Optimistic View | Pessimistic View |
|---|---|
| Services are used in composite applications. Mostly they are defined by using a BPMS that orchestrates them into effective business processes supporting the way the organization needs to operate. | Although business process management is increasingly important, few core business processes have been reengineered into a BPMS.<br><br>Some new applications are composite applications, but most are not, and business logic and other functionality are coded into each one. |
| Processes are monitored and tracked to see how the organization is doing against its key performance indicators, and those involved in the process have a rich set of information available to them. | Most reporting is from a data warehouse that's not current or complete. Analytics are rudimentary, with power users building their own reports and many standard reports of dubious value. Data mining is scattered and piecemeal. |
| Business activity monitoring is tightly integrated into processes to ensure that those managing them are immediately aware of issues or bottlenecks. | Monitoring is mostly by reports, and dashboards are limited in scope and are not as up to date or useful as needed. |
| The data used in services is integrated so that all information about customers or products is available in a single request, and data is available for summary and analytic reporting without performance implications. | Data is stored in several databases, and integration remains a problem. Technologies such as EAI and EII bring together some data sources in an application, but despite CDI and MDM initiatives, integrating metadata remains a problem. |
| The organization uses packaged enterprise applications for standard functionality—functionality that supports the organization but doesn't differentiate it. | Much of the functionality used is available only through large legacy applications running on a wide variety of platforms. |
| All this functionality is available as services and is easy to integrate with custom services the organization develops. | Enterprise applications for CRM or ERP are used, but various collections of functions are at different release levels, and few or none of them are available through services. |
| Some processes are outsourced, and integrating them is managed easily by using an SOA approach. Their performance is managed effectively alongside the performance of internally run, but related processes. | Some departments use software as a service (SaaS) providers to plug gaps in the information architecture, but there's little or no integration with internal systems. Similarly, outsourced processes are managed at arm's length, with reports going back and forth and no integration. |

*continues*

**Table 10.1    Continued**

| Optimistic View | Pessimistic View |
|---|---|
| Outside core processes, the organization is highly event-driven. Data on inbound events is processed, aggregated, and acted on immediately to notify staff and systems to act. Event-driven functionality reuses the services and service architecture that process-driven elements use. | Event-driven applications are simple and notify people to take action only through worklists and simple e-mail notifications.<br><br>Few, if any, parts of the business are managed by using a combination of events and processes. |
| Customer and employee-facing applications use dynamic Web interfaces on thin and mobile clients seamlessly. Wireless and other location-aware technology is used with customers and mobile staff. | Blackberries are the only mobile device of note in the organization that are connected to enterprise systems. The Web site has some features available to mobile device users, but management of mobile, location-aware devices as a channel is rudimentary. |
| Social networking technologies allow associates to use different aspects of the organization that matter to them in a unique mashup of functionality and information. | Some small projects are adopting Web 2.0 technologies to build more engaging and dynamic Web sites, but they don't affect core enterprise applications, and early attempts at social networking aren't integrated with anything else. |
| The IT architecture runs on a hardware platform that's interoperable and closely managed. | Every conceivable kind of hardware and operating system seems to be in use. Processes and applications often require more than one platform. |
| Requirements are managed in tools and combined with models. Systems development and maintenance work come from these models. | Projects use models, such as those defined in Unified Modeling Language (UML), in theory, but the models have little or no long-term value. Models are used in initial design and construction, but ongoing maintenance and modification are manual. Requirements are poorly defined and managed. |
| IT is a source of innovation and focuses its energy on new systems that add value to the business. | The application maintenance backlog is large and consumes the majority of IT resources to change existing systems to match new and revised requirements. |

If your organization looks more like the optimistic view, EDM can add value to your architecture. If your IT architecture looks more like the pessimistic view but you're trying to move toward a truly modern IT architecture, EDM can build on the architecture you *actually* have as well as the one you're building. Before considering the impact EDM can have on the IT department's concerns and issues, reviewing a brief summary of how decision services are deployed can be helpful.

## Decision Services and the EDM Ecosystem

Deploying a decision service into the production environment where other applications and services can access it is the final step in bringing EDM solutions into operation. Typically, this step means deploying decision services into an existing IT infrastructure and linking those decision services to business processes, enterprise applications, and Web sites. Figure 10.1 shows how one particular organization uses centralized business rules and analytic model infrastructure to deliver effective decision services to multiple operational systems. A number of key concepts, discussed in the following sections, are involved.

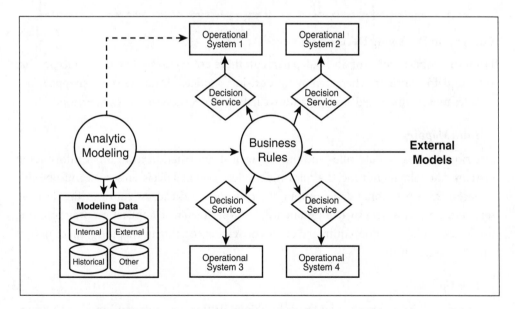

**Figure 10.1    An architecture showing how rules and models deliver decision services in a major credit card issuer**

---

### Role: Developers

Developers (programmers) build information systems and the "plumbing" for decision services. They need the following:

- A willingness to give up some control of their systems to improve them
- An understanding of business users' perspectives so that they can build effective rule maintenance environments for them
- An understanding of the value of analytics and the challenges in using them
- Communication skills and an ability to work with both analytical and business users

Developers do much of the construction work of a decision service and the setup to allow business users to be involved. On top of usual developer skills, they need a willingness to partner with business users on development.

---

## Concepts in Deploying Decision Services

From the point of view of an IT department, there are relatively few new concepts that you need to consider when deploying decision services. Data must be mapped, live updates must be managed, and the additive nature of decision services understood.

### Data Mapping

Decision services execute rules and models against information from other information systems. At deployment time, the rules and models used in a decision service must be able to access this operational data without any runtime overhead. At runtime, the decision service must access data by using standard, high-performance application programming interfaces (APIs) and not require data type conversion (casting or mapping) that imposes a performance burden.

### Live Updates

With most decision services, you must be able to deploy new rules and models to a running service without having to interrupt or restart it. Therefore, you need a way to schedule updates or specify an on-demand update mechanism that allows deploying tested rules and models. When these **live updates** happen, running transactions must be able to finish, using the rules and models they started with (although this capability might be overruled for some updates), and all new transactions must use the new rules and models. This capability is widespread in today's decision technology, and for highly agile systems it can be crucial.

### Additive Services

A key characteristic of decision services is that they tend to be additive. They aren't replacements for existing systems or services, nor are they **systems of record**—they don't manage the data that documents your business, such as orders and customers. They don't run the business directly; instead, they allow the systems you have running your business to run more effectively. Decision services typically don't *replace* existing systems but *enhance* them or replace only part of the existing system—hard-coded decision logic. When considering how to integrate decision services into your IT infrastructure, keep this characteristic in mind.

### Deployment Process

Figure 10.2 shows how a decision service responds to requests for decisions from production applications by executing rules and models against information, all in the context of your enterprise IT architecture. Getting decision services to this point involves quality assurance (QA) and test processes, deployment, and integration.

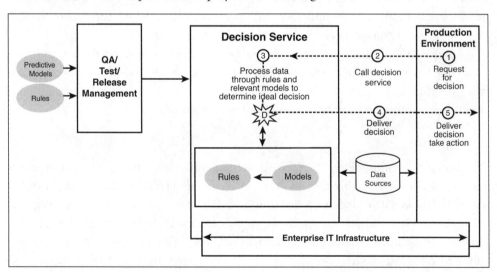

**Figure 10.2 Deploying decision services in EDM** *©Fair Isaac Corporation, reproduced with permission*

### QA/Test

Each version of a decision service is put through a quality assurance (QA) and test step that's usually the same as the QA/test for other services in the application portfolio and, like them, is concerned with integration and system test issues. If the rule maintenance environment enables business users to change rules in a running decision service, this capability probably isn't covered in standard QA/test plans. You need to develop suitable tests and checks to make sure that authenticating business users, limiting their edits, and redeploying rules to running services all work correctly. A separate QA/test step, focused only on rules changes, takes place *after* business users have made changes to the test system and before those changes are applied to the production decision service.

As discussed in Chapter 7, "Adaptive Control," champion and challenger strategies should be run through the QA/test process, and the whole environment needs to be tested to make sure the right percentage of transactions flow through each challenger. If the decision service will check for new rules or models automatically, this process needs to be tested, too.

### Deployment

How you deploy a decision service into a production environment depends largely on the production environment. If a decision service is deployed into several distinct environments without using an SOA approach, each deployment is separate, and part of the testing should ensure that all deployments stay synchronized correctly.

Many BRMS products support automated deployment of new, tested rules, and more modeling environments now include this capability for models. Deploying decision services that monitor for new rules or models typically requires deployed services to have access to repositories where these rules or models are stored.

### Integration

Decision services must be able to receive data from applications asking for answers and be able to pass information back. In addition, many decision services access internal and/or external data as part of making a decision, and these data sources need to be integrated with the service. Technologies such as enterprise service buses (ESBs) and business process management systems (BPMSs) might also need to be integrated. Integration usually isn't complex; modern decision-making technologies are built with integration in mind, but it must take place and be suitably robust. Figure 10.3 shows one form of decision service integration where decision services are deployed as Web services and accessed using standard interfaces. The applications calling the decision service treat it like any other service.

Integrating decision services into your IT architecture can have many benefits in terms of complementing and strengthening it, solving some persistent problems, and delivering some needed improvements in IT capabilities. These benefits are discussed in the following sections.

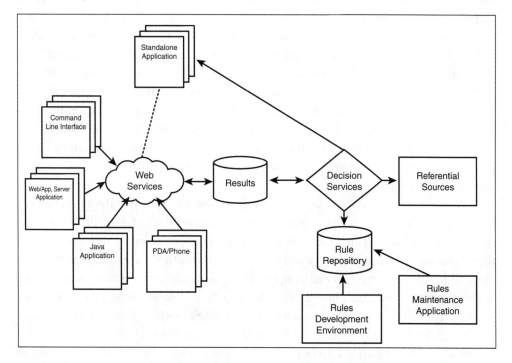

**Figure 10.3**    **An architecture for preventive maintenance decisions that uses Web services to integrate with systems**

## Complementing Your IT Architecture

The first area of IT architecture to consider is what EDM *complements*. EDM builds on and takes advantage of some current IT architectural trends:

- Service-oriented architecture (SOA)
- Business process management (BPM)
- Data integration (including CDI, MDM, EAI, and EII)
- Web 2.0 and social networking (tagging, mashups, wikis)

EDM builds on each trend in different but complementary ways, as explained in the following sections.

## Building on SOA

A major benefit of adopting an SOA is supposed to be an increase in business agility, mostly because of the reduced time, cost, and difficulty of making a change. The definition of functionality as coherent components or services with well-defined interfaces helps limit a change's impact to a single service, which makes change easier to control and implement. Well-defined services are loosely coupled—they use service contracts to allow services to interact without having to depend on interaction. These services change independently, and as long as the interface to the service doesn't need to be changed, independent service changes shouldn't affect other services. SOA contrasts with the typical result of changing monolithic applications—a change is likely to cause a ripple effect throughout the application stack. SOA also supports a more iterative approach to defining services because of this control over the impact of change, which also helps in agility by eliminating the need to define a complete set of requirements upfront. SOA makes more agile development possible.

When you define business services with SOA, you can decouple the business from automation of the business. Business services are independent of a particular process; they perform a business function you can use in many processes. In this way, you can define new composite applications and business processes that use existing business services, which increases reuse as well as agility. Now you can assemble a new process—such as for handling a new channel, for example—mostly by orchestrating existing business services, especially with entity-centered business services in which functionality is associated with a defined entity or set of information, such as customers or accounts.

In addition, using an ESB to implement an SOA can increase agility by providing an integration layer and enabling you to assemble services on different platforms and perhaps with different interface semantics. By making it easy to add new services, transform messages to allow services to interact, and so on, an ESB can increase the level of agility beyond what service orientation alone can offer. Figure 10.4 shows how one organization used publish/subscribe interfaces with a decision service to ensure that specific process steps and messages on the ESB could trigger the same decision. This infrastructure also enabled the decision service to publish additional messages onto the ESB, which allowed for easy integration with other services connected to the ESB.

Clearly, some services implement a business function that must change more often and be more capable of adapting to change than others. Some services increase value when changed. The costs of failing to change some or doing so in a way that can't be audited for compliance might also vary in services. These services are defined as decision

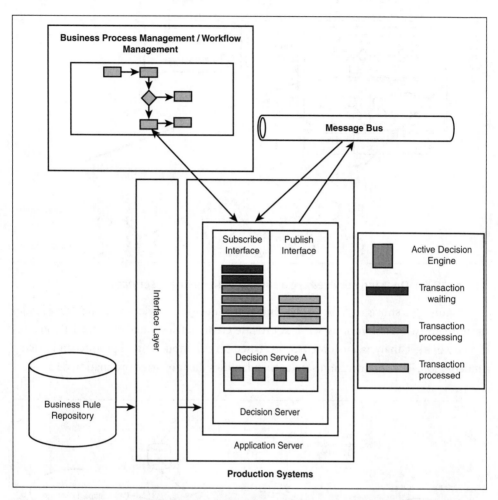

**Figure 10.4   How a decision service can communicate decisions with BPM or workflow software and a message bus by using a publish/subscribe approach**

services and usually implement business functions that are in constant flux, complex or voluminous business logic, or business functions that aren't easy for programmers to understand or for which business user control is critical. With decision services, business logic can be changed and shared more easily between services in the SOA and non-service-enabled applications in the portfolio. As shown in Figure 10.5, decision services are a subset of all possible business services as well as legacy services available for reuse.

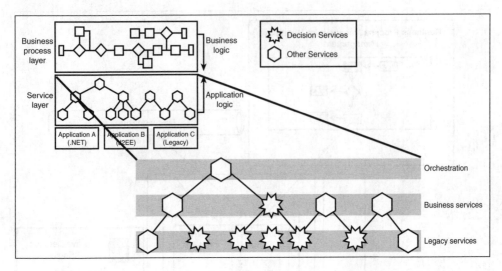

**Figure 10.5    Decision services are a subset of all business services**

Figure 10.6 shows an SOA implementation of decision services for a mortgage lender in the United States. Various services provide credit retrieval and summarization, secondary market analysis, customer scores (based on risk models), and product and pricing information. The core decision service then handles the mortgage origination decision.

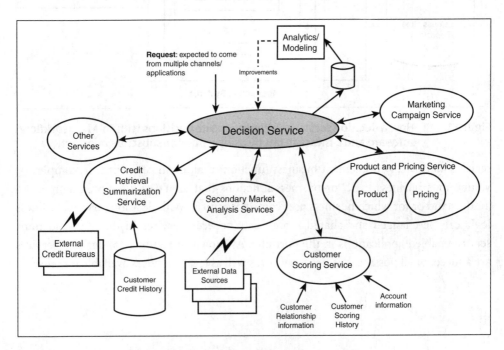

**Figure 10.6    An SOA for decision services in mortgage lending**

Decision services also allow a more effective "build or buy" decision. Organizations can buy services based on best practices and standards where the functionality of those services is not critical to the organizations' competitive differentiation. They can then build services with competitive potential and use an SOA infrastructure to compose them into effective applications and processes. Many services that differentiate an organization—that is, that define how it acts differently within a standard process framework—are decision services. Focusing on decision services can, therefore, make it possible to construct composite applications mostly from standard services that still deliver a unique and competitive customer experience. In addition, integrating analytics in decision services is a more effective way to apply data to improving processes than trying to "service-enable" traditional business intelligence (BI) tools.

## Completing Application Decomposition

If you embed decisions in your applications, you hide these decisions from view and delegate details to the wrong people—systems developers, not business users. Traditional application development techniques hide decision logic deep inside software, making development time-consuming and costly. Developers have to translate business requirements ("If this condition is encountered, respond in this manner") into abstract representations in programming languages—a laborious process full of possibilities for error.

By embedding decisions in applications, your decisions become a liability. By managing decisions, however, you can enable business users to make their own changes, which reduces the time to make changes and reduces maintenance expenses. Focusing on decisions as a separate component is, in many ways, the last step in the decomposition of traditional applications.

Not so long ago, applications were monolithic, containing data, user interfaces, business logic, and process flow in one block of code. Then the process of decomposition shown in Figure 10.7 began. With the advent of databases, managing and reusing data became easier if it was removed from applications. For the first time, data was defined so that people knew what it represented, which allowed business users to access data for themselves. Next, client/server, thin clients, portals, and rich interfaces improved and separated the interface from the application. The same interface could access multiple applications in more sophisticated ways. Most recently, BPMSs have been adopted, which makes it possible to externalize work flow and build cross-application flows effectively. All that's left in applications is technical code and business logic. Decomposing applications one more step by separating business logic into its own managed environment makes more sense now and could be the most important advance to date.

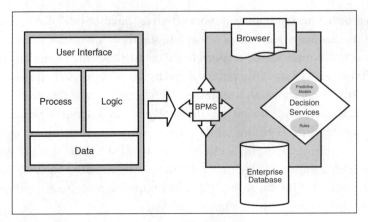

**Figure 10.7    The evolution of applications from monolithic to completely decomposed**

### Avoiding Brain-Dead Processes

As the monolithic application of old has been decomposed gradually, organizations are using BPMSs to design and build more processes. A BPMS focuses on *how* a process should be carried out. It helps standardize processes, facilitates collaboration and compliance, defines and manages workflow, automates steps, and provides activity monitoring, alerts, process reporting, and integration. What it doesn't do well is decide what should be done. A BPMS alone doesn't help standardize operational decisions, facilitate decision automation and maintenance, centralize business rules, or support straight-through processing in any but the most simple situations.

Adopting a BPMS without also adopting an EDM approach to decision automation has a number of risks, as described in the following list. You have probably spent time thinking about processes you're implementing in a BPMS but not as much about decisions in those processes—the "diamonds" in your process diagrams.

- A BPMS doesn't manage business rules or decisions properly. It manages process orchestration and process flow design, but not rules or policies. A BPMS does have some support for rules, but usually only as part of the definition of orchestration or composition. As a result, business rules and the decisions they automate are an afterthought.

- Without explicit management, business rules are reburied in the new process, which makes the process complex. Routing rules aren't business rules; decision-centered business rules are about the organization's underlying behavior, not its processes.

- Inconsistency in business rules is likely. This inconsistency is a problem, particularly if you need several kinds of BPMSs, and embedding policy rules in each BPMS means duplicating them and failing to manage them as an asset. Ensuring enterprise consistency in processes is hard unless you manage the decisions in them separately.

- Problems with consistency and rule management can cause trouble when regulators ask you to explain how you picked a particular branch in your process. Being able to explain just the process is not enough. Noncompliance caused by faulty business rules is likely, leading to fines.

- Although you can add process analytics to a process, you can improve the process only manually. Someone must examine and redesign the process. If you have automated decision points and manage them, you can use analytics to improve a process by adding analytic models to aid automated decision making.

- Personalizing transactions for customers is hard unless you make transaction-centered decisions in the process. You probably don't want to create a personalized process for each customer, but personalizing the decisions you make about customers as they run through a standard process might be just as effective.

- You might not get the business agility you're looking for. Although some problems require a change in process definition, others do not. Especially in a core process that doesn't change much, agile management of decisions could matter more.

---

### Compliance Issues

Some compliance is about processes—whether you follow certain steps or keep certain data—and some is about rules—whether you enforce certain rules or take only allowed actions. Often both types of compliance are required. In a healthcare claims process, for example, you might have to show how the claim was reviewed or referred for a second opinion, and show when you saved information and what information you saved. You might also have to show that the rules you followed for deciding to decline a claim were legitimate and appropriate. You can't get compliance correct without the right mix of flexible process automation and effective decision automation.

### European Health Insurer: Claims Handling

#### Old Way

Claims were processed with a 30-year-old system running on a mainframe combined with client/server systems. Business users had no understanding of the decision logic used in the systems and couldn't adjust it, so it became out of date. Any changes required costly IT projects.

#### EDM Way

Three decision services are integrated with a BPMS and a data integration hub. They handle claims adjudication and payment, among other decisions. Business users manage business rules for adjudication, for example, which ensures that rules are current and makes future product additions and enhancements straightforward. The centralized decision services provide consistent decisions and benefit calculations for all claim types and enable a high rate of auto-adjudication for maximum efficiency. Decision services can apply additional rules to route claims to the correct departments. These same rules deliver Web-based self-service for claimants. Figure 10.8 shows the architecture with three decision services.

#### Benefits

- Flexibility and agility in making changes and adding new products
- Consistency in decisions and benefit calculations
- Adjudicating claims automatically

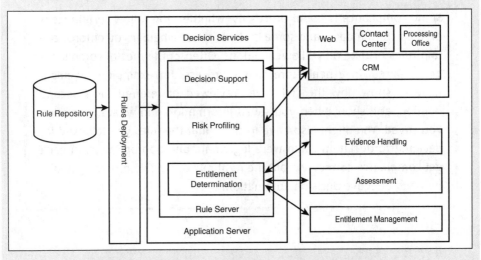

**Figure 10.8    An architecture for a claims-processing system**

Similarly, adopting a BPMS and EDM in parallel has several potential benefits:

- Using EDM to automate decisions in a new process can simplify the process dramatically. You can often eliminate several steps to have a single decision node in the process. When the automation percentage is high, the main process becomes the one without manual intervention, and the more complex one becomes the exception. Even if you can't reduce the steps in the design environment, the implementation complexity of a typical process is reduced. Figure 10.9 is an example of two decision services used to reduce the complexity of a process.

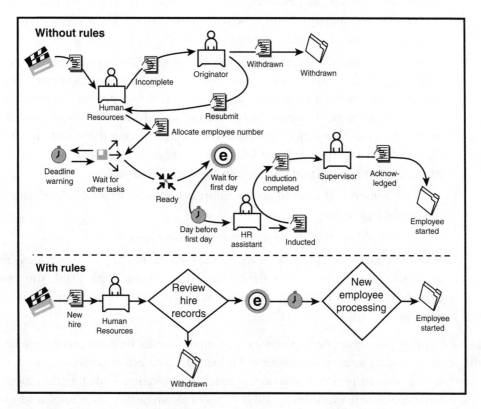

**Figure 10.9    A process simplified by automating critical decisions**

- Using business rules in an EDM approach to manage rules in a process's decisions makes management more effective. You can tie rule sets to business objectives and monitor them, and although rule sets are tied to a new process, your rules aren't buried in it. You can tie these same rule sets and decision services to other systems not built with a BPMS so that you can use the same decisions in several applications. For example, business rules for dealing with an order might affect your call center, processes for problem resolution in your BPMS, self-service applications on your Web site, and legacy systems for bill production.

- You can manage and deploy process and decision changes independently. There's no reason that the need to change a decision should correspond with a need to change process steps. When you have long-running processes, keeping decisions separate allows you to change work in progress. The process definition to be used to process an item of work is fixed for that item at the time it's instantiated. For long-running processes, a fixed process definition that embeds decisions is a problem because business rules and analytic models might not be current when they're evaluated. If you manage decisions separately and retrieve them when a process needs the decision, the decision is always current.

- If you want to use BI with business processes, especially those you're automating, you need to be clear what it is you want to do. To improve a process, do you want to analyze how you run the process, or do you want to use your store of information about products, customers, suppliers, and so on? Most BPMS tools handle analysis for you: They help you see how you run the process and what trends are identified and help you use that information to improve ongoing execution of the process. To use your store of information, you have two choices:

  - Use traditional BI tools to deliver information to someone who performs a manual step in the process.

  - Use an EDM approach to apply data insight to decision services.

  If you use only reporting-style BI tools to apply analytics to your process, you're limited to investigating and understanding your process. With EDM, you can embed data-driven and scientific decision making in your processes using decision services.

Using EDM to avoid brain-dead processes is common when a business process reaches the point of needing a complex automated business decision before continuing, such as origination, underwriting, fraud detection, or precision marketing. To do this, the process calls a decision service to examine applicable data and recommend actions, such as which products or services to offer or who should be notified of the current status. The BPMS uses the decision data to continue its flow through the process.

## Types of Agility

When focusing on agility, you need both process agility and decision agility. Some kinds of change require changing a process in response. A change in core processes usually has a major impact on the entire organization and could require organizational change and perhaps new audit procedures. Processes around a company's "edge"—those with lower transaction volumes, less repeatability, and more manual steps—must be easy to change, because they're likely to change often. To do this, you need **process agility**.

Sometimes the change required in a process isn't about the process itself. For instance, a change to rules for determining price discount eligibility doesn't change the process—it changes the decision of what discount to offer. To achieve **decision agility**, you must be able to change decisions in a process quickly without changing the process. This agility matters most in core business processes that are stable in steps and outcomes but can vary in decision making over time.

EDM can also take advantage of a BPMS when a decision service reaches the point of needing additional data in the decision process, which requires human intervention. The service initiates a BPMS process to bring the right users into the flow and step them through the required tasks. When the BPMS process finishes, it reinitiates the decision service with a saved state and new data. Similarly, a decision service can call for a complex business process to be started. It calls the appropriate BPMS process as the rule action, often while continuing to run the rest of the decision.

### Better Decisions, Not Just Better Data

Many organizations deploy a vast array of technology to better integrate data and deliver it more effectively to the part of the business where it's useful. These technologies usually fall into these broad categories:

- **Enterprise information integration (EII)**—EII technology creates a virtual object from a variety of data sources that other applications can use without having to worry about the original data source. EII can result in much looser coupling between data sources and the services that need the data.

- **Enterprise application integration (EAI)**—Similar to EII, EAI enables integrating enterprise applications to support a business process. Unlike EII, it's not just about integrating data in those applications; it's also about the process that runs through them.

- **Customer data integration (CDI)**—CDI technology gives companies a 360-degree view of their customers by reconciling different data sources with customer information so that all information the organization has about customers is accessible after the customer has been identified.

- **Master data management (MDM)**—In many ways a superset of CDI, MDM is an attempt to bring a company's reference or master data under control. This data is typically spread over many data sources and is hard to access coherently.

The challenge with these technologies is that you must *act* on the information to get value from them. Overestimating the value of making more information available is easy. No matter how easy you make it to use information, you still assume that users can put it into context and use it. For instance, if your doctor has an electronic medical record of your entire history, will she make a different treatment decision because of it? Will she have the time to read it all or be able to spot the crucial piece?

---

### Transaction-Centered Processes

Using EDM for decision automation in processes allows you to build processes that are driven by transactions. The data or metadata in the transaction determines what scores models generate, and the combination of scores and data determines which rule fires in your decision service. This in turn decides which steps to take to complete the transaction.

You have now "inverted" the process—it flows from the customer to the organization. An example of an inverted process is an origination process, in which data the customer enters affects the models and rules for determining which products are available and the process then executes to offer and fulfill those products. This kind of analytically driven, transaction-based process is a key component in customer focus and personalization strategies.

---

Making information more readily available is important, but making better decisions based on information is what pays the bills. Bill Gates was quoted recently as saying:

> *"Resolving the information overload and underload problem will take more than just better search tools. What's required is a comprehensive approach to enterprise information management that spans information creation, collection, and use and helps ensure that organizations can unlock the full value of their investments in both information and people."[1]*

You also need ways to turn better information into better decisions and, therefore, better outcomes. Better-informed organizations don't perform better automatically; they perform better if they can make better decisions with that information. In other words, having a 360-degree view of a customer results in better customer treatment only if you can, and do, use that view to *improve decisions*.

Another challenge in using data integration and management technologies is latency.[2] You can divide latency into three categories: capture latency, analysis latency, and decision latency, as shown in Figure 10.10. When many organizations talk about real-time data, they focus on capture latency—how long after the business event data is available for analysis. In reality, analysis latency (the time to analyze data) *and* decision latency (the time to decide how to act in response to analysis) also matter. EDM builds on the latency reduction of data integration and management technologies by reducing analysis and decision latency as well and adding business value, as shown in Figure 10.10.

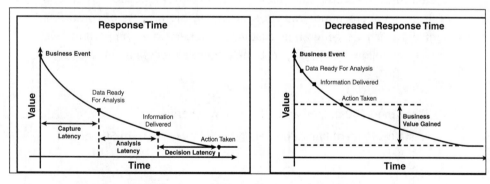

**Figure 10.10    Types of latency between events and responses**

---

[1] Bill Gates, "Beyond Business Intelligence: Delivering a Comprehensive Approach to Enterprise Information Management," 2006.

[2] Richard Hackathorn, "Active data warehousing: from nice to necessary," *Teradata* magazine, June 2006.

### U.S. State Tax Authority: Nonfilers

#### Old Way

The tax authority had more than 200 million pieces of information from federal and state sources on tax returns. It used this information to identify citizens who haven't filed all the required tax forms or who have made major mistakes in filing. A 30-year-old system failed to identify nonfilers correctly, missing some and misidentifying other taxpayers as nonfilers. Tax revenue was lost, and taxpayers were angered. Millions of nonfilers had to be handled, and changing the system to respond to new tax laws or data sources was hard. Hundreds of millions of dollars was at risk annually.

#### EDM Way

A decision service contains business rules that match filing information to other data sources to identify potential misfiling or nonfiling citizens. Business and technical staff collaborate on rules to make processing more accurate. Those who understand the tax system can edit rules. Changes can be made to rules whenever regulations or policies change, and all rules are stored and managed in a central repository. A second decision service contains rules for managing the process of contacting nonfilers (such as generating customized letters) and supporting self-service capabilities for taxpayers to help them correct filing problems.

#### Benefits

- More than $30 million annually in new revenue
- Mistakes in identifying nonfilers reduced by more than 50 percent

**Business Agility and Data Integration**   *When a decision service uses complex data, business agility is lost unless the integration is easy to manage in the face of change. An EDM approach's agility depends mostly on a stable object model. To improve business agility, integration technologies can ensure that the decision service "sees" a stable object model, even if underlying data sources change.*

One final note on how EDM builds on data integration technologies: Proving an ROI for some MDM/CDI initiatives can be difficult. How do you show the value of better decision making when you don't have a good definition of what "good" decision making is? Using an EDM approach, particularly the champion/challenger strategy, can be effective in proving an ROI. Comparing an account-based strategy with a customer-based one, for example, can show whether a new strategy is better and, if so, how much better. This comparison enables you to put a value on data integration, but only if the decision has been automated, of course.

### Using Customer Interests and Social Media

One trend made possible by the Internet is the growth in customer (and other associates) participation. Customers can write blogs, contribute content to wikis, develop their own mashups that include your content or reference your products, tag and review your products, or change the rules you use to interact with them. All this information tells you something about customers, but using the information often seems impossible without manual intervention, which isn't possible either if many people are involved. With EDM, however, you can get more value from this type of customer interaction.

When you're trying to use this kind of customer information, however, remember that the act of participation tells you something about customers. You can include information about how much they contribute (number of postings, number of reviews, average ratings, number of contributions to a wiki, and average length of contributions, for example) as part of their information profile. These characteristics might be highly predictive of a certain class of customer. Wikipedia, for instance, finds that some contributors make a few important edits (they could be considered subject experts), and others make many minor edits (they could be considered content stewards). Understanding your customers in this way can be helpful. You can also use these characteristics for rules-driven treatment of customers. For instance, you might route a call to more knowledgeable customer service representatives (CSRs) if the customer contributes regularly to your product wiki.

You might also be able to analyze what customers say to infer their opinions. This analysis might be as simple as using their ratings or as complex as text analysis of postings to look for competitors, product names, positive or negative words, and other details. With this analysis, you could separate customers into those who like your products and those who like your competitors' products, for example. In reality, only a small percentage of any community participates in this way—perhaps a maximum of 5 to 10 percent. If you can use participation to understand a group of your customers, however, you could find attributes known for all customers that predict the identified behavior. For instance, if analyzing your wiki identifies customers who like your products, you might find other aspects of your customer data, such as buying patterns, that are highly predictive of this behavior. You could then infer that customers showing those buying patterns probably think the same way, even though they aren't participating in the wiki.

> **Use Data Holistically**   *Remember that all customer data should be used together. Information about how customers interact with you (by phone, over the Web, in person), the way they change their preferences (and whether they do so), and their participation in social media tells you something about your customers. Using this information to affect how they're treated by rules and in analytic models can improve their experience and help you. The same advice about using data together holds true for other kinds of associates—employees and partners, for example.*

EDM and deploying decision services can complement current IT trends, but it can also help solve some of IT's most persistent problems, as discussed in the following sections.

## Solving IT Problems

EDM also has an impact on IT architecture by easing a number of well-established problems, such as maintenance backlogs, channel inconsistency, heterogeneous platforms, and the general level of "stupidity" of enterprise applications. Although solving these problems has value for the whole organization, many IT departments regard these problems as "their" domain, so they are often described as "IT problems."

### Ending Maintenance as You Know It

Most IT departments are drowning in maintenance work. This work, including changing systems to meet new or revised requirements, is often perceived as low-value work and a burden on the IT department that prevents it from doing more useful work. However, change is a constant, so maintenance might seem to be, too. After all, despite IT professionals' jokes, most change requests don't come from users too stupid to get it right or from users failing to decide what they want. Most changes are caused by users' business needs changing—new regulations, policies, competitors, products, and market opportunities, for example. Taking an EDM approach to new systems and to modernizing existing applications can dramatically reduce IT's maintenance burden.

An EDM approach allows you to fix the applications you already have incrementally to reduce maintenance. In many applications, the majority of the change requests come in a small area, such as the pricing or eligibility module. In these applications, the majority of the code typically has few change requests and is largely stable. The change requests are usually requests for changes to the business rules embedded in the code. Renovating this one piece by using EDM, developing a decision service to replace it, costs much less than replacing the whole application. The new decision service, built using business rules, will require fewer IT resources to maintain and will allow business users to make many, if not all, of the business changes they need themselves. The application remains stable, because much of the code is not edited, and the robust nature of business rules-based components minimizes the impact of rule changes on the system.

Fixing existing systems is part of the problem, but with EDM, you can prevent the problem from continuing to grow. Using an EDM approach means building decision services that encapsulate rules an application must run. These rules represent the single largest source of change requests, so an EDM approach minimizes the impact of these change requests. Indeed, using EDM to build decision services makes it possible to build changeable applications and design flexibility into the system. By enabling business users to maintain some rules, you can use user-configurable components that require fewer programmers to maintain. These new systems, like your old ones, will be in use much longer than you expect (perhaps 10 to 15 years) and will continue to evolve and change to meet new business needs. EDM can help make sure they don't contribute to your maintenance burden.

Another consequence of neverending maintenance work is that most IT organizations have a huge backlog of projects they're unable to start, let alone finish. With reported maintenance spending sometimes reaching 75 percent of software budgets, perhaps any new projects being taken on is more surprising than having a backlog. The ROI for eliminating maintenance comes in part from your "value backlog."

Projects in your backlog aren't progressing because of a lack of time or resources; other projects have higher priorities. Your organization has probably estimated the potential business value of projects in the backlog. Indeed, most projects don't even make it to the backlog unless they have a positive potential—the project's business value exceeds its cost. So being able to complete all projects in your backlog would add tremendous value to your business. By reducing maintenance work, you free up resources to work on the backlog, and the total net business value of completed projects is your value backlog and represents a potential return on an EDM investment.

## Large Field Services Organization: Managing Field Representatives

### Old Way

A network of more than 1,000 contractors performed property management activities for the company's clients. In a typical month, 150,000 properties were managed. A largely paper-based process involved faxing and shipping work orders to contractors. Ensuring compliance with federal and state regulations involved manual review of binders full of regulations. Updates to regulations were frequent and time-consuming to make. These regulations influenced what work should be done, the time frame for the work, and payment of contractors. A lack of integration resulted in frequent rekeying and manual review of information in legacy systems. Clients often wanted a customized service, but customizing a client process meant initiating a major programming project and producing specific instructions and workarounds.

### EDM Way

A decision service is integrated with a workflow engine and EAI software to support field representatives. Integrated data from several systems is fed into the decision service, which uses the workflow engine to route work orders and contains rules for work order decisions. Some rules implement state and federal regulations, account managers implement other rules representing a client's standard operating procedure, and contractor managers enter rules based on arrangements with contractors. Business users manage all rules. Regulatory, client, and contractor rules are applied in real time to generate instructions and orders for contractors, pricing and invoicing for clients, escalation, and new orders prompted by completing previous orders.

### Benefits

- Annual operating costs reduced by $1 million
- Time to market for a new client reduced from six months to a few weeks
- IT support staff reduced from 50 to 5

The Requirements Tar Pit

Much time and money are spent trying to improve the process of gathering and managing requirements for information systems. Widely perceived as a serious problem, requirements have the potential to bog down projects. The InfoWorld 2005 annual Programming Research Report[3] had a "Getting Applications Right" section containing this quotation:

> *"This gap [between user requirements and developer specifications] was one of the two principal [sic] challenges developers complained about in our survey, with 40 percent of respondents reporting that it was a major problem at their site."*

This gap has always been seen as a major cause of project failures. The graph in Figure 10.11 shows that although project failures are in decline overall, failures caused by requirement errors have remained steady.[4] At this rate, we might soon reach the point at which almost all project failures are caused by requirement errors. The rate of change is the prime culprit in this persistent failure to reduce the number of failures due to requirements errors. As Kulak and Guiney say:[5]

> *"The major difference between developing systems 20 years ago and doing it today is that change is much more pervasive now. Changes to business processes and rules, user personnel, and technology make application development seem like trying to land a Frisbee on the head of a wild dog."*

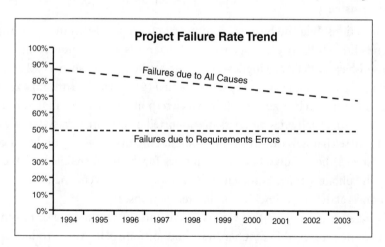

**Figure 10.11**    **The increasing importance of project failures caused by requirement errors, as overall failure rates drop**

---

[3] InfoWorld Programming Research Report, IDG, 2005.
[4] Joe Marasco, "Unraveling the Mystery of Software Development Success," www.sandhill.com, 2006.
[5] Daryl Kulak and Eamonn Guiney, *Use Cases—Requirements in Context*, Second Edition, Addison-Wesley, 2005.

However, not all requirements change more rapidly. In fact, requirements don't change very rapidly at all, but business rules do. Rules are "requirements" only if they are to be transformed into another format, such as a rule about how long to store information. Business rules—pieces of business logic that can be automated—aren't requirements; they're business statements.

Business rules change constantly because competitive pressure, market movements, and regulatory requirements change so often. Requirements for rules in a system never really stabilize. There's nothing you can do to stop changes in the way systems need to work, especially in how they need to make decisions, unless you can stop the world from changing.

If you enable business users to make their own changes to business rules in a controlled environment with EDM, the burden of this constant change can be reduced, however. The IT department's role then becomes one of supporting business users and focusing on technical requirements. So instead of investing in more detailed requirements, IT departments can solve many of their requirement problems if they invest in identifying what the system must do (business rules) and make it possible for business users to create, modify, and delete business rules. EDM, with its focus on business rules to manage this logic, can make a big difference in the scale of your requirement problems.

## Channel Consistency

Most organizations today do business through several channels: on the Web, by phone, in person, and through third-party agents. These channels are quite different in form and function and have widely varying levels of automation. Some, such as ATMs, are completely computerized, some are completely manual (personal advisors, for example), and many are a mixture, such as an interactive voice response (IVR) system that can refer you to a person for some activities or a person supported by information systems. The people involved in these channels can work for different employers; when you buy a cell phone plan, for instance, the person selling it might work for the phone retailer, not the company providing the phone service. Some customers always use one channel, but most use different channels at different times or for different purposes.

Different systems support this variety of channels. These systems are from different vendors and often run on different hardware and software platforms. Product pricing and availability, service eligibility, and other decisions critical to customer experience must be delivered to several channels, however. With an EDM approach, you can ensure consistent decision making in all channels without having a single system to support them. In addition, EDM lets you reuse some standard rules and models across channels while including channel-specific rules and models. For instance, you might apply special Internet pricing rules on your Web site in addition to the standard risk-based pricing rules you use in other channels. A multichannel environment is a reality for most organizations, and EDM can help ensure consistent decisions in all channels. Figure 10.12 shows a typical financial services organization's architecture, where many channels and business processes must deliver consistent decisions.

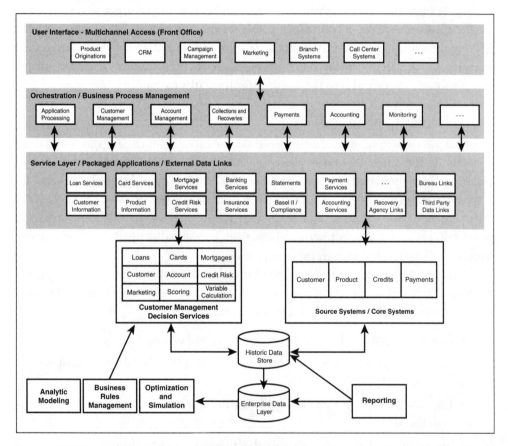

**Figure 10.12    An architecture showing the wide range of channels and business processes that need customer management decisions delivered by a core set of decision services**

### Multiplatform Consistency

Closely related to channel consistency is the problem of supporting heterogeneous platforms yet delivering a consistent experience in systems running on those platforms. A typical organization might have mainframes, UNIX servers, Java application servers, Windows PCs, and a modern SOA. It might own applications written in several languages and use both Java-based and Microsoft .NET approaches. Ensuring that different platforms run the same logic, calculate things the same way, and can be changed as a set is extremely difficult. Many organizations adopt an SOA approach to address this issue but still struggle with systems that aren't on SOA-enabled platforms or are hard to make available as useful, shared services.

Just as high-maintenance parts of systems can be, and often are, decision services, so are the pieces that need to be made available for cross-platform consistency. With the EDM approach of using a decision service as the point of platform consistency, or even using rules in services to ensure a level of consistency between services designed for specific platforms, you can address the multiplatform reality of your organization.

### Commodity Enterprise Applications

Organizations adopting enterprise applications for ERP, CRM, or SFA can find limited opportunity for differentiation in these applications. The standard processes and best practices these applications embody might be efficient, but they are mostly the same for everyone. Enterprise applications are, largely, a commodity. Indeed, Shai Agassi, formerly the president of SAP's Product and Technology group, once asserted that "more than 95 percent of business is common across all companies, in all industries."[6] The 5 percent difference is what provides strategic differentiation.

In a typical business process or application, almost every step has a best practice or template that is widely applied by your competitors. In contrast, how you make decisions in that process is unique to you for the following reasons:

- Customer segmentation is based on *your* data and profiles.
- *Your* policies and procedures are unique, even if they build on regulations and external rules.
- The data used for personalization is *yours*; no one else can duplicate the insight from that data.
- *Your* business users have experience that uniquely informs the rules they write, the way they treat customers, and so forth.

The 5 percent difference between companies *might* not be best represented in decision services, but decision-making approaches certainly aren't common across companies.

---

[6] Shai Agassi, in a keynote speech at SAP® TechEd 2006.

---

### Resisting Commoditization

The relentless commoditization of processes through process templates and outsourcing makes it harder for organizations to offer unique services. Drill into the problem, however, and you find two kinds of differentiation:

- Process differentiation means performing steps in a process in a radically different order or at a radically different pace. Adopting a build-to-order process could fall into this category.

- Decision differentiation means performing the same steps in a process in a similar order but choosing when to use which steps/branches or whether to price/approve transactions differently. Essentially, the transaction content determines how the process proceeds.

Decision differentiation is a way to give customers different experiences and outcomes yet use a standard process. For example, an organization that approves low-income customers more readily than its competitors represents decision differentiation, even if the organization and its competitors use the same loan paperwork-processing vendor. If the key decision points (approve/decline, complete/incomplete, treat as a good/average/poor customer) in a process are automated by using EDM, changing decision services differentiates the process, even if the process steps are standard.

---

Automating and improving them by using EDM to apply rules and analytic insights gives you strategic differentiation while still allowing you to purchase commodity components for the other 95%.

The other challenge of enterprise applications is, to quote Butler Group,[7] that "enterprise applications tend to be pretty dumb. They collect data, store it, and produce reports on it." Using an EDM approach to build decision services can make these applications smarter, as in these examples:

---

[7] Butler Group, "Exploiting Enterprise Applications," 2006.

- Using EDM to improve up-sell decisions in a call center system
- Using EDM to plan maintenance work based on predicted failure risk and maintenance schedules and to use a maintenance, repair, and operations (MRO) system to manage maintenance schedules
- Using EDM to devise optimal staffing plans for an HR system
- Using EDM to generate complex product masters and load them into an ERP system

Automating and managing decisions can make your enterprise applications much smarter.

**Large Chemical and Gas Supply Company: Streamline the Supply Chain**

**Old Way**

A largely manual process was used to create materials masters (used in complex supply-chain processes) in the company's ERP system. Because of the high number of products and manual handoffs, the process was slow, which created customer issues (delays to products) and transactional problems caused by inconsistent data. Teams had members from the United States, Europe, and Asia and relied on functional experts to handle issues such as bills of material, costing, inspections, and more. Excel-based forms were reviewed and forwarded manually until enough data was assembled to create a first version of materials masters, and then different groups updated the ERP system's records until the definition of the materials master was complete. Demand for new materials masters was anticipated to grow to 100 to 200 requests per day, resulting in the need to hire 15 more people. The average creation time should have been just 5 days, but it was running up to 45 days, causing unacceptable delays.

**EDM Way**

All business rules for creating materials masters are captured and stored in a rule repository. These rules are then applied by using a decision service at the point of data entry. The service ensures that valid and complete data is entered, even though different data is required, depending on the type of materials masters and circumstances. Rules are used to derive the right questions to ask to complete the data, based on the kind of request, its status, and so on. Additional rules are applied in a second decision service to route applications for approval and review using the ERP system's work flow and to ensure conformance with regulations and internal policies.

### Benefits

- All work is now handled online, with automatic validation and routing for approval.

- Data is controlled at the point of entry by rules.

- Rework is down and productivity is up, with many requests being completed the same day—a more than 95 percent reduction in elapsed time.

- Knowledge previously held by a few has been transformed into a corporate asset.

## Enabling IT Capabilities

EDM helps solve many IT problems inherited from the past, but it can also help the IT department offer some capabilities it's being pushed to deliver in the future, such as support for mobile devices, event-driven and model-driven architectures, outsourcing and business process outsourcing (BPO), performance management, consumerization, and location awareness.

### Self-Service

A large part of the workload for many IT departments is building self-service applications in response to pressure from associates. Sometimes these applications are simple forms or reports. Often, however, true self-service applications require decision automation.

IT departments focus on the infrastructure that's needed for self-service applications: portals, intranets, Asynchronous JavaScript and XML (Ajax), forms management software, and so on. However, decisions can be a bottleneck if they aren't automated. If you automate a form to request a service but the request still gets routed to someone's work queue, customers might not think the form is helpful. If your suppliers can request a delivery date extension on your Web site but the decision on allowing it or the cost implications can't be determined immediately, suppliers might phone instead.

By focusing on automating and improving associate-facing decisions, you can make self-service more rewarding and extensive. Customers who want to self-serve appreciate being able to do more without the need to seek approval from an employee. In general, nothing frustrates customers more than not being able to get things done. Creating an "always there for you" environment, in which the company makes rapid decisions about customers' needs, helps lure customers to self-service. Automating decisions helps meet the self-service mandate and in a way likely to reduce the demand for staff. Studies have shown that answering a question online can cost 4 to 40 times less than answering it on the phone. Imagine how much you could save by automating a decision.

### Making Mobile Matter

As the consumerization of enterprise IT continues, IT departments struggle with integrating mobile technology into their organizations. Mobile, consumer-friendly technology creates many issues, not just connectivity and security. How do mobile device users want to use them? What access to the enterprise IT infrastructure do they want and need?

An EDM approach to automating decisions can clarify what mobile device users want. When they want to go beyond simple notifications, they often want to make decisions. For instance, when they're notified of a delayed order to a major customer, they can see what options are available for rerouting and pick one, ideally having been recommended the most effective one. Simply displaying user interfaces of existing systems doesn't get it done, however, for these reasons:

- Using BI tools on mobile devices is a problem. How can you "slice and dice" data or view reports on a cell phone?

- Although seeing all notifications on your PC might make sense, you should see only urgent or critical ones on your mobile device.

- How many options should you display on devices? Being able to spot the best one easily is helpful for mobile users.

- Application users might use different mobile devices with varying capabilities, so their opinions on acceptable numbers of options or what requires an urgent notification might differ.

With EDM, an IT department can develop decision services to power mobile applications as readily as enterprise ones, and users and others can interact with the rules for an application, making it possible to personalize and configure mobile devices.

---

**Government Bureau: Ship Inspection**

**Old Way**

The bureau must certify many different kinds of vessels in several locations, so it needs a lot of inspectors who must be trained and given a list of regulations. Manual inspections could take a long time. Consistency and accuracy of inspections were hard to ensure, given the paper-based process.

**EDM Way**

A laptop-based decision service was created and kept up to date with the latest regulatory and safety rules. Experts who understand the regulations and have experience in inspecting vessels are responsible for entering rules. The service prompts tasks and questions to complete inspections quickly.

**Benefits**

- Consistent application of inspection rules
- Faster inspections, reduced paper and materials
- Verifying and recording status reduced from 15 days to 1 day

---

### Smart Event Processing and Business Activity Monitoring

IT departments are beginning to transition to an event-driven architecture or at least one that combines service orientation with event-driven styles of development. **Event-driven architectures (EDAs)** allow loose coupling between elements of IT architecture and real-time assessment of how to respond to incoming events. Sometimes called **complex event processing (CEP)**, these approaches analyze inbound events and then prompt a response based on those events. Similarly, organizations are adopting business activity monitoring (BAM) to assess their state in real time and use that assessment to alert people, or occasionally systems, to the need to take action. Organizations using a BPMS or an SOA to manage business processes might also use an EDA to link processes or trigger processes in response to events while processing some events directly. They might also use BAM to monitor processes they have automated.

### Telecommunications: Self-Repairing Network

#### Old Way

All network faults were reviewed manually, and an engineer was dispatched to make a repair. Meanwhile, an engineer in the control center reviewed the existing network and traffic and reassigned traffic around faulty equipment. Major customers with service-level agreements (SLAs) might be affected by a failure, but the company didn't know until the end-of-month analysis, which caused customer service problems.

#### EDM Way

A decision service handles network errors and alerts without requiring staff intervention. To respond to system failures, the service uses business rules to assign field service engineers based on region, product expertise, and urgency. The rules-based system ensures accurate assignment of field service engineers and allows easy modification and deployment of rules about new engineers or products. The service tracks and correlates systemwide alarm information to determine uptime and downtime for equipment on the network and routes calls through equipment that's running. The rules can also prioritize major customers.

As new equipment is added or company experts learn more about equipment, experts can add new rules to the service. Another decision service determines what compensation is owed to major customers in the case of system failure. The rules analyze system outage information against signed SLAs to determine whether an outage violated the agreement and what compensation is due to the customer. This proactive approach has increased customer satisfaction.

#### Benefits

- More effective assignment of engineers
- Faster response time to network faults and outages
- Proactive management of major customers

The essence of these approaches is to monitor events within and external to operational business processes. They are often used to link BI systems to everyday operations

more. The role of decision automation and EDM in supporting these approaches is clear. Although these specialized contexts—business process management, event processing, and activity monitoring—can take advantage of rules-based technology, it's not the same as using EDM to support them. Using rules for routing, activity monitoring, or event processing doesn't replace true decision automation.

First, if you embed rules in a CEP/BPMS/BAM solution, you make it impossible to reuse those rules in other parts of this group of solutions and in legacy applications. Rules for what makes a good customer or a fraudulent claim, for example, are the same throughout the enterprise and should be managed as the enterprise asset they are. Managing decisions in this way also allows you to invest in improving them and maximize the ROI. Some rules belong in each environment, but core rules for decisions don't.

Second, rules for routing and handling processes are synchronized with process definitions in the same way that rules for event handling are synchronized with event definitions. Rules for making business decisions in these processes or as a result of identifying an event are independent of the event or process definition. You shouldn't oversynchronize business decisions and processes or business decisions and event identifications. You must be able to change how your business responds to an event separately from how it processes and identifies the event. Similarly, you must be able to change how you manage a decision without having to change the processes that include it.

By adopting EDM, you can make the right parts of your architecture more event- or activity-oriented and still control, manage, and reuse your decisions.

## Model-Driven Engineering

**Model-driven engineering (MDE)** is the systematic use of models as primary artifacts throughout the software engineering life cycle. MDE involves building a platform-independent model (PIM) and translating it into a platform-specific model (PSM) automatically when deployment is required. (Chapter 6, "Business Rules," introduced PIMs and PSMs.) Ongoing maintenance and modification are performed on the PIM, and design is kept separate from architecture and implementation technologies. The design and implementation platforms can, therefore, evolve independently. Design addresses functional requirements without incorporating infrastructure issues, so ideally, round-trip engineering is possible, in which the model is always synchronized with the implementation.

Organizations adopting MDE should also adopt EDM. Not only do business rules represent a way to define business logic in a platform-independent way, but they also can be used in many different projects in a way that domain-specific languages (DSLs) might not. Rule management is also well established, so rules can be shared and modified coherently; most DSLs don't allow effective management of atomic units of logic. Many BRMSs support deploying the same rules to several platforms, which is critical to the MDE approach, and almost all rule syntaxes are platform-neutral. EDM and business rules extend MDE's power by making definitions of what the system should do more accessible to business users, as described in Chapter 6. Most PIMs aren't user friendly, but business rules are.

Additionally, predictive analytic models normally aren't considered in MDE. Using predictive analytics is important in many decisions, so this omission is a weakness in MDE. By formalizing decisions as separate but equal components alongside other models, you can include analytics more coherently. Finally, decisions can be considered somewhat orthogonal to objects in an object model. With EDM, you can treat decisions this way and still manage them, making impact analysis, for instance, much easier. MDE tends to wrap decision making into objects and lose the capability to manage decisions properly.

### Smart Outsourcing

IT departments are involved in outsourcing in two ways: They are often responsible for managing technical interactions with outsourcers running the organization's processes, and they are under pressure to outsource IT development or maintenance work.

BPO vendors can deliver innovation and optimize processes only if they make the key decision points in their processes available so that customers can control them. Organizations have their own way of doing business, and even a standard process varies in decision making that outsourcers need to support. With BPMSs, outsourcers can make these decisions available to clients yet still run standard processes. Although IT departments must care about visibility into processes in terms of data and reporting, they should also insist on visibility in how certain decisions are made.

In addition, for some regulated processes, organizations might be legally required to know the inner workings of a BPO vendor's system. Business rules are ideally suited to showing that a decision has been made in a compliant way. If you're audited on what you did and why, you should make sure your outsourcer is using business rules, and you can integrate their logs about how decisions were made into your own compliance infrastructure.

When outsourcing development, IT organizations worry about intellectual property (IP) infringement. Not all code in a system is core IP, but some is. Outsourcing development and maintenance of nondifferentiating code can be cost-effective, but outsourcing code representing your IP is a big risk.

The code that business rules replace is core IP, so one option is to develop core IP by using business rules, focusing on ownership and reuse of this IP, and to develop other code with the most inexpensive resources or tools. This way, business contributors to core IP can manage it directly, and you can still take advantage of low development costs for other code. Working with an outsourcer to take control of an existing system—while reengineering key business logic into a decision service that can be managed in-house—can increase cost and efficiency savings and business control.

### Global Logistics Company: Freight Management

#### Old Way

The company's clients wanted to customize their shipping requirements, but often divisions of the same client had different freight-forwarding methods, for instance. Allowing clients to control freight management required custom-built applications modified for each customer whenever customers requested changes.

#### EDM Way

A decision service handles data validation, event management, and logistics logic. The company's experts created baseline business rules, and each client sets up its own additional business rules. Clients can modify their rules directly within the bounds set for them. The complete set of relevant rules verifies each shipment as it's entered, based on the client's shipping requirements, goods requirements, and so on. Business rules for personnel allocation and material configuration are also applied to automate the shipping logistics definition.

#### Benefits

- Flexibility and customer satisfaction increased
- Reduced IT costs

## Corporate Performance Management

**Corporate performance management (CPM),** an important initiative for many IT departments, is a systematic, integrated management approach to linking enterprise strategy with core processes and activities. By providing planning, budgeting, analysis, and reporting capabilities, CPM lets you run your business "by the numbers" and use measurements to make management decisions. CPM typically takes the form of dashboards and other visualization tools for past results and perhaps trends and predictions, and these tools are designed for analytically minded people. What CPM doesn't do, in general, is help you take action in response to information. Many organizations use BPMSs for this purpose; when their CPM systems tell them things are going poorly, they can use their BPMSs to adapt and change processes to respond. When things are going well, they can use BPMSs to standardize best practices.

### Software as a Service and EDM

One form of software as a service (SaaS) is called a decision service provider (DSP), which offers on-demand delivery of analytic business decisions. In addition to the usual SaaS capabilities, a DSP also needs to

- Build and maintain analytic models and business rules
- Pool third-party and customer data to build models
- Access third-party information at runtime
- Ensure that regulations and industry guidelines are followed

A DSP offers value in part because many possible data sources are available for decisions, and an organization might have difficulty orchestrating access to them without a DSP. In addition, analytics and decision making can be based on pooled data and expertise rather than an understanding of the organization's own (potentially limited) experience. DSPs are already common in areas such as fraud, but they could become important in areas such as marketing, where shared data sources (such as customer panel data) can play a role in retailers' and Consumer Packaged Goods (CPG) firms' decision making.

EDM adds value to a CPM/BPMS environment when you start thinking about decision change rather than process change. For example, suppose your CPM environment tells you that bad debt in a customer segment is rising. The reason is unlikely to be a process—after all, you have standardized the process—so it's probably related to decisions for how you segment and treat customers. If these decisions are manual, managing them effectively is hard, because you must find all those responsible for the decision and retrain them. If you have automated them in your BPMS, however, you probably don't have as much control over the decision as you would like, because BPM environments are centered on processes, not decisions.

With EDM, you could develop decision services and make them readily available to processes implemented with a BPMS and to other legacy environments, Web sites, partners, and so on. By using business rules to develop these services, you can ensure that the business users who have access to the CPM environment could manage the rules to eliminate the time lag between CPM insight and BPMS action. What's more, as your CPM environment helps you learn more about your business, you can identify the potential to use embedded predictive analytics. If your CPM environment shows you how to predict that a customer has a high risk of cancelling her service, you could develop a model for this purpose and embed that prediction into decision services. Then your operational decisions and hence your operational processes are run by the numbers. Using EDM to automate key decisions acts as the glue between the insight CPM provides and the BPMS/SOA environment.

## Extending Your Software Development Life Cycle to Support EDM

Most IT organizations have a preferred software development life cycle (SDLC) approach as well as a formally documented methodology or group of methodologies. To reflect EDM adoption, these methodologies need to be adapted to include business rules, analytic models, and adaptive control. This section contains some general notes on these approaches, as well as specific guidance on adapting Rational Unified Process, Unified Modeling Language (UML), and agile methods.

### General Approach to Adapting an SDLC

When you're adapting an SDLC to include EDM, you need to consider four areas: identifying and managing decision services, managing business rules separately from requirements and as a model, integrating analytic models, and recognizing the impact of adaptive control.

#### Decision Services in an SDLC

Adopting EDM means building decision services and managing them over time, so this means treating decision services as a class of components or services in your SDLC. The classification scheme and design guidelines you use for services or components should be extended to include a decision service type, and you should document guidelines for creating and managing them.

In many ways, decision services have the same characteristics and requirements as other business-focused services or components. In addition, you need to document how rules are maintained and what rules in the service might be shared among decision services. Release management tasks should be updated to include releases that just involve an update to logic in a decision service and to handle updates to shared decision services.

> **Finding Decision Services**   *Your methodology should include activities to analyze reporting, worklist, and other services to see whether you have hidden decision services. Becoming more decision-centered should be a long-term goal of any methodology change.*

*Rules in an SDLC*

The most important change to your SDLC is the separation of rules and requirements. Most methodologies don't make this separation, so rules and requirements are intermingled. This mixing is always a bad idea, but it's particularly unhelpful when you're managing rules as explicitly as you do in EDM.

The first step is managing "source rules" and mapping them to the scenarios and design requirements you're documenting. Source rules are generally written in the language your business users use—in terms of being in English, for instance, and using business terminology. These rules are designed to be atomic and manageable, but they can't be implemented. Effective management of terms and vocabulary for these rules makes checking them and mapping them to analysis artifacts easier. Source rules should usually be kept general. Some source rules become production rules or sets of production rules; others map to templates for production rules. For instance, a source rule might describe typical knock-out (decline) rules for an applicant, which map to a rule template that constrains a rule set for eliminating applicants.

The second step is managing platform-independent but object-specific rules for your decision services. As you develop your object or data model, you can start to develop rules that run against that data. These rules must be managed in a repository, versioned, and structured to allow for reuse in other decision services. More production-oriented rules map back to source rules, although not usually in a simple fashion, and are collected into rule sets.

> **Rule Maintenance**    *You need to develop a separate rule maintenance process outside your regular SDLC, especially if business users maintain some rules in your decision service. Although you want to go through many of the usual test and QA steps, realistically, you need a different process, because the time frame is shorter and changes are more frequent than in a typical IT project.*

Logging rules as they execute to create a record of how a decision was made is a common requirement of decision services. They can be managed like a typical logging requirement, except that using business rules makes it easier. Using business rules also makes it possible to use the logged information in both customer-facing and regulatory conversations, because the rules are more user-friendly. Figure 10.13 shows a real, and typical, architecture for decision services with a strong compliance requirement. The architecture manages development and production environments, logging, reference data, and test scenarios to ensure that compliance can be demonstrated.

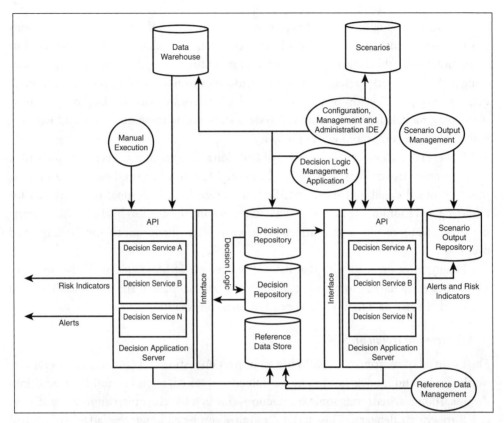

**Figure 10.13**   **Production (on the left) and development environments (on the right) for decision services handling regulatory compliance, showing scenarios, reference data, and alerts for compliance follow-up**

### Analytics in an SDLC

Most IT departments have made little effort to integrate analytics into their SDLCs, even in organizations that use predictive analytics. The need to write code to implement a predictive model has often meant that a predictive model was regarded simply as a kind of specification, and a complete programming project was followed to implement it. As predictive analytics become more automated in your organization and you use them more, this viewpoint needs to change. The need to synchronize models and rules also motivates change in an SDLC, because previous projects are likely to have used a model simply as a block of code.

Besides changing how model deployment is handled in the SDLC, IT departments must consider how predictive models can enhance their data or object model. The methodology should encourage the possibility of adding an attribute that predicts something about an object—retention risk for a customer or likelihood of return for a product, for example. The full benefit of predictive analytics can be realized only if those developing models for the operational system start asking these questions and working with analysts to understand what's possible.

IT departments must also be aware of additional data requirements that come with a focus on predictive models. In particular, you might need to keep and make accessible far more historical detail and more specific time-series data. Additional requirements for reporting and monitoring as well as data access at runtime are also likely. Without meeting these requirements, organizations can't ensure that these models can be improved over time.

Finally, most organizations that make extensive use of EDM and predictive analytics also use external data at some point. Integrating external data at runtime and delivering historical external data to modelers are additional considerations.

### Adaptive Control in an SDLC

The use of adaptive control in EDM has an impact on testing and operations. Several versions of rules and models need to be assembled and tested, often in parallel. In addition, the operational system runs some transactions through the champion approach and others through challengers. This testing requires understanding the adaptive control approach on the part of those developing and operating the production application. Adaptive control requires logging information for subsequent analysis, which affects data storage and APIs for the operational system.

The development process, when it's adapted to rules and analytics, also needs to support developing champion and challenger approaches simultaneously. It must also allow developing new challengers for a decision service already in production, promoting a challenger to champion status, and adding and removing challengers. Developing champions and challengers isn't a full-blown development project; it's a smaller, more focused effort. It does affect a running operational system, however, so you should schedule, manage, and track them.

### Rational Unified Process and UML

**Rational Unified Process (RUP)** and, more recently, **Enterprise Unified Process (EUP)** are methodologies designed to apply UML and development best practices in a formal way. In the past, these approaches haven't managed business rules in a way suitable for EDM but have considered them part of use cases or requirements. Generally, a more managed approach to business rules as separate artifacts is required for EDM, but adding this approach is easy.

RUP outlines six best practices, and business rules clearly support all six:

- **Develop software iteratively**—Declarative business rules are separate, testable decision-making units. EDM allows incremental development and testing of business rules, separate from the other software components. Software development is divided into manageable and measurable changes.

- **Verify software quality continuously**—Business rules are easier to verify, because they are close to the business. Rule management encourages constant validation and verification, which improve software walkthroughs and reduce test cycles.

- **Control changes to software**—Traditional software systems are "brittle"—meaning small changes can break them—but change is guaranteed and must be managed. Business rules are expected to change and can be traced to software more easily and updated separately, even in 24x7 environments.

- **Manage requirements**—Business rules shouldn't be managed like requirements, so separating them from requirements makes rule management and requirement management easier. Rule management replaces some requirements management with the management of explicit business rules, throughout and beyond the application life cycle.

- **Use component-based architectures**—Identifying and managing decision services separates business logic into reusable, manageable components.

- **Visually model software**—If a picture is worth a thousand words, business rules could be worth many lines of code. Business rules and their interrelationships can be visualized and managed more easily than code, so more of the application can be managed more visually.

### Integrating Rules

To bring business rules into RUP, several changes are required:

- Add a business rule-modeling activity alongside business modeling that emphasizes collecting and organizing business rules. This activity replaces a single focus on use cases with a more balanced view of use cases as a means of rule discovery. However, it doesn't provide a place to manage them (see the section "The Requirements Tar Pit" in this chapter). This activity also has highly compressed interactions between rule modeling and analysis, design, and implementation.

- Formally identify decision services as components that implement business rules.

- Consider additional software components and processes for future rule maintenance and testing.

In UML, business rules must appear at three different levels: business model or computation-independent model (CIM), PIM, and PSM. At the business model/CIM level, you need an unambiguous representation of business policies, procedures, and constraints as business rules in natural language and independent of assumptions about the platform on which an information system is delivered. At the PIM level, you need a representation of business rules targeted to a business rule engine—perhaps a format that's independent of a particular vendor.

Modeling business rules in UML is a broad topic, as you can see in these examples:

- Business rules defined as formal texts for documentation or requirement purposes are covered by the SBVR standard.

- Business rules, such as simple data relationships and constraints, have simple counterparts in a UML model. For example, the business rule "Orders must have at least one line item" is typically represented as a multiplicity constraint on an association. Other rules translate into constraint expressions easily. For example, the rule "An account can never have a negative balance" can be expressed as an invariant by using Object Constraint Language (OCL).

- Process-oriented business rules define conditional action, behavior, and state changes—those that OCL doesn't handle—as production rules. Business rules expressed by production rules are common, and representing (modeling) production rules in UML isn't standardized.

The two UML mechanisms for defining constraints and behavior are OCL and action semantics (AS). However, neither provides an out-of-the-box solution for representing production rules.

### Integrating Analytics

Analytic models and their integration into systems are a good conceptual match for the model-driven development promoted as part of a RUP/UML approach. That said, little or no clear guidance for bringing analytics into a UML model is available. Object attributes can be derived analytically, and model components can be manipulated in an interaction diagram to show when a real-time scoring service is used. These methods have no specific support in RUP/UML, but you can manage them by using existing artifacts.

## Agile Approaches

Describing agile approaches in detail is beyond the scope of this book. The basic principles of iterative development, collaboration, developing working software regularly, and test-driven design are well known and well documented. Using agile approaches with EDM requires integrating rules into the process, integrating analytic modeling, and considering adaptive control.

### Rules in Agility

Two key agile principles[8] apply to EDM:

- Welcome changing requirements, even late in (or after) development. Agile processes harness change for the customer's competitive advantage.
- Business users and developers must work together throughout the project.

Applying these principles can improve business agility by making sure you respond to changes that are needed because of a changing environment or competitor. There's a challenge when a new requirement isn't really a requirement but a new or changed business rule, however. For instance, new legislation might force new requirements on a project, but it's more likely to generate new rules. Business rules aren't the same as requirements, so your agile development processes must work as well for business rules as they do for other requirements. Furthermore, a core practice in agile modeling is **single source information**—that is, information required for development should be recorded once in a suitable artifact. Business rules should also be treated this way.

Scott Ambler once said that

*"Agile software development teams embrace change, accepting the idea that requirements will evolve throughout a project."[9]*

To embrace change in this way, agile projects focus on the highest-priority requirements in each iteration. To manage business rules separately from requirements, you must also manage business rules alongside your other requirements. You use three key artifacts in this process: decision services, rule templates (or definitions of kinds of rules), and actual rules. These artifacts usually require business users, developers, and business analysts to work together. The best way is for developers to define decision services, developers and business analysts to define rule templates and how they fit into processing the

---

[8] Agile Alliance, "Manifesto for Agile Software Development," www.agilealliance.org.
[9] Scott Ambler and Ron Jeffries, *Agile Modeling: Effective Practices for Extreme Programming and the Unified Process*, Wiley, 2001.

decision service, and business analysts and business users to manage rule instances. This method supports agility, because rule instances reflect the business users' understanding of the business at that time and the target range of test cases.

Test-driven development means writing the test before the program—thinking about how to use the component or what it's for *first,* and then thinking about how to implement it. For developing a decision service, the agile approach of test-driven development is ideal. Most decision services have a simple interface—a modest amount of data is passed in, and a simple answer is passed back. All the complexity is inside the decision service, so developing a test or set of tests for the decision service when it's first defined is straightforward. Business users can provide real examples and explain what decision was made in each case, which then becomes a test case. Typically, only a core set of cases is automated to start with, as described previously, and new test cases must be known before new rules are written (because rules are defined to handle specific cases not handled before). Therefore, adding test cases before making changes is completely logical.

The process of defining templates is iterative, and the process of defining rule instances is highly iterative, so these processes are well suited to agile approaches. An important benefit of using business rules in this way is that real collaboration is possible. When rules are written in a syntax everyone can understand, agreeing on them and editing them are much easier. In addition, domain experts can develop rules independently, so some change management during an iteration is in their hands. They can change as quickly or slowly as they like, and cost is controlled because there's a defined difference between change within expected boundaries (requires only new or changed rules) versus unexpected change (requires new decision services or templates). Modifying a system means targeting a certain percentage of decisions and then gradually increasing the percentage by automating exception handling, identifying patterns, and so forth.

By taking this approach, essentially you record a business rule once as human-readable but implementable code so that you can reuse it. This method helps improve business agility and matches the Agile Alliance's Manifesto for Agile Software Development, which has these key tenets:

- **Individuals and interactions over processes and tools**—A key interaction is between developers and business users. Using business rules facilitates this conversation.

- **Working software over comprehensive documentation**—Business rules can deliver working software that's easier for business users to read and change, which makes software more "self-documenting" and lessens the pressure for documentation.

---

**Pair Programming for Rules**

An interesting approach to bringing rules into an agile development process is "pair programming." In this method, rules are created by a pair—one member from IT and one from business. Because a rules environment allows both technical and business users to read and write rules, this kind of collaboration is possible. For rules that are too technical for business users to maintain on their own yet require a high degree of business content to manage effectively, pair programming can be successful. Building a majority of your rules quickly with this technique is often possible. Organizations unwilling to go this far might still find value in pairing a technical rule developer with a "pure" code developer.

---

- **Customer collaboration over contract negotiation**—Both developers and business users being able to read and understand business rules allows true collaboration in implementing business logic.
- **Responding to change over following a plan**—Business rules provide business agility by making the code you write easier to change during and after the project.

*Analytics and Agility*

Both analytic development and agile development are highly iterative. Most analysts developing models develop a "working" model at the end of each iteration, but it might not be particularly useful, because it generates poor lift or worse lift than a previous version. Actually deploying and integrating a model each time might not be worth the effort. The most effective way to bring iterations together is after the decision service has stabilized in its integration with the rest of the system. At this point, subsequent iterations involve only changes to rules and/or models in the decision service, which maps well to analytic iterations in model development.

Test-driven development is by far the most common approach to building analytics, with validation and test data sets created along with training data sets as part of the core process of developing a model. While the analytic staff focuses on these data sets, IT staff might find it helpful to similarly define their tests for the deployed model.

*Adaptive Control and Agility*

Adaptive control should be integrated into agile approaches by ensuring that part of iteration after initial deployment is a focus on the champion/challenger strategy. This strategy might run at a different pace than more technical iterations because you might have a noticeable lag time before results can be measured and compared between the champion and challengers.

---

**The EDM Wiki**

You can find more information on how EDM fits into the IT ecosystem in the EDM wiki at www.smartenoughsystems.com.

---

# CHAPTER ELEVEN

# Closing Thoughts

**T**he world is conspiring to force you to build smarter information systems—smart enough systems. The technology exists for you to get started, and you should.

## Recap: Smart Enough Systems

Smart enough systems ensure that the decisions your organization makes, especially the high-volume, front-line decisions your systems and staff make every day, are smart enough to help you survive and thrive in today's business and economic climate. In a very real way, your organization is the decisions it makes. Traditional approaches to information systems don't handle small, operational decisions well, which is a problem, because many small decisions add up and make the difference between success and failure. Smart enough systems enable you to manage decisions as a real corporate asset and ensure that they're made the way you expect and want them to be made.

The power of enterprise decision management is how it enables you to focus on and automate these high-volume, operational decisions. Automating them makes it possible to develop and change them to make sure they're precise, consistent, agile, speedy, and cost-effective. Enterprise decision management combines existing, proven technologies and approaches to solve the problem of operational decision making and does so in a way that complements and enhances your current and future IT architecture.

With its focus on constant management and improvement and its complementary technologies, EDM enables you to create a true virtuous cycle, as shown in Figure 11.1. Using business rules to automate decisions reduces development and maintenance costs and ends dependence on IT for systems updates. This platform for decisions enables you to embed more predictive analytic models into your systems quickly and inexpensively, materially improving the quality of your decisions and getting more value from your data assets. With deployment into an adaptive control environment, a business can track the effectiveness of decisions to find new rules that work better. A continual improvement loop is created, and IT resources are freed up at every stage to focus on new systems that add more value to the organization.

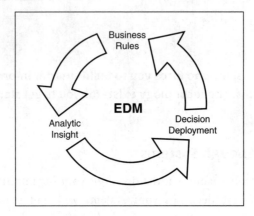

**Figure 11.1    The virtuous cycle of EDM** ©*Fair Isaac Corporation, reproduced with permission*

By using enterprise decision management to take control of your operational decisions, you can gain a real competitive advantage and extract more value from your existing technology and data investments. Figure 11.2 shows how taking control of an operational decision—in this case, a retention offer to telecom customers who want to discontinue their service—can deliver better results. More targeted, precise, flexible decisions get better, more profitable outcomes. Replicate this kind of improvement in the thousands or millions of operational decisions you make, and EDM can truly make a difference to your organization.

## Why Now?

Although EDM concepts and technologies have been around for a while, the reality is that now is the ideal time to adopt EDM. As Figure 11.3 shows, the increasing sophistication of business rules technology, analytic modeling techniques, optimization and simulation,

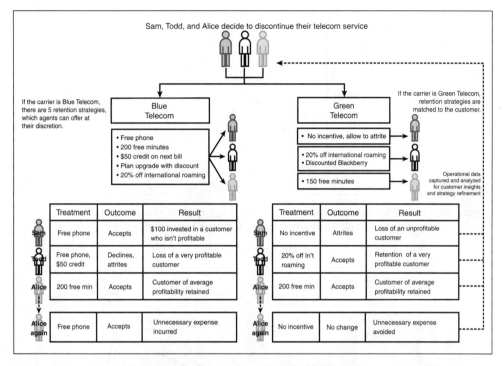

**Figure 11.2    Green Telecom makes better operational decisions and gets better results in retaining profitable customers**

and the rest of the EDM ecosystem has increased the range of decisions you can automate. Some decisions are, and will likely remain, the realm of experts, but very few must be manual decisions made by nonexperts because of their value or complexity. Most decisions can and should be automated by using EDM.

Not only is the technology more ready than ever before, but also the need for EDM and smart enough systems is greater than ever. The pace of change is, as you hear every day, at its highest rate and increasing. In these times, the organization that responds correctly first has a huge advantage. Take fraud as an example. Figure 11.4 shows the difference between a non-EDM and an EDM approach in responding to a new kind of fraud loss, a ploy developed by an organized crime syndicate. In the non-EDM approach, implementing new mitigation approaches and a final solution to a new fraud problem takes a long time, leading to a high cost (shown by the area under the curve). A more rapid, yet measured, EDM response makes a dramatic difference in total losses. As the world changes faster, the slope of these curves gets steeper, and the value of rapid EDM-based change increases.

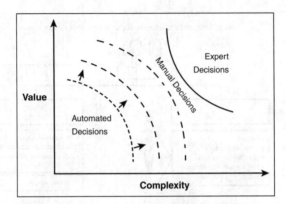

**Figure 11.3   The increasing power of technology makes replacing manual decisions with automated ones possible and effective**

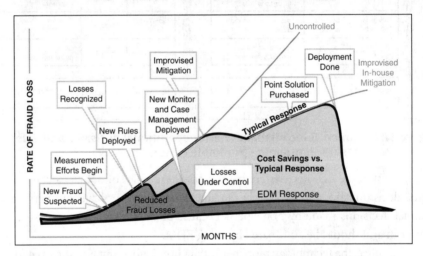

**Figure 11.4   A more rapid and accurate response to a new business situation can result in dramatic savings** *©Fair Isaac Corporation, reproduced with permission*

## What Next?

Begin. The biggest barrier to EDM adoption and, therefore, to developing smart enough systems in most organizations is simply that it hasn't been done yet. Anything new is hard to start, and EDM is no exception. Chapter 9 laid out an incremental approach to adopting EDM that makes sure you can show a good ROI at each stage. You can assess your readiness with the tools covered in Chapter 8 and you can assess the impact on your IT department with the guidelines in Chapter 10. You can also use the resources available at www.smartenoughsystems.com to learn more about EDM technologies and approaches. You can even contribute to the EDM wiki there. We look forward to hearing how it goes and what you learn.

One last thing: Lest you think that only dull systems can be improved with EDM, read one last case study about robots.

---

### Innovative Robotics Startup

#### Old Way

Although thinking of robotics as having an "old way" might seem odd, much of the programming for robots is still old-school. Even autonomous robots often had to be given detailed routing instructions. The navigation logic was applied manually to the desired destination, resulting in a list of instructions loaded into the robot. For this reason, route planning could be carried out only at the start of a journey; if the route needed to change along the way, the robot couldn't plan a completely new route. In addition, robots must avoid obstacles while navigating. The hard-coded obstacle-avoidance logic turned sensor data into an understanding of what obstacle was being sensed and useful avoidance actions. Consequently, each new obstacle required new code and ran the risk of breaking the existing code.

#### EDM Way

Business rules are used to encode expert judgment on navigation, such as how far away from the direct route is it worth going to find a road or how steep a slope should be avoided. These rules are run against the destination to generate detailed instructions. They can be changed easily and run repeatedly during the journey. If a robot is forced off its route, it can recalculate to find a new, better route from its current position. Obstacle-avoidance logic is developed by using business rules so that it can be changed easily and without breaking existing rules. An inferencing rules engine ensures that only rules that might be true are evaluated, which makes it possible to identify the few relevant rules for each obstacle quickly, despite the many obstacle types. Predictive analytics are applied to sensor data to help identify potential terrain and obstacle changes earlier.

#### Benefits

- More independence for robots
- Easier access to experts when configuring robots
- New experience added to working robots easily

# Decision Yield as a Way to Measure ROI

**A**lthough many standard approaches to calculating return on investment (ROI) are used in enterprise decision management, there's growing interest in a new one. Decision yield is a holistic measure of a decision's effectiveness in multiple dimensions being developed at Fair Isaac Corporation. Materials and graphs in this section are used with permission from Fair Isaac.

## Overview of Decision Yield

As noted in Chapter 2, "Enterprise Decision Management," you can't manage what you can't measure. One challenge in adopting enterprise decision management is measuring success. Some organizations find that focusing only on cost savings doesn't yield enough of a return to justify the investments required for EDM or adequately reflect the value they achieved. By comparing organizations that have adopted EDM with those that haven't, identifying some clear differences in the way they make investment decisions is possible. In particular, you can see more of a focus on revenue improvement and opportunity costs (costs of delaying a response to an opportunity). The challenge is how to turn this broader focus into a method for justifying EDM investments. Decision yield is the recommended approach for this challenge.

Decision yield, as introduced in Chapter 2, is a broad-based evaluation metric that reveals the quality of your current decisions and decision processes. It helps you plan, justify, and measure improvements to decision processes. Frank Rohde first described it, saying:

> *"We judge leaders by how well they make big, strategic decisions. But corporate success also depends on how well rank-and-file employees make thousands of small decisions. Do I give this customer a special price? How do I handle this customer's complaint? Should I offer a seat upgrade to this customer? By themselves, such daily calls—increasingly made with the help of enterprise decision management technology—have little impact on business performance. Taken together, they influence everything from profitability to reputation."[1]*

---

[1] Frank Rohde, "Little Decisions Add Up," *Harvard Business Review*, June 2005.

Although decision yield is a fairly general-purpose tool, it's designed to evaluate automated decisions with these characteristics:

- Made frequently, often many thousands of times a day
- Made in real time (such as approval for going over a credit limit) or in batch mode (matching an offer with a prospect)
- Delivered through another system, such as a Web site or call center—often the same decision is made in many such systems
- Made when interacting with associates, such as approving loans, pricing insurance, and determining cross-sell offers

In other words, decision yield can evaluate the kinds of decisions for which EDM is ideal, so it's an effective tool for organizations adopting EDM.

Decision yield's holistic approach involves comparing the following five dimensions—introduced in Chapter 2—of decision effectiveness to make a comprehensive assessment of an operational decision:

- **Precision**—How targeted is the decision?
- **Consistency**—How consistent across divisions, channels, and time is the decision?
- **Agility**—How quickly can you effectively change the way the decision is made when you need to?
- **Speed**—How quickly can you make the decision?
- **Cost**—How much does it cost you to make the decision?

Each dimension contributes to a decision's overall effectiveness and an organization's likely yield from the decision—the decision yield. The following list examines these dimensions in a little more detail:

- **Precision**—Precision is a measure of a decision's effectiveness. Different decisions require different ways to assess precision, but whatever is used should focus on effectiveness, not efficiency, or on targeting. You might need to consider financial outcomes, such as profit, customer lifetime value, revenue, or losses, as well as accuracy of predictions, comprehensiveness of factors, and level of specificity.
- **Consistency**—Consistency measures how well integrated and coordinated your decisions are throughout your enterprise. Do you make the same decision the same way unless you mean not to? You can measure consistency over time (Is today's price the same as yesterday's?), across channels (Is the offer on the Web site

the same as the offer the call center makes?), and within and across product lines (Do I offer the same interest rate for different unsecured credit products?). Highly consistent decisions need not be the same for all customers, all channels, or over time, but the variations should be deliberate and designed, not accidental.

- **Agility**—Agility is a measure of how quickly, inexpensively, and easily you can change the way you make a decision in your systems and organizational infrastructure. For example, if you want to introduce a new cross-sell strategy or pricing structure, how easily can you change the system specifications that support these decision strategies? How quickly would someone interacting with your organization notice that you had changed the way you make a decision? Agility should measure the total time and cost, from having data indicating you should change your decision process to actually effecting the change.

- **Speed**—Speed is one of the simpler measures; it simply tracks how quickly you can carry out a decision. It might be a measure of response time in an interactive system or elapsed time for a batch run. Speed should include any delays caused by waiting for additional data, such as third-party reports, and should be measured across the distribution curve for a decision—what is the mean, the median, and so forth?

- **Cost**—Cost is a pure efficiency measure of decision making that looks at the expenses of carrying out decisions. These costs include activity-based costs, the cost of data needed to make a decision (such as credit scores or motor vehicle reports), and the cost of system resources and other fixed and variable costs. These costs are separate from the costs of running the processes in which decisions are embedded. Cost must likewise be measured for the entire set of decisions, and median, mean, maximum, and so on might all be relevant.

Decision yield should be measured at a level that's specific and focused enough to be compelling to business decision makers. You can divide an organization in many different ways:

- **By segments or lines of business**—For example, in telecommunications, wireline, wireless, and Mobile Virtual Network Operator (MVNO) versus Internet Service Provider (ISP).

- **By nature of products delivered**—For example, in banking, credit cards versus savings accounts

- **By nature of the customers served**—For example, in long-distance telephony, consumer versus commercial

- **By functional area**—For example, in insurance, underwriting versus claims
- **By process**—Particularly when the process is considered "broken" or requires complex coordination in several parts of an organization, such as managing attrition in credit card customers

There's no right or wrong way to create these divisions. You should do what makes sense, particularly given the differences in the nature of decisions to be made. Thinking about enterprise-wide issues in a particular decision domain could be valuable, too. For example, identity fraud might be a compelling issue, even though it cuts across an organization's lines of business and products.

## Measuring Decision Yield

The process of measuring decision yield has a few steps: creating questions to assess decision performance, assigning weights to responses and calculating your organization's current state in the five dimensions, and then comparing your scores to other performance measures to create a decision yield chart.

### Develop Questions to Assess Decision Performance

The first step in measuring decision yield is finding the answers to questions about the decision. These questions are different for each decision, but they should follow these guidelines:

- The questions must be developed at a level specific enough to be compelling to business decision makers.
- Each question should take the form of a simple measurement of performance, in which the answer can be quantified or at least compared with a predefined standard.
- The dimensions of decision yield often give helpful prompts to the nature of questions to be asked, as shown in Table 1.

Ideally, you want to create 40 to 50 questions to ask mid- and senior-level managers from a range of functions related to the decision.

### Table 1 Questions Derived from Decision Yield Dimensions

| Decision Yield Dimension | Prompts for Questions |
| --- | --- |
| Precision | Making decisions that result in the most profitable outcomes, such as most reliably identifying and preventing fraudulent credit card activity yet minimizing the number of false positives |
| Consistency | Interacting with customers the same way, regardless of the means of interaction, such as ensuring that when insurers underwrite customers, the same risk is priced at the same rate, no matter what channel is used |
| Agility | Being able to adapt quickly to changing business conditions, such as putting an offer for your best customers into effect immediately in your call center when a competitor launches a new marketing program |
| Speed | Returning decisions in as near real time as possible to increase value for the organization and its customers, such as reducing the time to gather the necessary information and underwrite a mortgage application |
| Cost | Making it possible to increase decision management's scale and scope with only an incremental increase in cost, such as increasing the proportion of complex decisions made automatically rather than manually |

Beyond these dimensions, you can generate a list of questions by using these methods:

- You can consider metrics companies in the same industry use. Although these metrics are often a good starting point, they are unlikely to be adequate by themselves.

- You can identify metrics that equity and other analysts use to rate the performance of companies like yours. This approach is usually a rich source of questions for "decision-intensive" industries, such as banking and insurance, but less so in industries where analysts don't think of decision quality as a driver of success. Because senior management is likely to be familiar with these metrics, they are also valuable in highlighting decision yield's role in improving company value.

- You can also review annual reports or even advertising campaigns of leading companies to pinpoint the metrics they think are most important. These metrics can also be valuable when you're using decision yield to respond to competitive threats.

Using these approaches, you can come up with many different questions. Some examples include the following:

How finely segmented is your treatment of customers? (Precision)

How effective is the decision in achieving your short- and long-term financial goals? (Precision)

How well are associate-facing decisions made? (Precision)

Is the goal behind these decisions to manage customer lifetime value, long-term customer profitability, account profitability, or current product-line performance? (Precision)

Do your decisions take past and future decisions into account? (Consistency)

How well do different product lines coordinate customer marketing activities across channels and product lines? (Consistency)

Are customers or prospects receiving conflicting or confusing communications? (Consistency)

Are you leaving money on the table by not fully coordinating customer-facing marketing, cross-sell, and retention decisions? (Consistency)

How long does it take a business manager to change the way a decision is made all the way to implementation? (Agility)

How many resources (business and IT) need to be used to change a decision? (Agility)

How quickly can new information be brought to bear on a decision? (Agility)

How much time do you need to return a price quote to a customer or prospect? (Speed)

How long does it take you to design and implement a marketing campaign? (Speed)

How many customers do you lose because your decision turnaround times are too long? (Speed)

Are your decisions made through manual intervention or human review? (Cost)

What data elements are used in a decision, and how much do they cost? How many times is each piece of data purchased in relation to the number of decisions? (Cost)

When developing questions, identifying which dimensions of decision yield each one applies to is essential. Even when a question is prompted by considering one specific dimension of decision yield, the response might have implications in several dimensions. Most questions relate to a single dimension, but some relate to more than one.

### Calculate Your Yield for the Five Dimensions

While you're defining benchmarks, defining the overall weight given to responses to a question can be useful. You can get very precise in defining weights, but establishing the importance of each question along the following lines is usually more effective:

- **High**—Performance in this category is critical to the company's competitive position and overall financial performance.
- **Medium**—Although important, performance in this dimension isn't necessarily make-or-break, as long as it's offset by good performance elsewhere.
- **Low**—Strong performance is desirable, but poor performance isn't a "show-stopper."

To measure decision yield effectively, you need to develop a set of questions specific to the industry and decision area. For instance, if you're establishing the decision yield for an underwriting decision, you might ask "How many tiers do you use in rating risk?" or "How accurately do you predict the cost of claims for new customers?" These more specific questions drill into the precision, consistency, agility, speed, and cost of the *actual* decision you're trying to improve.

By gathering answers to these questions, you can come up with a measure of a decision's current state in all five dimensions. The most effective way to track the effectiveness of EDM projects is to plot these dimensions on a radar graphic.

### Compare Your Decision Yield to Others

One of the most effective ways to graph decision yield is to not just show your assessment of your current state. Instead, you can plot your current state, a potential future state—say, based on the expected outcome of a project, competitive average—how well a typical competitor does, and industry best practice. Plotting all these on a radar graphic such as Figure 1 can be very revealing.

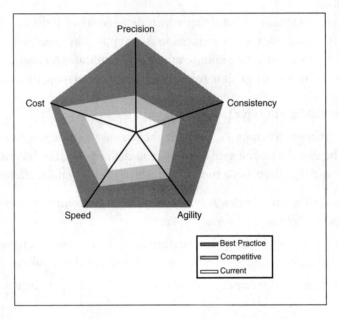

**Figure 1    Radar chart showing a decision yield for a specific decision**

The first step is considering how the industry leader in the particular area of your business under consideration would answer each question. By calculating a theoretical decision yield based on this information, you can plot the current best practice for this decision. Usually, this score is normalized as 100 to produce a regular pentagon.

Then you follow a similar process for what might be called "industry normal" or average. How well does a typical competitor do in this dimension? Calculate the decision yield for each dimension and compare it with best practices to yield a score in relation to the best practice's 100 points. Then plot these average points on your chart.

Finally, you calculate your current state scores in all dimensions and plot them in relation to the points for best practices and competitive averages. This information shows you where you are at present. If you're lucky, you might already have some points outside the competitive average that explain your current competitive edge.

> **Note**    *Any time you get a decision yield for your organization that lies outside the competitive average's boundary, you should have a competitive edge—in other words, you're doing better than the industry norm.*

You can also plot a project's results or expected results to see how it "expands" the decision yield for this decision. One of the key concepts in decision yield is measuring against best practices. Decision management is a neverending process; even if you make it to industry best practice on all five dimensions, the reality is that the standard will change, and more work is required to keep pushing the envelope.

For each operational decision, you must decide how close to industry best practice your business strategy needs to be in each dimension. This information is critical for successful EDM adoption and means you need to constantly reevaluate your decision yield because best practices improve over time. If you improve your decision yield to the best-practice score and assume you're finished, you might not notice that you're falling behind competitors when they meet and exceed the standard you have set.

> **Decision Yield for Competitive Analysis**  *You can also use this chart to calculate an approximate decision yield for a specific competitor and compare it to your own.*

## Using Decision Yield to Drive Planning

Decision yield is, in some respects, a "soft" measure because different stakeholders in an organization place different values on each dimension. One group might value consistency highly because it's constantly hearing complaints from agents about customers getting the wrong price on the Web site, another might be focused on the staff costs of manual decision making, and so on. The most effective way to use decision yield in this environment is to consider it a scorecard that combines the five dimensions based on the following factors:

- **Competitive importance**—Which dimensions will most improve your competitive position?

- **Financial value and impact**—Where are you losing money today? Why? Where are you leaving opportunities on the table?

- **Value to stakeholders (business, analysts, IT)**—Who has the most expensive business problems or is clearly under capacity for their workload?

- **Impact on customers and prospects**—What do customers complain about? Why do you lose prospects to competitors?

Groups vary in opinions on these factors, and converting a change in decision yield to an ROI involves assigning value to the five dimensions, given your unique circumstances.

After you have developed suitable questions, answered them to your satisfaction, and gone through a prioritization and valuation step, you can make several uses of decision yield. They include, but aren't limited to, conducting a decision audit, optimizing performance over time, and evaluating specific opportunities.

**Conduct a Decision Audit**

If your concern is simply to assess how you're doing in a particular decision area, a decision audit might be what you need. Having developed a set of questions for a decision area, you also need to identify the managers or other staff who should answer these questions. You might pose the same question to several managers. It doesn't matter if they give different responses; in fact, different answers can be revealing. You can also develop specific numeric measures for each question, but for an audit's purposes, defining three levels that equate to three points on a simple scale of 1 to 5 is often more effective:

1: The benchmark performance earning a score of 1 represents a "laggard," or the level of performance expected from a very poor performer.

3: The performance earning a score of 3 represents a "follower," or the level of performance expected from a company in the middle of the pack.

5: The benchmark performance earning a score of 5 represents a "leader," or the level of performance expected from a company that's an innovator and at the forefront of decision performance.

Table 2 shows some examples of benchmarking questions for insurance underwriting.

### Table 2    Benchmarking Questions for a Decision Audit

| What types of rating/underwriting decision tools are used as the basis of risk assessment? | | Precision | Consistency | Agility | Speed | Cost |
|---|---|---|---|---|---|---|
| Laggard | Written policy manuals only | | | | | |
| Follower | Common use of predictive models | High | | | | |
| Leader | Expert, pooled, and empirical models | | | | | |

| What proportion of the business you quote is issued at the same rate as what was originally underwritten? | | Precision | Consistency | Agility | Speed | Cost |
|---|---|---|---|---|---|---|
| Laggard | <85% | | | | | |
| Follower | >95% | Low | High | | | |
| Leader | >99% | | | | | |

**Note**   *The second question in Table 2 clearly shows that the five dimensions can be affected in different ways by the answer to a question.*

When conducting an audit, you have three stages: a prework stage, a workshop stage, and analysis and reporting. In the prework stage, you should identify the functions affected by the results of the decision audit that should be included in the study. For example, representatives of the following functions should be identified and tapped to participate:

- Executives
- Management and staff making the decisions being considered (usually from several departments)
- IT
- Downstream areas of the business affected by these decisions
- Any third parties affected by these decisions or the approach to making them

Each representative should be given a prework questionnaire on a "best-effort" basis, using knowledge commonly known in the organization or available through standard reports or easily run queries. If information isn't available, entering "Not Known" as the response to a question is acceptable. The people completing the survey can be told in general terms why their responses are necessary and important to the upcoming workshop effort, but little further explanation should be given at this point. Representatives can consult within their own function but shouldn't confer with representatives from other functions. Representatives of each function should answer the questionnaire separately from representatives of other functions because potential divergence in functions can provide valuable insight about opportunities and challenges.

Each questionnaire should be tailored to present only the questions relevant to the function answering it. After the questionnaires are returned, you need to aggregate the answers to get the following kinds of information:

- **Overall score**—Across the dimensions of decision yield
- **Comparisons**—How the company compares with measures such as "minimum competitive levels" and "market-leading levels"
- **Reasons**—What factors contribute positively to a company's rating for a dimension? What factors contribute negatively to the ratings?
- **Important functional differences**—What might different ratings from different functions for the same metrics reveal?

The next stage is to conduct a workshop with the same participants. You introduce everyone to the decision yield concept and its value in improving decision-making efficiency and effectiveness. For example, you could talk about companies in your industry that have staked out a dominant position in one or more decision yield dimensions. Who is the leader in precision? In credit cards, it might be Capital One. Who is the leader in cost? In insurance, Geico might rise to the top of your list. Who are the leaders in consistency, agility, and speed? These examples should help your participants understand the strategic value of decision yields.

You can then present the results of the prework questionnaire to spur discussion. Are people surprised by the results? Do they think the results reflect the company's policies and intent? A discussion on what could be done to address issues and what priorities seem appropriate is useful.

In the last stage, you deliver a report that summarizes findings and presents details on initiatives for improving decision making. If possible, provide an overall ranking of opportunities, based on factors such as ease of implementation, investment requirements, and expected payback.

## Optimize Decision Performance over Time

If your concern with a decision is to ensure that you maintain or improve the way you make decisions, measuring decision yield over time is helpful. To track decision yield in this way, you need to assign numeric weighting values to the five dimensions so that you can combine them into an overall score. You could track all five dimensions separately, but a single combined score is easier to use in your performance management environment and to show management its current value, trends, and so forth, similar to other key performance indicators. You can then assess each dimension regularly to track the values and convert them to an indicator by using these weights. For example, the weekly performance of an insurance underwriting system could be tracked with the decision yield score for the "underwrite new policy" decision.

You would use your existing performance management or business intelligence tools to collect data for answering quantitative questions, such as number of quotes issued or number of policies written, and some kind of online questionnaire to capture qualitative information, such as typical response of prospects to the quoted price. You then plug these answers into a formula to generate a number you can track as a graph.

This graph might show how a new Web site affected decision yield by reducing consistency or how a change in regulations led to much higher rates of manual review and, therefore, higher cost and lower decision yield. The graph also gives you early warnings of problems as you change and adapt your decision-making process.

You need to consider perspectives from different groups, too. Table 3 shows an example of a scorecard you can develop; it allows each group of stakeholders to weight each decision yield dimension. You typically measure a dimension in terms of how close it is to the best practice, which gives you a score from 0 to 1.00, with 1.00 being the best possible score.

> **Note** *Remember that a score on a dimension should decrease if you do nothing, because most industries continuously improve best practices.*

Applying weights from your stakeholders gives you a single number that you can track on a dashboard as a key performance indicator (KPI).

## Table 3 A Scorecard for Weighting Dimensions

|  | Sales | Marketing | Operations | Relative Score | Weighted Score |
|---|---|---|---|---|---|
| Precision | 20 | 40 |  | 0.72 | 43.2 |
| Consistency | 40 | 30 | 20 | 0.64 | 57.6 |
| Agility |  | 30 | 20 | 0.55 | 27.5 |
| Speed | 40 |  | 30 | 0.87 | 60.9 |
| Cost |  |  | 30 | 0.25 | 7.5 |
| **Total** | **100** | **100** | **100** |  | **196.7** |

A graph such as Figure 2 can show rises when the decision yield improves and declines when something goes wrong. You can use dashboards and business activity monitoring software to determine when to respond to changes in decision yield. Figure 2 shows that the decision yield has risen steadily, largely because of an improvement in speed. Precision jumped early and then stabilized, and consistency and cost have remained fairly constant. Agility had a large drop in the most recent period; this is probably worth investigating.

In addition, you can use a radar chart to plot current results against target and trailing average results—for the most recent quarter, for example—as shown in Figure 3.

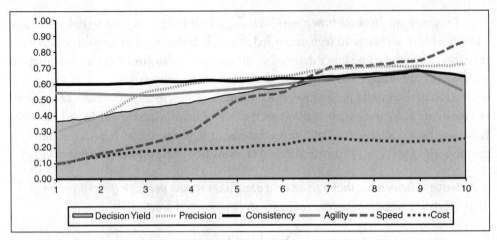

**Figure 2    A graph tracking decision yield over time**

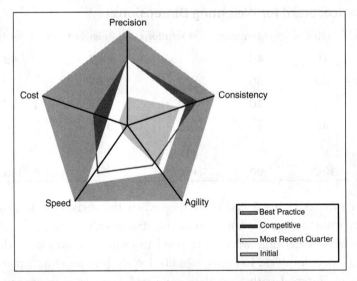

**Figure 3    Radar chart comparing target and trailing decision yield results**

## Evaluate Specific Opportunities

Decision yield can also be used when you have a variety of proposed decision projects to help you decide which is most appropriate. If you're taking a holistic view of decision making in your organization and are trying to focus your energies on a few projects, you need a way to compare likely or expected outcomes. Decision yield is an ideal tool for this purpose. To make it work, you have to be able to estimate likely improvement in each dimension for each project. Clearly, this estimate can be challenging, but scoping each project should include an assessment of hoped-for improvements, along with an idea of how likely or unlikely these improvements are.

You also need to get stakeholders to assign weights for each project, as described previously. (Remember, they will probably assign different weights to different projects.) To show the trade-off matrix, you need to plot each project to show three factors:

- **Decision yield**—The single numeric value calculated from your scorecard for each project

- **Estimated time to market**—Planned duration of the project, from inception to delivery of improvement

- **Estimated investment**—Total investment required, including staffing, resources, cost, and so on

With these factors, you can plot a universe of alternatives to consider. When considering decision projects, decision yield might be a better measure of value than other models, because it considers all five dimensions of decision making. Each project has different trade-offs in terms of time, cost, and decision yield, but at least by plotting these factors, you can show decision makers the range of alternatives.

Figure 4 shows five projects with different time and cost factors in relation to their decision yields.

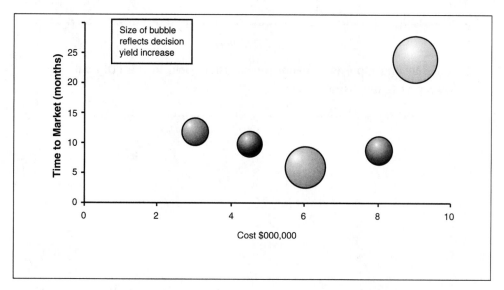

**Figure 4**    **The size of the bubble is the estimated decision yield, and the cost and time to market are the axes**

The classic representation of decision yield is the radar chart shown in Figure 1. Different projects and opportunities result in different decision yield charts, and you can compare charts when trying to choose between opportunities. One company's strategy could be focusing on agility projects rather than cost projects for a companywide effort to reduce IT costs, and another company focuses on top-line growth. In the first company, projects showing good growth on the agility axis in projected decision yield charts would be preferred, and projects showing growth on the precision axis would be prioritized in the second company. Again, the holistic approach of measuring decision yield instead of or with a more narrow definition of ROI makes showing the choices for decision projects easier.

## Closing Thoughts

Decision yield is just starting to be used in some of the ways discussed in this chapter. The basic ideas of the framework—focusing on precision, consistency, agility, speed, and cost for a decision—have been used qualitatively, but no real quantitative data is available yet. Determining how many and what kind of questions are needed to measure decision yield accurately isn't possible at this point. It's also difficult to say whether companies can trace competitive advantage to specific areas where decision yield says they're ahead of the market or use it as an effective tool for tracking decision performance over time. Decision yield looks promising, but the results will have to wait for another book.

---

### The EDM Wiki

You can find more information on decision yield in the EDM wiki at www.smartenoughsystems.com.

---

# Index

**Safari®**
**BOOKS ONLINE**
**ENABLED**

# THIS BOOK IS SAFARI ENABLED

## INCLUDES FREE 45-DAY ACCESS TO THE ONLINE EDITION

The Safari® Enabled icon on the cover of your favorite technology book means the book is available through Safari Bookshelf. When you buy this book, you get free access to the online edition for 45 days.

Safari Bookshelf is an electronic reference library that lets you easily search thousands of technical books, find code samples, download chapters, and access technical information whenever and wherever you need it.

**TO GAIN 45-DAY SAFARI ENABLED ACCESS TO THIS BOOK:**

- Go to **http://www.prenhallprofessional.com/safarienabled**
- Complete the brief registration form
- Enter the coupon code found in the front of this book on the "Copyright" page

**PRENTICE HALL**

If you have difficulty registering on Safari Bookshelf or accessing the online edition, please e-mail customer-service@safaribooksonline.com.